JEWELRY MAKING

FOR SCHOOLS • TRADESMEN • CRAFTSMEN

by
MURRAY BOVIN

revised by
PETER M. BOVIN

PUBLISHED BY BOVIN PUBLISHING

68-36 108th Street   Forest Hills, N.Y. 11375

Enlarged and Revised, May, 1971

Eighteenth Printing, February, 1974

Twentieth Printing, June, 1976

Enlarged and Revised, May, 1979

by Peter M. Bovin

Dedicated to my wife, Etta, without whose help this book would not have been possible.

Published by the author of

SILVERSMITHING AND ART METAL

For Schools — Tradesmen — Craftsmen

JEWELRY CASTING

For Schools — Tradesmen — Craftsmen

Printed in the United States of America

CONTENTS

CASTING

STONES AND SETTINGS

JEWELRY OBJECTS AND THEIR CONSTRUCTION

PREFACE

Jewelry making is one of the oldest, most fascinating, and respectable of crafts. Today the handmade jewelry craftsman is one of the few remaining hand-skilled workers left in the American economic system. The craft has been recently adopted by hobbyists, educators, and occupational therapists for its stimulating appeal and for its educational and therapeutic values. Unfortunately, until comparatively recent years, many of the jewelry making techniques have been closely guarded secrets of the jewelry craftsmen.

It is the purpose of this book to present thoroughly to both the beginner and advanced craftsman the most practical and contemporary methods of making handmade jewelry. The information and techniques presented have been gathered, tried, and developed through many years of actual work as a craftsman in the jewelry industry. All techniques have been tested and the method of presentation perfected through years of teaching in high schools and trade schools, colleges, and adult centers. It is hoped that all craftsmen, students, shop teachers, therapists, and tradesmen can gain useful, practical information about handmade jewelry making.

Those craftsmen that possess a little ingenuity and dexterity should find an adequate market for jewelry objects which they desire to sell. There is a good demand for well-designed and executed jewelry objects. Professionally, there are many individuals, men and women, engaged in jewelry making.

All jewelry objects, unless otherwise noted, were made by the author. The same is true of all the sketches and photographs except those submitted by craftsmen and manufacturers.

The author is indebted to many manufacturers who have supplied technical information and also to many craftsmen who have submitted pictures of their jewelry creations which are being used in this book.

ACKNOWLEDGMENTS

Many individuals contributed information, materials, and suggestions during the writing of the revised edition of my father's book. I am very grateful to the following for their assistance: Dudley Shannon, Bud Hesch, Ira Skalet, E. James Erwin, Roger Gesswein, Jack Ferris, Sam Howarth, Harry Adwar, Cliff Wilson, Anthony Paolerico, Dvora Horvitz, Kathryn Gough, Arthur Cohen, Larry Weiss, Ed Holownia, William Kalich, William Klein, and Sheldon Besher.

A special thanks to the following craftsmen: Janet Mainzer, Janet Vitkavage, Robert Browning, Tsun Tam, Cecelia Bauer, Antonia Schwed, Robert Nantel, Meryl Greenberg, and Joseph Finelli.

I am especially indebted to Katy Hanson and Tom Paré for their help and also their understanding of what this book means to me.

Peter M. Bovin

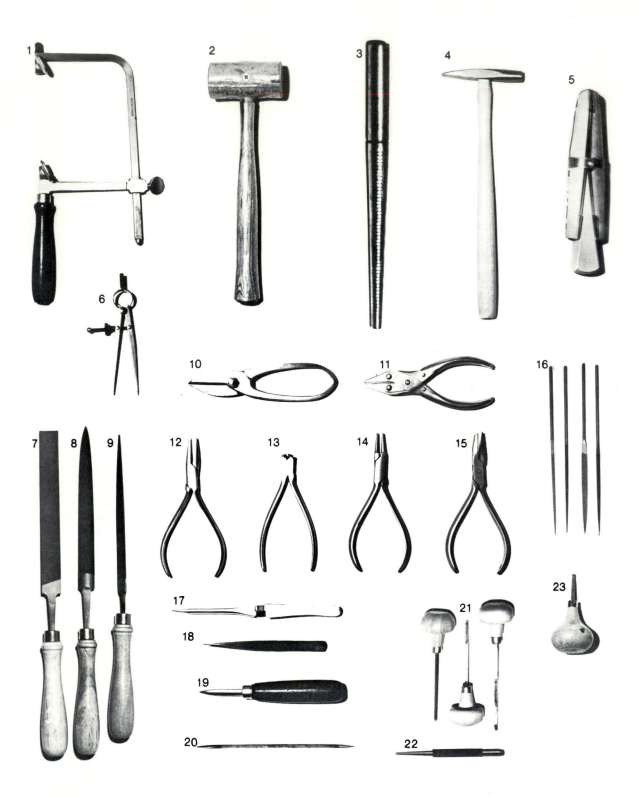

Fig. 1. Jeweler's saw, 2. Rawhide mallet, 3. Ring mandrel, 4. Riveting hammer, 5. Ring clamp, 6. Divider 7. Hand file, 8. Half-round file, 9. Three square file, 10. Brown's shears, 11. Bernard flat nose plier, 12. Chain nose plier, 13. End nippers, 14. Round nose plier, 15. Flat nose plier, 16. Needle files, 17. Cross-locking tweezer, 18. Tweezer, 19. Burnisher, 20. Scriber, 21. Engraving tools, 22. Center punch, 23. Stone setter.

TOOLS AND EQUIPMENT

TOOLS Surprisingly few and comparatively inexpensive hand tools are required to do successful jewelry work (fig. 1). Obtain as many tool catalogues from jewelry craft and supply firms (see Appendix) as possible. A good source of supply firms is a local classified telephone directory. It is good economy and safe practice to purchase a tool of high quality.

BASIC TOOLS

These tools are suggested for doing successful craft work. A thorough description of many of the tools will be found in subsequent chapters on processes.

Jeweler's saw frame, 2¼″ or 4″ depth
Hand shears (Brown's), 6″ for cutting solder
Flat nose plier, smooth jaws, 5″
Round nose plier, 5″
Divider, steel, 3″
Ring clamp
Scriber
Riveting or ball peen hammer, 7 or 8 ounce
Files, Swiss pattern, 6″, 0 and 2 cut, one each, hand, half-round, three square
Files, needle, 16 centimeter length, one set
Ring mandrel, graduated
Tweezer, 5″, pointed
Tweezer, cross lock type
Emery stick

PROFESSIONAL KIT Add the following tools to the above to form a minimum professional jeweler's working kit.

Flat nose plier, 5″, "Bernard" type
Spring gauge, lignes
Plate shears, 1½″ blade, 7″ long
End nippers and side nippers
Ring sizes
Chain or snipe nose plier, 5″
Engraving tools, onglette, flat, lozenge, round
Eye loupe, 3″ or 4″ focus
Ring stick
Pin vise

ADDITIONAL TOOLS It is impossible to list all the required tools, since many phases of jewelry work such as engraving, stone setting, and casting require specialized tools; however, the following should be added as the need arises:

Pliers, half-round
Draw plates
B. & S. gauge
Burnisher, curved or straight
Engraving block
Tinner's hand shear
Draw tongs

A small metal tool or fishing tackle box can be purchased to store and carry jewelry making tools (fig. 2). Plastic boxes should be obtained to keep findings, solder, gemstones, and filings (fig. 3).

Fig. 2 Tool box

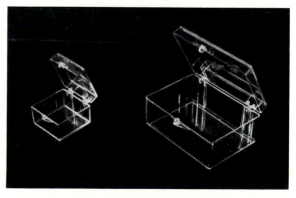

Fig. 3 Plastic finding boxes

EQUIPMENT

WORK BENCH The accompanying picture (fig. 4) is that of a typical jeweler's bench used professionally. Note the tray to catch filings and small pieces of metal, the sliding arm rest and the bench pin. Any bench can be used; however, it is essential that the bench have a tray to catch filings for gold and platinum work, since these metals are very expensive. The better benches have a hard wood (usually maple) top and a sliding tray of galvanized iron.

The jeweler's bench should be as near to a window as possible. Northern exposure is preferred since the light is constant. Where possible, it is best to hang the soldering torch from a hook on the work bench so that it can be used while one remains seated. The

Fig. 5 Metalsmith's bench

mounted a vise, drill press, stakes, and a surface plate (fig. 5). A metalworking bench should be at least two inches thick. It should be firmly attached to the floor, or sufficiently heavy so that the vises, stakes, and anvils that it supports do not reverberate unnecessarily when used. The height of an average metalworking bench is three feet.

A fixed ceiling, or an adjustable fluorescent or combination fluorescent-incandescent lamp (fig. 6) should be acquired since good lighting is essential for jewelry making.

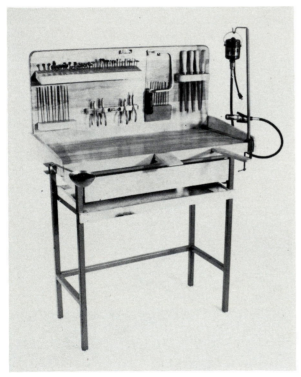
Fig. 4 Jeweler's work bench

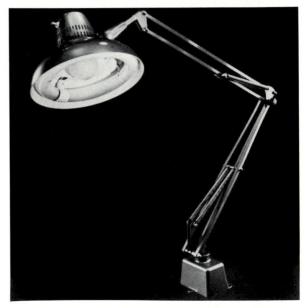
Fig. 6 Fluorescent-Incandescent bench lamp

flexible shaft should be hung from a hook or wire above the bench for easy accessibility. It is best to use a low chair or stool (14″ high) when working at the bench.

In addition to a jeweler's work bench, a jeweler should try to acquire a metalworking bench for heavy work on which can be

When making very fine jewelry, setting small precious gemstones, engraving, etc., it is essential to wear a clip-on magnifier which can be attached to regular glasses, or a headband magnifier which is available with interchangeable lenses (fig. 7); or to use an eye glass loupe, or an eye loupe (fig. 8).

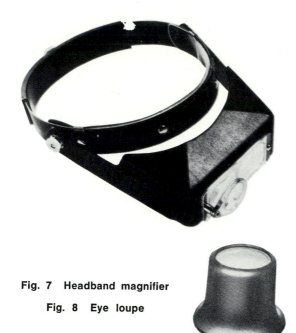

Fig. 7 Headband magnifier

Fig. 8 Eye loupe

sirable for flattening, forging and stamping metals (fig. 10).

BENCH ANVIL A small jeweler's anvil is handy for shaping and stretching bezel settings, and for forging thin wires (fig. 11).

Fig. 11 Bench anvil

COMBINATION BENCH PIN AND ANVIL — The combination bench pin and anvil for sawing, filing, and light hammering is recommended to craftsmen who do not have a regular jeweler's work bench with a bench pin (fig. 9).

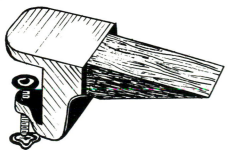

Fig. 9 Combination bench pin and anvil

BENCH BLOCK A 2½″ x 2½″ hardened steel bench block about 1″ thick is very de-

Fig. 10 Bench block

BENCH VISE A 3″ or larger jawed bench vise mounted on a utility or metalsmithing bench can be used advantageously (fig. 12).

A small vise with removable rubber jaws (2½″) is held to the jeweler's work bench by means of a vacuum base (fig. 13). The vise will hold a bench pin; thus it can be used for sawing, filing and stone settings.

Fig. 12 Bench vise

Fig. 13 Vacuum base vise

FLEXIBLE SHAFT Modern jewelers find the flexible shaft, controlled by a foot rheostat, to be an indispensible tool. It is used for drilling, setting, polishing, etc. (fig. 14). The outfit shown is either suspended from the jeweler's bench, a wall, or the ceiling.

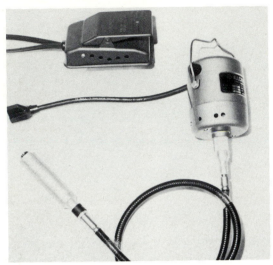

Fig. 14 Flexible shaft outfit with foot rheostat (speed regulator)

There are several types of chucks available for the flexible shaft which can accommodate various sizes of drills, burs, grinding stones, and polishing buffs (fig. 15).

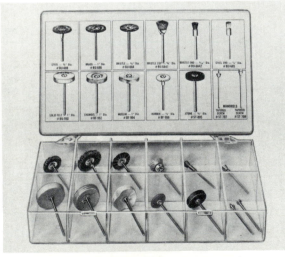

Fig. 15 Flexible shaft accessory set

DRILL PRESS A small high speed drill press controlled by a foot rheostat is excellent for drilling small, accurately placed holes (fig. 16).

Fig. 16 Drill press

POLISHING (Buffing) MACHINE (fig. 17) Almost any electric motor can be converted into a buffing machine by attaching a tapered spindle. A double shafted ⅓ horse power motor is preferred for craftsmen. A variable speed motor with speeds up to 3600 R.P.M. is desirable. Professional buffing machines should have suction dust collectors to safeguard the health of the worker who uses the machine for extended periods. Lights in

Fig. 17 Polishing machine

the dust pan are very desirable for better vision.

ROLLING MILL A rolling mill is indispensible for professional work (fig. 18). Geared hand mills are available for schools and small shops, though powered mills are preferred in a production shop. Flat and square mill combinations are recommended; the flat for reducing the thickness of sheet metal, the square for forming square bars which can be flattened into strips or drawn into wire. Plain and tiffany ring rolls are also available. With a mill, filings and small pieces of metal can be melted and easily rolled into sheet or wire.

Fig. 18 Rolling mill

BENCH SHEAR The bench shear is used for cutting metals up to 3/16" thick (fig. 19).

Fig. 19 Bench shear

JEWELER'S BALANCE The balance, or scale shown in the accompanying picture (fig. 20) is ideal for weighing gold and silver: If platinum and diamonds are to be weighed, more sensitive, glass enclosed balances are available that have a sensitivity of 1/200 of a carat.

Fig. 20 Jeweler's balance

Troy or metric weight sets can be purchased for use with the scale. The sets of weights are made up of the following: TROY— .1 dwt., .2 dwt., .5 dwt., 1 dwt., 10 dwt., 1 troy ounce, 2 troy ounces; METRIC—.1 gram, .2 gram, .5 gram, 1 gram, 2 grams, 5 grams, 10 grams, 20 grams, 50 grams, 100 grams. The

Fig. 21 Electronic digital scale

11

scale is accurate to one tenth of a dwt. (penny weight).

Many jewelry manufacturers who frequently weigh metal, castings, or finished jewelry use electric top loading balances that instantaneously record the weight on an electronic digital display. (fig. 21)

SOLDERING EQUIPMENT The purpose of soldering equipment is to provide a clean, hot flame quickly and inexpensively for rapid soldering. Since soldering is very important in jewelry work, the equipment should be selected carefully. When ordering a blowpipe or torch, specify the type of gas (natural or manufactured) available. Below are several suggestions:

FOR HOMECRAFT WORK Very intricate jewelry work can be done with an inexpensive mouth blowpipe (fig. 22). Gas is connected to the side of the pipe and air is blown in by mouth from the end to produce a hot, clean flame. The gas can be obtained from the kitchen gas range quickly by disconnecting one of the burners.

Fig. 22   Mouth blowpipe

Soldering torches using propane gas in small metal cylinders (fig. 23) are comparatively inexpensive and practical for home craft work, especially if one is squeamish about using a mouth blowpipe. The flame will melt silver and gold solders. The gas ignites immediately, the size of the flame can be controlled by means of a valve, and the small cylinders contain gas for 8 to 15 hours of use.

FOR SCHOOLS AND CRAFTSMEN Small jeweler's torches (with interchangeable tips for producing different sized flames) which use gas and compressed air or oxygen are recommended (fig. 24). A variety of gas-air torches are made for use with natural or manufactured gas (propane, acetylene) and either pure oxy-

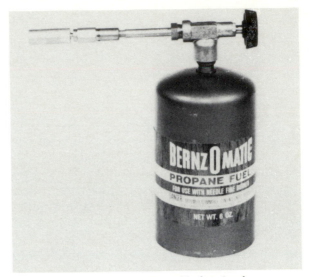

Fig. 23   Propane soldering torch

gen or atmospheric air. It is important that the proper torch be purchased for the specific gas/air supply that is available. A compressor with a storage tank (fig. 26) is recommended for providing a continuous supply of air to several torches. Air can also be supplied by means of foot bellows, an old vacuum cleaner, or a small rotary blower driven by an electric motor. Natural gas/with compressed air is the most practical for most jewelry work done in schools since it is the most economical. Unfortunately, natural gas is not available in many areas. In shops where gas is not avail-

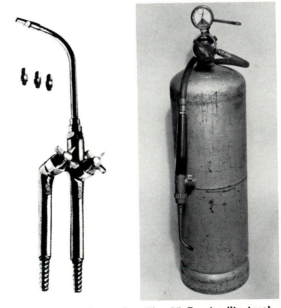

Fig. 24   Jeweler's torch   **Fig. 25 Prest-o-lite torch and gas outfit**

Fig. 26 Air compressor

able, a Prest-o-lite outfit is recommended (fig. 25). The Prest-o-lite tank contains acetylene gas, which gives a much hotter and superior soldering flame to the one produced by propane gas.

FOR CAMPS A Prest-o-lite torch and gas outfit with a pressure regulator valve is safe, comparatively inexpensive and easy to operate in rural areas (fig. 25). Soldering torches using propane gas are also recommended (fig. 23).

FOR COMMERCIAL JEWELERS Gas and compressed oxygen is preferred for gold and platinum. Pure oxygen increases the temperature produced by the torch by approximately

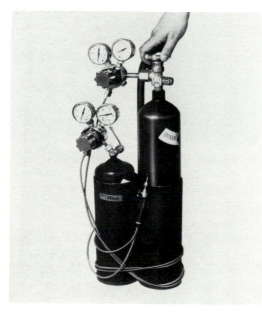

Fig. 27 Propane/oxygen soldering unit

1000°F. over atmospheric air, and also eliminates any water accumulation which sometimes causes sputtering and blowout. Propane/oxygen units with gas and air regulators (fig. 27) may be purchased at most supply companies. Acetylene/oxygen is used primarily for platinum. Here are some temperatures produced by popular gas mixtures:

Fuel	With Oxygen	With Air
Acetylene	5850°F.	3848°F.
Propane	5252°F.	3497°F.
Natural Gas	5120°F.	3565°F.

PLUMBER'S TORCH A plumber's torch using white, unleaded gasoline can be used for jewelry soldering (fig. 28). Mexican craftsmen use the plumber's torch exclusively for silver and gold soldering all their jewelry.

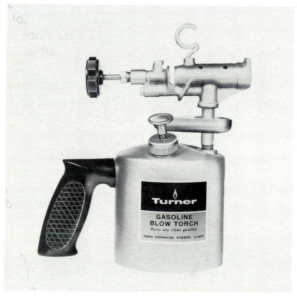

Fig. 28 Plumber's torch

Note: As a rule, the soldering copper or the alcohol torch is rarely used or recommended for jewelry soldering. The copper cannot melt gold or silver solder and with soft solder the results are unsatisfactory since too much solder can be seen. The alcohol torch is not very satisfactory since the flame cannot be regulated, alcohol is expensive, and too much time is wasted in the preheating process to make the torch work.

SOLDERING AREA A soldering area can either be made or purchased for soldering and annealing (fig. 29). Fireproof transite sheets surround the work, thus assuring maximum protection.

Fig. 29 Soldering area

SOLDERING AND ANNEALING PAN A soldering and annealing pan filled with small chunks of pumice (fig. 29) is very useful for silver soldering and also for annealing metals since it can be rotated easily so that one can get at all parts of the object being soldered or annealed. The pumice chunks can be shifted to hold objects in position and the pumice, since it will not conduct heat from the metal, shortens the annealing or soldering process.

Note: Be careful when soft soldering on the pan that no soft solder drops onto the pumice, for any soft solder that comes in contact with an object being silver soldered or annealed will pit or burn a hole into the metal.

WHAT TO SOLDER ON (fig. 30) Asbestos (millboard) Blocks: Most gold and silver jewelry objects can be soldered on asbestos blocks and, since they are long lasting, easy to clean, and comparatively inexpensive, they are recommended. Two blocks 6″ x 6″ x ½″ are ideal.

Charcoal Blocks: The blocks radiate heat well and, since their surfaces can be punctured easily, they are excellent for soldering prong settings. However, the charcoal blocks are expensive and deteriorate quickly.

Also used: 6″ x 3″ x 1½″ soft magnesia soldering blocks, fire bricks, and 1 inch high strips of asbestos coiled to fit into a 6½″ diameter pan. Several other soldering items will be described later.

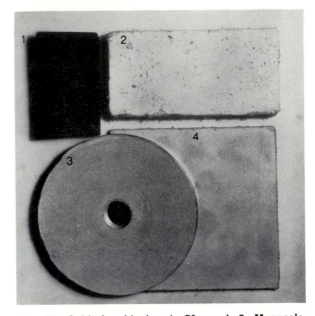

Fig. 30 Soldering blocks: 1. Charcoal, 2. Magnesia, 3. Coiled asbestos strips, 4. Asbestos (millboard) blocks

ADDITIONAL INFORMATION This additional information is presented in question and answer form especially for beginners since, it is felt, they may be somewhat taken back by the thorough presentation of the above chapter on jewelry tools and equipment.

1. How much money is required by beginners to purchase sufficient tools to get started?

Actually very little money is required, especially when compared to other crafts. As suggested, purchase only the tools needed immediately and add others as the need arises. The basic tools listed in this book for beginners can be bought for as little as fifty dollars.

2. What equipment, that is listed, is essential to beginners?

Only the equipment for soldering is absolutely essential to beginners. However, a mouth blowpipe can be purchased for as little as a dollar or a propane gas torch for about six dollars, and with them the finest silver and gold jewelry can be soldered. Almost any motor can be converted into a buffing machine, and if a machine is not available, as will be explained later in the book, many attractive finishes can be given by hand to jewelry objects. Of course, it is advantageous for craftsmen and schools to have the above equipment; to commercial jewelers they are essential.

3. Are there any occupational hazards in jewelry making?

Jewelry making is a comparatively clean craft. With normal precautions, no hazardous conditions that might injure one's health should exist.

4. Can jewelry be made by those living in apartment houses or confined quarters?

Jewelry making, since it is a clean craft, can be done in the kitchens of apartment houses or in confined quarters. A propane gas torch or a mouth blowpipe connected to the kitchen range can be used for soldering. By covering the kitchen table with paper an adequate work bench can be set up. A combination bench pin and anvil can be used for sawing and filing. The jewelry tools are compact and can easily be stored. Naturally, a regular shop or work room is preferred.

5. Is there a market for handmade jewelry?

Those craftsmen that possess a little ingenuity and dexterity should find an adequate market for jewelry objects which they desire to sell. There is a good demand for well designed and executed jewelry objects. Professionally, there are many individuals, male and female, engaged in jewelry making.

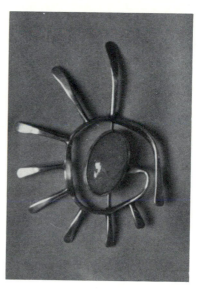

Pin　　　　　　　**Newbro-Wendell**

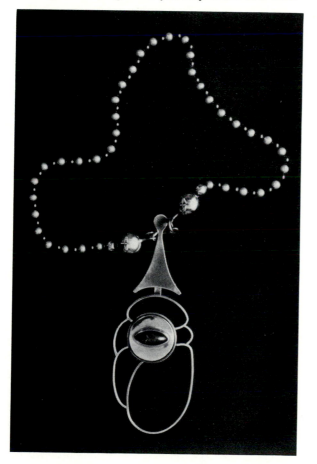

Necklace　　　　　　**Jonathan O. Parry**

Pendant　　　　　　**Ralph Murray**

15

THE METALS

WEIGHTS OF METALS Troy weights are used to weigh the precious metals: gold, silver, and platinum. Copper, brass, and nickel silver are weighed and sold by the standard (avoirdupois) pound. The troy ounce is about 10 per cent heavier than the avoirdupois ounce.

Troy Weight

24 grains	1 pennyweight
20 pennyweights	1 ounce
12 ounces	1 pound

The pennyweight is abbreviated "dwt."; "d" for the English penny and "wt" for weight.

THICKNESSES OF METALS The thickness of silver and copper and their alloys is measured by the American Standard or the Brown and Sharpe wire gauge (fig. 31). On one side of the gauge is a group of gauge numbers and on the other side is the thickness of those numbers in thousandths of an inch. The wire or sheet is inserted into the slot, not the hole, to find its thickness.

Gold and platinum workers use the spring gauge to measure the thickness of their metals (fig. 31). The gauge is divided into 72 sections called douziemes. One douzieme equals .0074 inches; 12 douziemes equals 1 ligne which equals .0888 inches. The micrometer, especially by precious metal supply concerns, is also used to measure the thickness of gold, silver, and platinum. The micrometer can measure the thickness of a metal to one ten-thousandth of an inch.

If a rolling mill is not available, several silver sheet metal thicknesses should be stocked. The following are recommended:

	B. & S. Gauge	Thickness in ins.	Weight per sq. in.
For men's rings	16	.051	.278
For rings and pins	18	.040	.221
	20	.032	.175
For earrings	22	.025	.139
	24	.020	.110
For bezels	28	.013	.071

The above weights are in troy ounces.

Wire thicknesses 10, 14, and 18 are popular. Wire may be purchased in many shapes including, round, square, and half-round.

Circles of almost any diameter and gauge can be ordered at a slight additional cost.

Fig. 31 (Top, left) B. & S. Gauge. (Bottom, left) Micrometer. (Right) Spring gauge

SILVER

PROPERTIES Pure silver is almost perfectly white, very ductile and malleable. It is the best conductor of electricity. Unfortunately, sulphur and its compounds tarnish it. Pure (fine) silver, for most jewelry use, is too soft—it will not hold its shape and will wear away quickly. It is hardened by alloying wth copper. Pure silver is mainly used for enameling and electroplating in jewelry work.

STERLING SILVER Sterling silver is an alloy of 92½% (.925) silver and 7½% (.075) copper. It is the silver that is used commercially and by craftsmen for jewelry and flatware.

COIN SILVER Formerly (before 1966) U.S. silver coins contained 90% silver and 10% copper. Today, dimes, quarters and half-dollars are made from two sheets of nickel with a center of copper—they contain no silver. The

Washington Quarter, the Kennedy Half Dollar and the Eisenhower Dollar (all limited editions) contain 40% silver—two outer sheets of silver and a center of nickel.

MEXICAN SILVER Mexican Silver is the name given to the silver used by many Mexican and American Indian craftsmen. Its silver content is generally above 90%.

SPRING SILVER Spring silver is sterling silver that has been reduced as much as ten times its original (last annealed) thickness by rolling or drawing to harden it. It is used to make tie and money clips, and where hardness and spring are desired.

ORDERING When ordering silver, the type, thickness, and width or shape must be specified. Sterling silver is the type usually used. It is sold soft, unless otherwise specified.

Silver may also be purchased half-hard, hard, and spring hard. Half-hard and hard silver are used for pins and pierced objects that are left flat and do not require silver soldering.

PRICE Pure (fine) silver's price has fluctuated from $1.37½ (a pre-1967 high) an ounce in 1919 to 25 cents (a record low) in 1932, to 45 cents in 1936, to $1.00 in 1955, to $1.85 in 1972, to $4.50 in 1977, and to over $30.00 in 1979.

The above is the market price for a 1000 ounce fine silver bar (bullion).

Silver dealers add a service charge to the above price for shaping, cutting, and handling small quantities of silver.

TEST FOR SILVER File a deep notch in the piece to be tested and apply a drop of nitric acid.

    Sterling silver turns cloudy cream.
    Plated ware—the base metal will turn green.
    Nickel silver turns green.
    Coin silver turns dark or blackish.

Silver when pickled (cleaned in hot sulfuric acid) becomes glittering white; nickel silver takes on a dull gray finish.

Pure silver, when heated to light red and then cooled, remains white; sterling silver turns black.

MELTING POINTS

fine (pure) silver	1762°F.
sterling silver	1640°F.
coin silver	1615°F.

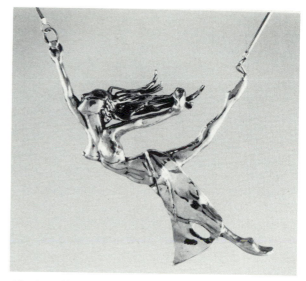

Fig. 32 Silver pendant   **Harriet Forman Barrett**

GOLD

Gold is found chiefly in the free state in the sands of streams or in the veins of quartz rock. Most gold is mined in the Rocky Mountains, Alaska, South Africa, Russia, and Canada. It is claimed that all the gold mined since the dawn of history would fit into a 100 foot cube.

PROPERTIES Pure (fine) gold is yellow in color. It is the most malleable and ductile of all metals. It can be hammered into sheets less than 1/300,000 of an inch thick, and one ounce of gold can be drawn into a wire 35 miles long. Gold is chemically inactive—it is not affected by oxygen, sulphur, or acids; however, it can be dissolved by aqua regia, a mixture of 1 part nitric and 3 parts hydrochloric acid.

USES Gold is used for jewelry, coinage, decorative, scientific, and dental purposes. Most gold is stored in treasury vaults to be used for balance of trade payments with foreign countries. Pure gold is very soft and to enable it to resist wear and for different color effects it is alloyed with other metals.

COLORS Yellow gold is popular for most jewelry, and is comparatively easy to work. Special yellow gold alloys that will retain their elasticity after soldering are available for tie clips, pin tongs, etc. White gold is usually used with diamonds, since its white color harmonizes with the stone. White gold is difficult to work—it is hard and brittle. Red gold is often used with yellow for contrasting effects. Green gold is used for antique jewelry. Below are the popular gold colors and the metals added to the fine gold to obtain the colors:

white ...... gold, nickel, copper, and zinc
yellow ..... gold, silver, copper, and zinc
green ...... more silver—less copper than yellow gold
red .... more copper—less silver than yellow gold

KARAT The amount of alloy (base) metal used with the gold depends upon the karat desired. The term karat denotes a measure of purity; 24 karat is pure gold. Thus, 14 karat gold is by weight 14/24 fine gold and the balance (10/24) is alloy metal.

PURITY AND MELTING POINTS OF GOLD

24K fine gold	1.000	1945°F.
18K white	.750	1730°F.
18K yellow	.750	1700°F.
14K white	.5833 ...	1825°F.
14K yellow	.5833 ...	1615°F.
10K yellow	.4167 ...	1665°F.

ALLOYING Various practices exist in different commercial jewelry plants for purchasing and alloying gold. Many jewelers prepare their own gold alloy by melting the proper weight of gold and base metal in a crucible; a small amount of boric acid powder is added to check oxidation of the base metal. When melted, the molten gold is mixed with a steel or carbon rod to obtain a uniform batch. The base metals and charts for preparing the various alloys can be purchased from gold suppliers. The above is common practice especially if the gold is to be used for castings. For handmade objects or stamping, the gold can be purchased already alloyed in the desired karat, color, shape, and gauge. See page 253 for additional information.

FILINGS Many jewelers send their filings to the refiner for cash or credit towards clean gold. Many, however, remelt the filings and then roll the gold into sheets or draw it into wire again. The filings, all of the same karat and color, are first cleaned of ferrous (iron) metals by means of a magnet. Then the filings are placed in an iron frying pan and heated until all organic (wood, etc.) materials burn off. Finally, the filings in the pan are left to cool, washed clean with water, dried in the pan, and then remelted in a crucible and poured into an ingot mold (page 25).

GOLD FILLED refers to metals made by welding a layer (or layers) of gold alloy to a base metal and then rolling or drawing the metal to the required thickness. Thus, 1/10 - 12K gold

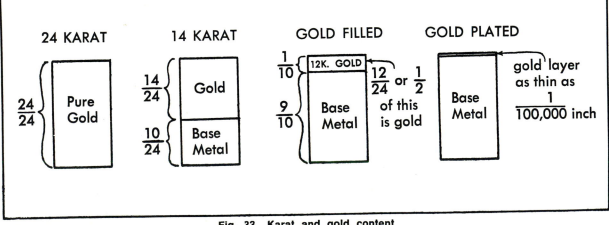

Fig. 33   Karat and gold content

18

filled means that the article consists of base metal covered on one or more surfaces with a gold alloy of 12K, and the covering comprises 1/10 part by weight of the metal in the entire acticle. Since 12K gold is only ½ fine gold, the gold filled object contains 1/20 fine gold.

ROLLED GOLD PLATE Rolled Gold Plate refers to the same type of gold covering on a base metal as gold filled; however, the gold content is lower. 1/30 - 10K rolled gold plate is a good example. A jewelry object with the above rolled gold plate content would have a 1/72 fine gold content for $1/30 \times 10/24 = 1/72$.

GOLD ELECTROPLATE is made by electrolytically depositing gold on a base metal. The gold deposited must not be less than 10 karat and it must have a thickness equivalent to at least 0.000007 inches of fine gold. Items with a gold thickness less than 0.000007 can be labeled gold washed or gold colored.

Note: The gold plated layer is very thin, often less than 1/100,000 of an inch.

PRICE From 1932 until 1968 the price of fine gold in the United States was established by an Act of Congress at 35 dollars an ounce. Fine gold had been worth 22 dollars an ounce before 1932. United States gold coins minted before 1932 contained 90% gold and a five dollar piece was worth $4.50. When gold was increased in value to 35 dollars an ounce in 1932 all gold pieces and bullion were called

in by the Federal Government. Since March, 1968, the price of gold has been permitted to rise to a dealer's market price: over $43 an ounce in 1968, $35 an ounce - 2/70, $50 - 3/72, $65 - 1/73. In 1975, when it became legal for individuals to buy and hold gold, the price rose to $195, 6/76 - $125, 11/77 - $165, and to over $700 in 1979. What the future price of gold will be is - ?

Note: Daily prices for gold are set by the London Bullion Exchange, and for silver and platinum by the New York Commodity Exchange. The price of the precious metals fluctuates from day to day. It is affected by the current worldwide economic situation and by intricate monetary manipulation and speculation.

TEST FOR GOLD The following equipment is required: a black stone slab, testing needles of different karats and colors, a bottle of nitric acid, and a bottle of aqua regia (1 part nitric and 3 parts hydrochloric acid). The testing procedure is as follows:

File a deep notch into the piece to be tested. Apply a drop of nitric acid. A bright green reaction indicates gold plate on copper or brass, a pinkish cream color indicates gold plate on silver. Ten karat gold will show a slight reaction—over ten karat, little or no reaction.

To find the karat of a gold object, rub it several times on the testing stone (fig. 34) to make a distinct mark about ¼ inch wide. Beside it make a mark equally heavy with a test

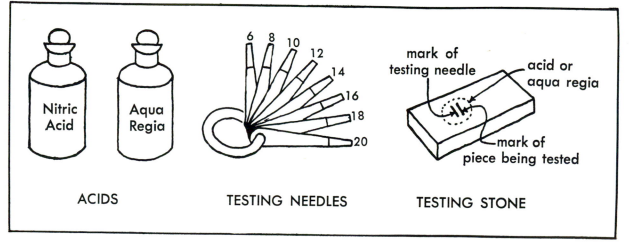

Fig. 34 **Testing the karat of a gold object**

needle nearest in karat and color to what you suppose the gold to be. Apply acid to both marks at the same time. Use nitric acid for 12 karat or less and aqua regia for higher karats. If the needle marking reacts (disappears) sooner than the gold, wipe the stone dry and retest with a higher karat needle—if slower try a lower karat needle. When you have matched the reactions you have determined the karat.

Green gold reacts more slowly than yellow gold because it contains more silver. White gold reacts slowly because of the nickel or palladium in the alloy. Some testers prefer to dilute the acids in order to get slower reactions, especially on the low karat golds.

Note: Many commercial gold buyers do not use testing needles—they use pieces of gold of known karat instead of the needles.

Fig. 35 Cast 14 Karat gold ring   Robert Browning

PLATINUM

Platinum is found in nugget form in Russia, Colombia, Trans-vaal and Canada. Most platinum, however, is obtained as a by-product, along with gold and silver, in the refining of nickel and copper in Canada.

It is grayish white in color, does not oxidize, can be cast, forged, and welded. Platinum is very ductile and malleable. Its melting point is very high—3224°F. This is a very desirable property for it permits the use of many different strong melting solders. A small amount, usually 10%, of iridium, a rare metal in the platinum family, is added to platinum to increase its hardness.

Platinum is the ideal metal for setting diamonds because of its white color, strength, and its excellent working properties. It is a very heavy metal (specific gravity—21.5). It is 1.624 times heavier than 14 karat gold and 1.825 times heavier than palladium.

Platinum was once used for coinage in Russia. Its value, especially during war emergencies, can fluctuate sharply; as much as twenty dollars an ounce in one day. Presently, most platinum is used for industrial and scientific purposes; only about 5% produced is used for manufacturing jewelry. Platinum's price: 1945 — $35, 6/73 — $155, 2/74 — $220, 6/76—$167, 4/79—$440 an ounce for 90% platinum - 10% iridium.

TEST FOR PLATINUM Platinum, since it is a heavy metal, can be distinguished from palladium and white gold by the feel of its weight when bounced in one's hand. Platinum, after being heated to red heat and cooled, does not oxidize; palladium and white gold oxidize and change color.

To test for platinum with testing needles, follow the same procedure used to test gold, using however, needles made of platinum, iridio-platinum, palladium—platinum, and palladium. Apply aqua regia and compare reactions. Iridio-platinum and platinum react very slowly. Lower grade alloys containing palladium, gold, and base metals react rapidly. To speed up testing, heat the stone until uncomfortable to hold, or use a white stone, which sometimes shows reactions better.

PALLADIUM belongs to the platinum family of metals and, since it is cheaper, is used as

Fig. 36 Diamond ring set in platinum
Courtesy of Tiffany & Co.

a substitute for platinum. Its melting point is 2831°F. It is much lighter in weight than platinum, approximately ½ (54.8%) its weight, and is used for light platinum jewelry such as earrings. An alloy of palladium (95.5%) hardened with ruthenium (4.5%) is generally used for jewelry objects. Its price: 1977 — $45 an ounce; 4/79 — $120 per ounce.

COPPER

Copper, due to its excellent working properties, its attractive color, and comparative low cost, is one of the most widely used craft metals. Historically, it was used as early as 4500 B.C. by the Babylonians and Egyptians.

PROPERTIES Copper can easily be recognized by its reddish color. Unfortunately, it tarnishes quickly; often it is lacquered to protect its finish. Commercial copper is practically pure: 99.9% copper and 0.1% arsenic, which is added to harden it. Its melting point is 1981°F. It is a very good conductor of heat and electricity—second to silver.

Copper is very malleable, more so than sterling silver (not pure silver), brass, bronze, and nickel silver, which means it can be formed or shaped easier than those metals. It can be forged at red heat, but it does not cast well. It is resistant to the action of sea water and the atmosphere. Copper can not be hardened by heating. When heated until red hot and dipped into water or left to cool in air it becomes soft. To harden, copper must be worked—that is, planished or hammered, rolled thinner, drawn into a wire, etc. Unfortunately too, silver soldering will leave the copper soft. Most copper jewelry objects must be planished after being silver soldered (not soft soldered) so that they will be sufficiently hard to retain their shape.

ORDERING When ordering copper, state the thickness, hardness, and size or shape desired. Copper and its alloys can be purchased soft, half-hard and hard.

Soft copper is classified into two groups: namely, hot rolled and cold rolled annealed. Hot rolled means, as the name implies, that the copper was rolled into sheets while it was hot and thus the final product (due to the heat) is soft. A harder and smoother copper

is obtained by rolling the copper into sheets while it is cold. The copper is then annealed (see page 31) if a soft smooth sheet is desired.

Cold rolled annealed copper should be ordered for most art metal and jewelry objects since it is smoother and more malleable than hot rolled copper, which is usually pitted with small imperfections.

Soft (annealed) copper is obtainable in rolls and in sheets. The rolls usually run from 8″ to 18″ wide and from 18 gauge to 36 gauge in thickness. The standard sheet size is 36″ by 96″ and the gauges run from 8 to 26.

Most craftsmen purchase 18 and 20 gauge copper. Copper is also obtainable in the form of wire, tubing, rods, circles, etc.

PRICE The price of copper has fluctuated from 18 cents a pound in 1933 to $1.88 in June, 1977. The above prices are the cost per pound when ordering 100 pounds of the same gauge (18) of copper. Copper dealers add a service charge to the above price for cutting, shaping, and handling small quantities of the metal.

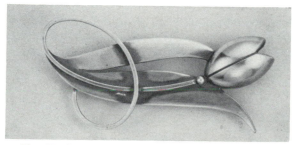

Fig. 37 Copper pin   **Paul Lobel**

BRASS

Brass is an alloy of copper and zinc—the zinc proportion varies from 5% to 40%. The proportion is changed for different uses, and occasionally small amounts of tin and lead are added for special purposes.

The brasses may be divided into two groups; namely, the low-Zinc Brasses with a zinc content of less than 30%, and the High-Zinc Brasses with a zinc content of 30% to 40%.

The color of brass varies widely with the composition—from the bronze and golden colors of the Low-Zinc Brasses to the yellow of the High-Zinc Brasses. **Note:** 5% zinc and 10% zinc-copper alloys, because of their color, are known as "commercial bronze" in supply houses, even though they are true brasses. The Low-Zinc Brasses are more ductile and corrosion resistant than the High-Zinc Brasses and also have superior cold working properties. The High-Zinc Brasses are stronger, harder, and wear better. Forging brass, 60% copper, 38% zinc, and 2% lead, has remarkable heat working properties but cannot be worked cold to any great extent.

Below are the composition and uses of four brasses important to art metal workers.

Gilding:
95% copper, 5% zinc; has a deep bronze color, used for costume jewelry, medals.

Commercial bronze:
90% copper, 10% zinc; has a typical bronze color. Used for store fronts, screens, costume jewelry.

Red brass:
85% copper, 15% zinc; looks like gold, used for costume jewelry, builders' hardware.

Yellow brass (Cartridge brass):
70% copper, 30% zinc; has a bright yellow color, most widely used of all brasses.

Brass is less malleable than copper but is harder, stronger, and can be filed and machined easier. Most brasses cannot be forged at red heat—they crack, can be cast and welded, and do not tarnish as easily as copper. Brass is the base metal for much of the gold plated costume jewelry. Yellow brass, especially when highly polished, has a

beauty of its own and is very popular for art metal objects such as lamps, vases, trays, boxes. Price of brass is approximately 10% less than copper's.

Melting Points

Gilding	1949°F.
Red brass	1877°F.
Yellow brass	1706°F.

BRONZE

Formerly, bronze was considered an alloy of copper and tin. The following two alloys were popular:

Coinage:
95% copper, 5% tin; for coins and statues

Bell Metal:
80% copper, 20% tin; for making bells

Today, modern bronzes contain, besides copper and tin, other elements such as phosphorus and aluminum, forming alloys which are rarely used by craftsmen. Several modern copper alloys are called bronzes, because they look like bronze, even though they do not contain tin. Example: Commercial bronze —90% copper, 10% zinc. This alloy can be worked cold and is recommended when a bronze-appearing object is desired.

Note: Bronze is tougher and harder to shape by hand processes than copper.

Fig. 39 Silver, copper and bronze brooch
Richard Helzer

NICKEL SILVER

Nickel silver, sometimes called German silver, is an alloy of copper, zinc, and nickel. Since it does not corrode readily, it is used for inexpensive tableware and imitation silver

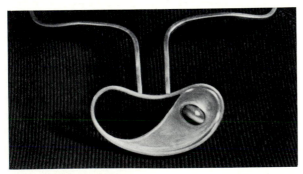

Fig. 38 Brass pendant   **Alyse Tartell**

objects. This alloy—65% copper, 17% zinc, 18% nickel—is a popular base metal for silver plated flat and holloware. The above alloy has a melting point of 2030°F. Nickel silver can be used when making delicate prong settings for models since it has a high melting point. Unfortunately, a ring made from nickel silver would tarnish one's finger.

ALUMINUM

Aluminum, the most abundant of all the metallic elements found in the earth's crust, was first isolated chemically in 1825 and produced commercially in 1886. It is a light metal—approximately ⅓ the weight of copper and ¼ the weight of silver. Its melting point is 1220°F.

Aluminum is a good conductor of electricity. It can be cast, forged, hammered, and spun. Aluminum pieces can be joined together by riveting, welding, and soldering. It is not attacked by sulfuric or nitric acid—hydrochloric acid and strong alkalies will dissolve it. Many alloys of aluminum are used in industry. For craft purposes "1100" aluminum—commercially pure with slight impurities of iron and silicon—is used.

The color of aluminum is a little duller than silver's. It is popular when planished and given either a high polish or a steel wool or wire brush satin finish.

Price: $1.25 per pound on 100 pound orders.

PEWTER — BRITANNIA METAL

Britannia metal, also known as white metal by jewelers, is the modern industrial name for pewter. It is used for white metal cast rhinestone and other low melting cast costume jewelry.

Modern pewter is a Britannia metal alloy of approximately 91% tin, 7½% antimony and 1½% copper. Its color is slightly duller than silver's, and it does not tarnish readily. Pewter is very malleable and does not require annealing. Pewter can be soldered easily; however, since its melting point (app. 495°F.) is not much higher than 63-37 soft solder (363°F.), care must be taken not to overheat and thus melt it when soldering with 63-37

solder. Pewter is soft and bends fairly easily and for that reason thicker gauges than those used for similar sized copper objects should be used. For general work, 14 and 16 gauge are the most popular.

Pewter's price, due to its high tin content, is comparatively high—approximately $8.00 a pound in 1977.

QUALITY STAMPING

Since the Civil War, most of the gold and silver jewelry sold in the United States has received a quality mark such as "14K", "10K gold filled", or "Sterling". The National Stamping Act was enacted in 1906 to provide standards for properly marking merchandise made of gold, silver, and platinum (see Appendix). The purpose of the law was to protect the purchasing public from fraudulent misrepresentation of the quality of such articles by some jewelers. In 1962 an amendment was made to the Stamping Act which required that trademarks accompany all quality marks.

Craftsmen and manufacturers can purchase quality stamps such as "14K", "18K", "Sterling", "Platinum", and "Handwrought" from their local equipment supplier. Several companies such as Allcraft will make a trademark stamp if a craftsman sends them a sketch of the insignia, name, or logo.

The metal surface to be stamped should be filed, sanded with emery, and polished with tripoli. Stamping should be done before the parts of the piece of jewelry are soldered together because delicate parts soldered to the piece being stamped could be damaged during the stamping process.

The metal to be stamped is placed on a polished steel surface plate and, with one firm blow of a ball peen hammer, the stamp is struck. The mark should be made where it will be clearly visible after all soldering operations have been completed. The stamp should be held firmly so that it does not move and cause a blurred image on the metal. If a blemish forms on the reverse side of the metal it can be removed with emery or pumice. Wax models can be hallmarked by pushing a warm stamp against the surface of the wax.

FUNDAMENTAL JEWELRY PROCESSES

INTRODUCTION

Although contemporary jewelry making has moved beyond the level of hand craftsmanship insofar as there have been technological developments in the processes that can be utilized to manipulate precious metals, the fact remains that there are only three basic ways of making jewelry. The first way of working metal is to cut or shape the metal when it is "cold." The metal can be cut, sawed, bent, filed, hammered, stamped, forged, pressed, or drawn into the desired shape. The second method is to heat the metal until it is molten, and then cast it into a mold. The mold can be made of a higher melting metal, rubber, sand, clay, a refractory investment, or a cuttle fish. The third method involves the addition, or joining, of metal to metal by means of solder, granulation, fusing, rivets, links, or chains. Most of the more complex pieces are constructed by using combinations of the above processes. After the metal has been fabricated, it may be decorated by chasing, engraving, inlaying, etching, enamel-ing, reticulating, plating, or electroforming; set with gemstones; or combined with other metals and materials.

Regardless of the processes and techniques used to make jewelry, the design is of utmost importance. Before attempting to construct a piece of jewelry, a sketch should be made, and all of the processes needed to complete the piece should be studied, understood, and practiced.

Fig. 41   Pendant   Harriet F. Barrett

Because the techniques, materials, and equipment used to create jewelry frequently vary, it is difficult to categorically list a sequence of operations that might be used to make a piece of jewelry. There are some processes, such as casting, that are employed in the manufacturing of much of the jewelry that is made today. There are other processes, such as niello, that are rarely used. Some processes, such as soldering and polishing, may be repeated several times during the construction of a piece of jewelry, while other processes, such as engraving, are usually only done once. It is possible for a piece of jewelry, such as a simple forged necklace, to be created by a single process (forging)

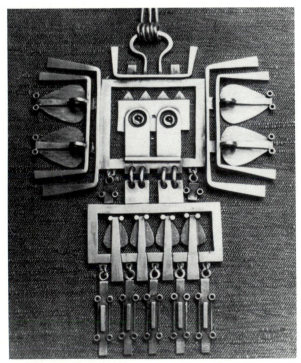

Fig. 40   Neckpiece   Klaus Kallenberger

and with a single tool (a hammer). Most of the time, however, to construct a piece of jewelry, it is necessary to lay out a design; cut pieces of metal into various shapes; hammer, tool, engrave, or form the metal pieces; fashion, fuse, or solder pieces of metal together; perhaps stamp or cast some pieces of metal; clean and polish the metal; and set gemstones into the metal.

The problem of completely describing the processes that are used to make jewelry is further complicated because the tools and equipment used by jewelers, even though designed for a specific purpose, can be used in many different ways. Various jewelry making processes are also frequently modified according to the individual requirements and methods of work of the jeweler. The tools and processes described in the pages that follow are therefore presented in terms of their most common usage.

1. INGOTS, USE OF ROLLING MILL, WIRE DRAWING, AND TUBE MAKING

Most of the melting, shaping, extruding, and casting of metal into standard sizes and shapes of sheet, wire, and tube are done by refiners and smelters. Few jewelry makers have the necessary equipment or time to make metal manufacturing economically feasible. There are, however, several operations related to metal processing that jewelers might need to know and wish to perform, if they want to alloy metal or fabricate odd-sized sheet metal, wire, or tubing.

POURING METAL INTO INGOTS New and scrap metal must be cast into square and rectangular bars in order to be rolled into sheet or wire. An adjustable ingot mold (fig. 42) is an ideal tool for forming the square or rectangular bar. When using the mold, apply a thin coat of oil to it to keep the metal from adhering. Prior to pouring the metal, warm the mold with a torch to prevent the metal from freezing and therefore to produce a smooth casting. Tilt the ingot mold slightly so that the metal flows down the wall of the mold, for if the molten metal is poured straight down it splashes and forms blisters (imperfections) in the bar.

Set the mold to form a square for wire or to the desired width for sheet, and, after the

Fig. 43 Wire ingot mold

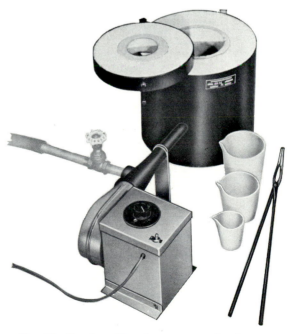

Fig. 44 Small melting furnace, pouring tongs, and crucibles

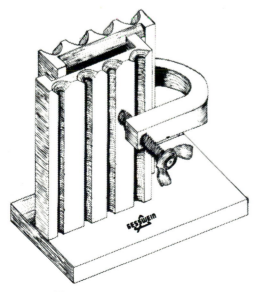

Fig. 42 Adjustable ingot mold

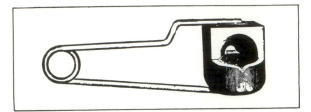

Fig. 45 Burno hand crucible

metal has been melted in a crucible, pour it into the mold. Remove all fins from the cast ingot with a file before rolling it.

Flat and wire ingot molds are also available.

Metal can be melted in graphite crucibles (fig. 44) in furnaces available in many school shops. If a furnace is not available, the metal can be melted with a large torch in the Burno type of hand crucible available from dealers. Metal can also be melted with an electrically heated graphite crucible unit such as the Kerr "Electro Melt" or the Jelrus "Handy Melt". With electric melting furnaces, undesirable metal oxidation is eliminated. A pyrometer records the temperature of the metal inside the crucible as it is melting.

When using a pouring crucible the inside should be coated with boric acid, in order to prevent small particles of the crucible from dropping into the molten metal. This is done by heating the crucible to melt he boric acid crystals and then swirling the crucible so that the boric acid adheres to the inside wall as a glaze.

Before melting the scrap metal, any iron filings should be removed with a magnet. The metal is heated until it begins to shine and spin. Its fluidity should be checked with a carbon stirring rod. **Note:** A small amount of boric acid is added to check oxidation of the metal when it is melted. Once the metal starts to "roll" like mercury, the torch should be lifted away from the molten metal and concentrated on the pouring lip of the crucible as the metal is poured into the ingot mold.

USE OF THE ROLLING MILL After the ingot has been removed from the ingot mold it should be forged on both sides with a forging hammer so that the metal is compressed and made stronger, planished smooth with a planishing hammer, filed and scraped to remove any blemishes and impurities, and finally annealed. The thickness of the metal is then reduced in a rolling mill.

A flat rolling mill with interchangeable square and half-round grooves is very essential for making handmade silver, gold, and platinum jewelry. With a mill, sheet metal can be shaped quickly and accurately, the cross-sectional shape of wire can be changed, and twisted wire can be flattened.

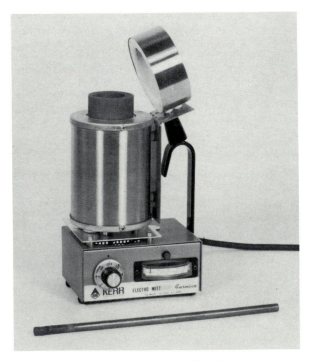

Fig. 46 Small electric melting furnace

Fig. 47 Reducing wire in a square wire mill

The flat mill (fig. 18) is easy to operate. The rollers should always be parallel. For the initial roll, the rollers should be adjusted so that the metal is easily pulled into the rollers. Feed the metal into the rollers slowly and after each rolling reduce the gap between the rollers slightly until the required thickness is reached. It is advisable to reverse and turn over the metal after each pass through the rollers to keep it flat. Anneal the metal occasionally to keep it soft and to prevent the formation of cracks. Rolling will make a metal longer but not wider, and if the metal must be slightly wider, feed it into the rollers at a slight angle.

Square wire or bar is easily reduced in the square wire mill (fig. 47). In each opening the wire is fed through at least twice and after each feeding the wire is turned ¼ of a turn. The square wire can be flattened in the flat mill to form rectangular pieces or it can be drawn easily into round wire through a drawplate.

The rolling mill can be used to imprint a design, texture, or line pattern into a sheet of annealed metal. Screens, iron wire formed into patterns, iron wire wrapped around a strip of iron, work-hardened coins, and even woven fabrics can be either rolled through the mill between two sheets of annealed metal so that both pieces are textured simul-taneously, or between a sheet of 16 gauge hard-rolled metal and a sheet of annealed metal if only one piece needs to be textured. Since the metal is stretched as it is rolled through the mill, this process should be done in one pass.

Hand operated mills are ideal for schools and small shops; electrically operated ones are indispensible for production shops.

WIRE DRAWING Wire can be thinned and shaped by means of a hardened steel draw-plate. Drawing wire keeps inventory down and also offers the craftsperson ready access to any shape and size of wire needed. Draw-plates are made with different shaped holes; the round, square, half-round, and rectangular ones are popular for jewelry work. Note from figure 50 that the holes in the drawplate become progressively smaller. The holes are numbered in specific Brown and Sharpe gauge sizes. Note, too, from the cross-sectional diagram (fig. 48) that each hole tapers from the back side of the drawplate almost to the front and then becomes straight for a short distance.

To draw down wire, first taper the end of the wire with a rough file, then insert it into the proper hole in the back of the drawplate, and pull it through with the aid of drawtongs. This hole is the first one that resists the easy

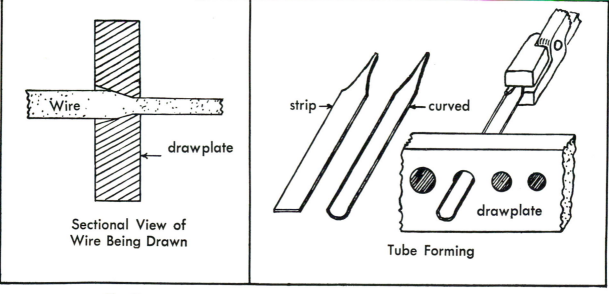

Sectional View of
Wire Being Drawn

Tube Forming

Fig. 48   Fig. 49

passage of the wire. The drawplate is placed in a vise to hold it securely. The wire is then pulled perpendicularly through the drawplate in an even and continuous motion with the drawtongs. Once the entire length of wire has passed through the drawplate, proceed to the next smaller hole, etc., until the desired gauge is reached.

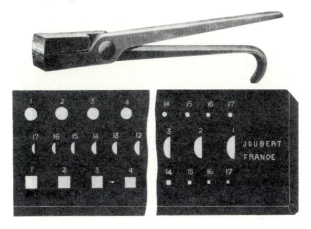

Fig. 50   Drawtongs and Drawplate

SUGGESTIONS: Annealing (see page 31) will keep the wire soft and thus keep it from breaking. Large gauge wire should be annealed after each draw through the plate. Smaller gauge wire is annealed after every other pass. It is recommended that the wire be drawn through a piece of beeswax before it is drawn through the drawplate. This lubrication will help prolong the life of the drawplate. It is best to warm the wire slightly, especially gold, when applying the wax. A draw bench can be used for drawing very thick wire. Half-round wire can be made by drawing two pieces of the same gauge square wire through a round hole in the drawplate. Triangular-shaped wire can be produced if two pieces of half-round wire are simultaneously drawn diagonally through a square hole in the drawplate.

TUBE FORMING A drawplate has a use other than reducing the gauge of, or shaping wire. Jewelers can use the drawplate to make hollow tubes that cannot be purchased commercially. Hollow tubing is used to make hinges, decorative links, clasps, findings, and gemstone settings. A tube is formed from a flat rectangular sheet of metal by pulling the

Fig. 51   Box with hinge made from tubing   Christine Thrower

sheet through the round holes of the drawplate. The width of the sheet should be 3 times the width of the required tube; the thickness of the sheet depends upon the desired wall thickness of the tube. **Note:** As the diameter of the tube is decreased, its wall thickness is increased.

TUBE FORMING PROCEDURE (fig. 49)

1. Mark off the required width with a divider along a straight edge of the metal and then cut this piece off with shears. File, if necessary, to make the sides parallel.

2. Point one end of the strip with shears into a taper approximately 1″ long.

3. Start forming the strip into a tube by placing it over a groove in a piece of wood or a swage block and then hammering down on the strip to curve it. Any narrow hammer with round edges (cross-peen) or even a rod can be used. Curve the strip sufficiently so that it can be pulled through a hole in the draw-

plate. Both edges of the tapered end should be brought close to each other, first in the swage block and then with a hammer so that they can be soldered together to form a point. This point should be tapered and smoothed with a file.

4. Apply beeswax to the strip and then pull it through holes, progressively smaller, in the drawplate until it is formed into a tube.

5. Just before the strip closes, a knife blade may be held in the opening to straighten the seam.

6. Draw the tube to the required diameter.

The tube may be straightened by annealing and then hammering or rolling on a flat, smooth surface. If desired, the seam of the tube may be soldered. It is best to cut sections off the tube with a jeweler's saw.

If a tube with an accurate inside diameter is required, the tube may be formed and drawn around a steel wire. The wire should be oiled so that it can be removed. To remove the wire, place the tube through a hole in the drawplate that will hold it and then pull the wire out.

The edges of the tube are usually soldered together with hard solder so that the tube does not open if additional soldering operations are required. Binding wire should be used to hold the tube tightly together. A length of tube can be cut into sections with a jeweler's saw either by placing the tube in a V-shaped groove made in a hardwood block, or by using a tube holding jig (fig. 53). Tubes can be bent without creasing their sides by first crimping one end in a vise, filling the tube with either molten wax or pitch, bending the piece into the desired curve, and then heating the tube to remove the wax or pitch. Sand can also be used.

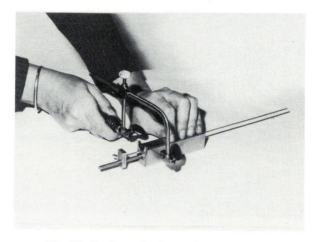

Fig. 53 Sawing tube in a tube holding jig

2. TEXTURING

The entire surface or large areas of a sheet of metal can be textured for contrasting decorative effects before it is shaped, cut into smaller sections, or soldered to another piece of metal. One reason for this is that when a similar texture is desired on many pieces of jewelry, it is usually easier to place a uniform texture on a large piece of metal and then cut it into smaller pieces, rather than try to duplicate the texture on small individual pieces. Also, areas of a piece of jewelry are sometimes inaccessible after assembly, and thus texturing must be done before the article is shaped. And finally, hammering a texture into a piece of assembled jewelry could distort its shape.

Ball peen hammers with different sized heads can be used to create textures in metal. Other hammer textures can be made with planishing, sinking and forging hammers. Textures can also be chiseled or engraved

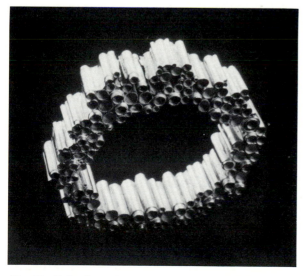

Fig. 52 Tube bracelet   Harriet Ackerman

29

Fig. 54 Textured pendant   **Neil Rosenblum**

with a smooth-faced hammer. Note that the hammer's face hits the metal at the taper angle desired. This type of forging will stretch the metal in length, width, and thickness.

Metal can be forged and stretched in one direction by using forging, raising, or cross-peen hammers. These hammers move the

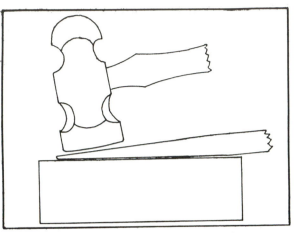

Fig. 55 Taper-forging a piece of wire

into the metal's surface. Power presses can be utilized to strike in a design. The smoothness and hardness of the surface that the metal is placed upon when hammered and the force of the hammer blows dictate the shape and depth of the indentations that are made in the metal. Most hammer texturing is done on a smooth steel surface plate. The hammer blows usually are done randomly and overlap each other. If the hammering is done on a softer surface such as wood, lead, or a sandbag, the front surface will be indented, while the back surface will be raised. Interesting textures can also be created by hammering nails, screws, bolts, iron wire, etc., into the metal until an impression is made. The metal should be periodically annealed if hammer texturing is done over a large surface area.

3. FORGING

The jewelry metals—platinum, gold, silver, copper and its alloys—are malleable, that is, they can be readily formed or hammered (forged) to various shapes. To spread and taper-forge a piece of wire, hold the metal (fig. 55) over a smooth piece of steel, an anvil, a mandrel, or a stake, and hammer it

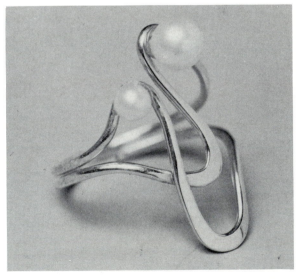

Fig. 56 Forged ring   **Phyllis**

metal outward at a right angle to the long axis of the hammer. The force and number of hammer blows should be increased gradually if the metal is to be thinned. By hammering one side of the metal, annealing, and then forging the other side of the metal, an even gradual taper can be easily achieved. The metal should be hammered systematically and its shape checked regularly against

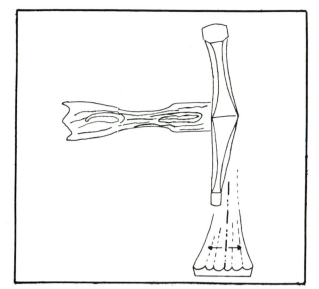

Fig. 57 Hammer used to widen metal strip

a sketch. A smooth-faced hammer is periodically used to true and even the surface of the piece.

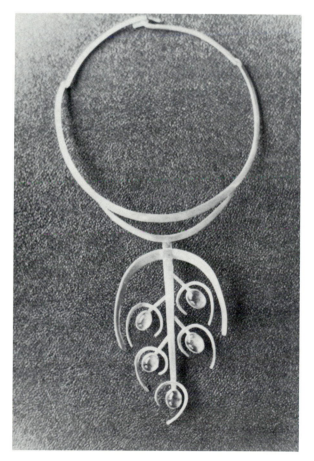

Fig. 58 Forged necklace   **Eleanor H. Cottrell**

To avoid cracking, heavy pieces of metal should be annealed several times while being forged. Copper, silver and gold can be forged easier if they are heated until they are red hot and forged while hot. Brass is forged cold; it will crack if forged red hot. If the metal is to be left hard, or have spring (such as a money clip or tie clip) the metal should not be annealed after the final forging and planishing. Some craftsmen prefer to leave hammer marks on a forged piece of jewelry, whereas others file the metal smooth.

4. ANNEALING

Metals when worked, that is, when hammered, forged, drawn into wire, or bent, become hard and brittle, so much so that with further working they will eventually crack or break. Annealing, the term for softening metal so that it is malleable again, is done by heating the metal. The temperature to which the metal is heated and the method of cooling varies with different metals.

Scientifically speaking, metals become soft at certain temperatures because the grain structure of the metal changes (recrystallization occurs).

The following should be observed when annealing:

No solder, especially soft, should be in contact with the metal for the solder will burn into it.

Objects that have hard soldered parts must be annealed at a temperature below the melting point of the solder.

All parts of the metal must be heated, though on large pieces not necessarily all over at the same time.

Do not drop gold below 14 karat, sterling silver, or brass into cold water when they are red hot for they are liable to crack.

STERLING SILVER Sterling silver is heated to a very light red (first red, 900°F., will do), permitted to cool to lose its redness, and then it may be dropped into water so that it may be handled quickly. Actually, sterling silver can be heated to a little below first red, at which point the silver is dull and does not reflect light.

GOLD Yellow, green, and red gold are heated to a dull red (1200°F.) and dipped immediately into water or, better yet, alcohol. The alcohol removes the oxide from the metal. White gold is heated to a cherry red (1400°F.) and permitted to cool slightly to avoid cracking and then it may be dipped into water.

PLATINUM Platinum is heated to white heat (2100°F.) and it may be dipped into water immediately.

PALLADIUM Palladium is heated to cherry red and immediately quenched in water, otherwise it will oxidize—turn bluish.

COPPER Copper is heated to red heat and dipped immediately into water, though it may be permitted to cool slowly.

BRASS Brass is heated to light red, cooled until the redness disappears, otherwise it may crack, and then dipped into water.

STEEL Steel is heated to cherry red and permitted to cool as slowly as possible in air or, better yet, powdered asbestos.

WIRE Wire, especially very thin, is coiled as shown in figure 59 in order to avoid melting. The wire can be annealed on a charcoal block or an asbestos pad. Note that the ends of the wire are wrapped around the coil to hold it together. Use a soft, almost yellow

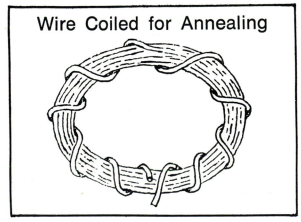

Wire Coiled for Annealing

Fig. 59 Wire coiled for annealing

flame when annealing; that is, a flame with very little air (reduction atmosphere). If binding wire is used to hold the coil of wire together, it should be removed prior to pickling.

To prevent the formation of fire scale (oxidation), silver, brass, bronze, and gold should be coated with boric acid or Handy Flux before they are annealed. Handy Flux becomes viscous at approximately 1020°F. When a glazed surface appears, it is a good indication that the annealing temperature has been, or soon will be, reached.

The metal can be pickled to remove any fire scale and to dissolve flux. Some craftsmen (especially silversmiths) prefer to anneal in a dimly lit room because then the low red color of the metal is easier to discern. Overheating the metal will increase the formation of fire scale and could possibly ruin the metal.

Fig. 60 Annealing silver

5. PICKLING

Alloy metals containing copper oxidize when heated, annealed, soldered or cast. The oxide formed is copper oxide. It is gray-black and since it interferes with soldering and polishing operations, it must be removed. In other words, when a 14 karat gold or a sterling silver object is soldered, the heat oxidizes the copper in the metal and therefore the object becomes black. The black oxide is generally called fire scale.

Pickling is the name given to the process of removing the oxide by means of acid. The pickle serves another useful purpose—it removes the hardened glazed flux so that the metal can better be worked and observed.

The following solution is used by commercial jewelers and craftsmen:

Water, 10 parts; sulfuric acid, 1 part.

Some jewelers add a little sodium bichromate to the above for pickling gold.

Heating speeds the pickling action of the solution, and the solution is most effective when heated to just below its boiling point.

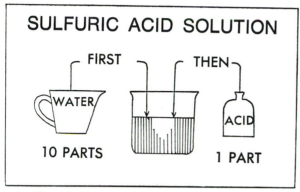

Fig. 61   Method of preparing acid solution

CAUTION When preparing the solution, first pour the water into the container and then add the acid (fig. 61). If water is poured into concentrated acid, the acid is apt to splash. Acid burns should be washed with water immediately and neutralized with bicarbonate of soda, or soap.

It is not advisable to drop very hot metal into the pickling solution since this will cause the acid to spatter and could even crack the metal. The pickling solution, with the jewelry object in it, is boiled in a copper pan (fig. 62) or a pyrex or ceramic crucible. Heat is supplied by either a hot plate or bunsen burner. When the metal appears clean (sterling turns almost pure white, copper turns a brighter red, and gold becomes brighter) it should be removed. If the metal is left in the pickling solution for a prolonged period of time, the acid will start to eat away the metal and attack the solder.

Note: Always remove binding wire from objects before pickling, otherwise the objects become coated with a thin layer of copper. Immerse and remove objects with copper wire or copper tweezers.

Fig. 62   Copper pickle pan

Do not pickle objects that have been soft soldered. Soft solder flux can be removed by brushing the object with a hot water and soap solution that has a few drops of ammonia added to it.

Electrically heated pickle pots and crocks are now available. They usually have a removable plastic sieve, an on-off switch with an indicating light, and a temperature control.

After the objects are removed from the pickling solution they should be rinsed in water. If the piece of jewelry contains crevices or hollows, it should be neutralized in a boiling solution of 1 tablespoon sodium bicarbonate to one cup of water, rinsed in water, and then dried with a towel. The acid, if not completely neutralized, will continue to corrode the metal and will also prevent the solder from flowing.

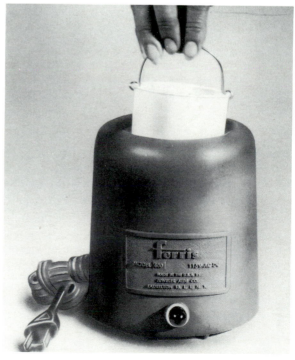

Fig. 63   Electrically heated pickle pot

33

When not in use, the pickling solution can be kept in an earthenware crock or a Pyrex glass jar. Several types of the new poly-ethylene plastic containers can also be used.

The pickling solution can be reused many times. Eventually, when enough metal is deposited in the solution to saturate it, the pickle will turn a dark blue-green color and should be discarded.

Sparex No. 2, a commercial preparation, can also be used for pickling. Though slower in action than sulfuric acid and a little more expensive, Sparex has the advantage of being less corrosive and is therefore recommended for schools, and also commercial establishments where ventilation is poor. Sparex solutions should be heated to make them more effective (one tablespoon to one quart of water).

Sulfamic Acid, an organic acid, or Sodium Bisulphate can be used for preparing pickle solutions. 1 teaspoon of either dissolved in a pint of water is as effective as the commercial preparation and both are less expensive.

OXIDATION PREVENTION Gold and sterling silver can be protected by chemicals to prevent the formation of the copper oxide (fire scale) while soldering.

For Gold Boric acid is mixed with alcohol and kept in a small covered jar (fig. 64). The gold object is dropped into the solution, removed, and heated to ignite and remove the alcohol, thus leaving a thin coating of boric acid.

For Silver The above can be used too. The following, however, is less expensive since alcohol is not required. An excessive amount of boric acid is dissolved in boiling water to form a saturated solution when the water is cooled to room temperature. The silver is warmed carefully with a soft flame until it turns light brown (not red), and then, while still hot, it is dropped into the solution. The metal is removed, heated to dry, and it can now be soldered without the formation of copper oxide or fire scale.

If formed, deep fire scale (cupric oxide) can be removed from silver by immersing the

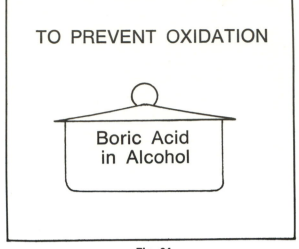

TO PREVENT OXIDATION

Boric Acid in Alcohol

Fig. 64

silver into a cold 50% water and 50% nitric acid solution. The solution is very strong and the object must be removed quickly. It is best not to use the above unless absolutely necessary.

Note: Pickling does not completely remove the fire scale from sterling silver; it merely cleans the gray cuprous oxide from the surface and leaves a fine thin layer of silver. After pickling, if the jewelry object is polished lightly, the silver layer will be removed, exposing any fire scale (a dark gray to reddish color). The cupric oxide (deep fire scale) can only be removed with pumice, emery, by stripping, bombing, or by "bright dipping" in the above nitric acid solution.

Though the fire scale can be prevented or removed as described above, on much of the handmade silver jewelry it is not objectionable.

6. CUTTING METAL

The easiest and quickest method of making straight cuts in sheet metal up to a thickness of 16 gauge is with a hand shear with a straight blade (fig. 65). Circles can be cut from a square piece of sheet metal with this type of shear. Although most straight and curved cuts can be made with a straight-bladed shear, there are other shears that a jeweler might use when cutting sheet metal. Compound lever shears, universal metal

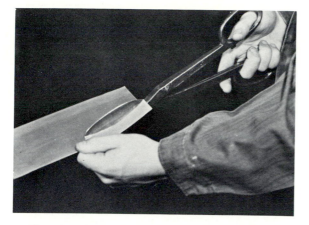

Fig. 65 Making a straight cut with a hand shear

shears, 7" plate shears with a curved blade (for concave cuts), 6" hand shears (for cutting solder), and large foot-squaring shears are among the most popular. To cut lengths of wire a jeweler can use an end-nipper plier, a combination plier, or a bench shear.

For easy cutting, the metal is held as near to the pivot point of the jaws of the shear as possible and also straight out, or perpendicular to the jaws. For long straight cuts, the metal is constantly pushed into the jaws of the shear as the cutting proceeds. When cutting curves, hold the metal perpendicular to the shear and as close to the pivot point as possible.

HACK SAWS The hack saw (fig 66) can be used for cutting large tubes, heavy bars, and thick metals. 8" hack saw blades with fine teeth (24 teeth per inch) are suggested for most required jobs. Suggestions when using a hack saw:

The teeth of the blade point away from the handle.

Fig. 66 Cutting a brass bar with a hack saw

Hold the frame with both hands.
Cut the metal with a steady (50 to 80 strokes per minute) even stroke.

7. THE JEWELER'S SAW AND BLADES

One of the most frequently used tools in jewelry making is the jeweler's saw. Sawing is the most accurate method of cutting metal. The jeweler's saw is used to cut out intricate shapes of metal, to remove an inner area of metal (known as piercing), to cut apart links for chain, and to make decorative cuts along the edge of a piece of metal. A jeweler's saw with a fine blade can even be used as a file in areas that are too small for the file to reach.

Fig. 67 Pierced pendant   Julian Wolff

PURCHASING Saw frames can be purchased with different depths, ranging from 2¼" up to 12". Purchase a good quality saw since it is used more than any other jewelry tool. The following are recommended:

The 2¼" frame for commercial jewelry work.

The 4" frame for general craft work.

Rarely is a frame with a depth greater than 4" required for jewelry work.

Jeweler's saw blades can be purchased in sizes from number 8/0, the thinnest, to number 14, the thickest. Number 8/0 is used for the finest pierced work; number 3/0 is used for general gold and platinum jewelry; number 0 and 2 for general silver work (fig.

35

68). The thicker blades are rarely used for hand sawing.

The blades are made from a good grade of tool steel. Rarely will a blade wear out. They usually break from misuse.

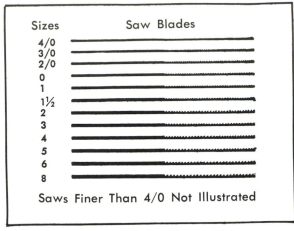

Fig. 68 Sizes of jeweler's saw blades

HOW TO INSERT THE BLADE Hold the frame as shown in figure 69. Insert the blade in the front (top) of the frame. The teeth of the blade should point out and down towards the handle. Tighten the wing screw to lock the blade in position. If necessary, adjust the length of the frame so that the blade extends to about the center of the lower jaws. Press the handle in with your hand; insert the blade between the jaws; and, while still pressing the frame in, tighten the jaws by means of

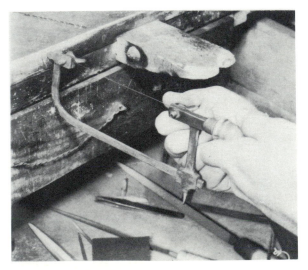

Fig. 69 Inserting the saw blade

the wing screw. This operation will leave the blade very taut, and a taut blade is essential for proper cutting.

Tighten the wing screw only by hand. The use of a plier should be avoided since it is slow and tends to damage the threads of the wing screw.

SAWING PROCEDURE Saw on a bench pin (fig. 70) a piece of wood with a "V" cut into it. Hold the metal down firmly over the "V" in the bench pin (fig. 70). If the metal slips, the jeweler's saw blade will snap. To make a straight cut, incline the saw frame forward no more than 5 degrees. Bring the frame up as far as possible (fig. 71) and then quickly bring the frame straight down with very little forward pressure on the metal. By repeating this operation and by using long even strokes, it is amazing how quickly and easily straight cuts can be made.

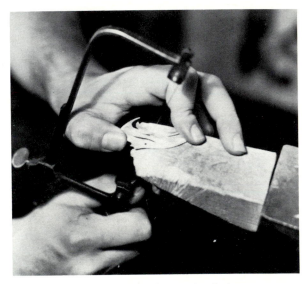

Fig. 70 Sawing in a school shop

To make a right angle cut or to turn, hold the saw straight up (perpendicular to the metal) and, without pressure forward or by almost cutting backwards, make a series of light cuts, each time turning the saw frame or work slightly until the right angle cut has been made. Saw as close to the line of design as possible but not directly on it. After the sawing has been completed, the line is used as a guide for filing. Accurate sawing calls for very little filing. A very taut blade can be used as a file when doing fine piercing if it is used on its side.

When piercing, that is, cutting inside the metal, a very small hole is first drilled through the metal. The blade is inserted through the hole and then tightened so that the necessary cutting can be accomplished.

Some jewelers prefer to add beeswax to the saw blade when cutting. A piece of beeswax is pressed against the side of the bench pin (fig. 69) and the blade is touched to it occasionally.

When sawing, the metal can be held by hand over the "V" in a bench pin or by a Bernard-type plier, with the plier pressed against the bench pin. The hand method is recommended for silver craft workers; the plier method is preferred by gold and platinum jewelers, especially for small objects. In both methods, the metal must be held firmly against the bench pin, for the saw blade will snap if the metal slips. **Caution:** Beginners should avoid clamping the metal to be sawed to the bench pin or vise since the clamping takes time and also does not permit proper manipulation of the metal.

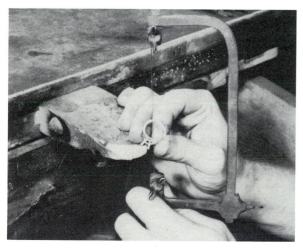

Fig. 71 Sawing on a bench pin

When backing out of a straight sawed line, move the saw frame up and down, slowly pulling the saw blade back along the saw kerf. The saw blade can be removed from the inside of an intricate cut by opening the upper clamp and releasing the blade, whereupon the frame can be pulled down until the blade is free. The blade should be released

from the lower clamp after all sawing has been completed so that the saw frame is not stored under tension.

The bench tray should be pulled out and a piece of paper placed in the tray to catch filings and scrap metal. After the piece has been filed, the filings should be carefully deposited into a jar so that when enough metal has accumulated, it can be sold to a refiner. Try to keep the various scrap metals separate.

8. DRILLS AND DRILLING

Drilling is the most common method used to make holes in metal for jewelry work.

SIZES Drills are sized several ways: by numbers, fractions, letters, metrically. The number system is the one used most often by jewelers. The drills in the number system run from number one, the largest, to number eighty, the smallest. Below are listed different sized drills and their equivalents in thousandths of an inch.

80	.013	60	.040	35	.110
1/64	.015	55	.052	1/8	.125
75	.021	1/16	.062	30	.128
70	.028	50	.070	15	.180
1/32	.031	45	.082	1	.228
65	.035	40	.098	1/4	.250

CENTER PUNCHING The exact spot to be drilled must be centerpunched or marked. This may be done several ways: with a spring center punch, an awl, or an engraving tool. The spring center punch is easy to use — merely press down on it at the desired position. The awl is pressed firmly and rotated slightly where desired. The engraving tool, a diamond or lozenge one, is rotated where desired to form the mark for the drill.

DRILLING METHODS Holes may be drilled by means of a hand drill, a drill press, or a flexible shaft.

The hand drill is the least desirable method for commercial work. When using a drill as small as No. 60, care must be taken not to press too hard to avoid breaking the drill. In spite of its shortcomings for professional work, amateur craftsmen will find the drill satisfactory for much of their work. To insert the drill, place it in the chuck, hold the chuck firmly with one hand, and, with the other hand, turn the handle clockwise to tighten the jaws of the chuck. The sheet of metal can be placed on a wooden block and secured with small brads hammered around the perimeter.

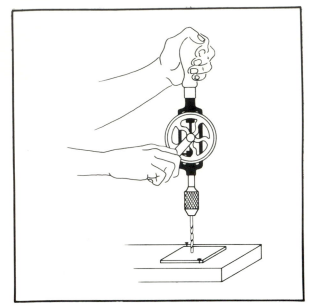

Fig. 72 Drilling with a hand drill

For commercial jewelry, a small high speed drill press (fig. 16), the speed of which can be controlled by a rheostat, is desirable. Most work to be drilled is clamped to a piece of wood on the drill press table or held securely in a vise. After the drill mark (the mark indicating where to drill) is aligned with the drill, the drill is slowly lowered by a lever to the metal. The object to be drilled may be held in

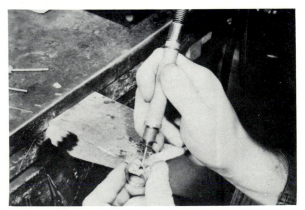

Fig. 73 Drilling with a flexible shaft

one's hand, and the hole is drilled by pressing the object up against the rotating drill. This method permits one to drill holes in curved objects that would be difficult to drill otherwise with a drill press.

The flexible shaft (fig. 73) is indispensible for professional jewelry work. With it, one may remain seated at the work bench. The accuracy, speed, and versatility of the flexible shaft more than repays its initial cost in a short time.

Small adaptor chucks, that fit into the larger chuck of a flexible shaft handpiece, can be purchased to hold very narrow drills.

DRILLING HINTS The drill or metal must be oiled often while drilling. Oil keeps the drill cool and sharp. A light machine oil is best. It is best to keep the oil in a small glass container. The tip of the drill is placed into the container so oil may be gathered.

Thin drills should protrude from the drill chuck as little as possible (¼″ for thin metals) since they tend to snap easily. Often the shank of the drill must be snapped off so the drill will not stick out too much.

Use higher speeds for smaller drills than for larger ones. However, the pressure applied (feed) must be less to avoid snapping

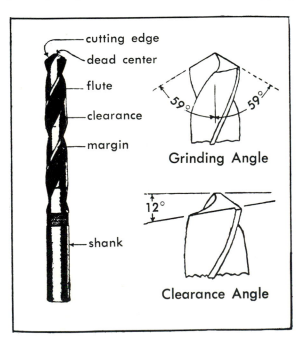

Fig. 74 A twist drill and its cutting angles

the drill. Small drills tend to snap when they break through the back of the metal being drilled.

Carbon steel drills are superior to high speed steel drills for jewelry work since they do not snap as easily. High speed drills are used mainly for drilling pearls.

SHARPENING DRILLS Drills eventually become dull and must be resharpened. They may be sharpened several ways: namely, by means of the grindstone, oilstone, or flexible shaft.

Note, from figure 74, the following:
1. The drill turns clockwise.
2. The actual cutting (drilling) is done at two cutting edges, the lips.
3. The twisted flute helps to form the cutting edge. It also removes the metal being cut, curls the chip within itself, and permits the oil to get down to the cutting edges.
4. The surface of the "point" is ground away from the lips at a 12 degree angle to give the lips a real cutting edge.
5. The angle of the lips (in relation to the axis of the drill) should be equal; 59 degrees is recommended for most work.
6. Both lips should be of the same length.

GRINDSTONE METHOD Drills that are larger than number 50 are best sharpened on an electric grindstone. Each lip is sharpened separately. The drill is held against the stone so that the lip forms the required 59° angle with the axis of the drill. Then, while grinding the 59° angle with the axis of the drill, the drill is twisted slightly to form the 12 degree lip clearance angle. Study the shape of a new drill. With a little practice, it should be easy to grind the drill properly.

OILSTONE METHOD The drill, held in a pin vise, is rubbed on a hard Arkansas stone. First adjust the pin vise to obtain the 59° angle on one of the lips and then incline the vise for the 12° angle. Sharpen the other lip the same way. The stone may be rubbed against the drill.

FLEXIBLE SHAFT METHOD This method is very easy with small drills. The drill is held in a pin vise. A small, flat emery wheel (¾″ dia. x ⅛″ wide will do) is placed in the chuck of the flexible shaft. The drill is held against the rotating emery wheel at the proper angles. With a little practice, drills can be sharpened very quickly and accurately this way.

HOW TO MAKE A SMALL DRILL (fig. 75). It is comparatively easy to make a small drill if a manufactured one is not available. A sewing needle or any good grade of tool steel rod is required. The rod is first ground, as shown in the diagram, to a screw driver point. Then the 59° lip clearance angle is ground to form each lip. The 12° lip clearance angle is ground to complete the grinding process. The drill, if drill rod is used, must be hardened and then tempered to dark brown. This drill, surprisingly practical, can be made quickly.

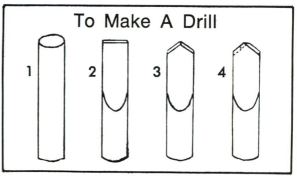

Fig 75 Steps in making a drill

PUNCHING HOLES Often it is easier to punch a small hole through a metal than it is to drill it. This is especially true on flat thin metal (up to 18 gauge) that is to be pierced (sawed) and where the punched hole is used for inserting the jeweler's saw. A sharply ground pointed pick or awl is used and the punching is best done over a lead block. Hammer the punch until the metal breaks through, then remove the tool and punch back lightly from the opposite side to enlarge the hole.

9. HARDENING AND TEMPERING STEEL

Although gravers, stamping, and chasing and repoussé tools can be purchased from jewelry supply and equipment companies, jewelers frequently have to create new tools, modify existing tools, and sharpen old tools. In order for jewelers to make their own punches, stamps, and cutting tools, it is necessary for them to be able to use the various processes described below on tool steel—the metal that these tools are made of.

Gravers, and stamping and chasing tools can quickly be ground to their approximate shape by using a carborundum or an emery wheel that is mounted on an electric grinding machine. These wheels should not be used for grinding nonferrous metals because they will clog the surface of the wheel.

Steel tools can also be shaped by forging. The metal is heated in a furnace or with a torch until it turns a glowing red color. It is then forged on an anvil.

Chasing and stamping tools are frequently made from square tool steel blanks, or drill rod. The design on the stamp is made by using assorted files, drills, and a jeweler's saw. Since steel drill rod is as hard as a file it must be softened before it can be filed. Tool steel is made soft by heating it to a cherry red color (approximately 1400°F.) with a torch and then allowing it to cool slowly. After the tool steel has been made soft and the design has been formed, the tool steel is returned to its original hardened state.

Tool steel is hardened by heating it until cherry red (approximately 1400°F.) and then dipping it very quickly into cold water. This makes the steel very hard but brittle. It must be heated again, that is—tempered, to remove some of the brittleness, otherwise it would snap while being used.

An engraving tool can be hardened and tempered as follows: Heat about one inch of the cutting end of the tool until it is cherry red and then quickly dip it into cold water. Move the tool around in the water so that it will always be in a cold section. This should make the cutting edge very hard but also too brittle to be used. The edge can be tested for hardness with a file. If it can be filed it is too soft.

Now polish the tool with emery paper. It is tempered by heating the steel about 1½" behind the cutting edge. The proper tempering temperature can be obtained by observing the oxidation colors which appear. These colors, caused by the oxidation of steel when heated, indicate different degrees of temperature. It has been found that the higher the temperature of the steel, the darker the oxidation color and the less brittle the steel is. Note the colors as they appear. First—a light straw, then in order, dark straw, dark brown, purple, blue, and finally steel gray. The proper tempering temperature for the engraving tool is approximately 420°F. At this temperature the steel is light straw.

Note: If the steel is overheated when tempering, that is, if it turns brown or blue, the entire process must be repeated. To soften hardened steel, heat the steel to cherry red and permit it to cool slowly in air, or better yet, in powdered asbestos.

Temp.	Color	Suggested Uses
420°F.	Light Straw	Engraving tools, scrapers
460°F.	Dark Straw	Chasing tools, punches
500°F.	Dark Brown	Drills
540°F.	Purple	Hammer heads
570°F.	Blue	Knives, screw drivers
630°F.	Black	Springs

GRINDING TOOLS When grinding a tool such as an engraving tool, the tool must be dipped constantly into cold water to avoid "burning" the steel. By burning is meant the appearance of a blue color on the steel. This color is formed by the heat generated by the friction of the grinding operation, and it indicates that the steel has been tempered or softened too much. The tool will have to be hardened and then tempered to restore its cutting properties.

The preferred grinding wheel is a soft emery or soapstone, and the wheels should be mounted on an electric machine.

SUGGESTIONS WHEN GRINDING Dip the tool constantly into cold water to keep it cool.

Do not press too hard against the wheel to avoid "burning" the steel.

Grind away from the cutting edge of a tool such as an engraving tool. If you grind towards the cutting edge you may carry the friction heat towards the thin edge and "burn" the steel.

10. FORMING METAL

Forming is the general name given to the processes that are used to shape the metal. Forming is not a working technique in itself but a combination of all the techniques that change a two-dimensional shape into a three-dimensional object. Under the heading of forming are such processes as bending, dapping, chasing, repoussé, sinking, hammering with or without stakes, using stamps and dies, forging, fusing, and engraving. All of the forming processes, with the exception of bending, will change not only the original shape and/or texture of the metal but also its thickness.

Fig. 76 Pin   **Jem Freyaldenhoven**

PLIERS AND THEIR USE

Although it is possible, and often advantageous, for jewelers to obtain many interesting shapes by bending thin wire or sheet with their fingers, much of the bending that is done on thin metal is accomplished with the aid of pliers. Smooth jawed pliers are preferred to pliers with serrated jaws for bending metal since they leave no nicks on the metal. Right angle bends may be made with flat nose pliers. Round-nose pliers are helpful when creating spirals and half-round pliers are used when bending curves.

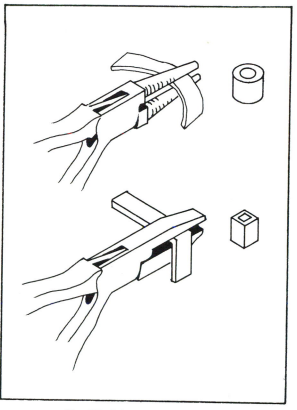

Fig. 77 Pliers bending metal

TYPES Pliers can be classified into two groups: those with parallel jaw action and those which have jaws that pivot around a rivet.

The jaws of the parallel jawed (Bernard) type, opened or closed, (fig. 78) are always parallel, and since they have strong gripping action they are very popular with commercial jewelers.

The jaws of the pivot type are parallel only when closed. Their gripping action when open (fig. 78) isn't as strong as the parallel jawed group. They, however, are manufactured with finer jaws and are superior to the parallel jawed type for bending thin wire; they also are excellent for bending thin flat strips of metal.

The box joint type (fig. 79) of pivot plier is recommended over the usual cross lap type

41

because the jaws of the box joint plier remain straight and aligned under the pressure required to bend metal, and also because they are often made from a better grade of steel.

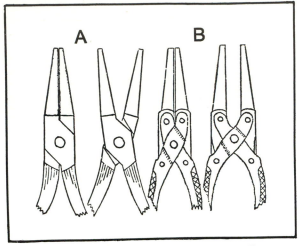

Fig. 78 Pivot (A) and parallel (B) type pliers, closed and open

LENGTHS Jeweler's pliers are manufactured in lengths from 3½ inches up to 6 inches. The 5 inch length is used by most commercial jewelers and is recommended for craftsmen.

SHAPES OF JAWS Flat, round, chain or snipe, and half-round pliers are the popular shapes of jewelry pliers (fig. 79). They are usually purchased with smooth jaws by craftsmen. The 5″ parallel jawed Bernard plier with serrated (grooved) jaws, due to its strong gripping action, is popular with gold and platinum jewelers. The jaws of the above plier also are grooved down the entire length so that wire and tubing can be held firmly for cutting and filing purposes.

Special pliers with jaws designed to hold rings to be filed or cut, and also pliers for bending heavy shanked rings are available.

RESHAPING THE JAWS The jaws of most jeweler's pliers are soft and can be filed to different shapes for special purposes. The Bernard type of parallel plier with smooth jaws can be converted into a useful half-round plier by filing and then emerying one jaw to a half-round shape. The snipe or chain nose plier also can be converted into a half-round type of plier for bending wire into spirals. The jaws of serrated jawed pliers can be filed smooth.

If pliers have heat hardened tool steel jaws, the jaws can be softened by heating them to light red (see page 40) and then permitting them to cool in air.

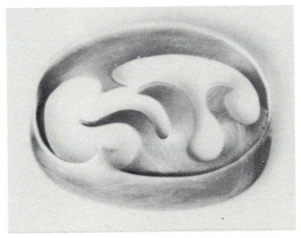

Fig. 80 Pin   **Ralph Murray**

SHAPING AND BENDING

When the metal is too thick to be bent with pliers, sharp bends can be made by placing the metal between the jaws of a smooth jawed vise and then hammering the metal with a rawhide or wooden mallet until the desired bend is achieved. Annealed metal can be curved over mandrels or stakes with a wooden mallet. **Note:** A wooden mallet will

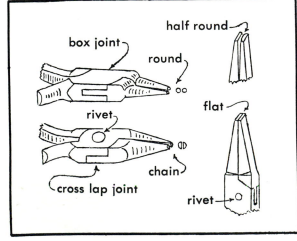

Fig. 79 Plier types and shapes

not nick or stretch the metal as much as a metal hammer. Starting at one end of the section or piece of metal to be bent, the metal is held firmly against the stake, and hammered on the appropriate curved part of the stake with the mallet. The metal is moved on the stake as the hammering continues until the metal, or the end of the section of metal, is formed into the desired curve. The curvature of the stake or mandrel should be slightly less than that of the inside curve of the section being formed. A stake that is too large, or has a radius that is too flat, will only stretch the metal. If the stake has too small a radius, the curve could become too closed.

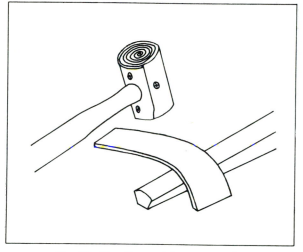

Fig. 81 Bending metal over a stake

Shallow hardwood hollow forms are used when forming contours, or when sinking metal into the shape of a dome if the hollows of a dapping block are either too small or too deep. Small commercial maple blocks with hollows of various sizes can be used, or the desired hollow can be made in a piece of hardwood by using assorted gouges and riffler files. The metal can be placed over the depression and then hammered into the depression with a shape that matches the depression, such as a wooden block or pestle, until the metal matches the depression curve in the wood. The metal can also be shaped by sinking it into the depression with a small forming hammer and then planishing it over a domed stake.

Metal can also be formed into various shapes by utilizing such techniques as straight raising, combination raising, and angular raising. These techniques are done with various hammers (forming, planishing, raising, forging, box, ball peen, and cross peen) and stakes (T-stake, cow-tongue, concave, valley, forming, raising, and dome). It

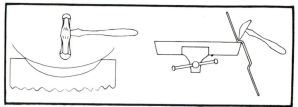

Fig. 82 Sinking metal   Fig. 82A Raising metal

is frequently advisable to make a stake (or a series of stakes) from hardwood that approximates the convex and concave contours being formed. This also minimizes the number of stakes that have to be purchased.

A piece is raised by hammering the metal in stages until a rough approximation of the desired contour has been formed. It is impossible to form a complex shape in a single raise. The metal should be hammered to various angles along its length. The angles are then rounded off by planishing the metal on a domed stake. To remove any irregularities and further smooth the metal, anneal and then replanish on an appropriate stake. Planishing also hardens the metal so that it will retain its shape.

Work with a template or a sketch to check the shape of the piece as it is being formed.

Fig. 83 Bracelet   Pahaka

Greatest leverage (mechanical advantage) is achieved when the metal that has been raised is held in contact with the front top corner of the stake. The greater the angle of elevation, the more the metal will be bent at the contact point with the stake. An area of metal that still has to be raised and bent is elevated slightly and then slowly hammered down until it conforms to the shape of the stake. If the metal is held too flat on the stake, or if the hammer blow is "pushed" outward too much on the stake, the metal will not be raised inward, but rather stretched.

Intricate pieces are usually formed by combining raising and sinking.

Note: Additional information on these processes can be found in the author's book "Silversmithing and Art Metal".

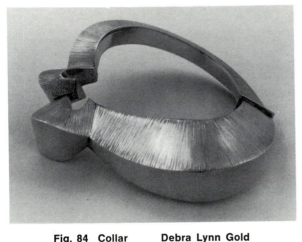

Fig. 84 Collar   Debra Lynn Gold

DOMES

Dapping is a term that is applied to the process of forming hemispheres or domes in sheet metal. While the blocks that are used to form the domes can be made of lead or wood, most jewelers prefer a steel constructed dapping block since it maintains its shape indefinitely. A dapping block is a cube that consists of a number of different sized hemispherical depressions. The depressions of the dapping block match spherical punches

The diameter of the circular disc used must be larger than the required dome, approxi-

Fig. 86 Circle cutter

mately ⅓ larger to make a half sphere. Circular discs may be purchased, or they may be cut to shape with a shear or sawed from a large piece of metal. The gauge of the metal depends upon the size and the design of the object. Circle cutters that will easily cut discs from sheet metal can be purchased. A sheet of brass should be placed under the metal being cut to prolong the life of the cutting die.

To form a dome, place the metal level in an appropriate hollow in the dapping block and hammer it to shape with steel dapping punches or, better yet, for larger domes, with wooden punches. The tops of many file handles make excellent punches. To make a semi-sphere, keep moving the metal while shaping it from larger to smaller hollows in the block until the required shape is obtained. The sphere may be filed while it is in the dapping block.

If a lead block is used to form the sphere, the hollows are punched into the lead with steel dapping tools. The procedure then is the same as above, only all traces of lead which may adhere to the metal must be removed with emery paper or a glass fiber brush.

A small dome may be formed on part of a flat sheet of metal (see mask on page 221) by placing the metal over the required hollow in the dapping block. A slightly smaller punch

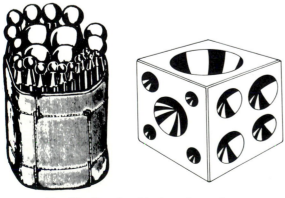

Fig. 85 Dapping block and punches

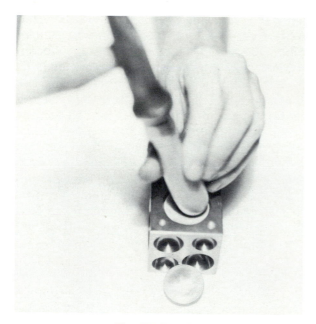

Fig. 87 Dapping

than the hollow in the block is hammered down to form the dome in the metal.

SPHERES Spheres are made by soldering two semi-spheres, made as described above, together. A tiny hole must be drilled in one to permit air to escape and re-enter during the soldering operation, otherwise the sphere may collapse as it cools or explode if re-heated.

SHOT

Shot are small, solid balls of metal which have many ornamental uses in silver and gold jewelry work. Although there is by no means a definition that differentiates exactly between a granule and shot, shot can be described as larger, with a diameter from 1/32″ to ¼″.

Shot are made by melting pure silver, sterling silver, or gold on a charcoal block. Pure silver will form into rounder and smoother shot than sterling silver. Scrap metal may be used to make shot; however, if many shot are required of the same size, it is best to use wire. The wire is wrapped around a rod, in a manner similar to link making, and after it is removed, the coiled wire is cut with a nipper to form rings. The rings, when melted, will form shot of equal size.

If perfectly round balls are desired, little concave impressions of the proper size are made in the charcoal with a small dapping punch, over which the metal is melted. If the concave impression is not made, the balls will be slightly flat on the bottom.

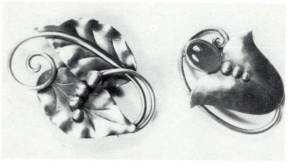

Fig. 88 Silver pins with shot and spirals

Before heating, coat the metal with borax flux to prevent oxidation of the surface and to assure that a perfect sphere is formed. Use a sharp flame to quickly melt the metal. As soon as the balls are formed, reduce the size of the flame. Slowly cooling the balls in this way should leave them smooth and oxide-free. The balls should be pickled before they are soldered to the jewelry object.

Excellent silver shot can be made by melting the silver on a piece of wood. The formed shot are unusually smooth, but slightly flat on the bottom. This method is worth trying, especially when charcoal is not available.

SPIRALS

A spiral is best formed from round, square, or rectangular wire as follows. File one end of the wire on one side only to taper it (fig. 90). The end of the wire may be forged, if desired, to a taper.

Grip the very end of the wire with smooth jawed round-nose or half-round chain nose pliers. Hold the wire fairly firm with the pliers and start to bend the wire in. While bending, permit the pliers to slip and snap off the end of the wire. By so doing, the spiral can be curved or started from the very end of the wire.

Now that the spiral has been started, hold the beginning of the spiral firmly with the plier and then bend the wire (or turn the plier) to form the spiral. A pleasingly shaped open spiral (fig. 90 top) can be formed in the above way. **Note:** The spiral is formed by holding the wire with the pliers at the very tip and no other place.

Fig. 89   Wire work   George Moore

The tip of the wire for a closed spiral (fig. 90 center) is started the same way as above. After the start, the tip is squeezed together with a plier until it is closed. Now the beginning of the spiral is held sideways between the flat jaws of a flat or snipe nose plier and it is then bent to form the spiral.

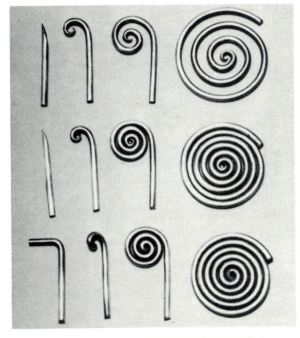

Fig. 90   Three methods of forming a spiral

After the wire has been coiled several times, the coil or spiral may be held in one's fingers and the coiling may be continued until the proper sized spiral has been achieved.

A closed spiral can be formed quickly by bending about ½ inch of one end of the wire to be spiraled at right angles (fig. 90 bottom). Then grip the bent end of the wire in the side jaws of a parallel jawed plier. Turn the long end of the wire to form the spiral. Wires 14 gauge or thicker may have to be annealed before the first turn is completed. After the spiral has been formed to the proper size, the bent starting end is nipped off leaving the spiral shown in figure 90 bottom.

Fig. 91   Silver pins with domed discs and spirals

CONES

Cones and sections of cones can be made from flat sheet as follows:

On the same center line, the front and top view of the cone is drawn as shown in figure 92. The top is divided into four equal parts and then with a divider one of the parts is divided into three equal parts. Distance 0 to 1 then represents 1/12 of the circumference of the top of the cone. Distance A-B is marked off on the metal, and, with a divider and A as center and A-B as radius, an arc is drawn. Along the arc, starting from B, 12 lengths, 0 to 1, are then marked off. At the twelfth point a line is drawn back to A, completing the pattern for the cone.

Transfer the pattern to a piece of metal and then cut it out with a jeweler's saw. File the two ends flat and straight with a needle file so that when they meet a perfect butt joint will be formed. The piece can be bent to shape with heavy round-nose pliers. Begin bending at the ends and work towards the middle. When a perfect fit has been achieved,

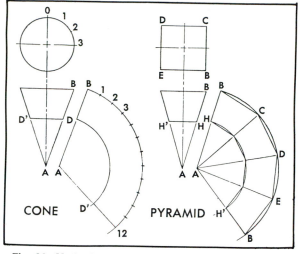

Fig. 92 Method of developing the cone and pyramid

PYRAMIDS

Sections (frustums) of pyramids can be made from flat sheet in a manner somewhat similar to that used for cones. Figure 92 shows how the front and top view are drawn. Then, on the metal, with A as center, the arcs are drawn and along the arc formed from B, distances B-C, C-D, D-E, and E-B are marked off and then connected to A with straight lines. Line H-H' is drawn. The bending lines are scored with a three corner file, and, after the metal is bent to shape, solder is applied to each corner to reinforce it. The ends are then soldered together. The pyramid can be planished on a flat tapered mandrel to define its shape.

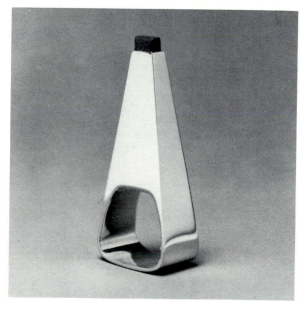

Fig. 94 Ring   Mary Ann Scherr

the joint can be soldered. The cone is forced onto a tapered mandrel that approximates its shape and then lightly planished. A center punch is frequently used as a mandrel.

A section (frustum) of a cone can be used to make a setting. The method of development is the same as the completed cone with the line D-D' added as shown in the diagram.

It is easy and practical, however, to form sections of cones for small settings by first making a cylinder and then, with a tapered punch and die, punching the cylinder to taper it. A large round plate may be used as the die.

11. RIVETING

Occasionally, in contemporary jewelry making, processes that do not require heat must be employed when joining two pieces of metal together. "Non-soldering" methods are also used when metal is combined with other materials such as wood, plastics, and gemstones. One technique of attaching materials is to use leather, wire, or cord, and then to string, tie, wrap, or weave the individual pieces together. Epoxies can be used to hold pearls, wood, and gemstones in settings.

Fig. 93 Gyroscope   Gerry Tuten

47

Fig. 95 Pendant with decorative rivets
Dennis de Jonghe

Screws, bolts, pins, nails, friction posts, interlocking joints, flanges, and wire knots can also be utilized to fasten materials together.

Rivets are excellent fasteners and thus are frequently used to join sheets of metal together. Some jewelers use rivets for purely decorative purposes. Rivets are also used in the construction of hinges. A simple hinge which will allow pieces of metal to move sideways can be made by riveting one piece of metal to another. A thin sheet of metal can be placed between the sheets during the riveting process to insure that the pieces are not pressed too closely together. In complex hinges, a rivet is inserted through tubes that have been alternately soldered to the two sections of metal.

Aluminum, copper, brass, and iron rivets can be purchased with round, oval, or flat heads in diameters of 1/16 to 1/4 inch and lengths from 1/4 to 1 inch.

Rivets can also be constructed from metal wire or rod. One end of the wire can be fused into a bead to form the head of the rivet. The heads of rivets can be textured or enlarged with a hammer. A hollow tube can be made into a rivet by countersinking holes in the metal and then flaring the ends of the tube with a tapered punch.

To rivet two pieces of metal together, first drill holes through them the same size as the rivet. Then place the rivet in position and, if necessary, cut the projecting part of the rivet (the shank) to the proper length — which for a round headed rivet is 1½ times the rivet's thickness. Now the clearance hole in the rivet set is placed over the rivet, and the set is hammered to force the two metals together (fig. 97).

Fig. 96 Bracelet   Phillip Johnson

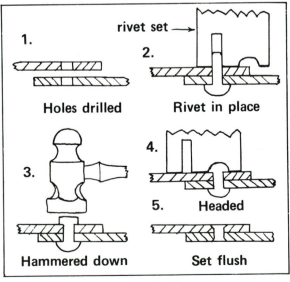

Fig. 97 Riveting

The rivet is set and headed as follows. With a flat face of a ball peen hammer, hammer down on the shank of the rivet to spread it as shown in figure 97. The round head is formed by placing the concave depression in the rivet set over the spread shank and then hammering the set firmly (fig. 97). If a faceted rivet head is desired, do not use the rivet set; round the spread shank of the rivet with the round head of the ball peen hammer.

If both sides of the rivet are to be round, set the rivet by placing the round head of the rivet over the concave depression in another rivet set. If the rivet is to be flush on one or both sides, countersink the metal on one or both sides and hammer the shank of the rivet to spread it into the countersunk area. If a number of rivets are to be used, drill the first set of holes and place a rivet in those holes. Then drill the other holes; thus all holes will be aligned.

12. FUSING

By carefully manipulating a soldering torch with a hot flame, pieces of metal can be fused together without solder. The disadvantage of joining two pieces of metal by fusing rather than soldering is that an orange-peel texture may be created on the surface of the metal. Also, the risk of melting the metal is increased because the metal is brought very close to its melting point.

Nevertheless, craftsmen can use the fusing process to join pieces of metal if the changes brought about by heating metal close to its melting point create effects that are desired for their jewelry pieces, or if they are very skilled with a soldering torch. The results of this process are difficult to control. By experimenting with different shapes and types of metals and observing the effects of heat on the metal, more control and artistic insight are gained. It is also important to learn the colors (see page 57) at which the metals melt.

The fusing process can be employed to fuse small pieces of metal together to form spheres, to create beads at the ends of wires, to join two pieces of metal, to join pieces of metal to a base sheet of metal, and to join

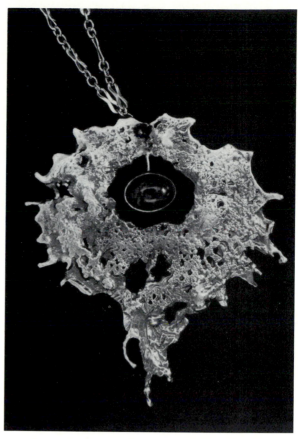

Fig. 98 Fused pendant   **Ross Coppelman**

many fragments of metal together into a unique form. In these last two cases, filings, shot, wires, and pieces of sheet metal can be used. Fragments can be cut out to the desired shape, shaped by heat before the final fusing, or fused into a shape from smaller fragments. Different metals can be fused together for different color effects.

Before fusing, clean the metals to be used in a pickling solution so that they are free from dirt, grease, and oxides. Then coat the pieces with flux to prevent oxidation. The metals can be fused on charcoal, asbestos, or fire brick. If necessary, pieces of metal can be moved into position for fusing with a poker, or, for smaller fragments, with tweezers. A torch with a hot, reducing flame provides the necessary heat. It is very important in the fusing process to heat the metals so that the points of contact become equally hot at the same time. As the metal reaches the fusing point, the flame can be adjusted to a needle point so that increased control over fusing

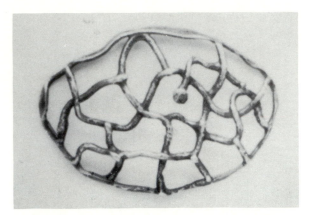

Fig. 99 Pin—fused wires—no solder was used

is possible. Avoid overheating the metal or carefully controlled designs will become molten pools of metal.

There are many different techniques that can be used to fuse metal, depending on the result desired. Regardless of the technique used, however, the basic principles of fusing described above apply and are important to remember.

Spheres can be formed from several pieces of metal by rotating the torch over the metal fragments until they fuse. Slow and even heating is essential. If necessary, make an indentation in the charcoal block to keep the metal from rolling off it.

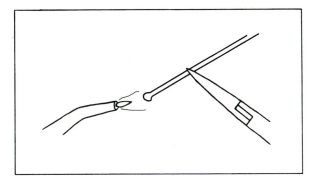

Fig. 100 Fusing a bead on the end of a piece of wire

A bead can be made on the end of a wire by coating the tip of the wire with flux; holding the wire, tip down, with tweezers; and quickly touching a small, hot flame to the tip. A bead will form when the end begins to melt. The bead will drop off when it reaches a certain size. A larger bead can be made by placing the wire on a charcoal block and

heating the end until it fuses to form a bead of the desired size.

The ends of two sheets of metal are best fused together by heating them separately but simultaneously. Use a torch with a large soft flame. When the pieces are approaching their melting point, push them together with a poker.

Small pieces of irregularly shaped sheet metal, different gauges of wire bent in various positions, and pieces of shot can be fused to a sheet of 20 gauge metal, which is used as a base. Both the sheet metal and the various small pieces of metal should be pickled before the pieces are fused. The base should be placed on a sheet of asbestos. After all the pieces have been coated with flux, the small pieces are arranged and intertwined on the base with tweezers. A broad torch flame is used to heat the entire piece. To bring all of the metal parts to a near molten condition at the same time, the heat should be concentrated mainly on the heavier parts and moved rapidly over the smaller parts. As soon as the edges of the smaller pieces have begun to fuse, the flame should be adjusted to a fine point and sections heated where necessary. The small pieces should be kept tightly pressed against the larger ones with a metal poker at this stage or they will melt prematurely.

Once fusing has been completed, allow the piece to cool, then pickle, and finally rinse it in water. Some craftsmen prefer to leave the "orange peel" texture on the surface of the metal, while others saw, file, and emery the piece to accent or smooth certain areas.

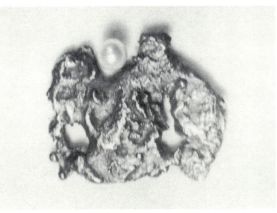

Fig. 101 Fused silver pin with pearl

13. SOLDERING

Soldering is a process that joins two pieces of metal together by heating a third metal, which has a lower melting point (known as solder), until that metal melts and then flows into the space between the metal pieces being soldered together. When the solder solidifies, a bond is created between the pieces of metal that is as strong as the metal it connects.

Soldering is generally classified into two divisions: hard and soft. Hard soldering is done with strong, high melting silver, gold, or platinum solders. Soft soldering is done with a comparatively weak, low melting, tin-lead alloy solder. Most pieces of precious metal are soldered together with hard solders. Soft solders are used when some part of the piece of jewelry will not stand the heat of hard soldering (e.g. enamels, certain findings, and some gemstones).

In both hard and soft soldering, there are certain rules that must be adhered to:

1. All metal surfaces to be soldered and the solder must be free from dirt and grease.
2. The surfaces to be soldered together and the solder must be coated with flux.
3. The proper solder must be used.
4. The surfaces of the metal to be soldered together must be shaped and then positioned so that they fit together perfectly, and they must be held together under tension.

Fig. 102 Necklace   Klaus Kallenberger

5. The solder must be correctly positioned on the metal.
6. The amount of heat must be regulated; from the torch, through the metal and to the solder.
7. The solder must flow into and across the joint in order to successfully join the pieces of metal together.

The purpose of the flux: most metals oxidize (turn black) when heated. The oxide prevents the solder from adhering and flowing. The flux facilitates the adherence and flow of the solder by:

1. Forming a protective film to keep the air away from the metal, thus checking oxidation.
2. Dissolving small amounts of oxide that have formed.
3. Wetting and lowering the surface tension of the metal.

HARD SOLDER FLUXES

BORAX — CONE Until comparatively recent times, practically all jewelers used borax as a flux. The borax, purchased in the form of a cone, is mixed with water to form a thin paste by rubbing on a hollowed slate. The flux is applied with a sable brush to both the joint and the solder. Ordinary household borax, mixed with water, can be used effectively.

COMMERCIAL PREPARATIONS In recent years, commercially prepared partially self pickling fluxes have become popular and are used by most commercial jewelers. These fluxes do not raise the solder and parts to be soldered as much as borax. The commercial liquid fluxes are recommended for most hard soldering operations. Borax, however, is preferred for copper and palladium.

BORAX AND BORIC ACID A 75% borax and 25% boric acid combination is used as a flux by some commercial jewelers for medium and high melting hard solders, for at high temperatures it is superior to borax in checking oxidation of the metal being soldered. A solution (saturated) of borax and boric acid may be formed by dissolving excessive amounts of the combination in boiling water. The solution, when cool, is applied with a brush.

1 ounce of **Ammonium Phosphate Dibasic** added to a quart of the above solution gives the composition of the commercial flux sold by many supply houses. The green color is obtained by means of a dye—sodium fluorescein. **Note:** The ammonium phosphate should be added to a cool solution to avoid a strong ammonia odor which would be obtained if added to a hot solution of borax and boric acid.

THE HARD SOLDERS

If the soldering process is to be performed successfully, it is important to use the correct solder for the metal that is being soldered. Hard solders are classified according to the name of the metal that they are intended to join together, the form in which they are sold, and their relative melting point. There are separate solders for gold, silver, and platinum. When choosing a solder, the jeweler must consider the color of the metal and using a solder that melts at the highest practical melting point possible so that the color of the solder seam will match the metal and so the bond is stronger. Hard solders melt at temperatures that are from 150° to 250°F. below the melting point of the metals being soldered.

SILVER SOLDER Silver solder, an alloy of silver, copper, and zinc, is the solder used for silver jewelry; and copper, brass, bronze, and nickel silver objects when very strong joints (tensile strength of silver solder—50,000 lbs.) are required. The melting point of the solder depends upon the percentage of zinc: as the percentage of zinc increases, the melting point of the solder decreases. Too much zinc, however, is detrimental to the metals being soldered, because zinc burns holes into metals at high temperatures. Jewelers buy silver solder in three different grades: hard, medium, and easy flow. The chart below lists the chemical composition, melting point, and flow point of the silver solders.

Solder	Silver	Copper	Zinc	Melting Point	Flow Point
Easy	65%	20%	15%	1280°F.	1325°F.
Medium	70%	20%	10%	1335°F.	1390°F.
Hard	75%	22%	3%	1365°F.	1450°F.

Note that the solders do not flow at the melting point but at a higher temperature—the flow point. On objects which require several soldered pieces, use a hard flow first and then an easier flow. However, easy flow solder alone can be used for making most simple silver jewelry objects if the seam is not visible.

A very low melting (1175°F.) silver solder, known as "Easy Flo", is available for soldering joints and catches to jewelry objects when strength is not critical, and for repair work if the gemstones have to be left in their settings. For objects to be enameled, a high strength, high temperature flowing solder (1460°F.), known as "I.T." is used.

Silver, gold, and platinum solders are available or can be made, in sheet, wire, strip rod, filed, powdered, or paste forms. The form of solder that is used depends upon the shape, size, and number of pieces that must be soldered together.

Sheet solder is the most popular form of solder with jewelers because of its versatility. 26 and 28 (preferred) gauge are the most practical thicknesses. The sheets of solder can be cut into smaller pieces of solder, or paillons, and these pieces can be placed at various points along the joint to be soldered with a tweezer or a moist flux brush.

Sheet solder is cut into approximately 1/16" squares by first cutting strips of the

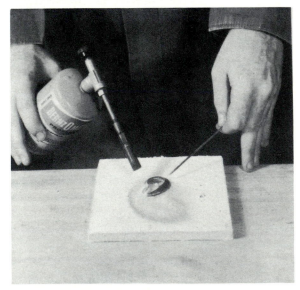

Fig. 103 Soldering with a propane gas torch

required width straight up the solder almost to the top. Then cut across the solder to form as many squares as the job requires (fig. 104). It is usually more efficient and cleaner to use several small, easily heated pieces of solder rather than one large piece of solder.

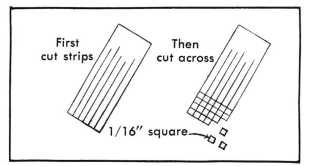

First cut strips   Then cut across

1/16″ square

Fig. 104   Method of cutting solder

18 gauge wire solder is popular with commercial silver jewelers for soldering large seams together. 24 gauge wire solder is frequently used in jewelry manufacturing. The joint is heated, and, when sufficiently hot, the wire solder (which has been dipped in flux) is quickly touched to the metal, where it will melt. Wire solders are often held in a small tube with an inside diameter the same gauge as the wire. This way it is easy to hold small pieces of wire, and on production work, since silver is a very good conductor of heat, the solder can be held without burning one's hand.

Soldering pastes are made commercially by blending together powdered solder, flux, and a binder. The pastes are used in high volume production soldering and are applied with an automatic paste dispenser or manually with a syringe type cartridge.

GOLD SOLDER At one time, jewelers would add silver and copper or brass to gold to lower its karat in order to make their solders. Today, practically all jewelers buy their solders prepared with the proper color and karat stamped on them.

Commercial jewelers use gold solders 2 to 4 karats lower, since they are less expensive than the karat gold being soldered. Recommended to craftsmen: for good color match on 14 karat gold jewelry use 14 karat solder

for first or primary soldering and lower karat solder for secondary soldering.

The karat of the solder does not necessarily indicate its flow point. A 14 karat solder can be made that will flow as easily as a 10 karat solder by varying the type of alloy metal added to the gold. Gold solders for the same karat jewelry can be purchased with two or more melting points. Note the colors, melting and flow points of some of the gold solders sold by Handy and Harman. Melting points are in degrees Fahrenheit.

Solder	Type	Color	Melting Point	Flow Point
8 kt. Y.	easy	light yellow	1165°F.	1275°F.
10 kt. Y.	easy	pale yellow	1335°F.	1390°F.
10 kt. Y.	hard	light yellow	1360°F.	1415°F.
12 kt. Y.	hard	yellow	1425°F.	1485°F.
14 kt. Y.	easy	pale yellow	1330°F.	1390°F.
10 kt. W.	easy	white	1295°F.	1350°F.
12 kt. W.	hard	white	1335°F.	1440°F.
14 kt. W.	easy	white	1300°F.	1375°F.

Note: For good color match, 16 karat hard solder can be used to fill in small pin holes or flaws on 14 karat cast objects. Joints and catches are soldered to gold jewelry objects with 6 or 8 karat solders.

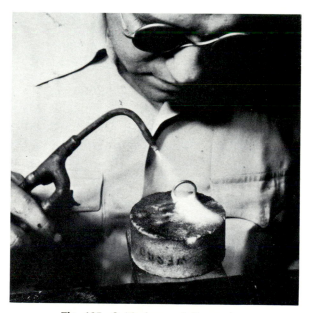

**Fig. 105   Soldering a platinum ring
Note blue goggles**

PLATINUM SOLDER Caution: Platinum has a very high melting point (3224°F.), and its solders require white heat to melt them. White heat is very detrimental to the eyes, so, for that reason, dark blue glasses (fig. 105) must be worn when soldering platinum.

Platinum can be welded. This often is done when joining the ends of a ring for a fishtail wedding band. The procedure is as follows. Place a small piece of platinum on the seam and heat until the platinum melts and fuses to the band. The required heat can be obtained with an oxygen and gas flame, but not with a compressed air and gas flame.

The usual platinum solders are 1200, 1300, 1400, and 1600 degrees Centigrade. A 1600°C. (2912°F.) welding solder is also available.

Since platinum will not oxidize, pickling is not required until the object is completed; the object is then pickled to remove the flux. A special commercially prepared flux is available for platinum soldering. It can also be soldered with the liquid self-pickling flux that is used for gold.

SOLDERING FLAME To obtain the proper soldering flame (fig. 106) with a jeweler's torch that has a separate supply of gas and air, first light the gas and then supply the air until the yellow color of the gas flame disappears and a yellow-blue flame appears. A flame that is too yellow will be too soft to concentrate the heat on a specific area, and therefore it will be difficult to control the melting of solder where needed. If a hissing sound is heard, too much air is being used. A flame that contains too much air (recognizable by its hard pointed blue flame) will cause the metal and solder to oxidize and prevent the solder from flowing. The air-gas mixture of the propane and acetylene torch flame is self-regulating.

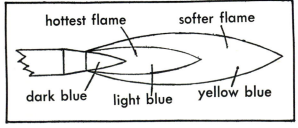
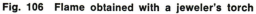

Fig. 106 Flame obtained with a jeweler's torch

Use a small flame for small objects and a larger flame for larger objects. Many soldering outfits can be purchased with interchangeable torch tips. Do not hold the flame too near the metals being soldered. Hold the torch so that the hottest part of the flame (light blue) is approximately 1 inch from the metal but does not touch the metal.

HARD SOLDERING HINTS

A flux must be used with all precious and semi-precious metals. Apply the flux to both the metal and the solder. It is best, after applying a coating of flux, to warm the metals slightly and then to apply more flux. Flux adheres better to the warm metal. The flux should be completely dry before beginning to solder.

Cleanliness is essential. Oxides, scratches, dirt, and grease must be removed by pickling, filing, emerying, or scraping. However, it is not necessary to pickle the object after each soldering for the flux will keep the metal clean. If the object looks clean—does not turn black—do not pickle until all the soldering operations are done.

The principle of capillary attraction governs the behavior of the liquid solder as it flows between the solid metal surfaces. Solder will not bridge the gap between two pieces of metal. The seams must fit perfectly. Do not attempt to fill in holes, for in subsequent soldering the solder will run out leaving objectionable spaces.

Gold and silver objects are soldered on a charcoal or asbestos soldering block. Platinum is soldered on a fire brick—often a piece of an old crucible (fig. 105). These materials reflect heat, thus accelerating the soldering process. Metal can not be used under the work because it dissipates and conducts heat.

A 4″ x 4″ iron screen frame (fig. 107) is useful for soldering flat jewelry objects. The screen is placed on an asbestos block, and the metal to be soldered is placed on the screen. Thus, when the metal is heated, the screen permits the heat to get underneath the flat metal to heat it evenly.

Irregularly shaped silver or gold objects often are soldered in powdered asbestos. The powdered asbestos is mixed with water and molded to the desired shape so that the

Fig. 107 Sweat soldering on an iron screen frame

small ball of iron binding wire (known as a soldering mop) can be made to support the work while it is being soldered.

Soft, high temperature, ceramic materials, known as soldering forms, can also be used to keep pieces of metal from shifting. Soldering forms can be invaluable when doing production soldering. The parts of the piece to be soldered together are pressed into the form until properly positioned. If possible, solder together a prototype so that the cavity

parts to be soldered lay properly. Sometimes the asbestos is formed into a thick, flat piece and a hollow is carved into it of the desired shape. Carborundum grains (No. 12 or 16) can also be used for soldering irregularly shaped objects.

In certain situations, the pieces of metal that are to be soldered together are kept in close contact with each other by embedding the pieces in an asbestos or a charcoal block. Pieces of asbestos or charcoal can be arranged so that the metal will not move. A

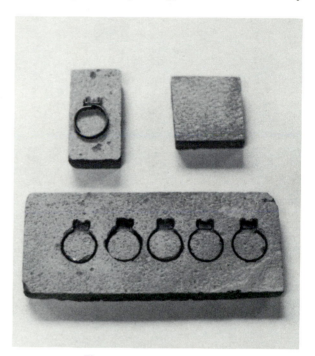

Fig. 109 Soldering forms

can be made in one impression. The pieces can be placed into the cavity with tweezers. If fine delicate work is being soldered together, the impressions should be made with a chasing, dapping, or engraving tool. Soaking the form in water before making the impressions will yield slightly better mold detail, and the parts will be held more securely. After the impression has been made, the form should be allowed to dry for 30 minutes at 400°F.

Most soldering operations require the use of a clamping device to hold the metal parts together, to prevent the pieces from shifting, and to keep the joint under tension, thereby promoting capillary attraction. Various me-

Fig. 108 Soldering on an asbestos block

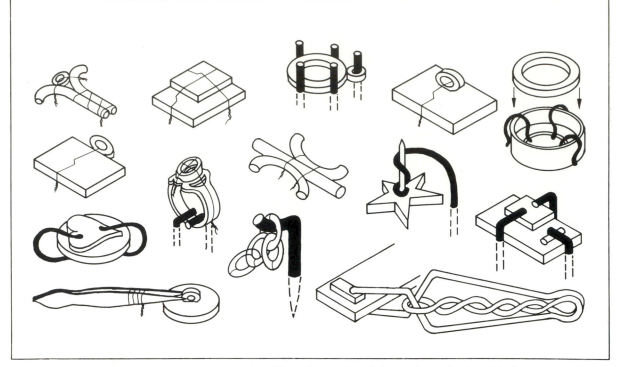

Fig. 110 Various methods of holding pieces of metal together prior to soldering

thods of employing binding wire, small clamps, pins, and soldering tweezers are illustrated in fig. 110. The iron binding wire (24 or 26 gauge) is tightened by twisting with a flat nose plier and pulling out with the plier while twisting. A bend is then made in the wire to tighten it more. This bend allows the wire to give slightly during soldering so that the metal can expand without distortion.

Soldering jigs such as a carbon ring stick or a pair of mounted cross-locking tweezers (fig. 111) are ideal and are recommended for holding metals together, or in position, while

soldering. Soldering jigs can be made by bending and then embedding pins in a soldering block.

Experienced jewelers often hold the jewelry piece with a soldering tweezer and solder it while it is held in the air (fig. 112). This is possible if the solder is first melted onto the smaller piece of metal. Next, both pieces are fluxed, positioned, and then held together with tweezers. The piece is lifted in the air and turned so that the heat of the torch can be concentrated where needed until the solder melts.

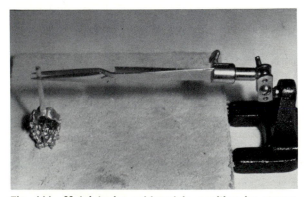

Fig. 111 Metal to be soldered in position by means of a cross-locking tweezer on a swivel base

Fig. 112 Holding object with tweezer while soldering

When soldering a very small piece of wire to a sheet of metal, a small amount of solder can be melted on the sheet. The solder is heated until it is molten, the fluxed wire is quickly positioned on the sheet with tweezers, the torch is removed, and the piece is held in place until the solder has solidified.

Solder with a soft blue flame. Too much air or oxygen will produce a sharp flame that tends to oxidize the solder and metals quickly.

Heat the metals, not only the solder, for the metals must be hot enough to melt the solder. You can not melt solder onto a cold metal. In other words, heat the area around the seam first (preheat) and then heat the seam and solder directly.

Solder will run to the hottest metal or part of a metal. When soldering a smaller part to a larger, apply the heat to the larger first, for if the smaller part is heated first, it will become red quickly and the solder will flow to it. The torch must be directed on both metals so that they become equally hot at the same time.

If the solder does not flow when sufficiently heated, it is possible that oxides and fire scale have formed on the surface of the metal. Pickle the metal, reflux, and then resolder the joint.

Occasionally, while soldering, lift the torch and thus the flame from the metal for a fraction of a second to permit the heat to travel evenly to the metals being soldered.

Balling or bunching of the solder is usually due to underheating or improper fluxing.

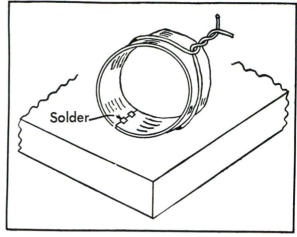

Fig. 114

The brown glaze material on the seam after soldering with borax is the flux. It is removed by pickling.

Do not attempt to hard solder an object that has soft solder on it. Soft solder, when heated to red heat, will burn into the metal.

When soldering, the temperature of the metal can be judged by its color. Below are approximate temperatures.

First red	900°F.
Dull red	1100°F.
Cherry red	1400°F.
Salmon red	1545°F.
14K yellow melts	1615°F.
Sterling silver melts	1640°F.
Copper melts	1981°F.
White heat	2100°F.

Most gold and silver solders flow at about cherry heat or lower. Care must be taken not to heat gold and silver much above cherry heat, or they will melt.

A large flat piece can best be soldered to the main part by first melting pieces of solder onto the back of the large piece. When cool, place the large piece where desired on the main part, clamp or bind in position if necessary, and then heat both metals until the solder remelts. This is known as sweat soldering (fig. 113). The back of cross lock tweezers can be used to press the two pieces of metal together until the solder appears at the edge of the work.

HARD SOLDERING PROCEDURE The actual hard soldering procedure is comparatively

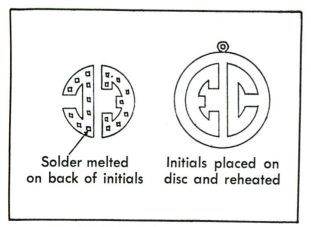

Solder melted on back of initials

Initials placed on disc and reheated

Fig. 113 Method of sweat soldering

easy. The following procedure for soldering a simple ring band should be valuable to beginners. The band is formed and joined as explained in the chapter on rings. Binding wire may be used to hold the band together. Apply flux and small pieces of solder along the seam (fig. 114). Place the band on a charcoal or asbestos block and then heat slowly until the water in the flux evaporates. Now apply the flame to both sides of the seam to preheat the metal evenly and then heat directly around the seam until the metal turns red and the solder melts and flows. Often the solder forms a small ball before it flows. Remove the heat immediately after the solder flows in order to avoid melting the band too. After the band has cooled sufficiently, remove the binding wire and pickle the band to clean it.

BEGINNER'S ERROR Beginners tend to heat the solder not the metals. This is wrong. The metals to be soldered must be heated until they are hot enough to melt the solder so that it will flow and adhere.

IMPORTANT A poker (usually a 6″ long piece of 3/32″ steel rod) is a very important tool when soldering. Quick, accurate, clean soldering can be done with it by heating a small piece of solder on an asbestos or charcoal block until the solder melts and forms a ball (fig. 115A). While still heating the solder,

touch the tip of poker to it (fig. 115B). The solder will adhere to the poker. Now heat the metal to be soldered to the proper temperature and, while heating, touch the solder, still on the tip of the poker, to the seam (fig. 115C). The solder will melt and flow into the seam. Immediately after the solder flows, remove the poker and the heat.

The poker can also be used to shift parts, while they are hot, that have moved out of position. An old three square needle file can be used as a poker.

CHECKING THE FLOW OF SOLDER To check the flow of solder into seams and other places, the seams or places can be covered or painted with a thin paste of yellow ochre or rouge mixed with water. India ink can also be used. **Note:** Careful, controlled soldering is the best prevention against the unwanted flow of solder.

Shot (see page 45) can be soldered to a jewelry object by first melting a small piece of solder onto the bottom of the shot. Place the shot where desired on object. Heat the metal around the shot until the solder on the shot remelts. Solder also can be applied to small shot as follows. Melt solder onto a flat piece of metal. Place small shot on metal and then heat metal until solder remelts and adheres to bottom of small shot. While heating the metal, pick the small shot off the metal with a tweezer.

Another popular method for soldering shot is to first affix it with flux and glue to the metal surface and then solder it. Apply a mixture (see page 110) of powdered borax flux, gum tragacanth and water to the desired contact areas and then attach the shot. The glue must be dry before soldering takes place. To solder the shot, place a small piece of solder against the base of the shot and heat the metal. Too much solder will distort its rounded appearance. To hold the shot in place without glue, coat the shot with flux and place it into a small depression made into the metal's surface by striking the metal with a small, rounded tool.

Filigree objects can be soldered by combining the solder with the flux. Sheet solder is filed in order to get very fine filings and the filings are mixed with the flux to form a

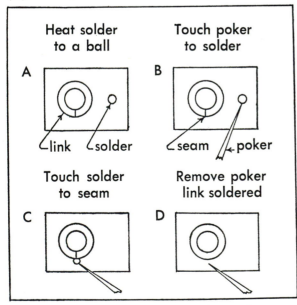

Fig. 115 **Method of soldering with a poker**

Heat solder to a ball — A — link — solder

Touch poker to solder — B — seam — poker

Touch solder to seam — C

Remove poker link soldered — D

paste. The mixture of flux and solder is then applied to the wires. A very soft flame (not much air) is used to heat the object.

INVESTMENT SOLDERING is frequently employed to solder small prong settings together to form a cluster setting. This method is used since it is very difficult to arrange, hold, or bind the small settings together without them shifting. The settings should be prepolished. Position the settings (prong side up) with tweezers on a sheet of utility wax. The wax can be shaped or built up with a warm spatula. When all of the settings have been arranged, they should be carefully pressed halfway into the wax. A wax or cardboard retaining wall approximately 1½" higher than and 1" from the outside of the settings should be constructed.

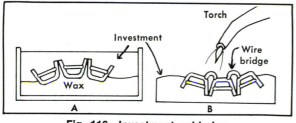

Fig. 116 Investment soldering

Investment casting plaster (Kerr Jewelers Plaster #2) is mixed and then slowly poured into the mold. Make sure that the plaster flows into all the crevices (lightly tap the mold) and that the settings are not disturbed. After approximately 20 minutes the wax base can be removed by warming it with a torch and then slowly prying it off. Any remaining wax can be eliminated by placing the plaster form in boiling water for 2 minutes. Slowly dry the plaster with a torch or in a burnout oven. Plaster in contact with an area to be soldered can be scraped away with a small needle tool.

The undersides of the settings should be examined to determine how they can be best soldered together. If the settings are in proper contact with one another, a small piece of solder can be placed on the joint. Settings that are not touching will require a wire bridge (often part of the design) to join them together. A reducing flame should be used to heat the metal and the investment until the

metal has turned a dull red. The flame is concentrated, and the settings are soldered together. After all of the settings have been successfully soldered, the plaster mold is placed under running water. This will cause the plaster to fall apart, releasing the settings.

PROTECTING STONES Generally speaking, all stones should be set after all hard soldering has been completed. However, occasionally a soldering operation must be made on a new piece of jewelry or while repairing an old object with the stone or stones in position. Precious stones like the diamond, synthetic ruby, and sapphire can be heated to a red heat without any fear of cracking or discoloration. It is best to cover the stones with a boric acid solution, formed by dissolving boric acid in alcohol. The stones must be permitted to cool slowly after soldering.

Semi-precious stones can best be protected by wetting powdered asbestos and then forming it into a ball around the stone. With the hot flame of an oxygen-gas soldering torch, often repair soldering can be accomplished while the stones are immersed in water.

Though many objects with semi-precious stones can be soldered the above way, if in doubt about the outcome, remove the stone in order to avoid cracking or discoloring it.

SOFT SOLDERS

Soft solders are alloys of tin and lead. They are used in the jewelry trade for soldering inexpensive copper, silver-plated, and rhinestone jewelry. Though they are comparatively easy to handle and have low melting points (approx. 400°F.), they do not possess great strength and their white color is very noticeable. They are not suitable, nor should they be used for gold, platinum, or good silver jewelry.

SOFT SOLDER FLUXES

ZINC AND MURIATIC ACID This popular, effective flux is prepared by dropping small pieces of zinc into muriatic acid until all chemical action ceases and the solution turns white.

GLYCERINE AND MURIATIC ACID This is a very good flux for pewter and copper. To one oz. of glycerine, add 5 drops of muriatic acid.

COMMERCIAL PREPARATIONS There are several good commercial preparations that can be purchased in the form of a paste, salt, or liquid. "No-Ko-Rode" is the paste form that is recommended. Schwerter's "Soft Soldering Fluid" is an excellent liquid soft soldering flux.

THE SOFT SOLDERS

Tin and lead may be mixed in any proportion to produce a soft solder. The most popular soft solder for jewelry is 60-40, 60 per cent tin and 40 per cent lead. 62 per cent tin and 38 per cent lead is the soft solder with the lowest possible melting point. Note from the melting points below that soft solder has a lower melting point than its components.

Melting Points

Tin .... 450°F.
Lead .... 620°F.
50-50 solder .... 442°F.
60-40 solder .... 395°F.
62-38 solder .... 356°F.

Soft solders can be purchased as a thin wire, a bar, as a hollow wire with the flux in the hollow, cut into small pieces, or powdered and mixed with a flux. The thin wire or powdered and mixed with a flux solder is recommended for jewelry work by craftsmen and in school.

Note: Bismuth solder, a very low melting (approx. 200°F.) soft solder alloy of bismuth, tin, and lead, is available and recommended for repairing white metal costume jewelry.

Allcraft silver color soft solder (96½% tin, 3½% silver—melting point 430°F.) is stronger than ordinary soft solder and is excellent for soldering findings to enameled pieces.

SOFT SOLDERING PROCEDURE

A general procedure for soft soldering is as follows. Clean the metals thoroughly. Make sure the edges fit exactly. If necessary, clamp or bind together the parts to be soldered. Apply the flux and then the solder to the metals. Apply heat, and only enough heat

to the metals to make the solder flow. If the metals are overheated, the flux will evaporate, the metals then will oxidize quickly, and the solder will not flow. The proper temperature is reached when the flux begins to turn to a very light brown. Remove the heat then, and only reapply when needed. Let the metals cool for a moment until the solder hardens; then they may be placed in water.

SOFT SOLDER HINTS

When two large pieces are to be soft soldered together, one piece is first tinned; that is, a thin layer of solder is melted onto it. The two pieces are then clamped together and heated until the solder remelts and fuses them.

Avoid the use of a soldering copper in jewelry work, for the process is slow and it leaves too much solder outside the seam.

Earwires can be soft soldered to earrings very cleanly and quickly by first melting a small piece of solder in the cup of the earwire. This can be done by holding the earwire over a bunsen burner flame with a tweezer until the solder melts. Then cool the earwire in water and clamp it to the earring with a tweezer. Now heat the earring over the bunsen burner until the solder remelts (fig. 116).

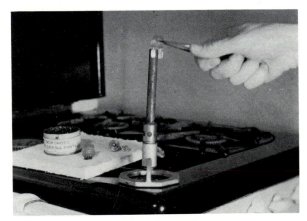

Fig. 116A Soft soldering in a kitchen workshop

Very small objects such as initials or thin wire work can be soft soldered to a larger piece by the following method. First melt a thin layer of solder onto a flat piece of scrap copper. The solder can be spread thin by rubbing it with a damp cloth or with fine steel wool. Then place the small objects on the solder on the copper. Reheat the metal so the solder will melt and stick to the small objects and, while the solder is still liquid, push or pick the small objects off the copper with a tweezer. The small objects will have a thin layer of solder on their bottom side. Now place the small objects where desired and reheat to solder them permanently. Remember, a flux must be used.

ELECTRIC SOLDERING and welding machines are used in certain soldering situations, when the heating of the entire piece of metal might damage thin sections or cause soldered joints to flow. They are particularly well suited for soldering small rings, links, or chain. The ring being soldered is held on a graphite ring mandrel, solder and flux are applied to the joint, and then a second graphite electrode is touched to the piece of metal. Current is activated by a foot pedal. The metal which is resisting the flow of electricity becomes hot in a matter of seconds and the solder melts.

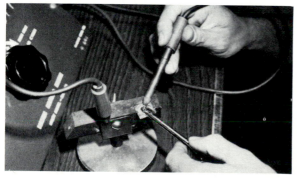

Fig. 117 Soldering with an electric soldering machine

14. FILIGREE

Filigree is a process in which thin, flat fine silver or high karat gold wires are arranged together to form complex designs. The wires are then joined together by solder. The wire used for filigree is usually 30 gauge. Fancy filigree wire can be made by twisting two pieces of round wire together and then flattening the braided wire in a rolling mill. A somewhat thicker wire (26 gauge, 1/16 inch wide) is usually used for the frame work of the design. There are two types of filigree:

open and closed. Closed filigree refers to filigree wires that are soldered to a flat metal base.

After a filigree pattern has been designed on paper, the framework is constructed with pliers so that it matches the outside of the

Fig. 118 Filigree neckpiece   Dvora Horvitz

design. Filigree wire must always be annealed. Bezel shears or end nippers can be used to cut the filigree wire. The framework is soldered together with medium solder.

The inside filigree lattice is made by winding and/or bending wire around drill rod; small round, flat, or snipe nose pliers; or watchmaker's, jeweler's, or soldering tweezers to create open spirals, closed spirals, scrolls, links, or curved designs.

Repetitive spiral and scroll designs can be made by constructing a winding jig. Headless brads are lightly hammered into a piece of wood until they form the perimeter of the curve or spiral. Brads can be positioned around the outside of the outer row to help maintain the shape of the wire. The wire is wrapped around the brads until the spiral is completed, and then the wire is carefully lifted from the jig with tweezers. If necessary, some of the brads can be pulled out before lifting the wire from the jig. Intricate filigree curves must be periodically annealed as they are formed. A repetitive design can also be made by running the wire between two gears. Flat wire can be cut diagonally to form small diamonds.

After being formed, the filigree wires are placed inside the frame with tweezers. The larger wires should be positioned first. If the piece has been properly designed there will be no large open areas and the wires should be held together by tension inside the frame. Adjustments can be made by opening some of the spirals. The piece is carefully picked up (by the frame) with tweezers and placed on a perfectly flat charcoal block. The metal is fluxed and allowed to dry. Gum tragacanth is not needed since the flux acts as a binder. Powdered solder is sprinkled slowly over the entire piece. Soldering should be carefully done with a soft flame. Experienced craftsmen lift the piece with tweezers as they are soldering and heat the bottom of the metal so that the solder can easily flow through the joints.

Filigree wires can also be soldered together in a block of investment. The wires are assembled together in a sheet of wax; investment is poured over the metal and the mass is placed in a burnout kiln to melt the wax, expose the metal, and dry out the plaster. After the wires have been fluxed and powdered solder applied, the dried block, with its exposed metal side up, is heated with a torch to fuse the solder. The investment soldering method should be used if filigree wires are soldered to the outside of the frame or if wire tension is difficult to achieve.

15. FILES AND FILING TECHNIQUES

Files are used to remove irregularities left in the metal by sawing and cutting, to help define shapes, to cut curves, to round contours, to bevel edges, to smooth surfaces, and to remove excess solder.

Filing is a very important operation in jewelry work that is often neglected by beginners. Accurate and rapid filing can only be developed through study and practice. Jewelry objects to be filed are held by hand or pliers against the bench pin (fig. 119). If the object is very small it can be held in a ring clamp. Use the entire cutting length of the file where possible. Firm pressure is required for quick filing. A clean smooth cut can be made by filing with the edge of the file resting against the bench pin. A properly used bench pin becomes well grooved from the edge of the file and eventually must be replaced.

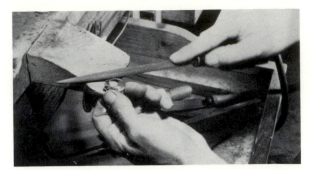

Fig. 119 Filing on a bench pin

MAKES Files may be divided into two classifications—Swiss and American. The Swiss files are considered superior for jewelry work. The coarseness of a Swiss file is marked by a number. Number 00 is the coarsest and, becoming progressively smoother, the other files are numbered 0, 1, 2, up to 6. Number 6 file is a very smooth file used for final filing before emerying and polishing. Number 2 is the most commonly used file.

The coarseness or fineness of American files is specified by name. Rough, bastard, second cut, smooth and super smooth are the standard cuts. Though the Swiss files are more expensive than the American, their additional cost is warranted for professional work. Several American firms are now making Swiss type files.

CUTS Single, double, vixen, and rasp are the common cuts of files. Single cut files have a single row of parallel teeth running the entire

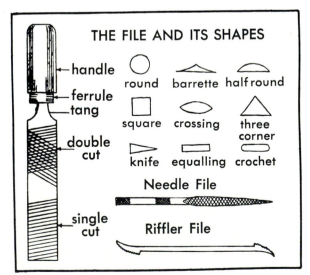

Fig. 120 File terminology

cutting length of the file. The American mill file is a single cut file. Double cut files have an additional row of teeth cut at an angle of 60 degrees to the first row. Swiss jewelry files are double cut. Vixen cut files have a single row of curved teeth running across the file for its entire length. Rasp cut files have short, raised teeth that are spaced at even intervals over the cutting length of the file. Rasp and vixen files are used on soft metals like lead, aluminum, and tin, and on wood and plastics.

SHAPES Files can be purchased in almost any geometric cross-sectional shape and size in order to fit the contours that are being worked on. Standard files used in jewelry making have a cutting surface length of six inches. Many of the popular shapes are shown in figure 120. The barrette, half-round, three corner triangular, round, and flat equalling are the most popular shapes of files used by jewelers.

NEEDLE FILES Needle files are especially adapted for file finishing small and delicate objects. A popular size is the 16 centimeter, which has an overall length of 5½″ and a cutting length of 2¾″. Note (fig. 120) that the round end of the needle file forms its handle.

RIFFLER FILES Riffler or die sinker's files are tool steel rods with a very small file on both ends. These files can be bought with many curved and odd shaped surfaces. With the introduction of the flexible shaft, the need for

riffler files by most jewelers has diminished, for with the small grinding and polishing wheels available for the shaft it is now possible to get to surfaces formerly only possible with riffler files.

Filing Techniques

1. Use a rough file (#0) to remove metal quickly and then a fine file (#2 to 4) for finishing.

2. File on the bench pin.

3. Files cut on the forward stroke only. Press as hard or firm as possible on the file as it is pushed forward. Reduce your pressure on the file if you do not lift it when you draw it back.

4. On long narrow edges, as the file is pushed forward, it is also moved sideways to get even, smooth edges that are free of grooves.

5. Small objects can be held while being filed with pliers or a ring clamp. However, when possible, it is best to hold the objects in one's hand and the hand or objects should rest on the bench pin for quick, accurate filing.

6. While filing, occasionally tap the file on the bench pin to remove particles of metal that may stick to the file's teeth. A file card or cleaner, which is a steel wire brush, can also be used for removing metals from files.

16. EMERY AND ITS USES

Jewelry objects, after they are filed and before they are polished, are rubbed with emery paper to remove all file marks and scratches. Emery is a natural form of aluminum oxide mixed with iron oxide. It can be purchased as a powder, or glued to paper or cloth, or imbedded in rubber. Emery glued to paper or embedded in rubber are the types used by jewelers. Emery paper is graded by numbers as follows: 4/0 (the finest) 3/0, 2/0, 1/0, ½, 1, 1½, 2, and 3 (the coarsest). Numbers ½ to 2 are recommended for removing file marks and fine scratches from metals so that they can be polished. The finer grits are used by engravers and setters (explained later) and

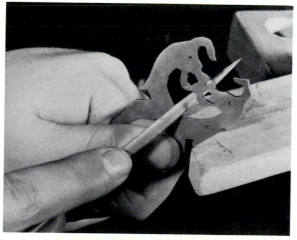

Fig. 121 Filing with a needle file

for fine hand finishes. Ways of using commercial emery products and attachments that can be purchased or made for their use are now described.

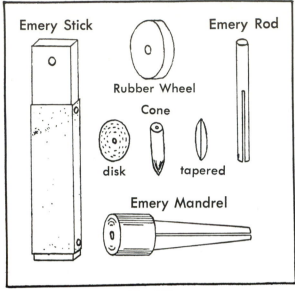

Fig. 122

EMERY STICK The emery paper is used similarly to a file by wrapping it around a piece of wood 3/16 x 1 x 12 inches (fig. 122). This is best done by laying the emery paper with the emery side down on a bench. Then, with a knife or sharp edge of a barrette file, score the paper where it is to be bent around the stick. Wrap the paper around the stick and repeat the process until the entire sheet of emery is wrapped firmly around the stick. The scoring of the paper will give it sharp edges where it is bent. The end of the paper is tacked to the narrow side of the stick or a piece of binding wire can be used on both ends. As the paper wears down, rip off the top layer and use the one beneath.

EMERY ROD Fine emery paper can be wrapped around a 1/8″ rod held in the chuck of a flexible shaft, and then it can be used to remove scratches on flat and concave flat surfaces. The rod, usually brass, is slotted on its length for about 1″ with a jeweler's saw (fig. 122). A 1″ strip of emery paper 2 to 3 inches long is wrapped around the rod counter-clockwise and then used where desired.

EMERY MANDREL The emery mandrel (fig. 122) is used to smooth the inside of rings. The end of the mandrel screws onto the tapered spindle of the polishing machine. The end of a strip of emery paper is inserted into the slot in the mandrel and then wrapped around it.

RUBBER WHEELS Rubber wheels mixed with emery are also available for the flexible shaft. The wheels are excellent for removing scratches from places, such as the inside of a cast ring, which are not accessible to files. A rubber wheel can be shaped by holding a file against it while it revolves. Rubber wheels can be used to impart a textured surface by pressing the wheel against the metal, quickly removing the wheel, and then repeating the process until the desired pattern is created.

EMERY DISKS Emery disks, similar to the type used by dentists, are excellent for getting into narrow slits. These inexpensive disks can have a tremendous amount of working time. Small emery stones also have many uses when used with a flexible shaft outfit.

SCOTCH STONE Scotch stone, a natural abrasive, was once popular with jewelers for removing scratches. It has been supplanted by the disks described above or, where a flexible shaft is not available, by emery imbedded rubber tablets or sticks which are used by hand.

ROUGE AND CROCUS PAPER Rouge and crocus paper are used by craftsmen to get fine satin and polished hand finishes. They are also used, as explained later, by stone setters and engravers to obtain bright cuts.

BURS Setting burs (fig. 194), especially the bud and round, can be used with a flexible shaft outfit (fig. 14) to remove efficiently excess metal or sprues from concave or hollow areas which can not be removed easily with files. Burs can also be used for texturing the metal.

17. PRE-POLISHING

A jeweler should employ a sequence of pickling, filing, pre-polishing, polishing, cleaning and metal coloring operations that are best suited for the metal they have been working with, the surface condition of the metal, the desired finish, the equipment available, and the design of the jewelry. Since the surface of the metal inevitably becomes dull and marred with fire scale due to its frequent exposure to the heat of the torch, the first step in the finishing of a piece of jewelry is usually pickling. If necessary, the metal can be refiled and/or rubbed again with emery paper.

STRIPPING AND BOMBING

Commercial concerns occasionally strip their yellow gold, silver and white gold jewelry after pickling and before polishing. Stripping leaves the metal bright by removing firescale so that less polishing is required. Stripping is done electrically and is a reverse plating operation—metal is removed instead of being plated (see Plating). This process is also used to strip old plating before replating.

Stripping to remove firescale should not be continued longer than necessary (15 seconds to 1 minute) or else the piece will start to corrode and diminish in size.

The following solution can be used at boiling temperature with a voltage of 9 to 12 volts:

1 gallon water
¼ lb. sodium cyanide
1 teaspoon sodium carbonate

Add the cyanide and carbonate to the boiling water. The stripping effect of the solution improves with use. Water is added when necessary and occasionally a little cyanide.

Caution: Sodium cyanide is a poison; handle it carefully.

Prepared cyanide stripping solutions such as Gesswein's stripping salts #120 can also be purchased. When the pieces start to appear dull, the electrostripping bath should be replenished by adding 2 to 3 additional ounces of stripping salts. If the bath changes color, from dark to light brown, it should be set aside for reclaiming.

The solution is kept in a stainless steel pot. The objects to be stripped are suspended from the anode (+) bar by a stainless steel or copper wire. The negative wire is attached to the stainless steel pot which thus becomes the cathode (—). The solution should be occasionally agitated by moving the anode wire and "shaking the pieces" during the stripping process. The stripped gold, platinum, or silver (use separate pots for each) will collect at the bottom of the pots and are eventually removed and sent to the refiner.

The pieces should be rinsed and washed immediately after the stripping process has been completed. They are then polished or tumbled with steel shot. If the work is to be plated, it should be electrocleaned (page 131) in order to eliminate grease or other impurities.

BOMBING The following process is recommended to professional jewelers only. Since there is an element of danger involved in its use, the process should not be used in schools nor should it be used by beginning craftsmen.

Bombing is used instead of stripping on yellow gold or silver jewelry which has deep recesses. Stripping will leave the gold object clean but shaded—the recessed areas will be darker. Bombing will leave the object clean and with a uniform color. The process is used after all soldering, assembling, and ornamentation (florentining, blasting, etc.) have been completed.

Bombing is done as follows. Heat (to 180°F.) a sodium cyanide solution (one egg

Fig. 123 Bombing

65

or ounce to a quart) almost to the boiling point. Cover gold objects placed in a Corning ware (or enameled) pot with the solution. Pour a small amount (1 oz.) of hydrogen peroxide (30% solution) into the Corning ware pot. Shake the pot; the solution will foam (fig. 123) and then in a few seconds it will burst. The bursting is safe, however; do not get scared and drop the pot.

Caution: Sodium cyanide is a poison; handle it carefully. Keep acids away from cyanide solutions—a poisonous, odorless gas (hydrocyanic) is formed. It is best to do bombing right in a sink so that the solution can be poured down the drain easily.

Bombing will leave a very thin 24 karat gold coating on the jewelry objects. The objects can be dipped into a cyanide solution to restore the 14 karat finish. The finish will be uniform throughout.

Sometimes it is necessary to repeat the bombing operation in order to obtain the desired finish.

Florentine finishes, pearls, and stones (except opals, turquoise) are not affected by bombing.

18. POLISHING AND BUFFING

Polishing is a general term that is used to denote the process of smoothing and shining the surface of a piece of metal. Polishing begins after all of the scratches have been removed from the metals' surface. The first phase in polishing a piece of jewelry is known as cutting down. Metal is removed by an abrasive compound such as tripoli or white diamond. These compounds will leave the surface of the metal very smooth but also dull in appearance.

Buffing is a combination of a cutting and burnishing action; some metal is removed but most is burnished to a high, bright finish. Polishing and buffing are very important phases of the jewelry industry for it is the glitter or finish of an object that first catches the customer's eye.

POLISHING AND BUFFING COMPOUNDS Tripoli and rouge are the two standard compounds used by jewelers. Tripoli is a silicon substance formed by the natural decomposition of siliceous sandstone. Rouge is a fine synthetic iron oxide. Both are mixed with a binder composed of fats and waxes to form bars or cakes which are convenient to handle and apply.

Tripoli is a fast cutting abrasive compound which is used to remove emery marks and fine scratches. When used properly, it leaves the metal very smooth but still dull in appearance. The color of tripoli is brown; a white tripoli is available for platinum and white gold.

Rouge produces the final high color or luster and it does this primarily by burnishing the metal. By means of the rouge, high surface speed, and heat caused by friction, the metal actually flows to fill in minute scratches, thus producing the final lustrous coloring. Gold and silver rouges are red; a white rouge is used for platinum and white gold. These rouges—black (for yellow gold and silver) and green (for white gold and platinum)—sometimes are used by commercial jewelers after the red rouge to obtain very bright finishes on commercial jewelry.

Note: White diamond, a compound formed from amorphous silica, is used by some craftsmen and jewelers between the tripoli and rouge operations. White diamond is a combination compound—it cuts and also buffs (colors) the metal. Greystar and bobbing compound also are used by some polishers. Most commercial jewelers, and craftsmen, however, use only tripoli and rouge on silver, gold, and platinum.

POLISHING AND BUFFING WHEELS Commercial polishing is usually done on a polishing machine that has a 1/3 H.P. motor which rotates at 3450 rpm, a suction dust collector and two tapered spindles that will accommodate various wheels of different sizes. The diameter of the polishing wheel has a direct relationship to the surface area of the wheel (surface feet per minute) that will come in contact with the surface of the metal within a certain time period. For example, the sfpm of a 4 inch wheel revolving at 3450 rpm is 3614 sfpm, and the sfpm of a 6 inch wheel revolving at the same speed is 5420 sfpm.

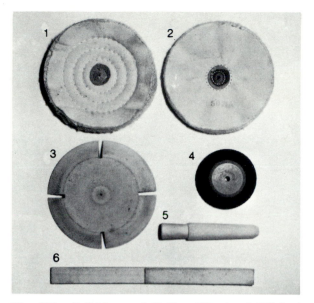

Fig. 124 Polishing and Buffing Wheels. 1 Stitched muslin, 2. Unstitched muslin, 3. Slotted, rock-hard felt, 4. Bristle, 5. Felt ring buff, 6. Felt stick for hand polishing.

The popular diameters of the wheels for jewelry are the 3, 4, or 5 inch ones. It is difficult to control larger wheels without damaging fine parts or settings. Smaller wheels than the 3″ ones are used for very delicate work. Generally, the harder, close stitched wheels are used with tripoli for fast cutting, and the softer, loosely stitched or unstitched wheels are used with rouge. Coarse (48/48) muslin wheels are used with tripoli; canton flannel or fine (80/92) muslin wheels are used with rouge.

Bristle brushes are used to get into corners and crevices not accessible to other wheels.

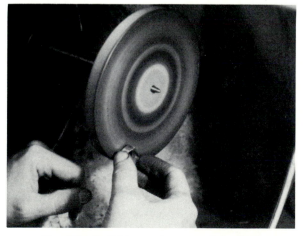

Fig. 125 Polishing a ring on a felt wheel

To even the bristle on the side and edge, the wheels should be singed (burnt) by rotating them over the flame of a torch or bunsen burner. The burnt part is then removed by holding a steel rod against the wheels while they revolve on the polishing machine. The burning also makes the bristle firmer so that more pressure can be applied against the wheel for faster cutting action.

Felt and wood wheels are used to maintain sharp corners and flat surfaces.

The inside of rings are polished with tapered felt or wood mandrels or with bristle brushes. Commercial polishers hold the ring with a piece of soft leather.

Sheepskin buffs are popular for buffing soft metals such as white metal jewelry.

Fine wire wheels (brass or nickel silver) are used to obtain satin finishes. The piece is occasionally dipped in a soap and water solution. Periodically reversing the wire wheel will prolong its use. Light pressure should be used when wire brush polishing.

Fig. 126 Polishing a ring with a bristle brush

LAPPING Lapping is the term for polishing on firm wheels, usually of wood or rock-hard felt. Since these wheels will not give under the pressure of the object being polished (as flannel, muslin, and bristle wheels will) smooth flat surfaces with sharp corners can be obtained and sharp step effects can be achieved. Lapping wheels measure from 3 to 6 inches in diameter and from ½ to 1 inch in width.

Slotted, knife edge, rock-hard felt wheels are popular for lapping. The wheel is mounted on a motor so that it turns almost in a horizontal position. The object to be lapped is pressed up against the side of the wheel; the slots permit one to look through the revolving wheel so that the object being lapped can be held at the proper angle (fig. 127).

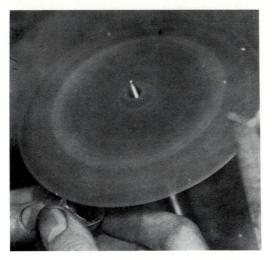

Fig. 127 Lapping a ring on a slotted rock-hard felt wheel

Wood laps may be dressed (sharpened and shaped) by means of wood turning tools; however, the tool shown in figure 128 is excellent for the purpose. It is made from an old flat file which is shortened by breaking it in a vise. It is then sharpened to the shape shown. The dressing is accomplished by holding the tool against the wheel while it rotates, and the wood or felt is thus removed until the desired shape is obtained.

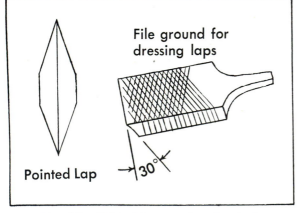

Fig. 128 Pointed lap and dressing tool

Since practically all lapping should be done on the sides of the wheel, the laps are pointed (fig. 128) with flat or slightly convex sides.

The wheels are charged with tripoli for polishing and sometimes with rouge for coloring, though most coloring is done by pressing lightly on flannel or muslin wheels.

Felt wheels are best dressed (shaped) by means of an old emery wheel or by an emery stick—1″ x 1″ x 6″ is recommended.

Lapping is employed by professional polishers, rarely is it used by craftsmen.

POLISHING AND BUFFING TECHNIQUES

1. It is faster and better to remove deep scratches with a file and file marks with emery paper than it is to attempt to remove them by polishing.

2. The top of the polishing wheel must turn towards the operator. The object to be polished is held below the horizontal

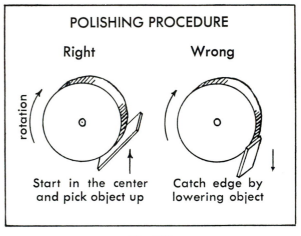

Fig. 129

center line of the wheel in the position shown in figure 129. **Note:** The metal will become hot while it is being polished.

3. Press the object being polished as firmly as possible against the revolving wheel for rapid polishing. If the object is pressed too lightly, often the polishing compound will adhere to the object.

4. Avoid holding objects too long in one position, otherwise undesirable grooves may be formed. It is best to turn or move the metal quickly while polishing.

Fig. 130   Polishing a silver pendant

5. It takes longer to tripoli an object than it does to rouge it. Spend 90% of the time on the tripoli wheel.

6. Do not apply too much tripoli to the wheel for this will glaze it (make it smooth) and a glazed wheel will not polish efficiently. The glaze can be removed from a wheel by pressing a thick old file, a notched piece of steel, or even a file card against it while it revolves.

7. Chains are best polished on a flat piece of wood around which the chains may be wrapped. A nail or hook may be attached to the wood to hold one end of the chain.

8. Small flat objects also can be polished safely on a flat piece of wood.

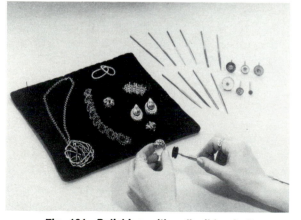

**Fig. 131   Polishing with a flexible shaft
Courtesy of Kerr Manufacturing Co.**

9. Small intricate pieces of jewelry can be buffed and polished by using a flexible shaft.

TRUMMING The inner surfaces of delicate settings and fine pierced jewelry can only be polished by trumming with cord or twine. One end in one's hand. The polishing compound end on one's hand. The polishing compound is rubbed onto the cord, which is then placed through the setting or pierced object. The polishing is done by pressing and sliding the jewelry back and forth on the cord.

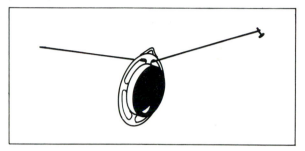

Fig. 132   Trumming

CLEANING PROCEDURE Cleanliness is essential for successful polishing. It should be apparent that the wheels must be used with one compound and that they should not be contaminated by other compounds. In large commercial concerns separate machines are used for tripoli and rouge. If objects have been hard soldered, they must be pickled and, as previously explained, much of the commercial work is stripped before being polished.

After using tripoli and rouge, objects should be cleaned in a hot water solution of soap and a few drops of ammonia. A jeweler's bristle brush is used to wash out the tripoli from crevices and corners. An old tooth brush can be used by craftsmen. Commercial jewelers use steam under pressure to completely remove all dirt, and the steam also dries the jewelry. Craftsmen may dry their jewelry with a rag, in warmed boxwood sawdust, or in crushed corncobs.

Chamois skins or prepared polishing cloths can be used to handle jewelry objects after they have been polished and washed.

ULTRASONIC CLEANING In recent years, ultrasonic cleaning machines have appeared

Fig. 133 Steam machine for cleaning and drying jewelry

on the market for rapid cleaning of polished jewelry objects. These machines convert 120 volt line current to high frequency electrical energy which is then converted into high frequency (80 kc) sound waves above the range of human hearing. These sound waves, when introduced into a cleaning solution, cause rapid formation and collapse of minute bubbles. This process (bubble formation and collapse) is called cavitation. Its purpose is to accelerate the chemical cleaning action

Fig. 134 An ultrasonic cleaner

of an ammoniated detergent (Joy) cleaning solution and to provide an intense scrubbing action, especially in inaccessible crevices, on the jewelry object to be cleaned. A solution with a neutral pH should be used when cleaning jewelry that contains opals and pearls.

BARREL TUMBLING

BARREL TUMBLING Small jewelry objects (findings, settings, castings, etc.) can be given a bright finish by tumbling. The objects to be tumbled are first loaded into the tumbling barrel (drum) and covered with the small irregularly-shaped (½″ to ¼″ in diameter) abrasive media. The ratio of the abrasive media to the castings should be at least 3 to 1. For optimal efficiency, the tumbler should be half full. Water and one tablespoon of a commercial abrasive compound are then added to the barrel so that the entire load is covered by one inch of liquid.

A tumbling machine has an action similar to that of a rock rolling down a hill. The castings are carried up to the top of the hill by rotation of the barrel. Upon reaching the apex, the castings and the media then tumble end over end down the hill. The castings are rubbed by the stationary media layer underneath and by the media tumbling with them.

Note: A ceramic abrasive media that contains aluminum oxide is used when refining gold castings. Silver and white metal castings are deburred with plastic media that contain quartz.

The tumbling machine shown in figure 135 can hold 50 to 60 rings. The drum is rotated overnight for gold castings, and from 4-6 hours for white metal and silver castings at a slow speed (28-35 rpm) so that the abrasive media and the castings can tumble over one another. Abrasive tumbling invariably darkens the metal. Most commercial casters remove the dark spots by either electro-stripping or bombing before polishing or tumble-polishing the castings.

Abrasive tumbling can help eliminate a finishing defect known as acid bleeding. Acid bleeding can occur if the acid used in pickling remains in the minute porosity holes of the casting. After the casting has been plated, the acid will begin to react on the thin plated layer of metal and will eventually remove it, thus exposing the base metal.

Tumble-polishing is a burnishing process-no metal is removed by abrasion. The process is ideal for small castings with concave or convex surfaces, but it is not suitable for ob-

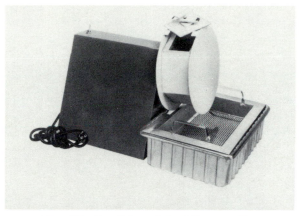
Fig. 135 Small barrel tumbling machine

jects with large flat surfaces. It is also ideal for castings requiring a nugget-type finish. The objects to be tumbled are placed in the drum (barrel) with small (3/32″) round, oval, and pin-shaped steel balls and a commercial burnishing compound such as Kramco #910, or a soap compound such as Oakite #23. A cleaning detergent (Joy) can also be used. In most cases, 30 minutes to one hour is an adequate tumbling time.

BURNISHING is a method of smoothing and polishing metal with a highly polished tool known as a steel burnisher. The tool is oval-shaped and tapers to a straight or curved point. A burnisher can be used for polishing beveled edges since it will not round off the metal. The burnished finish is applied by stroking the tool across the surface of the metal. Since a burnisher moves and compresses the metal, it is also used to remove deep scratches. The blade should be rubbed at a slight diagonal across the scratch. A lubricant of soap and water can be used.

SAND BLASTING is occasionally used to remove hardened investment and/or to texture the surface of the metal with a matt, satin, or frosty finish. The work is held inside a metal or fiberglass box with rubber gloves and can

be monitored through an illuminated glass window. Fine particles of abrasive—such as glass beads, silica sand, or aluminum oxide—are picked up by compressed air and sprayed on the work by a blast gun. Most machines can deliver the abrasive materials in either a wet or a dry state.

Fig. 136 Sand blaster

19. CHEMICAL FINISHING

The external surface of jewelry objects can be treated chemically to obtain several practical and interesting finishes. These finishes are usually applied to silver or copper and occasionally to gold jewelry.

Objects to be treated are first polished with tripoli and rouge; however much craft work may be prepared for the chemicals merely by rubbing with fine emery cloth and steel wool.

Cleanliness is essential. After polishing, remove all traces of the compounds by brushing objects in a hot water and soap solution that has a few drops of ammonia added to it.

Antique (bluish-black) Finish on Silver and Copper The chemical used is potassium sul-

71

phide, commonly called liver of sulphur. The solution, the most popular and easiest to prepare, is made by dropping a ½″ cube of the chemical into a pint of hot water. Drop the object into the solution and remove it when it turns bluish-black. If the finish did not take in spots, clean these spots with steel wool and return the object to the solution. The finish can also be applied by dipping steel wool or a nylon tooth brush into the solution and then rubbing the solution and finish into the object.

When the desired color has been obtained, wipe the object with a rag until it is dry. Then with dry fine steel wool, pumice powder, or on the buffing machine, tone the object to get bright contrasting spots.

Note: It is often advisable especially in school shops, to make a concentrated liquid solution of potassium sulphide by dropping large pieces of the solid chemical (potassium sulphide) into a bottle or jar (which can be capped) of hot water. When a usable solution is desired, pour some of the concentrated solution into hot water.

Black on Silver, Gold, Copper and its Alloys
Dissolve 1 oz. of tellurium dioxide in ½ pint of hydrochloric acid, then dilute with water. Dilute with 2 parts of water for silver and gold; six parts water for copper, brass, nickel silver. If the solution is too strong, the black color will peel off the copper.

Objects may be dipped into the solution or the solution may be brushed onto the object with an old tooth brush. Caution should be used in handling the solution since it contains hydrochloric acid. Hot solutions work best on gold.

Manufacturing jewelers now obtain a black finish in recessed areas of gold jewelry by plating a black nickel finish (available from supply houses) onto the gold. The surface of the object is then polished; the black finish remains in the crevices.

Blue to Black on Brass or Nickel Silver Brass or nickel silver immersed in a boiling solution of butter of antimony (antimony trichloride) will turn black.

Antique Finish on Gold. An easy way to get an antique finish on gold is to dab the gold with iodine. When the desired color, blue to black, has been obtained, wash off the iodine, wipe dry, and then tone the gold object by polishing or with fine steel wool.

Many gold finishes are applied by plating.

PROTECTING THE FINISH—LACQUERING
Copper, brass and silver jewelry objects will tarnish (darken) if left exposed to the air. This is due to the fact that a small amount of sulfur is in the air, and the sulfur combines with the copper, the copper in the brass, and with the silver to form, respectively, copper and silver sulfides, which are black.

The finish of copper and brass jewelry objects (not rings) can be protected by covering with a transparent lacquer. Lacquering is not recommended for most handmade silver objects since the finish looks better without the lacquer and tarnished objects can easily be refinished by hand.

Lacquer can be applied by brushing (good for earrings), spraying, or dipping. The dipping method, which is applied as follows, is recommended for pins.

Into a small jar (with a tight cover) pour a clear lacquer and then dilute (thin) with a lacquer thinner—about ⅓ lacquer thinner. Tie a piece (about 18 inches) of any thin wire around the joint or catch of the pin to be lacquered. Dip the pin into the lacquer; remove and twirl (spin) it quickly for three or four revolutions—this will remove the excess lacquer. Now place the pin on a flat surface to dry. The lacquer should harden sufficiently within five minutes for handling purposes.

Lacquer can be removed from jewelry objects by boiling in a strong pickling or lye solution.

DECORATIVE PROCESSES

INTRODUCTION

Many pieces of metal do not consist simply of single-colored, smooth, flat sheets of metal. To exploit the full potential of metal—its malleability, its reflective qualities, its hardness and rigidity, its conductivity, and its ability to be fused together with colored enamels—the surface of the metal is frequently decorated.

Designs can be modeled in relief or sunk into the metal by the processes of repoussé and chasing. Patterns or designs can be stamped or embossed into the metal. Ornamentation can be cut into the metal by the process of engraving. Etching is a method of creating a design by removing metal with

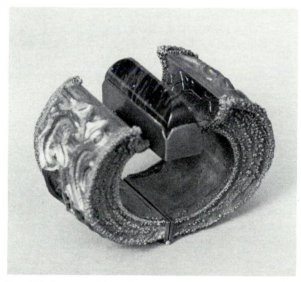

Fig. 137 Repousséd, etched and electroformed bracelet Pauline Warg

acid. The surface of the metal can be textured with heat by a process known as reticulation.

Contrasting pieces of metal can be inlaid into a design that has been cut into a sheet of metal. Areas of metal can be decorated with enamels in order to color the surface. A thin layer of metal can be electroplated onto the surface of a piece of jewelry to give the illusion that the metal is more expensive than it actually is, or to create a two-tone effect. Electroforming is a process that can be used to deposit metal onto either a metallic or a

treated nonmetallic surface in order to create textures, designs, or new forms.

Decoration is done at different times as the piece is being made. Texture hammering and stamping are usually done before the metal is shaped and/or assembled since it is easier to perform these processes on a flat sheet of metal. Chasing, etching, and reticulation, can be done either before or after the metal has been shaped. Inlaying, mokume, and granulation are done separately as the piece is being constructed. Enameling and engraving are usually done after the piece has been assembled. Electroplating is done after all of the jewelry making processes have been completed.

1. CHASING AND REPOUSSÉ

Chasing and repoussé are the terms used to describe the process of applying ornamentation by modeling and embossing sheet metal with steel tools struck with a hammer. Chasing is that phase of the work that is done from the top side of the metal in order to indent a linear design, define contours, or to emphasize a design. Repoussé is done from the reverse or back surface of the metal. Lines or patterns are pushed or embossed into the metal so that when viewed from the front a three dimensional relief design is seen. In many instances, chasing and repoussé are

Fig. 138 Chased pin — Mexican

combined, since one method complements the other. The tools used are known as chasing tools, and the metal is held in a substance known as pitch or over a lead block.

CHASING TOOLS Chasing tools can be purchased from many jewelry supply houses. It is suggested, however, that the tools be made. Since 50 or more tools are required for professional work, it is best to make a few of the fundamental shapes first and add other shapes as the need arises.

The tools (fig. 139) may be divided into the following categories:

TRACERS OR LINERS As the name indicates, these tools are used for forming lines, straight or curved, on metals. The tools are filed to the shapes shown in figure 139. **Note:** They do not cut through the metal but merely indent it.

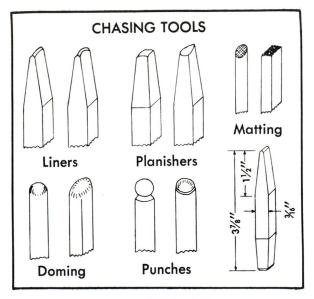

Fig. 139 Chasing tools

EMBOSSING OR DOMING These tools are used for raising metal, generally from the back or reverse side. Some of the tools are round, others are rectangular, but all have smoothly rounded edges so that they will not cut or nick the surface of the metal.

PLANISHING OR SMOOTHING These tools are used to smooth (planish) the metal from the top surface. The working faces of the tools are perfectly flat with the exception of

the square ones, which have slightly rounded edges. These tools, when used properly, impart to the metal a pleasing texture that makes good chased work so desirable.

MATTING OR BACKGROUND These tools are used to give fine dotted or cross lined effects on depressed or lowered surfaces. They are often used on the background metal of small transparent enameled objects and on the depressed surface of etched metal work.

DAPPING AND HOLLOW PUNCHES Dapping punches are round punches used to form spherical shapes on metals. The metal is punched from the reverse side, and the hollow punch is then used on the front side to form a perfect spherical shape. Hammer the tool lightly to avoid cutting through the metal. Large dapping punches can be made from wood.

HOW TO MAKE CHASING TOOLS Required: square tool steel bars, 3/16″ wide for most liners and planishers; 1/4″ square bars for the slightly larger tools; 3/8″ and larger bars and rods for the few required large embossing or doming tools. Use round rods for the round doming tools. Round tool steel rods may be used for the small liners and planishers; however, they tend to slip and turn, whereas the square tools will not. Cut the steel to 3⅞″ lengths with the exception of the larger embossing tools which should be cut 4½″ long.

A straight tracer is made from 3/16″ square bar 3⅞″ long, as follows: Starting 1½″ from one end, taper the steel as shown in figure 139 to 1/16″; then file to the edge (a blunt cold chisel one) shown in the enlarged view. Note that the tool is rounded very lightly at the ends so that the tool, when used, will slip along the metal and not cut into it. After filing, smooth the tool, especially the edge, with very fine emery paper. Harden the edge (see Hardening and Tempering) and then temper to a dark straw color to complete the tool. If a better appearing and balanced tool is desired, taper the four top sides as shown in the diagram and then chamfer them slightly. It is best to do the filing in a vise.

The other liners are made in a somewhat similar manner; however, smaller, larger, and even curved edged ones may be required. The planishers, embossing, etc., can be figured out from the diagrams.

Occasionally it is necessary to forge some of the tools, especially the embossing ones, to flatten and widen the steel. This is done by heating the steel to cherry red and hammering it while it is still red on an anvil or heavy piece of steel. After the steel is forged and then cooled slowly, it is filed to shape.

CHASING HAMMERS These hammers (fig. 140) have broad flat faces and long thin-necked handles to give the tool elasticity for rapid hammering. The 1 inch face hammer is popular. The hammer may be used for hammer-setting stones, as shown in figure 367.

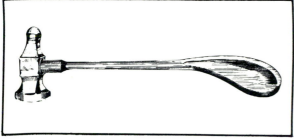

Fig. 140   Chasing hammer

PITCH Pitch is the ideal compound as a base or support material for chasing and repousséing metal. It is sufficiently hard to retain the general shape of the metal, yet it can quickly be softened in spots for the metal to give only in those spots under the chasing tool. It is adhesive, elastic, and easy to apply and remove.

If quantities up to five pounds are required, it is suggested that the pitch be purchased prepared from a reliable supply house. The actual making of pitch is a messy job; however, it is economical to make large quantities.

Pitch is composed of:

    Pitch . . . . 3 pounds
    Plaster of paris . . . . 2 pounds
    Tallow . . . . 2 ounces

Burgundy pitch is preferred for preparing Chaser's pitch. It can be purchased from chemical supply houses. Plaster of paris hardens the pitch, whereas tallow (common candles will do) tends to soften it. Lard oil may be substituted for the tallow. In the winter, tallow may be added to the pitch to keep it soft; in the summer, more plaster of paris may be added to harden it. The pitch is best prepared in an old pail. Warm the pitch slowly until it melts, and then, while mixing continuously, slowly add the plaster of paris and then the tallow.

HOLDING THE PITCH The ideal form for holding pitch for chasing jewelry objects is the chaser's pitch bowl (fig. 141). The bowls are made from cast iron to give them weight, come in 6 and 8 inch diameters, and are set on a cord or leather ring base so that they may be placed in any convenient position for good chasing. Avoid the thin metal bowls. They are too light and vibrate annoyingly when used, and their edges are too sharp.

Tin pie pans, round and rectangular, may be used by home craftsmen. Rectangular blocks of wood may be used with pitch piled on top, and the block may be held in an engraver's ball or a vise.

The design should be transferred onto the sheet of metal before it is embedded into the pitch. Leave extra metal around the outside areas of the design. This extra metal can be sawed off after the chasing and repoussé have been completed. Also, the metal should be annealed before it is placed in the pitch. Shaping the metal is frequently done before, or at the same time, as the repoussé process.

PLACING THE METAL IN THE PITCH Oil the back surface of the metal object to be chased in order to prevent the pitch from adhering when it is removed from the pitch. Heat the surface of the pitch slowly, moving the torch (use a large flame with little air) continuously to avoid burning the pitch. When the pitch is sufficiently soft, drop the metal on it and then wiggle the metal sideways to remove air pockets underneath. Raise some of the pitch over the edge of the metal to hold it down firmly while chasing. The pitch now can be air cooled or cooled quickly by placing the bowl under a running cold water faucet. **Note:** If the metal has been warmed before it is placed onto the pitch it will adhere better. After several hours the pitch will become very brittle and must be reheated.

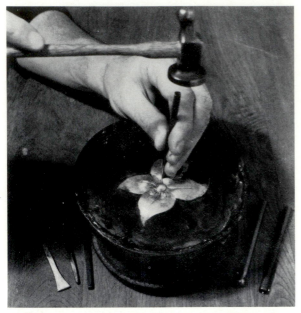

Fig. 141 Method of holding the chasing tool

CHASING AND REPOUSSÉ PROCEDURE

The actual chasing and repoussé procedure is comparatively easy. Patience, common sense, and artistic ability are the important requisites.

18-26 gauge metal can readily be chased. 20 gauge metal is frequently used, especially if chasing and repoussé are combined. The thinner gauge metals are used when doing fine or low-relief chasing.

STRAIGHT LINES Straight lines (which usually outline the design) are formed, or chased in, by means of a straight liner or tracer. Hold the tool between the thumb and first two fingers, with the other fingers resting on the metal to keep the tool from slipping, as shown in figure 141. Tilt the tool back about five degrees and then strike the back of the tool lightly with a hammer. The back corner of the tracer, known as the heel, will be driven into the metal, and the tool will move forward slightly towards the craftsman. Repeated gentle and rapid hammer blows (hammer from the wrist) will move the tool forward to form a sharp straight line. The depth of the chased line varies with the force of the hammer blow. Note that the chasing tool is not lifted; the hammer blow moves it forward. If the tool is held perpendicular to the surface, it will not move forward. Instead, it will dig into, and

perhaps cut through, the metal. If held at too great an angle, the tool will slide across the metal.

Cracks and holes, which are caused by the metal becoming work-hardened or from over zealous hammering, should be repaired immediately. They can be repaired by either drilling or filing out the hole so that it is no longer irregular, inserting a piece of wire or wedge of metal into the opening so that it protrudes slightly, soldering with hard solder, pickling, and then filing the metal smooth.

CURVED LINES Most curved lines are also formed with straight liners or tracers. Use a tool with a small and slightly rounded edge. Hold the tool as described above; however, while hammering the tool, twist it gradually to form the curved line. When making curves that have a small radius, it is necessary to tilt the tracer back further than usual.

Occasionally, curved tools may be used for forming very sharp curved lines. Circles may be hammered in with dapping cutters.

Fig. 142 Chased pendant   Carl Podszus

76

Fig. 142A Chased pin

RAISED OR DOMED SURFACES Raised or domed surfaces are formed from the back of the objects (repoussé). First, on the front, line-chase all necessary outlines. Then, remove the object from the pitch, remove the pitch from the metal, anneal the metal, and then place it in the pitch back side up.

Mark the areas of the metal that are to be depressed. Doming and embossing punches, and occasionally even ball peen hammers are used to raise the metal. When doing repoussé, the tools are held at right angles to the curves being modeled. The metal is pushed down with overlapping blows. The curves of the various punches should approximate the different curves of the form.

Larger punches are used to make deep wide hollows. Smaller punches are used for sharper, straighter curves. The hammer blows can also vary. The metal must be periodically annealed when doing high relief repoussé.

If the punches are too small, or if the tool is moved too quickly, smooth contours cannot be created and bumps will be visible on the metal. The piece must be removed from the pitch, annealed, returned to the pitch, and the "high spots" tapped lightly with a small domed punch.

After embossing, the metal is removed from the pitch, annealed, reversed, and chased from the front with planishing tools to smooth and further define the contours. It is very important that any hollow repoussé area be filled with pitch before it is hammered from the front in order to prevent the metal from becoming distorted. The metal can be tapped lightly to determine if there are any air pockets. Heating the softened pitch should

eliminate this problem. If necessary, after the piece has been removed from the pitch, it can be further planished with a small hammer on a dapping punch. The punch can be held in a vise.

TO FORM STEP EFFECTS (fig. 143) Step effects are formed by first line-chasing the object where the step is desired. The metal is lowered on one side of the chased line with a flat planishing tool having slightly rounded edges. Hammer the tool rapidly and move it continuously to avoid nicking the metal.

The line chasing tool is again employed, this time inwards at an angle at the bottom of the step. Often the metal is reversed on the pitch and shaped from the back in order to sharpen the design.

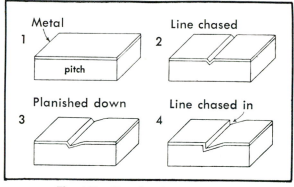

Fig. 143 Step forming procedure

REMOVING THE METAL FROM THE PITCH The metal is removed from the pitch by warming the pitch slightly with a large soft flame. Pick out the metal with an old tweezer and the pitch may then be wiped off. However, on most jewelry objects, it is best to heat the metal to a light red, and at that temperature the pitch will burn off the metal and turn into a white ash. The metal is also annealed by the light red heat, and, after cooling, the original color of the metal can be restored by pickling. **Reminder:** If the metal is covered with oil, the pitch will not stick to it. Benzine will dissolve pitch.

LEAD BLOCK Small objects, such as earrings, can be chased over a lead block. The lead will give slightly under the chasing tool; however, it is sufficiently hard to maintain the shape of the object. Chasing can also be done on a piece of wood or a linoleum block. Small headless nails can be positioned around the metal to keep it from moving.

2. STAMPING

Stamping is a decorative texturing process that affects only one side of the metal's surface. The variety of designs that can be made depends upon the shapes of the tools available and the ingenuity of the craftsman in combining them to form a motif. Chasing tools, commercial matting tools, stamping tools, and some leatherworking tools can be used as stamps to produce various design imprints on the metal. Nails and steel rods can easily be made into stamps by first heating and annealing the steel (page 39), forging and shaping the steel on an anvil, filing and then polishing the face of the tool with emery paper, using engraving tools and/or needle files to make a design on the face of the tool, polishing the tool with tripoli and rouge, and finally hardening and tempering the tool.

Before stamping in the design with these tools, the metal to be stamped should be annealed. Its surface should then be sanded with fine emery paper and crocus cloth; and finally, it should be buffed with tripoli and rouge. When a design has been decided upon, it can be transferred onto the metal with carbon paper or drawn on freehand. **Note:** It is advisable to practice stamping on a piece of copper in order to test the amount of force needed. Since it is difficult to hold a small piece of metal while stamping, it is advisable to trace an outline of the small piece of jewelry on a larger sheet of metal,

stamp in the design, and then saw or cut out the stamped piece. It is also easier to first stamp a design into a flat sheet of metal before shaping and assembling.

The piece of metal to be stamped is placed on a polished steel plate, block, or anvil. The steel stamp is placed on the metal, and held firmly in a perpendicular position. The stamp is struck with one sharp blow from a ball peen hammer. This compresses the metal and leaves an impression. The stamp should only be struck once, as a second blow may leave a blurred impression or crack the metal. The design may be stamped on the metal once, or stamped a number of times to form a pattern. Also, different stamps can be used to create an interesting motif.

Note: The larger the area of the stamping die, the heavier the blow of the hammer.

Embossing is a process that is very similar to stamping, except that the metal is pushed out to form a textured pattern by placing it on a soft surface such as a lead block, pitch block, or a piece of wood. Different sized smooth polished punches that have round, oval, square, or diamond shapes are usually used. The process is very similar to repoussé. Embossing is done by striking an embossing punch with a chasing hammer.

Fig. 145 "Flying Pin" with stamped decoration
Pahaka

Fig. 144 Decorative stamps

78

Tooling is another forming process where three dimensional designs are molded on metal. Since the metal used in metal tooling is a thin 36 gauge sheet, hammering is necessary. Sufficient pressure applied on a metal or wooden tracer or spatula model tool will cause the metal to stretch. The design is drawn on the back of the metal. The metal can be tooled on a soft felt pad so that high or low relief can be achieved.

3. ENGRAVING

Engraving is a highly specialized process in which a linear pattern or a design is produced on the surface of a piece of metal by incising and cutting away the surface with a sharp tool. Many jewelers do not attempt to do their own engraving but send the work out to professional engravers. Actually, with some practice and study, the average craftsman or jeweler should encounter no difficulty in developing an ability to engrave well.

THE ENGRAVING TOOLS The cutting tools that are used in engraving are called gravers or burins. The tools are made from a good grade of tool steel. There are several important shapes that can be purchased and each shape can be had in many different sizes. The sizes are specified by numbers, the smaller number being the thinner tool. Standard shaped tools are shown in figure 146.

The knife graver with its triangular shaft makes a very thin line with a V-bottom. The flat graver produces a line with a flat bottom. It can also be used to flatten and smooth an area of metal where a recessed design has been cut, make decorative wiggle cuts; and to form bevels. The square graver is used to make V-cuts and to remove large areas of metal. Lozenge gravers are used to cut V-shaped lines, scrolls, and diamond patterns. Half-round gravers leave a line that has an oval bottom. Onglette gravers are used for fine line engraving, shading, and when undercutting a line for inlaying. Line gravers are used to cut the parallel lines for Florentine textures.

Beginners can get started with the following tools: flat, Nos. 38 and 42; round, Nos.

51 and 53; square, No. 4 or lozenge, No. 4.

Engraving tools are also used to create surface textures, to remove excess solder, to

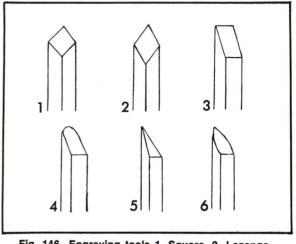

Fig. 146 Engraving tools 1. Square, 2. Lozenge, 3. Flat, 4. Round, 5. Knife, 6. Onglette

make lines and depressions for enameling and metal inlaying, to make the sides and bottom of a depression smooth and even when doing champlevé enameling and metal inlaying, to make diamond and other gemstone settings, to enlarge settings, and to finish settings. These operations are described in more detail in other sections of the book.

HANDLES Handles can be purchased in several shapes. One with the bottom part cut off is very popular for line engraving flat surfaces. The all round handles can be used on tools that have been bent or heeled.

SETTING HANDLE ON TOOL A hole is drilled into the handle slightly smaller than the tang (back) of the tool. The tool is set in a vise with the tang projecting, and then the handle is hammered on. Often the tang must be pointed more by grinding on a grind stone.

SHARPENING ENGRAVING TOOLS Engraving tools are always sharpened and frequently must be reshaped after they have been purchased. Gravers also need to be sharpened when their cutting edges become dull or break.

Detailed information about the sharpening and reshaping of specific tools for specific uses is beyond the scope of this book, but the information given will suffice for the average craftsman and jeweler.

Note: Most engravers shorten their new gravers approximately 2 inches (the original length of most gravers is 6 inches) for greater control of the tool. This is done before the graver is sharpened. Place the tool in a vise with the tang protruding from the top. A sharp hammer blow will snap off the unwanted portion of the tool, whereupon a new tang can easily be ground.

For normal engraving work, the face is usually ground at a 45 degree angle from the bottom edge of the graver. When working with softer metals, or for finer lines and deeper cuts, the face can be sharpened at a more acute angle. If the face angle exceeds 45 degrees, a shallow cut is produced, and the point is more likely to break. The face of the engraving tool is ground to shape on a soft emery wheel. Care must be taken not to burn (remove the temper) the tool. Keep the tool cool by dipping it constantly into water. The uppermost portion of the face is usually cut down during the rough grinding. Since this grinding reduces the thickness of the tool near the cutting edge, it permits quick sharpening; and it is easier to see the cut when using the tool. The face should be square with the length of the tool.

The face of the engraving tool is the only area of the tool that is usually ground by machine. The heel, belly (bottom) and cutting edge are ground and sharpened by rubbing (stoning) the tool on an Arkansas or Indian stone (fig. 147). Oil must be applied to the stone. A light oil, such as 3-in-1, is preferred. Depending on the shape of the cutting edge, the tool is either firmly rubbed back and forth, sideways, or rotated on the stone. It is important that the graver is not twisted as it is being sharpened. The cutting surface of a graver should be smooth, with no facets.

The graver is heeled to increase the strength of its cutting point and so that it can be held at its most efficient cutting angle. Also many of the tools must be heeled or bellied in order to best cut curves and spirals and to engrave flat surfaces. To heel the tool, lift it approximately 10 degrees from the surface of the stone and stone the belly

Fig. 147 Sharpening a flat tool

(or bellies separately) until a heel, roughly 1/16″ in length is made.

Tools can also be bellied by heating one inch of the tool at the cutting end until red hot and, while red hot, pressing the tool down against a piece of steel until the desired belly is obtained. The cutting edge must be hardened and tempered again (see page 39).

Sometimes it is necessary to both heel a tool and change the shape of the cutting edge. This is often done to a number 53 round which is changed to a V-shaped cutting edge tool for slanting or beveling curved lines (fig. 148-3).

Occasionally one side of the cutting edge is made slightly longer by grinding the face at a slight angle. This is advantageous when cutting a narrow line that becomes broader. The cutting point can be made narrower and

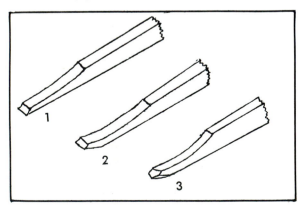

Fig. 148 Sharpening engraving tools 1. Back of tool ground away 2. Belly of tool heeled 3. Tool heeled and cutting angle changed

can be given more clearance by grinding more metal from the belly of the tool. If one side of the belly of the tool is ground back slightly more than the other side, the tool will be easier to turn in that direction.

Note: Before engraving, the face of the tool is always lightly stoned to hone its cutting edge. Excessive stoning at this stage will round the cutting edge of the graver, leaving it dull.

After rubbing the tool, dig it into a piece of wood quickly to remove the bur on its edge. The engraving tool is now ready to be used.

A sharp engraving tool when touched lightly to one's thumbnail will not slip, whereas a dull tool will.

The graver sharpening jig (fig. 149) can be adjusted and then locked to firmly hold the graver at whatever angle is needed for stoning its various planes. Most engravers prefer to sharpen their tools by hand.

Fig. 149   Graver sharpening jig

BRIGHT CUTTING When engraving, if a bright cut is desired, the bottom of the tool at the cutting edge must be rubbed on crocus or very fine emery paper. Hold the tool perfectly flat and rub it back away from the cutting edge. The tool, of course, is sharpened first, as explained previously, before it is rubbed for bright cutting.
Note: When engraving platinum and bright cutting is desired, the tool must be rubbed on paper after each cut. Some craftsmen prefer to rub the tool on a dry, hard Arkansas stone.

EYE LOUPE Some engravers, not all, use an eye loupe (fig. 151) for magnifying purposes when engraving. The 3 inch (magnifies 3.3 times) or the 4 inch (magnifies 2.5) are popular. 3 inch means that the loupe, held next to the eye, is used 3 inches from the metal being engraved.

TRANSFERRING DESIGNS Designs may be applied to a metal for engraving the same way as explained later in the chapter on transferring designs to a metal. Several additional specialized techniques especially suitable for engraving are described below:

1. Chinese White: Chinese white is applied to the metal so that a pencil mark will stand out clearly. The Chinese white is applied by either wetting one's finger, then gathering whiting on the finger and dabbing it on the metal, or, especially on large surfaces, by means of a camel's hair brush. Simple monograms and designs are drawn directly onto the Chinese white with a sharp pencil.

2. Calcium Carbonate: The following mixture is preferred to Chinese white since it does not chip as readily and since it also covers the metal more uniformly. Add alcohol (50%) to white shellac. To this add a sufficient amount of calcium carbonate (powdered) to turn the mixture white. Mix well. Apply to the metal with a soft brush. The mixture will dry quickly and leave a clean smooth white film on the metal that will take a pencil, carbon paper, or printer's ink (see below) impression clearly. When the engraving has been completed, the mixture is removed with alcohol.

3. Transfer Pads: A transfer pad can be purchased or made from a piece of uncured rubber. The rubber used for centrifugal casting is ideal. The pads are used when engraving identical pieces such as monograms or initials on silverware. Talc powder is dusted onto an already engraved object. The object is pressed into the transfer pad and removed, thus leaving a talc impression on the pad. The piece to be engraved is covered with transfer wax or beeswax and is then pressed over the talc impression. When removed the talc design will be on it, and the metal then can be engraved.

Fig. 150   The engraving block

Fig. 151   Engraving a bracelet

4. Paper Impressions: To copy an elaborately engraved object a paper impression can be used. Hold a good grade of paper over the engraving and then rub it firmly with a burnisher or round shaped tool to get an impression of the engraving onto the paper. Now rub a soft pencil over the raised impression in order to cover it with graphite. Cover the metal with a thin coating of engraver's transfer wax, beeswax or Chinese white. Place the paper over the metal and re-rub it to get the design onto the wax or Chinese white so that it can be engraved.

Instead of the graphite from a pencil, printer's proofing ink can be applied to the raised impression with a small proof roller. The paper is placed where required and pressed down onto the metal. This will leave a clean black impression on Chinese white or (better yet) the calcium carbonate, alcohol, and shellac mixture.

THE ENGRAVING BLOCK Figure 150 shows the shape of a good engraving block. Its purpose is merely to hold the object to be engraved; and since it can be rotated easily and can be held at any desired angle due to its leather ring base, it facilitates the hand engraving process. The top part of the engraving block has jaws which have numerous holes into which a variety of attachments can be fitted to hold work that has odd shapes.

OTHER METHODS OF HOLDING OBJECTS

1. Many objects can be held by hand on the bench top or on a sand bag or cloth.
2. The ring clamp can be used rather advantageously.
3. Shellac is ideal for holding objects to be engraved. The shellac, by means of heat, is melted onto a round, flat topped stick (fig. 152), and the object to be engraved is placed on the stick while the shellac is still soft. The shellac may be hardened quickly by placing it in cold water. When engraving, the stick is held against the V-cut in the bench pin so that it can be rotated easily. Objects can be removed by warming the shellac, and to remove all traces of shellac drop objects into alcohol.

Fig. 152
Shellac stick

4. A square block of wood with shellac on the top is often employed. The block, with object to be engraved, is set into

a steel engraver's ball and is held there by a clamp. The ball may be placed in different positions.

5. For engraving and carving rings, a block of wood with a top similar to a ring clamp but with a square bottom that can be clamped in an engraving block or ball, is very practical. The block can be made from a solid piece of maple.

HOLDING THE TOOL The engraving tool is held as shown in figure 153. Note that the thumb of the hand holding the tool rests on the metal in order to have complete control of the tool's cutting angle. The other hand's thumb may be held against the first thumb and acts as a pressure check; that is, it can prevent the tool from overcutting and slipping. Hold the rest of the other hand below the level of the engraver's block to avoid receiving a nasty jab from a tool that may slip.

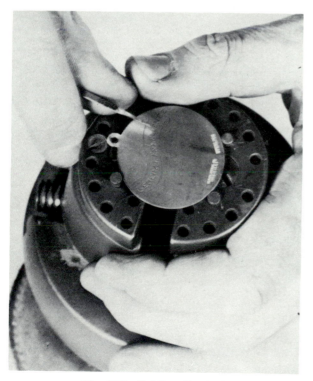

Fig. 153 Holding the tool

OIL OF WINTERGREEN Oil of wintergreen acts as a lubricant and also keeps the cutting edge of the tool sharper longer. The oil is kept as follows. Place a piece of absorbent cotton in a small glass container or jar and then saturate the cotton with oil of wintergreen. Touch the cutting edge of the engraving tool often to the oil while engraving.

THE ENGRAVING CUTS All engravings are composed of combinations of the few possible cuts which the engraving tools can make. The cuts are explained below.

STRAIGHT LINE CUTS (fig. 154) A flat or round bottom tool will normally give a parallel sided "U" straight cut with a flat or round bottom, respectively. A square, knife, lozenge, or onglette tool will give a "V" straight cut, and, if the same depth of cut is maintained, the sides of the cut will be parallel. Very narrow fine lines can be made with these tools. If the depth of the cut is varied the width of the cut will also change (fig. 154-C) and interesting effects can be had that way.

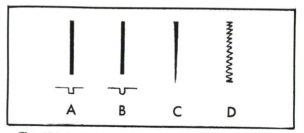

Fig. 154 A. Flat tool, B. Round tool, C. Varied cut D. Wiggle cut

To start the cut, hold the tool as explained previously. The back of the tool is raised approximately 15 degrees so that the face will be at a 45 degree angle from the surface of the metal. Press the tool into the metal to the desired depth. The line is cut by pressing the tool slowly forward. Even pressure must be maintained. A ½" cut can be made before the position of the thumbs must be changed in order to continue the cut. End the cut abruptly by snapping the tool up to remove the metal being cut. If necessary, cut back to the start of the cut and snap out the metal there too. Do not try to remove too much metal in one cut. Deep lines can be made by repeating the cut.

WIGGLE CUTS Wiggle cutting (fig. 154) is very easy to do, and, when used in conjunction with some of the other cuts, has many interesting possibilities. Flat engraving tools are used. The tool is held at a 45 degree angle and is actually wiggled as it is slowly pushed forward. One should be able to develop proficiency in wiggle cutting with a little practice.

CURVED LINE CUTS (fig. 155) Curved line cuts require more skill and practice than the other cuts; however, with a little patience, sufficient proficiency can be achieved to do the most attractive and interesting engraving. All tools should be heeled for curved line cuts.

A narrow half-round or flat graver can be used to form a parallel sided "U" or "C" curved line cut. To form the cut when the work is mounted in an engraving block (or shellac stick), raise the angle of the tool slightly and, while pressing the tool forward, turn the block.

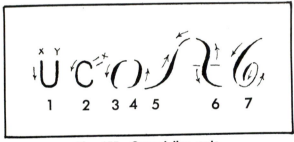

Fig. 155   Curved line cuts

Engraving cuts are made counterclockwise. Therefore, to cut the letter "U" (fig. 155-1), start at X and finish at Y. At Y, end the cut abruptly by snapping the graver up; cut back to X and snap out the metal there also. To cut the letter "C" (fig. 155-2), start where shown and cut counterclockwise; at X, cut back to finish the letter.

For slanted or beveled cuts, a square, a reshaped round, or even occasionally a flat graver can be used. The choice of the tool often depends upon the engraver's whim and training, for all of the above tools must be bellied and sometimes reshaped before they can be used. The cutting edge angle between the sides of the graver should be approximately 80 degrees.

To make the cut shown in figure 155-3, hold the tool as previously explained, and as the tool cuts and the engraving block is re-

volved, gradually turn the graver to the right side to get a wider slanted cut. Then, near the end of the cut, gradually turn the tool back again.

The cut in figure 155-4 is cut similarly; however, since the graver cuts counterclockwise, the cut is made in the direction shown by the arrow.

The cut in figure 155-5 is also made by gradually turning the graver to the right side. However, since the top of the cut goes in a clockwise direction, that part is made by back cutting. The cut in figure 155-6 is made by two slanted cuts, both starting from the center as shown by the arrows. The cut in figure 155-7 is made by 3 cuts in the direction shown by the arrows. These cuts (fig. 155-3 to 7) are the foundation cuts for script letter (fig. 160) engraving.

SPURRING Spurring is an inverted "V"-like cut that is used to form the serif on block letters and also has many uses in ornamental engraving and carving. The cut is made with a flat tool. If possible, study the cut on engraved objects. Note that on the wide top part the cut is level with the metal and that it is deepest at the sharp point. To make the cut, push the flat tool deeply into the metal and then snap the metal out abruptly to form the inverted "V". A little practice will be required to get the cut perfectly.

APPLYING THE CUTS The actual application of the cuts once they have been mastered is not difficult. It is suggested that a good book on monograms and lettering be obtained (see Index) since a thorough study of monograms and lettering is beyond the scope of this book. Another suggestion is to examine many engraved pieces and to study the letter styles and composition used. The method of engraving some of the important lettering styles is explained below.

PLAIN (EGYPTIAN) BLOCK LETTERS These letters (fig. 156) are comparatively easy to make, though very effective where inexpensive lettering is required. Flat engravers are used, and the width of the tool depends upon the size of the required letter. Note that only straight cuts are used and that the letters are as simple as possible.

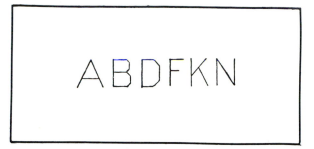

Fig. 156   Egyptian block

GOTHIC PLAIN BLOCK LETTERS (Curved Variety) (fig. 157) The straight letters are the same as the Egyptian block but letters such as C, D and O are curved. A round bottom tool may be used.

Fig. 157 Plain Gothic block

CAPPED BLOCK (fig. 158) These letters are similar to the Egyptian block with the caps added. Often the caps are put on with a narrower tool.

Fig. 158 Capped block

SERIF BLOCK (fig. 159) The serif is applied with a flat tool as explained under spurring.

Fig. 159 Serif block

SCRIPT (fig. 160) Script letters are cut with the same type of tools used to make curved cuts.

Fig. 160 Script

OLD ENGLISH (fig. 161) Old English capital letters are generally cut with the same tools as the script letters. The shaded line, if desired, is made by angling the tool. The fine lines run at a 60 degree angle and are cut individually. A wiggle effect may be substituted for the fine lines.

Fig. 161 Old English

Other popular styles such as Blackstone and Roman, and a complete study of the letters and monograms, as previously stated, can be had from a standard text book on lettering.

CARVING INITIALS Initials can be carved into rings and other jewelry items by removing the background metal around the initials (fig. 162) so that they stand out. The outline of the initials is first lined with a diamond or lozenge engraver, and then the background metal is removed with flat engravers. The background may be wiggled, matted, left plain, or enameled.

ITALIAN OR FLORENTINE FINISH This finish is obtained by means of fine line (8, 10, etc.) gravers. Heavy cuts are made in one direction. Lighter cuts are then made at a right angle to the first cuts to obtain the finish.

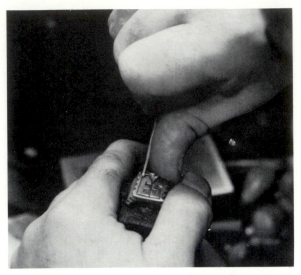

Fig. 162 Carving initials into a ring

The 14/8 graver is popular. The bottom number (8) stands for the number of lines; the top number (14) indicates the width of the space between the lines. A number 16 graver would have wider spaces; 12, narrower.

MACHINE ENGRAVING Hand engraving jewelry is often a long, tedious, and expensive process. If a jeweler frequently engraves, it is probably advisable to use a mechanical engraving machine. There are several basic types of mechanical engraving machines.

PANTOGRAPH ENGRAVING Pantograph engraving machines transfer human motion mechanically. A diamond graver is tracer-guided on a prescribed course, and it is virtually impossible to deviate from the desired inscription. The machine consists of four connected levers in the shape of a parallelogram, with an engraving tool attached to one of the

levers and a tracer tool affixed to the diagonally opposite lever.

When a piece is to be lettered, the engraver composes the inscription by setting individual master letters or designs into an adjustable self-centering slide. The engraver then places the engraving tool on a section of the metal and the movement of the graver is guided by the tracer tool as it follows the engraved master template. A template pattern can be reproduced on a smaller, larger, or equal scale on the metal. The depth and width of the cutter can be regulated.

In pantograph engraving, metal is not removed but rather depressed by the engraving tool. Insignias and other complex designs still have to be hand engraved into a brass plate, and then reproductions can be quickly engraved by the pantograph machine.

Fig. 164 Carving a figure onto a silver plate
Courtesy of Jack Staloff

GRAVERMEISTER The Gravermeister is a small precision-controlled pneumatic chisel that operates on the same principle as a jack hammer. The pressure-vacuum valving system of its pump sends controlled alternating vacuum/air pressure into a piston chamber in order to create a reciprocal action in the hand piece tube, which, in turn, delivers the impact to the engraving tool being held in the chuck. The number of strokes (cuts) per minute that the engraving tool can make can be varied between 800 and 1200 strokes per

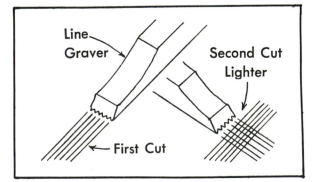

Fig. 163 Method of producing a Florentine finish

Fig. 165 Pantograph engraving machine

minute. As the number of the strokes per minute is increased, the cut made by the engraving tool will become lighter. Any of the tools that a hand engraver would use, such as liners, knives, onglettes, point and bevel gravers, can fit into the Gravermeister. The Gravermeister can considerably shorten the time needed to master the art of engraving.

Fig. 166 Gravermeister

4. ETCHING

Etching is a way of ornamenting metal by means of an acid and an acid resisting substance. It has gained popularity among crafts-

men as a simple and attractive means of embellishing jewelry.

The technique of etching is based on the fact that an acid solution, called a mordant, will remove or "bite" metal. Resists or grounds are used which, when applied to selected parts of the metal, protect these areas from attack by the mordant.

Essentially there are two types of etching used in jewelry making: open bite and intaglio. In open bite etching, large areas are left exposed to the mordant (fig. 167). The resulting depressions are used for inlaying other metals or stones, for champlevé and bassetaille enameling, or left to stand on their own decorative merits. In intaglio etching, the entire surface to be decorated is covered with a ground. A design is incised through the ground, leaving fine lines exposed to the mordant.

Fig. 167 Three simple pins with black asphaltum. An example of pieces prepared for open bite

Once the etching process has been mastered, it can be effective when used alone or in combination with other decorative processes.

PREPARING THE METAL Although it is possible to etch a curved surface, usually the piece is etched flat and shaped afterwards.

Remove any scratches from the metal with fine carborundum paper. Resists adhere better to a grease-free surface. Therefore,

87

grease and oxidation are scrubbed off with abrasive cleansing powder and water. Rinse well without touching the surface to be etched. Grease can also be removed by rubbing the metal with a generous amount of paste made from isopropyl alcohol and talcum powder. Rinse well.

The water break test described on page 131 is used to determine whether the metal is free from grease.

If the etch will be open bite, transfer the design onto the prepared metal with carbon paper. For intaglio, apply the ground first, let it dry, and transfer the design onto the ground with white or colored carbon paper which is available at artists' supply stores.

GROUNDS AND RESISTS There are several kinds of grounds and resists available at art stores and jewelry suppliers. Stop-out varnish and liquid asphaltum are used primarily for open bite. The parts of the design that are to be raised are painted with resist. Sometimes more than one coat is necessary. For best results use a sable brush which is kept soft by dipping it occasionally into the solvent recommended by the manufacturer. Usually a drying time of at least four hours is required. The drying time can be shortened by placing a piece in front of an electric fan. Accidental drips of resist are removed from parts to be etched with a knife or etching needle. Edges are straightened in the same manner.

Commercial brush-on "hard grounds" are used for intaglio work. The ground is painted over the entire surface to be decorated, the

Fig. 168 Black asphaltum applied to a pin

design is transferred and then the design is incised through the ground with an etching needle (fig. 169). Hard ground offers little resistance to the needle, allowing great freedom in drawing. Corrections are made by painting a thin coat of liquid asphaltum over the offending area. Allow this to dry and incise the correction through the asphaltum. Asphaltum offers more resistance to the etching needle than does hard ground.

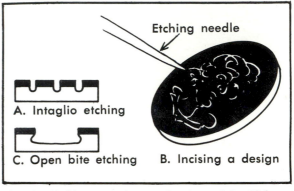
Fig. 169 Etching procedure   Courtesy of Jan Mainzer

Soft ground etching is a variety of intaglio, and, as the name implies, the consistency of the ground is softer than that of hard ground. The design is pressed rather than incised through the ground, which makes a wide variety of textural effects possible. Paint on the ground, allow it to dry and then place material such as lace, burlap, or leaves on top. Cover this with wax paper and gently press the lace, etc., into the ground. Carefully remove the wax paper and the lace with the aid of an etching needle, and paint the areas around the impressed design as needed to prevent false bite (accidental and unwanted bite). **Note:** It is often a good idea to press and dry plant material before using it in soft ground etching.

Most of the commercial paint-on grounds and resists work well, but most are also flammable and have toxic fumes. Keep them away from heat or flame and use them only in a well-ventilated area.

These fumes can be avoided by using liquid asphaltum with a turpentine vehicle, and/or ball grounds. Although ball grounds are commercially available, some craftsmen, feeling they get better results in soft ground and intricate intaglio work, make their own.

Formulas for ball grounds and liquid asphaltum with a turpentine base are given on page 93.

Ball grounds have essentially the same composition as the paint-on ones. The difference is that ball grounds come in lump rather than solution form, there are no fumes, and they are melted onto the metal. They can be more easily applied to curved or bumpy surfaces since they do not tend to pool or run off, as do the paint-on grounds.

Wrap the ground in a piece of taffeta as shown in fig. 170. Tie the top tightly with cord and then cover with tape to prevent unraveling. This is called a waxer. When the ground is melted onto the metal the taffeta strains out the lumps and lint. To avoid confusion, use different colors of taffeta for the hard and soft grounds.

Hold the metal briefly over an alcohol lamp with a cross lock tweezer. The grease-free side should face up. Touch the heated metal with the waxer, spreading a thin coat of ground as evenly as possible over the surface. Allow this to cool. Don't touch the newly applied ground. Now hold the metal, ground side down, over a candle until the ground remelts, moving the metal as necessary. The tip of the flame should touch the ground. This process, called smoking, smooths out the irregularities and darkens the ground by the admixture of carbon, so that the incised lines will be more clearly visible.

If, after smoking, there are translucent areas or breaks in the ground, probably the metal was not clean or came in contact with something greasy. Smoke it again. If the breaks remain, remove the ground, clean the metal, and reapply the ground.

When applying ground to metal that is too large to hold with tweezers, place it on a metal grill high enough to accommodate an alcohol lamp underneath. It is difficult to apply a thin even coat of ground to a large area with the waxer alone. Therefore, another tool, called a dauber, is used after the ground has been applied. It is constructed, as shown in fig. 170, of cotton, two disks of cardboard (2″ diam.) and two squares of taffeta, color coded according to the type of ground being applied. The dauber is used to remove excess ground from the metal and, more importantly,

to smooth the ground into a regular pattern of small bumps that are easily flattened by the smoking process.

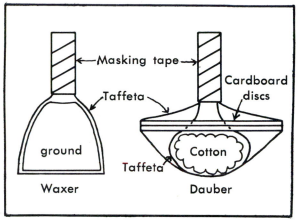

Fig. 170 Waxer and dauber

After applying the ground, warm the dauber briefly over the alcohol lamp. A cold dauber pulls too much ground from the metal. Then slide the lamp under one corner of the metal. When the ground melts pat it gently with the dauber. Continue to heat and dab following a zig zag pattern until the entire surface has been treated. As the dauber becomes saturated with ground, strike it on a clean sheet of paper (not newspaper) to remove the excess.

Suspend the metal, ground side down, between two wire hoops for smoking. A large surface area requires a large flame: twist together about six thin tapers (available at art or religious supply stores) to form a candle with many wicks. Start the smoking at one corner of the metal and allow the ground to remelt before moving the flame to an adjoining area. Once more, follow a zig zag pattern.

There is also transparent or "white" ball ground which is used to make additions to designs (often soft ground ones) that have already been etched. Smoke with an alcohol lamp and, as with soft ground, stop out areas around the incised design to prevent false bite.

Note: If, after application of the ball ground, it is difficult to incise the design, the coat of ground is too thick and should be removed and reapplied.

PROTECTION OF BACK AND SIDES When the resist has been applied to the front of the metal, dried, and the intaglio design incised, the back and sides of the piece are also covered. There are several methods of doing this. The first (and often messiest way) is to apply a generous amount of stop-out varnish or liquid asphaltum to these areas. Molten beeswax, paraffin, or candle stubs also work well. Melt the wax in a double boiler, keeping the heat as low as possible for wax can ignite if taken to a high temperature. Apply with an old brush. A third method, in which contact paper is used, cuts down on the application and clean-up time and reduces the possibility of false bite. Cut a sheet of contact paper slightly larger than the piece of metal, stick it to the back of the metal, paint the edges with liquid asphaltum or stop-out varnish, and then allow the resist to dry.

Before placing the metal in the mordant, check for accidental scratches or thin areas in the ground or resist and touch up where necessary with liquid asphaltum or stop-out varnish.

Provision should be made for taking the piece out of the mordant. Some craftsmen remove the object with copper or brass tweezers. Others stick one end of a strip of contact paper to the back of the metal, and the other end to the lip of the acid tray. This allows the piece to be removed without disturbing the resist.

ETCHING THE METAL Different mordants and grounds have varying characteristics. Until you are at ease with the etching process and materials, it is wise to first make a small test strip with the same metal and resist before etching the piece of jewelry.

Carefully slide the test piece into the mordant, front side up. The metal should be covered by about a half inch of acid solution. The time it remains in the bath varies with the type of mordant.

Depth of bite should be checked periodically. Remove the metal from the bath, rinse it with cold water and test the depth with an etching needle. Judging the depth becomes easier with practice. If the etch is not deep enough, return the metal to the acid.

Line thickness is governed partly by the width of the incised line, and partly by the length of time the metal remains in the bath. Mordants tend to bite horizontally as well as vertically.

For a pattern of thick and thin lines, incise the entire design and etch the metal until the finest lines are etched to the desired depth. Remove the piece from the mordant, rinse, dry, and cover the lines that are to remain thin with stop-out varnish or liquid asphaltum. Allow the varnish to dry and return the metal to the mordant. This process can be repeated several times. The same principle is applied to open bite to achieve the step effect used in bassetaille enameling. Usually, intaglio is not etched as deeply as open bite.

Keep a record of your experiments so that good results can be reproduced.

MORDANTS: ACIDS ARE DANGEROUS AND SHOULD BE HANDLED CAREFULLY. When preparing a mordant, pour the water into the mixing container FIRST, and then slowly pour the acid into the water. If the acid is poured first, it may spatter or could explode when water is added. Stir with a glass or wooden rod. Use a glass or pyrex baking dish, a polyethylene container or an enameled photo tray as an acid tray. Wear rubber gloves. Treat acid burns immediately with cold water and bicarbonate of soda (baking soda) or soap. Acid fumes are toxic: prepare mordants and do the etching in a well-ventilated area.

If the mordant is to be used frequently in the studio or classroom, store it in a large glass or polyethylene container or stoneware crock. Use a large polyethylene funnel to return the acid solution to the storage jar.

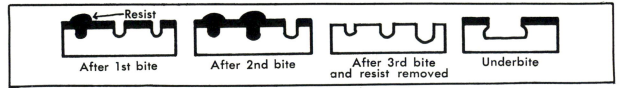

Fig. 171 Step etching and underbite

For occasional home use, prepare a small amount of mordant and dispose of it after use. Store the concentrated acid and the acid tray in a safe place.

DISPOSAL OF MORDANTS Place the jar containing the mordant into a sink and add cold water until the container is three quarters full. Slowly pour in bicarbonate of soda. This causes violent bubbling; the gas released is carbon dioxide. When the further addition of sodium bicarbonate does not cause bubbling, the solution is neutralized. Turn on the cold water again so that the contents of the jar overflow, and let the water run for several minutes to ensure that what goes down the drain is very diluted. The neutralized solution can also be poured down the toilet. Flush three or four times.

FORMULAS Listed below are formulas for several mordants. The choice of mordant depends on the metal being etched, the type of bite desired, and the quality of ventilation in the work area.

Usually, if a deep etch is required, it is best to use a weak acid solution which takes longer but results in a cleaner, more regular etched area with less underbite (fig. 171). Also, the resist is less likely to peel away from the metal. If a strong mordant is desired, use the fewest parts of water given in the formula, or gently rock the tray while the piece is being etched.

Sometimes the same acid solution is used to etch more than one metal. The various metals cannot, however, be etched in the same batch of mordant. Mix as many batches of mordant as necessary; label, use, and store them separately.

GOLD

hydrochloric acid	8 parts
nitric acid	4 parts
iron perchloride	1 part
water	40-50 parts

SILVER

nitric acid	1 part
water	2-4 parts

COPPER AND BRASS

1.	nitric acid	1 part
	water	2 parts
2.	ferric chloride crystals	13 ounces
	water	1 quart
3.	**Dutch mordant**	
	hydrochloric acid	1 part
	water	9 parts
	potassium chlorate (granular)	stirred into water until the saturation point is reached
	table salt	1 teaspoon per gallon

NICKEL AND NICKEL SILVER

mordants 1 and 2 for copper and brass

IRON AND STEEL

hydrochloric acid	2 parts
water	1 part

TIN, LEAD, AND PEWTER

nitric acid	1 part
water	4 parts

Of the acids listed above, nitric has the most toxic fumes.

Fig. 172 Etched pendant   **Lynda Watson**

When metal is placed into a nitric acid solution, small bubbles appear. Absence of bubbles indicates that the solution is too

91

weak. If the mordant is too strong, a brown gas (nitrogen tetroxide) is produced, and the bubbling is violent. Water should be slowly added.

If the bubbles are left undisturbed on the metal, the result is a pebbled effect on the bottom and sides of the bite. For a smoother etch, remove the bubbles with a feather or small brush, or by gently rocking the tray.

Another way of texturing an open bite is to etch the piece in the usual manner and then place it into a more concentrated acid solution for a few minutes. The result is an interesting matted effect.

A few minutes to about three hours are required for a satisfactory etch. The difference in time will be due to the strength of the mordant and the required etched depth.

Nitric acid tends to underbite, widening intaglio lines more than do most other mordants.

Dutch mordant works slowly, taking from one to four hours, depending on the depth of bite. There is little underbite, and for this reason many prefer it to nitric acid. The slow action does, however, make it impractical for open bite, which is usually deeper than intaglio. Bubbles do not accompany the etching process.

To prepare Dutch mordant, mix the warm water to saturation with potassium chlorate, add the acid, and then the salt. Allow the solution to cool to room temperature before using.

Ferric chloride is a salt rather than an acid, and behaves and is handled differently from acids. Although the solution itself is toxic, it does not give off any fumes. This makes it particularly suitable for classroom or extensive studio use. Five to six hours are required for a deep etch, with underbite developing after several hours.

Any grease left on the metal will act as a resist to the ferric chloride solution. Clean the plate well before applying the ground, and don't touch the areas to be etched. Ferric chloride crystals come in lump form. Weigh out the correct amount and place it in an acid tray. A wide shallow pan seems to give the best results. Slowly pour in the warm water and allow the mixture to stand. Usually it takes about half an hour for the lumps to dissolve. The solution is neutralized with sodium bicarbonate.

The piece is etched face down, suspended just below the surface of the mordant: Tape two to four loops of electrical wire (plastic coated copper wire) to the back of the metal, and paint the back and sides with molten wax. Another way is to stick contact paper to the back as described above, tape the loops to that and secure them with molten wax. Thread a piece of wire through the loops and hook the ends over the edges of the acid tray. The depth of the etch will be irregular unless the metal is level; therefore the metal itself must be flat. Usually another mordant is chosen for jewelry pieces shaped prior to etching.

Fig. 173 Neckpiece etched in ferric chloride in preparation for champlevé enameling
Antonia Schwed

CLEANING AND FINISHING When the piece is satisfactorily etched, take it from the mordant and place it in ammonia for five to ten minutes. This stops the action of the acid, and when the metal is copper, removes the discoloration caused by the mordant. Rinse with water after, not before, the piece has been in ammonia. This is especially important when preparing copper for enameling.

To remove the resist, soak the piece in the appropriate solvent for several minutes. Use an old toothbrush on the stubborn spots. Another way is to place the metal on newspaper, pour a small amount of solvent over it, and allow it to stand for several minutes. When the resist has softened, rub with paper towels and toothbrush, adding more solvent as necessary. Complete the cleaning with soap and water.

Wax is removed with benzine, acetone, or with hot water and a paper towel. Don't let wax go down the drain.

Slight imperfections in the etch may be touched up with engraving tools, and the background textured with standard matting tools.

The etched piece can be given a high polish or antique finish.

FORMULAS FOR BALL GROUNDS AND LIQUID ASPHALTUM Making grounds can be messy. It's a good idea to use an old pot and keep it exclusively for making grounds. All the formulas call for a double boiler: a cakepan partly filled with water for the bottom half and the old pot for the top work well.

Asphaltum, beeswax and rosin are available at art stores and chemical companies. Rosin comes either in lump form or already ground. To grind rosin, place the lumps between two pieces of newspaper and roll over this with a bottle or rolling pin until the rosin is a fine powder. Sift it through a fine strainer to remove the remaining lumps.

The solvents for the grounds described below are kerosene and turpentine.

LIQUID ASPHALTUM

asphaltum powder	1 part
turpentine	1 part
melted ground rosin	1 teaspoon per cup of liquid asphaltum

In the old pot mix the turpentine and asphaltum together, stirring constantly to avoid lumps. Then heat the mixture in the double boiler, continuing to stir until the liquid asphaltum has thickened to the consistency of thin honey. If necessary, add more asphaltum powder. Then add the melted rosin.

HARD GROUND

white beeswax	8 parts
asphaltum powder	5 parts
ground rosin	3 parts

Melt the wax in a double boiler, measure out the correct amount, and pour the excess into liquid soap-lined paper cups. Return the measured wax to the double boiler and slowly add the asphaltum powder, stirring constantly. Add the rosin in the same manner. The mixture should be free from lumps. Pour the ground into soap-lined paper cups and allow it to cool.

TRANSPARENT GROUND

white beeswax	11 parts
ground rosin	5 parts

Melt and measure the wax and add the rosin as described above.

SOFT GROUND

Summer formula

hard ground	3 parts
melted suet	1 part

Winter formula

hard ground	1 part
melted suet	2 parts

Melt the ground in the double boiler and stir in the melted suet. Suet is animal fat which has been cut in small pieces, melted, and the gristle strained out. Experiment with the proportions of ground to suet. Leftover suet can be kept in a refrigerator for a year.

Metal with summer formula soft ground on it can be passed through an etching press. This pushes the textured material into the ground more evenly than is possible by hand. Place a clean sheet of paper on the bed of the press. On it put the metal, ground side up, and arrange the textured material on top. Cover with wax paper and heavy cardboard (not corrugated). Over this put a thin etchers' blanket, then a thick one and pass the "sandwich" through the press. Experiment to find the right pressure.

On very hot days the ground may stick to the wax paper and pull away from the metal. Melt the lump of ground, add more hard ground, clean the metal, and apply again.

PHOTOETCHING

Some contemporary jewelers are experimenting with the process of photoetching, where designs used for the etching of metal are derived from photographs. The technique of photoetching is preferable to hand etching when the design to be etched consists of very fine detail. Fine detailed designs can be reproduced using the hand method, but photoetching is faster and can reproduce the design almost exactly.

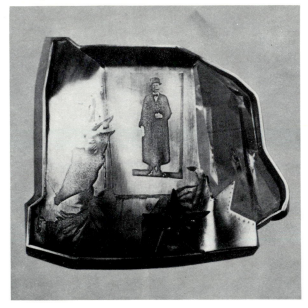

Fig. 174 Photoetched pin   **Eleanor Moty**

Photoetching differs from the manually-applied resist etching techniques in that the designs or ornaments are photographically reproduced on the metal's surface. Instead of applying asphaltum as a resist to the mordant, photoresists are used. These materials are resinous formulations of organic origin and are photosensitive to ultraviolet (U.V.) radiation. Once the metal is coated with photoresist, a contact "print" from a photographic transparency is made on the metal by exposure of the metal and transparency to U.V. light. The metal is then placed in a

developing solution (trichlorethylene - TCE); and at this time, depending on the type of transparency used and the type of resist used, certain areas of the metal are left exposed while other areas retain the resist coating. After developing the metal in TCE, the metal is etched. Only the exposed metal with no resist will be etched. This process is part of a much broader area known as photofabrication.

There are two variables that must be considered to achieve the etching effect desired: whether a positive or negative transparency is used and whether a negative-working or positive-working photoresist is applied to the metal. When using a negative-working resist (e.g. Kodak KPR), the areas of the resist exposed to U.V. light remain on the metal after development; when using a positive-working resist (e.g. Kodak KAR 3), the unexposed areas of the resist remain on the metal.

In figure 175, note that the two types of transparency were used with Kodak KPR. In example A, most of the face was not exposed to U.V. light and thus the resist there was

A   B

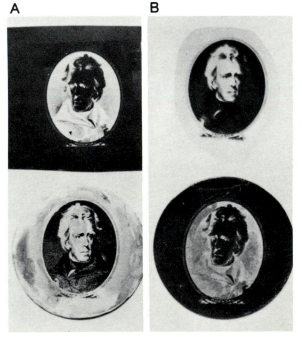

Fig. 175 A. Example of negative half-tone transparency B. Example of positive half-tone transparency Both transparencies were used to transfer design onto copper disks. Disks shown were developed in Kodak KPR and dyed.

removed by the KPR. The face therefore became the sunken part of the design after etching (fig. 179-A). In example B, the face was exposed, the resist remained there, and the face therefore became the raised part of the design after etching (fig. 179-B). Be sure to inquire as to whether the resist bought and used is negative or positive-working in order to choose the method for achieving the effect desired. Also, different resist solutions and developers are used for different metals.

IMPORTANT: All of the chemical solutions used in photoetching are toxic to the skin, eyes, and lungs. The same safety measures that apply for etching, apply for photoetching.

TRANSPARENCY PREPARATION A high contrast photographic pattern is required to reproduce artwork (or a photograph) onto the metal's surface. A high contrast graphic arts film (e.g. Kodalith Ortho Film, Type 3) is recommended for this purpose. This Kodalith emulsion is capable of recording extremely fine detail and is readily obtainable at graphic arts suppliers. It is commonly available in popular sizes (35mm, 4 x 5, 5 x 7, 8 x 10, etc.).

A negative Kodalith transparency is obtained by photographing the desired object, drawing, or photograph using Kodalith film and then developing the film in Kodalith developer. A positive Kodalith transparency can be made by contact printing from the first generation Kodalith negative onto Kodalith film. Certain Polaroid cameras and films and Kodak High Speed Duplicating Film 2575 can be used to make the positive transparency directly. Photographs can only be etched if a half-tone negative or half-tone positive transparency is then made. This is a complicated procedure, and it is better to "farm out" the job to a commercial firm.

COATING PHOTORESIST Before the photoresist can be applied to the metal surface, it must be thoroughly degreased and cleaned. Handle the cleaned metal by its edges.

A darkroom or suitably darkened room with the correct safelight is required for the coating procedure, since photoresists are sensitive to U.V. light.

For dipping and drying purposes, especially with larger pieces, it is advisable to make a cradle of wire to support the metal sheet. When coating smaller pieces, it is practical to wrap masking tape around a thin wooden dowel stick, sticky side out, and use the tape as a means of holding the metal when coating it.

Photoresists are applied by various methods such as spraying, whirling, dipping, and flowing. Flowing is the most practical way to coat metal. A small quantity of photoresist is poured onto the center of the piece of metal. The piece is then manipulated by tilting it at various angles to distribute the photoresist evenly on the metal surface (fig. 176). If bubbles appear they can be removed with a feather or a small brush. The coated piece is then held in a vertical position in a light-

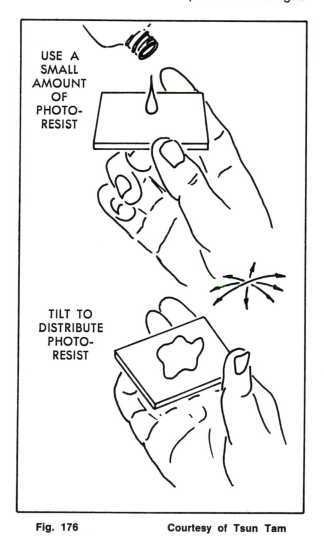

USE A SMALL AMOUNT OF PHOTO-RESIST

TILT TO DISTRIBUTE PHOTO-RESIST

Fig. 176   **Courtesy of Tsun Tam**

proof cabinet or box and is allowed to dry completely in the dark at room temperature (68°-72°F.). This usually takes about 24 hours. To dry a larger piece, use a cradle of cloth or metal that can be hung in a cabinet for drying. For smaller pieces, simply tape a "circle" of masking tape to the back of a lightproof box so that it sticks to the box and can also hold the metal in an upright position for drying.

After the metal has dried, it is suggested that it be prebaked at 250°F. for 10 minutes. This step is optional, but is necessary, especially if a deep etch is desired. A hot plate (with no visible heating elements) with a rheostat, or a small oven, are suitable. The metal is baked with the surface to be etched up. Care must be taken, when baking, not to overheat the metal or the photoresist may become fogged. This procedure must be done in a darkroom under safe lighted conditions to prevent exposure of the photoresist to light.

EXPOSURE As photoresists are sensitive to "light" sources rich in ultraviolet radiation, unfiltered fluorescent lamps (Type BL), high-pressure mercury-vapor lamps, and carbon arc lamps may be used to expose the metal. A slide projector that is equipped with a 500 watt lamp is a highly recommended "light" source.

The dried, treated metal and transparency are prepared for U.V. exposure by placing them together in a contact frame. The frame is obtainable through photo suppliers. Figure

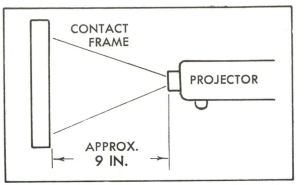

Fig. 178 Exposing the metal   Courtesy of Tsun Tam

177 shows the orientation of the transparency in relation to the metal.

It is best to make several test exposures using scrap pieces of metal to standardize the exposure time with the chosen "light" source. If a slide projector with a 6 inch lens (f3.5) is used, it should be placed about 9 inches from the upright contact frame (fig. 178). First start with a 5 minute exposure. Then develop and dye the image. Should the metal be underexposed—image not distinct, broken lines, incomplete detail—increase the exposure by minute intervals until a good image is obtained. On the other hand, if the metal is overexposed—image is dark, fine details filled in and lost—decrease the exposure time for a better image. A well-exposed design should appear similar to the original. When examining the contact "print" on the metal, it is best to judge its quality by observing the quality of the reproduction of the fine details.

DEVELOPING AND DYEING Developing and dyeing are best done in an open tray. Use a glass tray of a suitable size and pour in a workable quantity of developer. The exposed piece is totally immersed in the developer and is then processed for two minutes using constant agitation. This is accomplished by gently rocking the tray. **Caution:** The developer is a toxic and volatile material. Be sure to use it in a well-ventilated room.

The image is still invisible at this stage and must be dyed to render it visible. A 15 second immersion in KPR Dye will allow the previewing of the quality of the photoresist image prior to etching so that the underexposure or overexposure of the image can be judged and

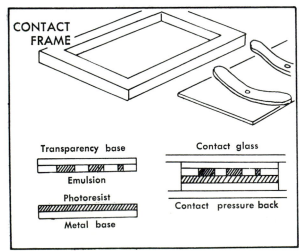

Fig. 177 Contact frame and preparation for exposure
Courtesy of Tsun Tam

corrected if necessary. Use tongs when immersing the metal in the dye. If the dye gets on the hands, wash them immediately with a waterless hand cleaner. This dyeing procedure is optional, but it is not time consuming and can be considered to be an integral part of the developing phase.

In order to examine the quality of the image on the metal, rinse it in water and examine it. If the quality of the image is satisfactory, post baking is recommended for increased image durability in the acid solution. As in prebaking, the metal should be baked, image side up at 250°F. for 10 minutes on a hot plate or in a small oven.

After the metal has cooled, a coating of liquid asphaltum or beeswax, should be painted onto the edges and back of the metal as described on page 90. The resist coating must be set before etching can begin. Last minute touch-ups can be done with molten beeswax. Excess resist on the surface of the metal to be etched can be removed as described on page 88.

ETCHING Proper etching requires using the correct mordant. See page 91 for a listing of the various metals and their suggested mordants. Also, see pages 90-92 for information on the etching procedure.

A   B

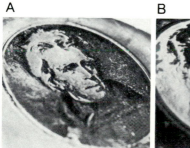 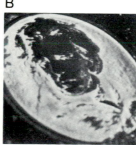

Fig. 179   Copper disks etched with dye unremoved
A. Note sunken design and raised background (used negative half-tone transparency, Kodak KPR)
B. Note raised design and sunken background (used positive half-tone transparency, Kodak KPR)

CLEANING AND FINISHING Information on cleaning and finishing procedures can be found on page 92. To remove the photoresist, wipe the metal with the developer or heat it for 15 minutes at 750°-950°F. Further information on photoetching can be obtained by writing Department 454, Eastman Kodak Company, Rochester, New York 14650 and requesting Eastman Kodak Company Pamphlet P246, "Photofabrication Methods".

Fig. 180   Photoetched pin   Holly Sparkman

5.   COMBINING METALS

There are many decorative techniques that use contrasting metals and nonmetallic materials with metals. In this section, the tech-

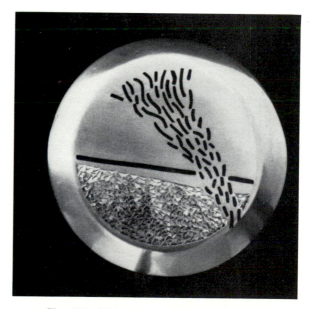

Fig. 181   Silver brooch with copper inlay
Gene & Hiroko Sato Pijanowski

niques of marriage of metals, inlaying, and mokume will be discussed, as they are the techniques most frequently used by craftsmen.

Marriage of metals and metal inlay are methods for joining different metals together or setting different metals into a larger base sheet of metal for the purpose of achieving contrasting color effects. Sheet metal, metal strips, and metal wire can be used. The basic problems presented by the marrying and inlaying of metals are achieving a perfect fit between the metal pieces, and/or successfully soldering together metals with different melting points and physical properties so that a multi-metal sheet is created.

MARRIAGE OF METALS

The "marriage of metals" is a term usually used to describe the process of joining different metals together to create a flat smooth sheet of contrasting metals. There are two basic techniques used to create a "married metal" piece. Either smaller pieces of contrasting metal are soldered together, or a design is pierced out in a larger sheet of metal and a piece of contrasting metal is soldered into that area. In both techniques, sections of compatible metals (metals that can be soldered together) are sawed out, fitted together, and then soldered.

When joining pieces of different metals to make a larger piece, the following procedure can be used. First, it is very important to make sure that all metal pieces to be used are flat. To flatten the metal, anneal it if necessary and then hammer it flat on a steel plate or stake with a mallet. Also, use a slightly thicker gauge of metal than desired for the finished piece, because much filing will be necessary after the metals have been soldered together.

Once the design is made, transfer the first section of the design onto the chosen metal (see page 206), saw it out, and file it to the line. To assure a perfect fit with the next piece of metal, place the first piece on the second piece of metal. Then, with a sharp scribe, trace the border that will be common to both pieces onto the second piece, saw it out just outside the scribed line, and file it so that the second piece fits perfectly with the first piece. The edges to be joined should be filed so that they are perpendicular to the surface of the metal (not rounded) and so that there is no space between the two butting edges. Once this is done, scribe in the rest of the design on the second piece, saw, and file. This procedure is continued until all pieces of the design have been fitted and filed.

To solder the pieces together, coat the inside edges of the pieces with flux and assemble them on a perfectly flat asbestos sheet or charcoal block, front side up. Steel pins can be placed around the pieces to help hold them in position. **Note:** A small space should be left between the metal and the pins since the metal will expand when heated. Soldering can also be done front side down, but when up, it is easier to see and control the flow of solder on this more important side. Coat the front surface with flux and place small pieces of hard solder along the seams about 1/8″ apart. It is better to use too much solder and flood the joints, than not enough. Heat the piece and use a poker to keep the solder close to the joints and flowing into all parts of the seams. After the metals have been soldered together, the piece should be turned over to make sure that the solder has flowed through the seams to the back.

If, after this initial soldering, some gaps remain in the seams, pickle and then rinse the piece in hot water, coat the front surface with flux, and solder with easy solder. If resoldering does not initially work, take a flat broad punch and lightly hammer the metal along both sides of the seams (from the back) to bring them together. After planishing, solder the seams with easy silver solder. Pits can be filled with medium solder.

Another common problem is that the solder may run during subsequent soldering operations. If this occurs, repair as described above.

After all soldering operations have been completed, pickle, wash, and dry the piece. Filing is necessary to remove high spots and solder. Filing should be done after all soldering has been completed in order to alleviate the problem of solder sinking away from the

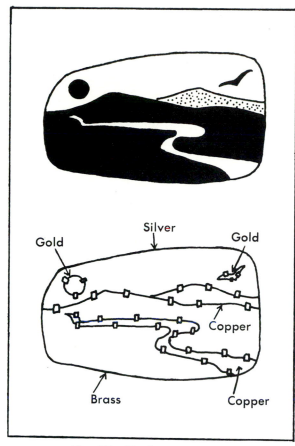

Gold   Silver   Gold

Copper

Brass   Copper

Fig. 182 Marriage of metals

be set in or pieces overlap, start with the piece that is largest), saw out the design, and then file the piece to the desired shape. Use this metal piece to scribe the design on the base metal. Pierce the base metal and saw out the design just inside the scribed outline so that the slight enlargement of the design due to tracing is accounted for. Then file as needed so that the "inlay" metal fits in perfectly. **Remember:** The edges to be joined must be parallel to each other and perpendicular to the top and bottom surfaces. As described before, solder and pickle the piece and then proceed by adding other metal pieces as required by the design, using the same method as for the first piece of metal. Repair any seams after all pieces have been soldered in place. Then file and finish the piece.

When thin lines are part of the design, it is possible to set thin metal strips into the base metal so that only the edges are visible. To set in a metal strip, first transfer the line design to the base metal. For sawing, it is necessary to drill a hole as small as possible at the beginning of the line so that the right size blade can be inserted (the width of the saw blade will determine the thickness of the metal strip used). **Note:** The diameter of the drilled hole will always be larger than the

edges when doing repeated soldering. Once the piece has been filed, use emery to remove the scratches and to give the piece a satin finish. The piece can also be highlighted after finishing.

When setting pieces of metal inside a base sheet of a different metal, various methods can be used. Planning the sequence of additions of different metals is very important. If, for example, the design requires one piece of metal to be set into another piece of metal as well as into the base metal, the metal part that appears largest must be sawed out, fitted into the base metal and soldered first, before the second smaller part is "inlaid".

One method that can be used for "marrying" pieces of metal sheet into a base sheet of metal is described below. **Note:** As when joining pieces of metal together, the pieces used should be flat and the thickness and size desired calculated to account for the effects of filing. First, transfer the design to the inlay metal (if more than one piece is to

Fig. 183 Stick pin   Arthur Cohen

99

saw cut. The gap between the strip and the base metal can be closed by spreading the base metal with a flat punch. If the dulled hole is too large it is difficult to close the gap. Saw forward as evenly as possible on the scribed line.

A sheet of metal is passed through the rolling mill to obtain a sheet that is slightly thinner than the width of the cut. Cut a strip from the sheet metal that is slightly wider than the thickness of the base metal. Small pliers can be used to push the strip down into the cut. Then solder the strip to the metal and file the piece so that the edge of the metal strip is flush with the base metal.

If several metal strips cross each other, it is necessary to solder the first inserted metal strip into place and then make saw cuts for the additional strips. Always use lower melting solder when soldering these additional strips in so that previously soldered strips

will not fall out. Yellow ochre can also be used to protect previously soldered seams.

It is easy to use wire of different gauges to create circle designs in the metal base. Drill appropriately sized holes in the metal and then cut short sections of wire that will fit into the holes. Drill sizes and wire gauges can be matched. Also, wire tubing with a wire rod of a different metal soldered in the middle can be used to create designs with more contrasting colors.

INLAYING

Inlaying is an old metal working technique used to set pieces of annealed metal into depressions or grooves in a base metal. These recesses for inlaying can be prepared by casting, etching, stamping, or cutting with gravers. Inlaying is different from "marriage of metals" because solder is not used to secure the pieces in place. Instead, a depression is made, with undercuts added, so that when a piece of metal—slightly thicker than the depth of the depression—is hammered in, it will spread into the undercuts and be held in place. The same basic principles hold for inlaying sheet metal or wire. Many contemporary craftsmen prefer to use marriage of metal techniques rather than traditional inlay techniques for surface decoration because the desired results are more quickly and easily obtained.

One basic inlaying method requires the removal of metal from the base sheet with engraving tools. (For more detailed information on engraving tools and techniques, see page 79). It is essential that the base metal used is thick enough to support the thickness of the cut desired. The type and size of graver used depends on whether the cut made is a straight line, a curved line as in scrolls, or a depression that can accommodate a piece of sheet metal; and whether the cut made is the main cut or the undercut.

For example, to engrave a straight line about 1/64" wide, a number 5 onglette could be used for the main cut and a number 0 onglette for the undercuts. For finer work—straight or curved lines—a lozenge or square graver could be used for the main cut and

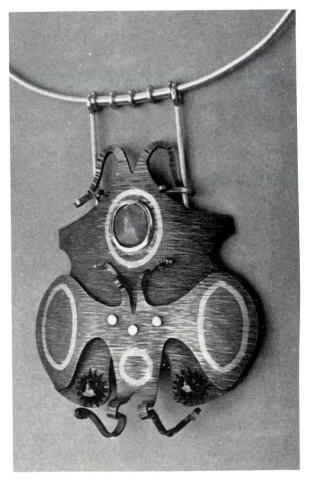

Fig. 184   Pendant   Chuck Evans

a number 00 onglette or number 1 knife for the undercuts. These gravers also need to be sharpened correctly for greatest control and best results. Sharpening procedures differ depending on whether the cut is to be straight or curved.

Inlaying wire into a straight line cut is the easiest type of inlaying. First transfer the line design onto the base metal. Then move the graver along the line so that metal is removed and a groove of the desired depth remains. With experience, judging the correct depth of the cut made with the graver will become easier. Using a finer graver, make undercuts on both sides of the main cut. The graver should be slanted sharply so that it just misses hitting the opposite lip of the groove and makes the main cut a bit wider and deeper along the bottom edges of the groove.

The wire to be inlaid should have a diameter about half the depth of the cut. To set in the wire, use a hammer and a broad punch. A hard brass punch which has a square end and a very fine textured unpolished face is recommended. The face can be textured by holding the punch on a piece of carborundum paper laid on a steel plate and tapping the punch lightly on the paper with a chasing hammer until the face is dull. This type of face holds the metal slightly so that it is forced down into the cut rather than pressed outward. Some craftsmen prefer to set in the wire by hammering on a block of wood placed over the wire and base metal. In either case, the wire should be annealed before it is hammered into the cut.

Some metal will remain above the surface of the base metal after the cut has been completely filled. To remove the extra metal so that the inlaid metal lies flush with the surface of the base metal, use a flat graver that is just a bit wider than the wire inlay, or a jeweler's file. Be careful to avoid marring the base metal during this procedure. Then stone the piece to remove file marks and polish with 500 or 600 carborundum paper wrapped around a polishing stick.

Scrolls and curved lines can also be cut and inlaid. The procedure is generally the same. Making the undercuts is more difficult, especially on the outside edge. The gravers used must be specially sharpened for this purpose.

When the design to be inlaid is relatively

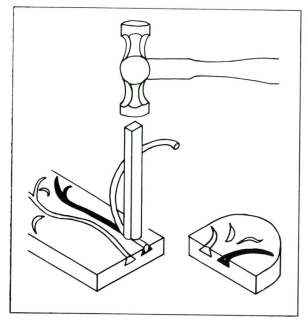

Fig. 185   Metal inlay

Fig. 186   Pendant   Gene & Hiroko Sato Pijanowski

large, sheet metal is usually used for the inlay. When inlaying with metal sheet, transfer the design to the base metal. With the appropriate gravers, make the outside cut, the cuts across the inside of the design to remove metal (flat or round graver), and the undercut along the outside edge (square or onglette). To flatten the bottom of the depression, use a flat graver. A small knife graver can be used to force up small projections of metal (burs) along the bottom of the depression for holding the metal in place.

Transfer the design to the sheet metal to be inlaid. Carefully saw out the design so that the fit will be perfect. The metal sheet used should be approximately one gauge thicker than the depression. Anneal the metal piece and then hammer it into the depression. If the sheet metal is difficult to fit, it can be domed slightly so that the perimeter is made smaller, whereupon it then can be hammered into the metal.

There is a technique for making the inlay recesses that is easier than either etching or engraving. Begin by sawing (piercing) out the designs in a piece of sheet metal. Saw and file the necessary contrasting metal inlay pieces (they should be slightly thicker) so that they fit perfectly into the open areas of the sheet metal. The cavities for receiving the inlay metal are created by sweat soldering the base to a metal backing sheet that is the same size and shape (see fig. 188-C). Any excess solder that may have flowed into the cavities can be removed with a flat graver. **Note:** Do not forget to make the undercuts. The contrasting metal is then inlaid by using the traditional techniques previously described.

There is another method of inlaying that utilizes soldering in the beginning stages. The pieces to be "inlaid" are soldered to the base metal, and then the whole piece is rolled through a rolling mill to force the "inlay" pieces partway (so that they are flush) into the base metal. Usually, it is best to use a base sheet of metal that is softer than the metal being set into it. Also, the metal to be "inlaid" should be a thinner gauge than the base sheet. For example, 26 gauge 14 karat gold pieces could be married to a sheet of 20 gauge fine silver.

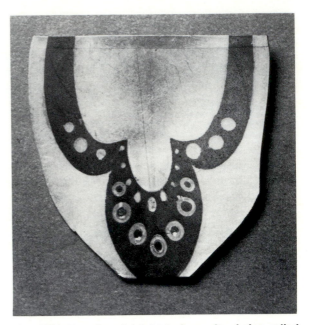

Fig. 186A Experimental inlaid piece after being rolled through a mill   Meryl Greenberg

After the design is made, cut out the metal pieces needed. These may be pieces of sheet metal; or tubing, wire, or combinations of tubing and wire which have been cut into short flat sections. When using this method it is important to take into consideration that the metals will stretch according to the direction that the piece is passed through the rolling mill. With experimentation and experience, it becomes easier to judge exactly how much smaller to cut the metal "inlay" pieces to allow for this stretching and therefore preserve the dimensions originally intended in the design.

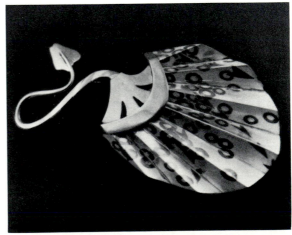

Fig. 187   Brooch   Meryl Greenberg

Sweat solder the pieces to the base metal with medium solder. Avoid using too much solder, for it will flow out of the sides and require extra filing. Check the seams and re-solder if necessary. After cooling, the piece is pickled and annealed. It is then put through the rolling mill two or three times to achieve the desired thickness of metal, usually about 20 gauge. If properly soldered, the pieces should not buckle or warp. After this initial soldering and rolling operation, other metal pieces can be added to complete the design. In any case, layers are added one at a time. If, for instance, a design requires a piece of gold sheet with rings of copper married to a sterling silver backing, the sheet should be soldered on first and rolled to the desired gauge, and then the copper tube sections should be soldered onto the sheet and the piece rolled again. Each time the stack is rolled, it is generally rolled to a thickness of about 20 gauge. **Note:** It is important that all filing operations be done after all soldering has been completed.

INLAYING NONMETALLIC MATERIALS The technique of inlaying also includes the inlaying of materials such as wood, ivory, bone, plastics, and gemstones into metal for color and textural contrast. Enameling can also be considered an inlaying technique, and is discussed later, on page 112. Inlaying nonmetallic materials requires basically the same procedures as inlaying and marriage of metals. In one method used, the desired shape and thickness of the inlay material is determined and then the shape is cut out of the appropriate sized metal sheet. That sheet is soldered to another sheet, which serves as the backing. Wire channel frameworks can also be used for inlaying.

A wire channel framework can be made using flat wire and a flat metal backing. The wires are shaped with pliers and cut with shears to form the design, and then they are soldered to the backing sheet. The outer wire framework is often heavier. It can be soldered in place first with medium solder. The inner channels can then be positioned on the backing sheet and soldered to it using easy solder. Small notches can be made in the heavier wire with an engraving tool or a file to help hold the smaller channels in position during soldering.

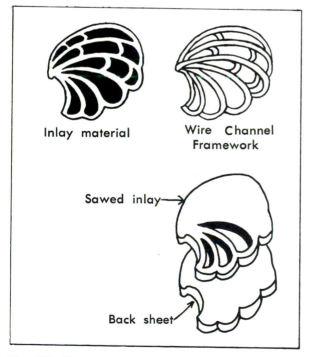

Inlay material   Wire Channel Framework

Sawed inlay →

Back sheet →

Fig. 188   Two methods of constructing recesses for inlaying nonmetallic materials

Fig. 189   Pin   **Holly Sparkman**

103

Fig. 190   Pendant   Christine Thrower

The materials to be inlaid should either be filed or ground to fit the cavities exactly or else the cavities can be shaped to fit the exact shape of the material.

The materials are held in place using cement, epoxy, pins, or rivets, as well as pressure. When working with nonmetallic materials, all soldering and as much finishing as possible should be completed before the

Fig. 191   Pin   Castillo

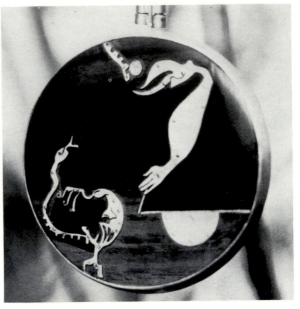

Fig. 192   Pendant   Bev deJong

materials are added so that they will not be damaged.

Another popular technique is to use chips or fragments (1/16″ in diameter or less) of gemstones (turquoise, lapis lazuli, tiger eye, malachite) for inlay. The channels are first filled with Clear Casting Polyester Resin to a level where the chips, when inlaid, will be slightly above the metal surface. A pointed file can be used to deposit the resin into the channels. The gemstone chips are then quickly placed close together on the resin. It is best to arrange the chips so that the flat surfaces are on top. The file, coated with resin, is an excellent tool for picking up and depositing the small chips into the channels. Extra resin can be added to fill any voids. When the resin has hardened, the surface is ground level with pumice blocks or carborundum stone while being held under running water.

MOKUME

Mokume is an ancient technique developed by the Japanese that creates patterns on metal surfaces that are impossible to achieve using traditional inlay techniques. The technique is aptly named, as mokume means "wood grain". With this technique, geometric

Fig. 193 Pendant   **Holly Sparkman**

and wood grain-like patterns can be created on the surface of the metal by laminating different metals together and then exposing the layers in various ways.

Usually two to six different types of metal are used for inlaying in mokume—gold, silver, copper, brass, bronze, and nickel silver. These metals can be sandwiched together in any order, depending on the desired effect. The size of the metal sheets or strips used depends on the size of the mokume piece(s) desired. **Note:** For beginners, it is advisable to work with small sheets of metal first. In any case, the metals used must be of the same size and shape. The layers can be of different thicknesses (usually between 14 and 20 gauge), and are usually stacked to create pleasing color contrasts among the materials.

Lamination proceeds as follows. The metal sheets or strips to be used are annealed, pickled, and cleaned if necessary to remove all grease. All pieces should thereafter be handled by the edges. Also, it is important to make sure that all of the metal pieces are completely flat.

Before stacking the pieces, one surface of each piece (except the top piece) should be coated with solder. This can be done by either applying a light, even coat of borax flux to the surface, sprinkling on hard solder

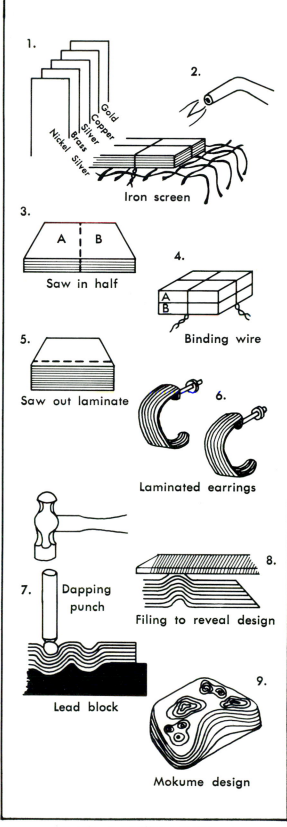

Fig. 194   Lamination and Mokume

filings, and then allowing it to dry; or by following the procedure for sweat soldering using medium solder. The pieces are then stacked, usually bound together with binding wire, and then placed as a completed stack on a wire soldering grid on top of a refractory surface.

To insure proper and even heating during soldering, a torch with a large, soft flame should be rotated all around the stack. The stack can also be turned over to assure even heating of all surfaces. As the stack is being heated, pressure can be applied to the top of the stack with a rod. This pressure helps push the metal surfaces together and removes air pockets. The flame is removed when the solder starts to flow at all the seams.

After cooling, the stack should be pickled and then rinsed in hot water. The seams are checked for gaps. If there are any gaps, the stack is lightly planished, flux is reapplied, and the stack is reheated to flow the solder. When the stack appears to be well soldered, it should be cooled, pickled, rinsed, and dried.

Once the soldering operations have been successfully completed, many alternatives are available to the craftsman. The stack may be cut into strips about ⅛″ thick with a jeweler's saw or a hacksaw. These banded multi-colored metal strips can be filed and used at that thickness, or, after filing, rolled in a rolling mill to reduce their thickness. When working with smaller, thinner blocks, it is possible to planish the metal on both sides to reduce thickness.

Remember: Anneal before and during rolling or planishing to prevent work hardening of the metal. Usually, the final thickness of mokume pieces is 16 to 20 gauge. The strips can be used singly, inlaid, or soldered together to make larger sheets or interesting geometric patterns.

Another alternative is to roll the entire soldered stack in a rolling mill to about a 20 gauge thickness, saw it in half, file the sawed edges smooth, stack one on top of the other, tie the stacks together with binding wire, and then solder the two pieces together using medium solder and the sweat soldering

procedure described above. These steps can be repeated to build up a stack of many layers.

Note: It is suggested that no more than 40 to 50 layers be produced. Each time a stack is soldered to another stack, the resulting larger stack is generally rolled to a thickness of about 20 gauge. As more layers are produced, each layer necessarily becomes thinner, which produces finer mokume effects and eventually less apparent contrast.

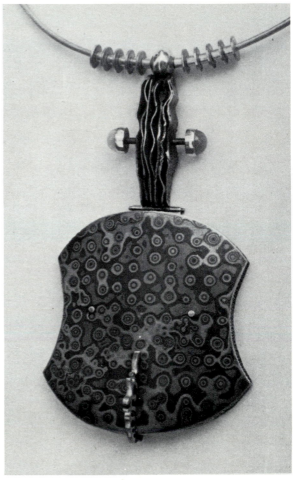

Fig. 195 Mokume pendant   Chuck Evans

To create interesting patterns, irregularly shaped bands, and rings, the different layers of metal must be exposed. It is possible to file or saw the laminate at different angles, or curves, or to form grooves; to drill holes in the surface either straight down or at an angle; and to twist and fold the metal strips. Rolling out or hammering the metal that has

106

been treated this way produces intriguing effects.

The familiar irregular "wood grain" pattern can be made by doming or punching the surface of metal, as in repoussé work. Different punch sizes can be used, punching can be done to different depths, and regular or irregular indentations can be formed. The protrusions in the top surface are then filed flush with the surface, thereby revealing the layers of metal that have been pushed up as a result of the doming procedure (fig. 194).

Note: Indentations should not be made too deep or else holes may appear in the metal. As a rule, do not punch deeper than half the thickness of the metal. If small holes are formed during doming or filing, fill them with solder. Patch larger holes by soldering in a piece of metal. The mokume piece is then rolled once again to eliminate the indentations on the bottom surface. Using techniques similar to mokume, multicolored metal spirals can be produced by twisting thin wires of various metals together, coiling the twisted wire into a spiral, soldering, and then hammering or rolling the spiral flat.

Once the desired mokume effects have been achieved, the mokume pieces are assembled, formed, or joined to other pieces of metal. **Note:** When soldering parts of the laminate to other metals, use easy solder to avoid causing separation of the metal layers. The mokume pieces are then finished by filing, sanding, buffing, and polishing. The metal's surface can be treated, if desired, by oxidizing or coloring the metals to bring out the desired colors.

6. RETICULATION

Reticulation is a technique whereby a rippled texture is created on a sheet of metal with a torch. Reticulation is possible because if a higher melting, outer surface layer of metal is formed on a sheet of metal, the inner surface layer of metal will become molten first when the metal is reheated. Upon cooling, the lower melting inner core will contract as it solidifies, causing the metal sheet to ripple, or reticulate.

Fig. 196   Reticulated pin   Harold O'Connor

Although sterling silver is relatively easy to reticulate, the preferred alloy for reticulation is 83 parts fine silver to 17 parts copper. If this alloy is not available, it can be made by first melting the copper in a flux-lined graphite crucible in a gas muffle furnace. As soon as the copper becomes molten, the silver should be quickly added in order to minimize oxidation. Once the silver has melted, the molten alloy should be stirred with a graphite rod, and a small amount of borax flux should be added to the melt. The metal is then quickly poured into a heated, oiled ingot mold. The ingot is formed and rolled into a metal sheet that is either 18 or 20 gauge thick and at least 2 inches wide. Any bending or shaping should be done before the reticulating process begins.

The outer layer of fine silver (which has a higher melting point) is created on the alloy by first placing the metal sheet in an annealing pan filled with pumice and then slowly heating (5-10 minutes) the metal with a torch that has a soft flame (less air and more gas) until it turns a dark cherry red color (its annealing point—approximately 1200°F.). The metal is then either quenched in a boiling solution of 10% sulfuric acid or in a solution of 33% sulfuric acid. The acid quench removes the copper oxide layer formed during annealing and leaves a pure silver layer on the metal sheet.

107

This process can be repeated as many as four times. Each time the metal sheet is heated and pickled, the silver layer is built up more. **Note:** Reticulation is not an exact science. The number of times and the length of time the metal sheet is reheated and

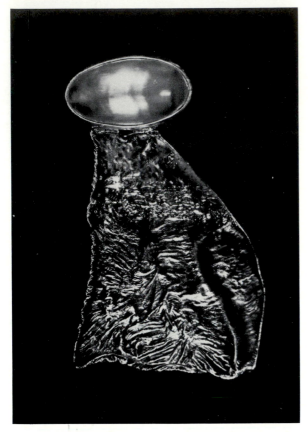

Fig. 197   Reticulated pin   Komelia Hongja Okim

pickled can be varied in order to experiment in producing different types of reticulation. Copper tongs should be used. Avoid handling the metal.

Before beginning to reticulate, make sure that the prepared metal sheet is flat. Yellow ochre can be painted on selected areas of both sides of the metal sheet to prevent reticulation of those areas. Place the metal sheet on a smooth, moisture-free asbestos pad. Begin to slowly heat the metal with a torch that has a medium-hot neutralized flame (an equal amount of gas and air). Move the torch slowly across the sheet, gradually increasing the heat of the flame until the surface of the metal turns a dull red and begins to wrinkle. This should take several minutes.

Once reticulation has started, the torch should again be made slightly hotter, and then slowly moved either across the sheet, up and down, or diagonally, in one direction and then the other. The torch should also be held at an angle.

Holes may sometimes be burned through the metal. If this occurs, do not stop playing the torch. Hopefully there will be either enough good metal left for the design or the hole can be incorporated into the design.

After the sheet of metal has been reticulated, it is pickled in a solution of 10% sulfuric acid and water.

Reticulated metal is very brittle and is therefore very difficult to form, bend, or twist. When soldering a sheet of reticulated metal to another metal, only low melting solders should be used. A reticulated piece of jewelry may be finished by oxidizing, wire brushing, or plating. Yellow or red 14 karat gold can also be reticulated by following the procedures described above.

7. GRANULATION

Granulation is a process whereby round granules or tiny pieces of metal are attached, without solder, to the surface of a sheet of metal by fusion. Many granules can be used to create reliefs in the form of lines, patterns, or shapes; or single granules can be attached to certain areas of the metal's surface.

The advantage of the granulation process over soldering—when adding tiny pieces of metal for decoration—is that the granules are bonded only at their point of contact to the base metal. Therefore, the appearance of the tiny granules is not marred by solder. 22 karat gold and fine silver are ideal metals to granulate, but lower karat gold (14 and 18 karat) and sterling silver can also be used. The techniques explained below are most successfully used with higher melting metals.

MAKING THE GRANULES Although there are no definitions that differentiate a granule from a shot, a granule can be described as a sphere of metal with a diameter of from 1/200″ to 1/32″, whereas shot is larger, with

Fig. 198   Ring   Fretz

a diameter from 1/32" to 1/4". For information on making shot, see page 45.

Granules are made from small pieces of metal that are heated until they melt and form spheres. Before making the granules, clean and pickle the metal. To produce very tiny granules (grains) file a piece of metal with a coarse file. For larger granules, cut metal sheet or wire into small pieces (paillons) with shears. If granules of approximately the same size are needed, the metal cuttings should be made the same size. Sprinkle these grains or chips of metal into a high, narrow crucible containing a layer of ¾" of powdered charcoal. The metal should be sprinkled so that all the filings or paillons remain separate. This prevents fusion into larger granules than needed. If more granules are needed, add an additional layer of charcoal and then sprinkle on the metal pieces. Each layer of metal should be separated by a ½" layer of charcoal.

The crucible should be placed in a preheated gas or electric kiln or furnace. When heated properly, the metal paillons become spheres because of capillary attraction. For gold, the crucible is heated for at least 30 minutes at 1900°F. For silver, the crucible is heated for 10-20 minutes at 1750°-1800°F.

The time that it takes the metal to form into spheres depends upon the size of the crucible.

To check the development of the granules, remove the crucible from the kiln, drop a small amount of charcoal into cool water, and observe the shape of the granules. If more time is needed (the pieces are not spherical), return the crucible to the kiln. When the grains are observed to be perfectly spherical, cool the crucible slowly. Once cool, place the contents in a pan containing detergent (for cleaning) and water. The granules should drop to the bottom of the pan, and the charcoal should float to the top, where it can be collected. The granules are then removed, washed, and sized by using sieves of different sized mesh.

To make a smaller number of granules, and for experimental purposes, place some tiny pieces of metal on a charcoal block and heat them using a torch with a reducing flame until the metal forms into spheroids. To assure spherically-shaped granules, make small depressions in the charcoal block one-half the size of the desired granule. Once the granules have matured, gradually turn off the air and slowly remove the torch so that the granules do not oxidize or cool too quickly.

In both methods of forming granules, the reducing atmosphere created by the charcoal should leave the granules smooth and oxide-free. If necessary, however, the granules can be pickled.

PRINCIPLES OF GRANULATION When doing granulation it is important to understand the principle of eutectics. A eutectic alloy is an alloy composed of two or three metals which has a lower melting point than any of the metals which make up the alloy. Many metal alloys and solders are eutectic alloys. By varying the percentage of the different metals which compose an alloy, the melting point can be lowered until the eutectic point (the lowest possible melting point) of that alloy is reached. A small percentage of copper when alloyed with either silver or gold will form a eutectic alloy. Therefore, if the granules are coated with a copper salt and glued to the piece, thereby creating a eutectic alloy at the contact points, the granules will fuse to the piece at their contact points when heated to a temperature that causes the eutectic alloy to melt. This temperature is below the melting point of the metal sheet and the granules.

The actual fusing of the granules and the sheet metal is thought to occur as a result of molecular exchange. When heated with a reducing flame, the copper salt forms an oxide and the glue carbonizes. The oxygen from the copper oxide combines with the carbon to form carbon dioxide gas and changes the copper oxide to a pure copper film. This copper film fills in the space between the granules and the sheet metal and then alloys itself with the granules and the piece, bonding them together. Eventually, at a higher temperature the copper diffuses into the gold so that the fusion is almost invisible.

22 karat gold and fine silver are easier to granulate because the melting point of the eutectic alloy is not as close to the melting point of these metals as it is to the lower karat golds and sterling silver. This allows for a wider margin of error when fusing granules and lessens the chances of damaging the piece.

PREPARING THE BASE METAL All the forming should be completed before the piece is granulated.

Note: Most soldering operations are done after the piece has been granulated. More heat is necessary for granulation than for soldering. Easy solder is used. Ochre can be applied to protect the granules. If soldering must take place before granulation, a high melting solder should be used. It is important to clean and pickle the metal to be granulated so that it is free of dirt and oxides. After cleaning, the metal should be handled with tweezers only. The base metal should be prepolished with fine carborundum paper so that after granulation only high polishing and buffing are necessary. In this way there is less of a chance of damaging the granules.

APPLYING THE GRANULES The granulation process can be used for fusing all types of small metal pieces—spheres, bits of wire, rectangular or square-shaped chips, etc. —

to jewelry objects. In the explanation below, the term "granule" should be understood as meaning any very small piece of metal to be joined to a larger object.

To apply the granules, make a glue from a mixture of organic glue and distilled water. Gum tragacanth, gum arabic, and hide or fish glue all work well. A formula that can be used to make the glue is:

For flat surfaces: 1 part hide glue
                      15 parts water

For domed surfaces: 1 part hide glue
                     2 parts flux
                     12 parts water

At this point the type of metal used must be considered. When working with high karat gold and fine silver, this glue must be mixed with equal parts of copper carbonate or cupric hydroxide and some distilled water to form another paste.

When using gold alloys with a high percentage of copper (14 and 18 karat), the addition of a copper salt to the paste is not necessary. Instead the granules to be used should be heated in an oxidizing atmosphere until they are covered with black copper oxide. Then the granules are affixed to the piece with glue. If the lower karat gold has been repeatedly pickled, however, which brings the gold to the surface, it is advisable to add the copper salt to the glue. There are, however, craftsmen who have fused granules onto fine and sterling silver successfully using unoxidized granules and glue only. In any case, adding the copper salt will probably assure a better fusion.

The granules can be fastened to the piece using different methods. One way is to coat the areas to be decorated with the correct glue and then to place the granules on the metal with tweezers or a small camel-hair brush dipped in glue. Another method is to coat the granules with glue using a camel-hair brush and then to use the brush to place the granules on the metal. Excess glue, especially that containing flux, should be removed with a damp brush. The glue must be thoroughly dry before granulation can take place. The piece is then carefully placed on a charcoal soldering block.

Fig. 199 Granulated pendant   John Paul Miller

flame to heat the metal. Ochre is applied to the back of the base metal, the granules are positioned, and the piece is carefully placed on the floor of the kiln or on a piece of steel or mica. The metal is heated in the kiln until a faint red color appears on its surface. The torch is then moved over the granules so that the piece is heated evenly from the top and the bottom. This heating process must be carefully monitored to prevent overheating. Once the granules are fused, immediately remove the torch and unplug the kiln.

Fig. 200 Granulating in a beehive kiln
Courtesy of Cecelia Bauer

FUSING THE GRANULES The greatest technical problem presented by the granulation process is heating both the granules and the base metal evenly to the correct temperature so that they will fuse without sagging or melting. Overheating can also leave a sometimes undesirable orange-peel texture on the metal.

A good way to judge when the metals have reached the correct temperature is to look at the piece, and, when the surface metal appears shiny and bright, remove the torch immediately. **Note:** High karat gold liquifies on the surface before it sags; sterling silver sags before it liquifies. Also, judging the fusing points of lower karat golds and silver alloys is more difficult because the melting points of the base metal and the contact points are very close. Of course, the ability to judge at precisely what point to remove the flame is difficult but can be learned through experience.

Some craftsmen use a beehive kiln with the top removed and a torch with a reducing

If possible, join all the granules to the piece in one firing. If more granules need to be added to an area after one firing, the piece must be cleaned before another firing is done. When granulation has been completed, the piece should be cooled slowly. To test whether the granules are well attached, tweezers can be used. If granules cannot be pulled off with tweezers, the granulation has been accomplished.

FINISHING Care must be taken in the final finishing stage to avoid removing or distorting the granules. To finish the piece, first pickle, and then wash it in water. If the piece has been well polished before granulation, further finishing may not be needed. If it is, for a satin finish, scratch-brush it lightly on a fine brass or nickel silver wire brush wheel rotating at a slow speed. Be sure to use soap and water to lubricate the piece. If a bright finish is desired, polish the piece with rouge on a soft buffing wheel or else by hand with a rouge cloth.

8. ENAMELING

Enameling is the name given to the technique of applying specially formulated colored glass compounds (known as enamels) to metal, and then fusing the enamels to the metal by means of heat. Enamels, chemically, are composed of sand or flint, red lead, borax, and soda or potash. Fusing these chemicals produces an almost colorless material known as flux or frit. By adding various percentages of metallic oxides to the frit (cobalt for blue, copper for green, iron for

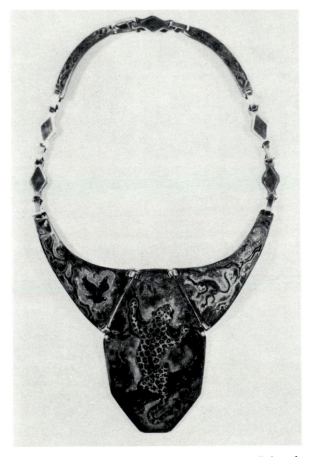

Fig. 201 Enameled pendant   Antonia Schwed

brown), colored enamels are produced. The colored enamels may be sub-divided into two main groups—the transparent and opaque. In addition, there are also opalescent and translucent enamels.

The actual technical operations of enameling are fairly simple and can be acquired easily. Those who have artistic ability and discriminating taste in the use of colors should find enameling an ideal medium.

PREPARING THE ENAMELS Enamels may be purchased either in lumps or crushed. The lumps, which resemble thick pieces of broken glass, are crushed and ground in a porcelain or wedgewood mortar with a pestle. Keep the enamels covered with water during the crushing and grinding operation. The water will prevent the enamel from flying about and also acts as a wash to remove impurities from the ground enamel. The enamel should be ground to the consistency of a very fine sand or until it can be passed through an 80 mesh screen. Agate mortar and pestles are used for the finest grinding operations.

The ground enamel is washed by adding more water (distilled water is preferred) to the mortar and then permitting the enamel to settle. The resulting milky water is poured off slowly and the washing operation is repeated until the water does not turn milky. Opaque enamels can be ground finer than transparent; however, transparent enamels should be washed more thoroughly. If transparent enamels are ground too fine they lose some of their brilliance.

After washing, the enamel can be very slowly dried in a small aluminum pan which is heated over an electric hot plate. Dry powdered enamel should be applied immediately or stored dry in glass or plastic containers with screw top lids so that they remain in a thoroughly dry state until used. Excess paste enamel can be stored wet for several days if covered. Enamels that have been previously prepared and stored should be washed again before reusing.

By buying the enamels crushed, at a slight additional charge, the tedious job of grinding the enamels can be avoided. Pre-crushed enamels are suitable for all enameling but the finest, artistic, transparent gold enameling. The opaque crushed enamels can be used for most jobs without being washed. Many enamelists however, will thoroughly wash and regrind all of their enamels. **Note:** Always wash the flux.

Note: Enamel colors cannot be mixed together in order to obtain different shades.

The color of transparent enamels can be made lighter by adding various percentages of clear flux.

80 mesh enamel—enamel that passes through a screen with 80 holes to the square inch—is recommended and should be purchased for most work. 150 to 200 mesh (powdered) enamel is used for painting.

Fig. 202 Enameled neckpiece   **Astrid Fog**

Most enamels are considered "medium fusing" and are fired (fused) at approximately 1500°F., for two to four minutes. Several of the enamels—flux (clear transparent), black, white—can be purchased "soft or hard fusing". The soft fusing enamels fire at temperatures approximately 50°F. below the medium fusing enamels; the hard fusing fire at 50°F. above. The hard fusing enamels are used as base enamels over which medium enamels are applied.

Colorless transparent enamel fluxes are often applied directly onto the metal first to protect the metal surface against oxidation, serve as the base layer for colored enamels, and/or to fuse cloisonné wire, foil or threads to the piece. Soft low fusing flux is sometimes used as a cover coat to protect painted enamel, or to obtain a smooth or brilliant surface. The type of flux used depends on the enamel work being done and the enamels being used.

PREPARING THE METALS The metals—copper, silver or gold—before they are enameled may be annealed (see Annealing) and pickled (cleaned in acid) to remove internal stresses, grease, and oxides. Some enamelers wash the pickled metal with a weak household ammonia solution to completely neutralize all traces of acid.

Note: Small silver and copper jewelry objects can be enameled without being annealed.

COPPER Copper is pickled in a nitric acid solution consisting of 1 part acid to 5 parts water (see Pickling, page 32) or Sparex. The copper is removed from the acid, washed in water, and dried as quickly as possible so that no water spots remain. When dry, the copper is cleaned and brightened by rubbing it with fine (00) steel wool, or with a detergent such as Comet and the finest grade (white) Scotch Brite. If steel wool is used, the piece should be washed to remove any small particles, and then immediately dried. It is important not to touch the surface of the piece about to be enameled with one's fingers since any oil deposited on the metal could cause problems during the first enamel firing.

Fig. 203 Cloisonné neckpiece   **Nancy Finelli**

113

Heating the metal during an enameling firing will cause fire scale to form once again. This fire scale must be removed before any counter-enamel is applied to that area. Once a coat of enamel has been applied to a piece, most enamelists remove fire scale with emery or a file rather than with acid. Commercial fire scale inhibitors can be painted on the metal prior to enameling. Fire scale can be removed with acid by dabbing on the acid with a swab so that the acid does not come in contact with the enamel. Contact paper, masking tape, or wax can also be used to protect the enamel from acid.

Note: The enamels will adhere to copper that has turned black (oxidized) when annealed. By applying transparent and opaque enamels over the black oxide, interesting results may be obtained.

GOLD The higher karat golds are usually preferred by enamelists. Fine gold is used for cloisonné wires.

Gold is pickled the same as copper; however, after the gold has been dried it is best brightened by scratch brushing with a glass fiber brush. Special gold alloys without any zinc are available and should be used for enameling. Enamel will pop or crack off gold containing zinc since zinc vaporizes when the gold is heated to red heat.

SILVER Most enamelists prefer to use pure silver, not sterling, since it does not oxidize when heated and therefore does not have to be pickled. It also has a higher melting point (1762°F.) than sterling silver (1640°F.)

Sterling silver, if used, is pickled in a hot sulphuric acid solution of one part acid to 10 parts water, as explained on page 33 and 34.

SOLDERING INFORMATION All parts must be soldered to objects before they are enameled. Use high melting silver solder (Handy "IT") for silver and copper so that the solder will not melt and flow during the enameling process. Special gold solders are also available for enameling on gold. To keep a solder from flowing, it is advisable to apply a coating of yellow ochre to soldered surfaces that are not covered by enamels. All excess solder

Fig. 204 Silver "Eagle Box Pendant" with champlevé and cloisonné enameling   Jo-An Smith

must be scraped or filed off the metal, otherwise the enamel may chip after firing.

Soft solders may be used to solder earwires and pin backs to the metal surfaces of finished enameled objects. Hard solders will crack the enamels. Soft soldering (see page 59) can be accomplished by means of a bunsen burner or a torch, and the object must be heated with a soft flame to avoid cracking the enamel.

Earwires and pin backs can be soldered to counter-enameled objects by grinding away small areas of the counter-enamel. A small area of the back can also be left enamel-free. By means of an electric soldering iron, solder is then applied to those areas. Then the earwire or pin back is held in position with a tweezer. A hot, clean soldering iron is touched to the earwire or pin back where the solder is, thus soldering them in position without cracking the enamel.

APPLYING THE ENAMEL The enamel may be applied (known as charging) to the metal by means of a spatula, a fine sable brush, or it may be sieved on. The method of application depends on the type of enamel project. The enamel is applied wet with the spatula or brush, or it is sieved on dry. Wet enamel is usually applied to small areas such as cloisons or champlevé recesses; dry enamel is usually used as a base coat or it is dusted onto larger objects such as bowls and trays.

The spatula can be made from a 3/16" piece of tool steel, or if available, stainless steel. One end of the steel is forged until flat (1/32" thick) and then filed so that it can pick up enamel; the other end is pointed (fig. 205). The wet enamel (mixed with water to form a thin paste) is picked up with the flat part of the spatula or a brush and applied where desired. It is then leveled and spread to different positions with a spreader, a 3/32" rod bent slightly or a brush as shown in fig. 205.

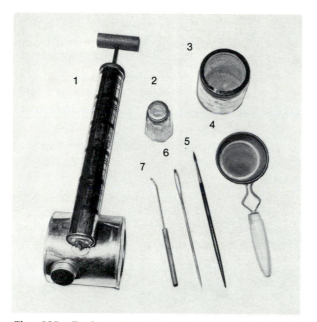

Fig. 205 Equipment for applying enamels 1. Hand sprayer, 2. Small shaker, 3. Jar shaker, 4. Strainer, 5. Brush, 6. Spatula, 7. Spreader

Dry enamel, placed in a jar, can easily be sieved onto objects (fig. 205). Note that part of the cover of the jar and saltshaker in figure 205 has been removed and replaced with 80 mesh screen. The salt shaker is ideal for small objects and for sieving enamel onto small areas of larger objects. The strainer in figure 205 is also recommended. Plastic containers with 80 mesh screen covers can be purchased from dealers.

Slush enamels—200 to 250 mesh enamel mixed with water—can be sprayed onto the metal or the metal can be dipped into the slush and removed slowly in order to obtain an even enamel coating which can be used as a base color.

GUM TRAGACANTH A gum tragacanth solution is often mixed with the enamel or sprayed onto the metal before applying the enamel. The gum acts as a glue and holds the enamel to the metal.

The gum solution is prepared by adding one teaspoon of powdered gum tragacanth (can be purchased in a drug store) to a quart jar filled with water. Shake the jar thoroughly and then permit it to stand over night. The result is a clear gum solution with a thicker solution on the bottom of the jar. The thin solution is poured into a different container and used when needed for spraying; the thicker solution is used to hold glass threads, beads, cloisonné wires etc. in position. A few drops of carbolic acid added to the solution will check the growth of bacteria.

A solution of ½ Klyr Fire and ½ water is also excellent for holding enamel in place.

SPRAYING The gum may be sprayed onto the metal by means of an atomizer, hand sprayer (fig. 205) or an electric spray outfit. The atomizer or hand sprayer is suitable for craftsmen; professional enamelers prefer spray outfits.

A properly sprayed metal surface is completely covered with small globules of the gum solution. Large globules can cause trouble and should be broken by blowing on them. If the metal is over-sprayed, the globules will form into patches of water. If so, wipe dry and respray.

As explained later, the enamel is sieved onto the metal while the metal is still wet.

Note: Flat objects and shallow bowls may be sprayed with plain water.

ENAMELING TYPES There are five distinct classical types of enameling techniques: namely, limoges, cloisonné, champlevé, bassetaille, and plique-a-jour. In recent years several other interesting techniques have been developed by craftsmen. The new techniques, since they are easier for beginners to master, will be explained first.

COLOR SAMPLERS It is advisable, if much enameling is to be done, to make color samplers so that one can tell how the colors will appear after firing. The enamel colors may be applied to small rectangular pieces of copper or silver. An excellent sampler for transparent enamels is made by dividing a rectangular piece of copper, 1″ by 1½″, into three sections and applying and firing the enamels as shown in figure 206. Across the white enamel and flux a piece of silver foil is placed, and on top of this and the white enamel and flux, the sample color is applied and then fired. Thus the color of the sample enamel can be observed as it will appear over copper, silver, flux and white enamel.

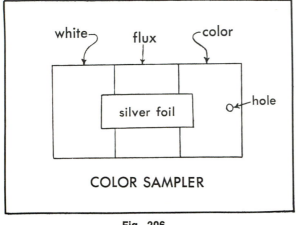

Fig. 206

FOIL Silver and gold foil are used in enameling for decorative and background purposes. The foil must be applied on top of a base of enamel that has already been fired. After a design is drawn on a sheet of tracing paper, the foil is placed between the design sheet and another sheet of tracing paper. It is then carefully cut to shape with a sharp pair of scissors so that it will not wrinkle. Before the foil is positioned, it must be pierced many times with a small needle so that steam and gas can escape as it is being fused to the enamel base. A thin coating of gum tragacanth is brushed or sprayed onto the enameled object. The foil is picked up with a damp brush and then placed in position with the brush. Then the foil is lightly rubbed smooth with the brush. Once the gum solution has dried, the piece is fired to 1450°F., or just to the fusion point of the base enamel. If the foil wrinkles during the firing, the piece can be refired and pulled out when the enamel is molten. The foil is then quickly flattened with a burnisher. By following the above procedure, the foil can be fired onto

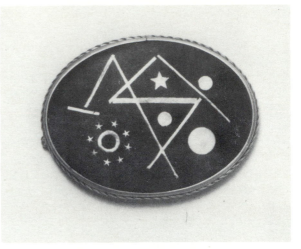

Fig. 207   Enameled pin with silver foil   Harold Tishler

the enamel without it becoming wrinkled. The foil is usually covered with transparent enamels.

SIEVING OR DUSTING The sieving or dusting method of applying enamels is by far the easiest and fastest method. The formed metal object—earring, tray, pendant, etc.—is sprayed with a solution of gum tragacanth or plain water and the desired enamel color is sieved on while the gum is still wet.

Note: On small flat jewelry objects, the enamel can be sieved onto dry metal; no spraying is required.

Spread paper—newspaper or paper towels will do—underneath the metal object being dusted to catch excess enamel. After the enamel has been applied to the piece, the newspaper should be rolled to form a funnel and the excess enamel returned to its jar. The newspaper should be changed every time a new enamel is used to avoid contamination.

It is often easiest to hold the metal object in one's hand for better manipulation. First sieve the enamel around the edges of the object and then sieve in towards the center in a spiralling motion. When the enamel covers the object so that no metal can be seen, a sufficient amount has been applied. For proper enamel coverage, sometimes it is necessary to carefully respray the object with gum tragacanth again and then to apply ad-

116

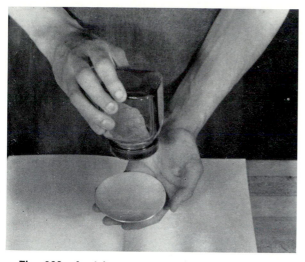

Fig. 208 Applying enamel by the sieve method

ditional enamel. If only one color is desired, the object may now be fired (page 124).

Note: If it is not practical to apply enamel by holding the object, the piece can be placed directly on newspaper. After the enamel has been sieved on the piece, it can be lifted by carefully wedging a thin spatula underneath it. The object can also be placed directly on a stilt or leaned against a prop.

Interesting effects may be obtained by re-spraying the sieved on enamel before firing and applying additional colors.

Note: If the desired effect is not obtained after the first firing, the object may be re-sprayed with gum tragacanth, enamel can be sieved on in spots, and the object can then be refired. Objects often require several firings until a satisfactory result is obtained.

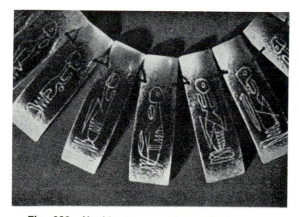

Fig. 209 Necklace—enamel on silver
Miriam Smith Peck

Fine lines may be dusted onto a base color as follows. With a pen dipped into squeegee oil or oil of lavender, draw the lines as desired onto the enamel base color. Then through an 80 mesh screen, dust the enamel onto the lines. Turn the enameled object over and tap its edges lightly on the work bench; enamel not adhering to the oil will drop off and the fine lines now can be fired on permanently.

SGRAFFITO In the sgraffito or the scratch enameling technique, an enamel base color is sieved onto the metal object and then fired. The fired enamel object is sprayed with gum tragacanth and one or more enamel colors are sieved evenly onto it. The object is then re-sprayed with gum.

With a scriber, or pointed handle of a small paint brush, lines are scratched through the sieved enamels to create the desired design (fig. 210). A damp fine brush can be used to remove any excess enamel from the sgraffito area or the piece can be held, turned over, and lightly tapped. Now the object is fired carefully and removed immediately from the furnace after the enamel has melted in order to retain the sgraffito design.

Fig. 210 Sgraffito pendant   Harold Tishler

STENCILS The enamel pin in figure 211 illustrates the stencil technique. Both positive and negative patterns can be used as stencils. The resulting designs can have either hard knife edged areas of delineation or soft muted ones. After the enameled areas have thoroughly dried the design can be modified by using sgraffito.

The object shown was first designed on paper. The stencil was cut to shape with a scissor and an exacto knife. Any sturdy thin paper can be used for stencils and if only a few copies are desired institutional paper toweling or blotting paper may be used.

The piece was first counter-enameled and then an enamel base color was fired onto the metal. The stencil was moistened with water and placed in position. Excess water was removed by blotting the stencil with a tissue. Gum tragacanth was sprayed over the stencil and object. Enamel was then sieved through the stencil opening. **Note:** The coating of enamel should not be as thick as the stencil to avoid ragged edges when the stencil is removed. The stencil was lifted carefully with a tweezer, leaving the sieved enamel where desired. The piece was then fired.

After counter-enameling, the enamel pin was fired three times, first for the base color,

then the border, and finally the enamel in the center, all with the same stencil.

STRING AND NETTING Interesting effects can be obtained by placing string or netting separately or in combination on a base enamel and sieving one or more colors over them. The string or netting is soaked in water and placed as desired over the previously fired base enamel. After the enamels have been sieved onto the base enamel, the string or netting is lifted carefully, and then the object is fired.

Fig. 212   Pin and earring set—frit applied
Harold Tishler

FRIT AND GLASS THREADS Frit, small pieces of crushed enamel—and glass beads or threads also can be applied to a base enamel. It is best to apply a thin layer of enamel (the same color) to the base enamel and then to place the frit and glass threads where desired. The frit and glass threads can also be dipped into a thick gum tragacanth solution and then applied where wanted (fig. 212 and 213). The threads can be shaped and bent by warming them on a block of asbestos or charcoal.

SWIRLING While the enameled object, often one with frit and glass threads applied, is still being heated in the furnace, the enamels can be quickly (problems can occur if the enamel cools, causing the rod to adhere to the enamel) swirled (moved around). This can be done with a metal rod that has been pointed

Fig. 211   Stencil and stencil pin

and bent one inch from the point at a right angle. By swirling the melted enamels with the pointed rod, interesting effects can be achieved. The swirling rod should not be pressed too heavily into the enamel.

LIMOGES OR PAINTED Limoges or painted enameling is an artistic and classical type. The metal — usually copper, since it is completely covered — is cut and formed before it is enameled. After forming, the metal is sprayed with a tragacanth solution and the base enamel color, usually white, is sieved on while the gum is still wet. Most objects require counter-enameling after the first firing, which is explained later. The object is now fired to fuse the powdered enamel. When cool, the design is transferred and scratched into the enamel base. Colors may then be applied.

The enamel colors for limoges enameling used by some craftsmen are very finely powdered (500 mesh) Chinese overglazes of the type used in ceramic work. The enamel colors are mixed on a flat piece of glass with a little oil of lavender and are painted on with a fine sable brush. A little oil of turpentine added to the above keeps them from drying too quickly. The enamel must be thoroughly dried under a heat lamp or in the kiln for a few seconds before refiring.

The refiring is done at a slightly lower temperature than that used for the base enamel otherwise the base enamel will melt and flow, thus ruining the painted design.

Steel tiles with a pre-enameled gloss surface can be purchased from supply houses. These tiles usually have to be re-enameled with a white undercoat enamel which acts as the background for the painted enamels. These tiles are recommended since they will not usually warp. Graphite pencils, for black, and underglaze ceramic pencils, for yellow, green and other colors, are available for drawing onto the white surfaces after they have been matted.

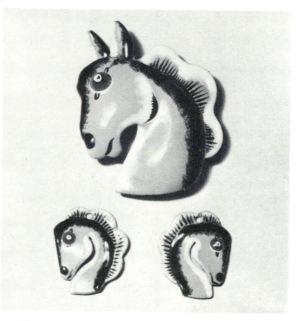

Fig. 214 Painted enameled pin and earrings
Harold Tishler

A clear transparent enamel flux may be applied over the entire object to protect the design. This is done by spraying the object with a gum solution and then sieving on the flux and firing. The flux, however, is not necessary for most ornamental inexpensive jewelry.

Gold, platinum, and palladium luster solutions are now available for painting onto enamels. They are applied last—that is when all other enamel colors have been applied, and they are fired at a low temperature—approximately 1200°F. Lusters should be allowed to dry for 24 hours to permit the oils

Fig. 215 Limoges enamels   Harold Tishler

to evaporate. The door of the kiln should be opened several times during the luster firing to allow the fumes to escape.

CLOISONNÉ In cloisonné enameling thin fine silver or gold wires are formed into the required design shape and then either soldered or fused with enamel to a background piece of metal. The spaces (cells or cloisons) between the strips are then filled in with enamels, which are then fused by firing. The resulting object is easily identified by the thin strips of metal that separate the enamels.

The thickness and height of the strips depends on the design of the object and the metal to be used. They may be as thin as 1/100 of an inch and more than ⅛ of an inch high. The strips can be formed in a rectangular drawplate or can be cut with a shear from a sheet of metal. The strips can be soldered together with as high a melting solder as possible. They may also be tacked (soldered in a few spots) to the background piece. Usually, the outer cloison is fused or soldered to the background piece. It is advisable to not file the edge of the backsheet flush with the bezel until all the enameling has been completed. After enameling, the piece is frequently set in a bezel setting.

The wires or cloisons do not have to be soldered to the background piece. The background may be covered with an enamel flux and fired. Then the strips are placed in position and held there by means of a gum tragacanth solution and fired so that they fuse

Fig. 216 Cloisonné pendant "My Watch"
Hiroko Swornik

into the enamel. Another method of attaching the cloisons is to position them on the metal (except copper), spray on a coating of gum, then a layer of flux enamel, and finally fire the piece until the cloisons are fused into place.

Pure silver (it is soft and will not oxidize) should be used for the cloisons in this technique since sterling silver, especially on larger cloisons, will snap out of the enamel as it cools.

A spatula or sable brush is used to fill in the cloisons with enamel (known as wet charging). The washed enamels are mixed with water to form a wet paste. The brush can also be moistened to pack the enamel into the cloisons. The brush should be rinsed in clean water after each application of enamel. **Note:** After the bezel has been soldered into place, but before the cloisons are positioned and fused to the backsheet, the backsheet can be slightly opened so that the front is slightly convex. This will minimize the possibilities of the enamels cracking.

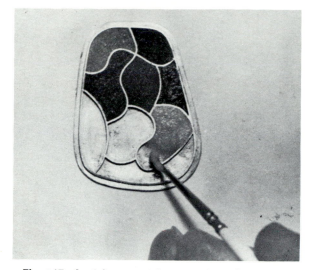

Fig. 217 Applying enamel to a cloisonné pin with a brush

Care must be taken to pack the enamel against the strips and in the corners in order to prevent bubbles. After the enamel has been applied and leveled, excessive moisture is removed by means of a blotter or tissue; then the object is fired. Most enamelists counter-enamel after the first layer of enamel has been fused to the front.

Examine the object carefully after it has been fired. Uncovered fire scale spots should be scraped with a scriber or engraving tool to remove discoloration and, if necessary, pickle the object. More enamel is applied and

Fig. 218 Cloisonné pendant   Dvora Horvitz

fired, and this is repeated several times if necessary in order to build up the required enamel thickness. The object may be ground and polished as described later on page 125.

Some contemporary cloisonné jewelry, however, is not ground and polished to a flat surface but is fired so that the enamel is left concave in the cloisons.

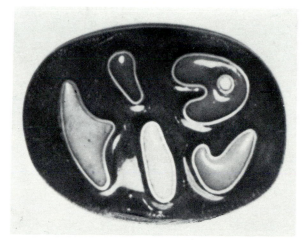

Fig. 219 Pin, cloisonné wires melted into background enamel

CHAMPLEVÉ ENAMELING In champlevé enameling, recesses are carved, etched, or stamped, and then filled in with enamels. The carving method by means of engraving tools is the richest type and is used on the finest handmade jewelry. The depth of the recess may be as little as 1/50 of an inch. The design should be executed so that a thin line of metal remains around each color. The background metal looks and holds the enamel best when it is given a wiggle or fine engraved line effect. Undercutting the separation lines also helps to hold the enamel. The enamel is applied similarly to cloisonné enameling. The pieces are usually counter-enameled after the first firing.

Some contemporary enamelists such as Antonia Schwed create the recesses for their champlevé pieces entirely by the etching process. The design is transferred onto a sheet of metal (usually 14 gauge). Resist is painted on the metal where needed and the metal is etched in its appropriate mordant (see Etching.) Often the piece is etched 3 or 4 times to create different depths. It is not

121

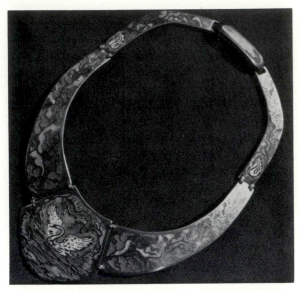

Fig. 220 Champlevé neckpiece Antonia Schwed

Fig. 221 Bassetaille neckpiece Antonia Schwed

advisable to etch the metal deeper than half its thickness. After the piece has been removed from the acid, it is neutralized and thoroughly cleaned. A flexible shaft or a file can be used to define the recesses.

The enamels are inlaid wet in thin layers into the recessed areas. A new layer of enamel is inlaid before each firing. Intricate pieces are often refired twenty-five times. Before the last firing a light coating of flux can be sprinkled over the piece, especially if the piece is to be left with a matt finish. After the last firing the enamel has usually been built up so that it is slightly higher than the metal. The piece is finished by stoning it with various abrasives until the enamel and metal are flush.

BASSETAILLE ENAMELING Here too the design is carved, stamped, etched, or chased into the metal. However, the different enamel colors are not separated by metal lines as they are in champlevé enameling. Also the recesses are not as deep as in champlevé enameling.

Transparent enamels are used so that the background design will show through. The design, since it is seen, must be executed very carefully and the time required for bassetaille enameling is usually only warranted for the better gold and silver jewelry.

The enamels are mixed with a little gum

tragacanth. Each color is placed in position carefully and permitted to dry or is dried with a blotter before the next color is placed in position. The procedure from here on is the same as champlevé enameling.

PLIQUE-A-JOUR or INLAID ENAMELING This enamel type is somewhat like miniature stained glass windows; the metal cloisons in the enamel represent the lead lines in the windows. The design is formed from rectangular wire or may be pierced into a piece

Fig. 222 Plique-a-jour cross and pendant
Jean Jacques d'ela Verriers

of metal of the proper thickness. The sides of the cloisons should be undercut with a round engraving tool. The metal cloisons are then placed on a smooth surface such as mica, stainless steel, or phosphor bronze, surfaces to which the enamel will not adhere. Mica should be placed on a flat piece of steel to keep it from warping. "U" clamps, preferably ones made from stainless steel, can be used to hold the metal to be enameled in position so that it will not warp. Then the cloisons are filled in with enamel and fired. More enamel is applied and fired, and this is repeated several times if necessary in order to build up the required enamel thickness. The background piece is removed by tapping it lightly, and then the back of the object is ground and polished as described later.

GRISAILLE is enamel painting in shades of gray. An opaque black enamel base is fused onto a sheet of metal. A thin coat of white opaque enamel (200 mesh) is sieved onto the base, the design is scratched through the white enamel using the sgraffito technique, and then the piece is fired. When the white

Fig. 223 Grisaille enameling   Kathryn Gough

enamel fuses into the black enamel, a dark gray color results. Each subsequent layer of white enamel is applied with a brush by wet charging, and then the piece is refired. The design develops as the layers of white enamel fuse into the base creating various shades of gray. Where many layers of white have

been applied, that area of the design will be white. For stronger outlines, opaque black enamel can be painted over the white enamel.

COUNTER-ENAMELING Enamels and metals have different expansion and contraction rates. The enamels on flat or slightly convex objects, therefore, will tend to crack and even chip after being enameled on thin metal. To prevent cracking and chipping, these objects can be counter-enameled on the back or reverse side.

Counter enamels can be made from the remains of several colors that are mixed together. Although the counter enamel can be applied before the front surface is enameled, many enamelists apply counter enamel (usually by dry sieving over a layer of gum) after the first coat of enamel has been fired. Some enamelists (especially in cloisonné) continue to apply a thin layer of counter enamel after every firing. This is done 3 or 4 times, and then the piece is only enameled on its front surface. The counter enamel can be slightly underfired initially since subsequent firings of the piece will cause the counter enamel to mature.

RACKS The four racks in figure 224 are made from heavy wire mesh and 24 gauge stainless steel. The wire mesh and steel are cut to shape with tinner's snips and bent to shape in a vise.

Number 1 is used for flat objects and trays that are not counter-enameled.

Number 2 is for counter-enameled trays. The ends of three machine screws are ground to a point and then bolted to the wire mesh. Three small pin holes will be left in the counter-enameled base of the object after firing.

Number 3 is for counter-enameled small objects, and number 4 is for counter-enameled large objects. The stainless steel in 3 and 4 is bolted to the wire mesh. The work required to make the racks is warranted if perfectly fired counter-enameled objects are desired.

Small pieces can be supported by steel-tipped star stilts or button stilts. Enamel will not adhere to mica. Stilts for problem shapes

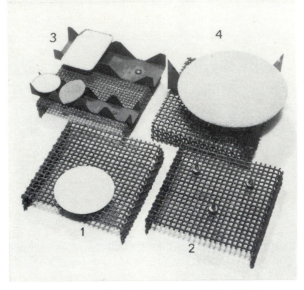

Fig. 224   Racks for firing enameled objects

Fig. 225   Firing an enameled tray

can be made by inserting stainless steel wire at various angles into a piece of fire brick. Planches can be used for panels or trays.

FIRING PROCEDURE The purpose of firing is to melt and fuse the enamel so that when it cools it becomes a solid, glossy, glass body. The required temperature for copper enameled objects is 1500°F., and is a little lower, 1400°F., for gold and silver. The time required depends on the size of the object and the temperature of the furnace; two to four minutes is ample for most objects. The object being fired must be watched carefully by repeatedly opening the kiln door slightly, and it should be removed from the furnace as soon as the surface of the enamel has a glossy appearance. An unequal firing can occur if the piece is placed too near the elements of the kiln.

Very small objects (up to two inches in diameter) can be fired by means of a blow torch with the flame applied to the bottom surface of the object. A flat smaller disc of metal should be placed between the work and the flame so that the flame of the torch is deflected.

Electric or gas muffle furnaces, however, offer the best and cleanest methods of firing the enamels. A good enameling furnace should have a door that can be raised vertically (fig. 225) or swung open sideways.

Small ceramic kilns can be used. A kiln whose door swings out and downwards is not recommended since the heat from the door is very annoying. Asbestos gloves are desirable to avoid burns from the heat of the furnace, especially when working with larger kilns.

Small table-top kilns can be used for firing most small pieces of enameled jewelry.

The enameled object is placed on a stilt or trivet which is placed on the heavy wire

Fig. 226   Small beehive enameling kiln
Courtesy of Cecelia Bauer

Fig. 227   Rack for firing rings

rack. The rack is picked up with a large spatula, a firing fork with a shield, or a flat piece of metal and deposited carefully in the furnace. The moisture must be removed from the enamel. This can be done by preheating the object on top of the furnace or by placing the object in the furnace for five or ten seconds, removing, and repeating until no steam rises from the enamel.

Fig. 228   Method of firing a bracelet

When the enamel has matured, the piece is quickly removed from the furnace by placing the spatula under the rack and then carefully removing it from the kiln. The rack is placed on a fire resistant surface such as fire brick or transite, where it can cool slowly. If an object has warped, remove it quickly, place it on a flat steel or stone surface, and hold its edges with a spatula, or place a flattening iron on the piece until the enamel hardens.

FINISHING The metal edges of enameled objects can be filed lightly with a single cut smooth file to brighten them. If the back or bottom of the object is to be seen, it is pickled to remove the oxide.

Pickling is done in a cold sparex or nitric acid solution. To protect the surface from the acid which will dull the enamel, it may be covered with wax as follows. Melt wax (candle wax will do) in a container and with a brush, paint the wax over the enameled surface. After pickling, the wax is rubbed off under hot water.

In cloisonné enameling, if a flat, smooth enamel and cloison metal surface is desired, the enamel is ground under water with a flat emery stone until it touches the cloisons. Use a coarse carborundum stone first and finish with a fine stone. After grinding (called stoning), the enameled object is further ground and smoothed with 240, 320, and 600 wet-dry

Fig. 229   Champlevé enamel pendant
Katharine S. Wood

sandpaper and scotch stone, and then it is scrubbed under water with a brush. It can be left this way if a matt finish is desired. Any emery or metal inbedded in the surface of the enamel may be removed by means of a quick dip in hydrofluoric acid. Rinse immediately in water. When dry, another firing (known as fire-polishing) will restore the glossy surface of the enamel. A high polish finish can be given to the enamel by rubbing it with a soft leather cloth that has been dipped in a diluted solution of chrome oxide and water.

PROBLEMS Most enameling defects are usually caused by using improper procedures before the piece is fired. Listed below are common enameling flaws, their causes, and how to correct them.

1. A thin, uneven enameled surface could result if not enough enamel or if an uneven coating of enamel was applied to the metal. Additional enamel should be dusted on the thin areas and the piece refired.

2. Pin holes, bubbles, or pock marks on the surface of the enamel could be caused by excessive heat or too rapid a firing cycle, dirt or grease on the surface of the metal prior to applying the enamels, exposure of stored enamels to excessive humidity, failure to anneal the metal before enameling, too thick an application of enamel, failure to sufficiently dry the enamel or gum before the piece was fired, or the insufficient washing of the enamels. The bubbles should be first broken with a file or pointed tool, excess enamel scraped or filed away, enamel reapplied if necessary, and then the piece is refired.

3. If the enamel appears rough or dull, the firing time was either too short or the kiln temperature too low. Refire the piece at a higher temperature.

4. If cracks appear in the surface of the enamel, it is possible that the piece was either cooled too quickly, was not counter-enameled, or too heavy a layer of enamel was applied. Counter-enamel and/or refire the piece.

5. If the enamel burns off, changes color, or if opaque enamel becomes transparent, the piece was probably over-fired. There is usually no remedy for restoring an enamel's color after it has been fired to too high a temperature. Some enamelists use a flexible shaft and grind off the enamel with a bur.

6. If large pieces of enamel begin to chip off while the piece is cooling, it is possible that the metal was not properly cleaned prior to enameling, the layer of enamel was too thick, the metal used was too thin, or the piece was not counter-enameled.

7. Black spots (fire scale) along the outside edge of, or in an enameled piece could be caused by over-firing, fire scale on the metal prior to enameling, contaminated enamel, or too thin an application of enamel. Grind, stone with carborundum, or file the specks until they are eliminated, and then refire.

If necessary, the damaged enamel can be removed by firing until the enamel is mature,

Fig. 230 Champlevé enamel pendant   **Kathryn Gough**

126

and then quickly quenching the piece in a basin of cold water. This procedure should cause the enamel to crack away from the metal.

9. PLATING AND ELECTROFORMING

By means of electroplating, thin deposits (as thin as 5 millionths of an inch) of gold, rhodium, silver, copper, and nickel can be plated onto jewelry objects. When very thick deposits of metal are plated onto a nonconductive substance such as wax or styrofoam, and the model is removed, the process is known as electroforming.

Gold plating enjoys its greatest popularity in the costume (inexpensive) jewelry trade because of its beauty, and resistance to tarnish, oxidation, and attack by most chemicals. Usually as little gold as possible is deposited on the metal; 1 to 3 millionth of an inch is sufficient. The cost of a thin (flash) deposit is as low as 12 to 36 cents per square foot of the area plated.

Fig. 231 Electroformed brooch   Stanley Lechtzin

A thin layer of gold can be plated onto a piece of gold jewelry in order to obtain a more desirable color and also to cover variations due to solder joints. Various antique and coloring gold plating solutions such as antique green gold, dark rose gold, and Hamilton gold are also available for color plating and antiquing gold jewelry.

Gold flash and color plating is usually employed on silver costume jewelry such as earrings, pins, bracelets, and other items which will not receive much wear or abrasion. Objects that have very thin gold deposits are often given a protective coating of clear lacquer.

Rhodium, the whitest of all metals, belongs to the platinum family of metals. It is ideal for jewelry plating since it will not tarnish, is not attacked by acids or perspiration, and is very hard and durable. Rhodium plating gives the metal a silver blue reflective surface which enhances the brilliance of faceted gemstones. Rhodium is plated over platinum and white gold jewelry (especially after the piece has been sized and soldered together), and over costume jewelry for a very low square foot cost.

Silver is plated onto sterling silver, brass, copper, and white metal costume jewelry. It is also used to increase the thickness of model rings (see page 165) and for electroforming.

Copper is used for electroforming and for decorative plating. A cyanide copper plating solution is the only satisfactory bath for plating soft solder, lead, iron, steel, and white metal. It produces a smooth fine-grained deposit which is an excellent base for the final plate of gold. Nickel should be plated on the copper if silver or rhodium is desired for the final plate. Acid copper baths are used in electroforming when a heavy, rapid buildup is desired without the dangers of cyanide.

Nickel is plated onto brass, silver, and white metal jewelry before they are rhodium plated. Bright (English) gold and green gold are also plated over a nickel plate.

THEORY OF PLATING A direct electric current when passed through a solution containing certain compounds of gold, rhodium, silver, etc. will deposit some of these metals on an item to be plated. The solution is called the electrolyte; the current enters the solution at the anode (+) terminal and leaves at the cathode (—) terminal, and the passage of a current through a solution is known as electrolysis.

As electrolysis proceeds, oxygen is liberated at the anode, and metal from the solution deposits out on the object being plated, which is the cathode. The anode will constantly add new metal to the plating solution and replace the metal being deposited on the cathode if the anode is a metal similar to the plating metal. Soluble anode plates are available in fine gold, fine silver, pure copper, and pure nickel. Platinum clad anodes (for rhodium) are nonsoluble and the strength of the plating bath must be maintained by the addition of metal salts in a replenishing solution.

Stainless steel anodes can be used with gold baths, but should not be used with rhodium, as the acid in the rhodium solution eventually will attack the stainless steel alloy. When a stainless steel alloy is used, the metal in the solution will plate out without being replaced by the anode. The reason that a stainless steel anode and/or a platinumized titanium anode is usually used for gold plating is that gold alloy solutions are composed of a combination of metals. It is difficult to control the dissolving rate of the various metals if a gold alloy anode is used. Replenishing anodes are used only when the color of the plating solution is exactly the same as the color of the anode.

SOURCE OF CURRENT A direct current is required for plating. If only a few objects are to be plated, the current can be obtained from storage batteries. Dry cells are not recommended due to their extremely short life. Professional jewelry platers use rectifiers or motor generator sets.

The required amperage capacity of the plating outfit depends on the number and size of the objects being plated at the same time. Small 10 ampere outfits are ample for most jewelry plating. Frequently plating voltages are given, generally 2-6 for gold and 2-5 for rhodium. These voltages are not as important as maintaining the correct current density.

Fig. 232 A selenium rectifier

An ammeter is necessary to measure the amount of current being used—the amperage —and a voltmeter is required to measure the amount of pressure—the voltage. The instruments are connected as shown in figure 233.

The distance that the electrical current must travel through the electrolyte from the anode to the cathode is a determining factor influencing the thickness of the metal deposited on the piece. If some parts of the piece are further from the anode, then the quantity of electrically charged metal particles reaching these areas will be less since

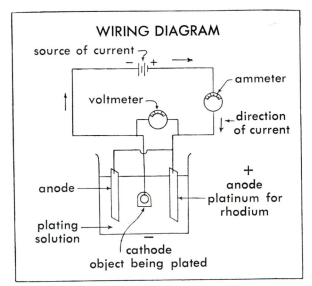

Fig. 233 Wiring diagram for plating

the path that the electrical current must travel is longer, and therefore not as much current reaches these areas of the piece due to resistance. This could result in a thinner deposit on the more distant portions of the piece, or under extreme conditions, no deposit at all.

With certain plating baths (rhodium), it is very critical that a uniform distance is maintained between all parts of the piece and the anode. These baths are said to have poor "throwing power".

In order to ensure a uniform thick deposit on the work, care should be taken to see that there is approximately uniform spacing between the anode and the surface to be plated. With flat work and a flat anode, this is a relatively simple requirement—periodically rotate the piece. If the piece is curved, the anode can be bent to conform to the shape of the piece. In some cases, it may be necessary to use anodes on opposite sides of the piece, or to frame the piece with more than two anodes. The anodes are all connected together to the positive terminal of the rectifier. **Note:** The area of the anode surface should not be less than the work area.

The anode and the piece to be plated are usually suspended in the solution with 18 or 20 gauge annealed copper wire. The cathode wire is either looped around the shank of a ring, through an opening of the piece, or through a jump ring so that it makes contact at a point where discoloration of the metal will not be noticeable. Coated copper wire plating racks that hold many pieces can be purchased. A good contact must be established between the piece and the cathode wire.

To electroplate to a selective thickness, four factors must be considered:

1. Area of the article to be electroplated in square centimeters, square inches, or square feet.
2. Cathode current density or plating amperage to be applied to the article.
3. Thickness of the electroplate required.
4. Time in seconds, minutes, or hours that the article will be plated.

CURRENT DENSITY The number of amperes that is required to plate an object is called optimum cathode current density. Successful controlled electroplating is accomplished by conducting the proper amount of current (amperes) to a given surface area which is calculated in square centimeters, square inches, or square feet. Standard optimum cathode current densities (in amperes per square foot of surface area) or a recommended voltage guideline are given by manufacturers for their plating solutions so that the amperage or voltage can be determined. This information applies whether only one small piece is being plated or whether there is a large amount of work in the tank. However, a greater number of pieces will, at the same voltage, draw more current (amperes) from the rectifier than a smaller number of pieces. Doubling the amount of surface area to be plated should approximately double the number of amperes needed.

To determine the current density of an object being plated: calculate the plating surface area (in square inches) of the jewelry object, then divide this by one square foot (144 sq. in.). This quotient times the recommended cathode current density equals the amperage at which the rectifier should be set.

$$A \times CD = I$$

A represents area in sq. ft., sq. in., etc.
CD represents current density (amps/sq. ft., etc.)
I = intensity of current

For example: You have determined that the area you are going to plate comes to 50 square inches. Cathode current density is optimum at 4 amps/sq. ft., so you must translate your square inches into square feet.

$$\frac{50}{144} = .35 \text{ sq. ft.}$$

Now $A \times CD = I$
$.35 \times 4 = 1.4$ amperes of current

Note: Many professional electroplaters control their processing on the basis of current density and read the tank voltage only as a check to make sure that they are within the voltage range where good results can be expected. Others simply maintain the recommended voltage across the tank and pay little attention to the amperes. Most of the plating solutions and systems are easy to operate, and calculations are not extremely critical for craftsmen. Therefore, provided the solution is of proper strength and is operated at the correct temperature, it is less important in small installations if the tank voltage (voltmeter) or current density is used as a guide to ensure uniform results.

The current density must be controlled for bright smooth deposits. If the voltage is increased, the amperage is increased and the current density also is increased (in direct proportion), and this eventually results, if the current density becomes too great, in rough granular deposits which will not adhere to the object being plated. When plating jewelry objects, if rough deposits occur, lower the voltage. This lowers the amperage until a smooth deposit is obtained. **Note:** Too high a plating voltage, or a piece too close to the anode, will "burn", (darken), the extremities (such as prongs) of the objects being plated.

Note: If the plating voltage is too high or a piece is too close to the anode, the extremities of the object being plated will "burn" (darken).

THICKNESS OF DEPOSIT The thickness of the metal deposited is in direct proportion to the amperes used. 2 amperes of electricity will deposit twice the metal thickness of one ampere; and a plate of 2 minutes with the same amperage will be twice as thick as a plate of one minute.

Below is the approximate time in ampere hours to deposit a thickness of 0.001 inches:

Gold	6.2	Copper	8.8
Silver	6.2	Nickel	18.7

100 ampere hours will deposit the following approximate thicknesses:

Gold	0.0163	Copper	0.0113
Silver	0.0163	Nickel	0.0053

CONTAINERS AND TEMPERATURE For jewelry plating solutions, pyrex glass containers or stainless steel tanks (pots) are ideal. Stainless steel tanks (they become the anode) can be used for gold plating and electrocleaning. Pyrex glass must be used for rhodium; it can also be used for other jewelry plating solutions including gold.

Several of the plating solutions must be heated. In commercial plants, gas heat, where available, is recommended since gas heat can be controlled easily by regulating the size of the flame. Electric stoves can be used by craftsmen that plate occasionally.

Although plating temperatures are not always a critical factor, best results are obtained by following the temperature recommendations of the manufacturers. An immersion thermometer, available in photographic supply stores, can be used.

Plating solutions should be kept covered when not in use in order to minimize evaporation and dust contamination. The solutions should be filtered when the presence of dust or dirt is apparent. This prevents floating particles from settling on the work and causing spots.

An asbestos pad (which acts as an insulator) should be placed between a stainless steel tank and a metal hot plate. An electric immersion heater can be used to regulate the temperature of a small plating tank.

PREPARATION FOR PLATING The jewelry object to be plated must be completed—all soldering finished, stones set, etc. Then it is pickled, polished, and cleaned perfectly. An ultrasonic cleaning machine is frequently used. **Note:** Plating will not cover imperfections that have not been removed by polishing.

Note: Genuine, cultured, or imitation pearls; shell cameos; imitation stones made of plastic; turquoise, opals, and other similar soft or non-heat resistant materials may be attacked by plating solutions. Do not plate any jewelry that contains these materials. They should be set after the plating process has been completed.

The jewelry objects are cleaned, after polishing, in a boiling solution of ¼ ounce of ivory soap and 1 ounce of ammonia hydroxide dissolved in a pint of water. Attach a thin (22 gauge) copper wire to the object so that it may be suspended into the solution. Rub the object with a jeweler's tampico or soft bristle brush to effectively remove the polishing compounds. The brushing may be done on a clean towel wrapped around a board. The object is then washed in hot and finally cold water.

Do not touch the work until the entire plating process has been completed. After cleaning, handle the work by the copper wire which should remain attached to the work during all subsequent plating operations.

ELECTROSTRIPPING (see page 65) is used to remove old plating before replating, clean inaccessible areas, brighten an oxidized surface, or remove fire scale. The procedure is the reverse of plating. Articles of jewelry should be thoroughly washed after they have been removed from the stripping solution. They should then be dried, buffed, and finally electrocleaned before plating.

ELECTROCLEANING After cleaning in the above solution, the jewelry object should be electrocleaned to completely remove all traces of buffing compounds and grease. This is done in a solution (electrolyte) formed by dissolving 1 ounce of Oakite, No. 90, in a quart of water or 2 ounces of sodium carbonate (washing soda) and ½ ounce of sodium hydroxide (lye) in a quart of water. ¼ ounce of sodium cyanide may be added to the above to remove any stains that may be formed while electrocleaning. Proprietary solutions are available for those who wish to buy rather than make the solutions.

A pyrex container with a stainless steel anode or a stainless steel pot (which becomes the anode) can be used to hold the cleaning solution. The solution is heated to 180°F., which is near the boiling point of water.

The object being cleaned is suspended into the solution by means of a copper wire to form the cathode. The cleaning voltage is 6 volts, though higher voltages may be used, and the anode and cathode may be connected directly to the terminals of the source of direct current in order to receive maximum current. A 15 second electrocleaning immersion is ample.

The cleaning is done by the evolution of hydrogen on the jewelry object. The hydrogen tends to lift the dirt and grease film from the object, and it also agitates the solution so

that the soap can dissolve (emulsify) the dirt quicker. Wash the object in cold water when it is removed from the electrocleaning solution.

Finally, the object is dipped into a cold 5% sulphuric acid solution to remove any tarnish acquired during cleaning and to neutralize the soap; then it is washed in cold water again.

WATER BREAK TEST After the electrocleaning process has been completed, there is a method of testing the metal's surface to see if it is free from oil and grease. The "water break" test is based on the principle that water will not adhere to a surface that is greasy. To test the piece that has been electrocleaned, dip it into clean water, remove it, and then carefully inspect it. If the piece has been properly cleaned, a uniform film of water should be visible. If the water does not adhere (or breaks), the electrocleaning operation should be continued until the water break test can be passed. The jewelry object is then ready to be plated.

A thorough rinsing in clean or running water is very important. It must be done after every cleaning and plating operation.

Electrocleaning solutions must be fresh and should be changed every week.

TO PREPARE OR BUY SOLUTIONS In former years it was customary for platers to prepare their own plating solutions. Now it is easier and more economical (considering the value of the time and equipment required) to purchase plating solutions from supply houses.

REPLENISHING PLATING BATHS During plating, metal is deposited out of the solution, and this loss must be replaced if the solution is to retain its original concentration or normal working strength. If a soluble anode is being used, metal loss is constantly being replenished by the anode as it dissolves into the solution. But when an insoluble anode is used (as in rhodium or gold plating with a cyanide solution), metal loss must be replaced by periodically pouring replenishers into the tank.

To compensate for evaporation, indicate the level of the solution in a new bath by marking the outside of the beaker with either a diamond scratch tool or nail polish. Heat and natural elements cause evaporation (only the water evaporates). Maintain the original level of the bath by adding distilled water when necessary.

For craftsmen and others who wish, especially in schools, to make their own solutions, several tested and proven formulas are listed.

GOLD PLATING The gold plating solutions are made from prepared concentrated liquid gold solutions or gold cyanide salts which can be purchased from dealers in practically every large city (see Index). They usually only require the addition of clean tap water to form the required plating solution concentration.

Can the required solution be made from gold directly by the user? Yes. The formula below can be used. Is it warranted? Usually not. Practically all jewelry platers buy their solutions prepared, and all desired colors and karats of gold can be obtained.

The anode is stainless steel, if pyrex is used, and its immersed area should approximate the area of the objects being plated. The anode can also be the stainless steel tank itself.

Potassium gold cyanide (67.5%) 1.5 oz.
Potassium cyanide . . . . 4 oz.
Potassium carbonate . . . . 4 oz.
Phosphate dibasic . . . . 4 oz.
Water . . . . 1 gallon
Temp. of solution . . . . . . 140° to 160°F.
Voltage . . . . 4 to 6 volts
Current density . . . . .5-10 amp./ft.^{2}
Time . . . . 5 to 30 seconds
Agitation . . . . None except for 24 K

Flash Gold Plating Formula for Jewelry
Potassium gold cyanide (67.5%) . .5 oz.
Potassium cyanide . . . . 2 oz.
Water . . . . 1 gallon

By adding small amounts of copper cyanide (for red), silver cyanide (for green), etc., the other gold colors can be obtained.

Warning: The cyanides are poisonous. They should not be handled by children. Avoid undue breathing of plating fumes. Avoid contact with skin. After using, wash hands. To carry off odors, the plating bench should be set under a ventilating hood or near a window where an electric fan can be used to dispel the fumes. If ingested a physician should be called immediately. The victim should be removed to fresh air. An Amyl Nitrite pearl should be broken in a cloth and held lightly under the nose for 15 seconds. If the victim is still conscious, he/she should be given a tablespoon of salt in a glass of warm water to induce vomiting. The inhalation of Amyl Nitrite hould be repeated 5 times at 5 minute intervals. Rubber gloves and a rubber apron should be worn when plating. Hands should be thoroughly washed after plating. A cyanide antidote kit should be on hand.

Acid plating baths should never be allowed to come in contact with cyanide plating baths. An extremely noxious and deadly gas—hydrocyanic acid gas—will be generated. Make sure the pieces have been thoroughly washed before they are plated in cyanide baths.

Gold may be plated directly over gold-filled and silver objects. On base metals such as nickel silver or brass, and objects that have been soft soldered, nickel is first plated on and then the gold is plated.

Why nickel? A good and uniform gold color can be obtained by plating over nickel. Also, the gold layer is very thin and porous. Brass and silver eventually will tarnish (discolor) under the gold plate; nickel will not tarnish.

Note: Cyanide gold plating solutions are used for thin (flash) deposits. For heavy deposits, acid gold plating solutions are now available. Good procedure: Acid plate for thickness, then cyanide plate for the desired gold color. If it becomes more difficult, or longer, to obtain a bright gold color, add more gold concentrate to the plating solution.

STOPPING-OFF, or masking, is done to prevent deposition of metal on that portion of the work by applying a stop-off lacquer. A soft camel's hair or sable brush is used to apply the lacquer. The work should be cleaned before masking and might have to be recleaned to remove finger grease. After plating, the piece is washed thoroughly, dipped into a commercial lacquer or nail polish remover for a few minutes, and then the lacquer is removed with a soft brush or cloth under running water.

TWO-TONE FINISHES Two color effects can be obtained by lacquering portions of jewelry objects and then plating. The lacquering surface will not be affected; the unlacquered will be plated. If, for example, you have a 10 karat gold ring with a white gold insignia emblem and you wish to plate the shank of the ring to a 14 karat color and rhodium plate the emblem, the first step is to polish and clean the ring. Apply the stop-off lacquer to the emblem. When the lacquer is dry, dip in electrocleaner, rinse, then plate the ring in the 14K gold solution. The lacquer, after plating, is then removed. Coat the shank that has been gold plated with the stop-off lacquer and then plate the emblem with rhodium. Remove the lacquer from the shank and if necessary lightly polish the ring with rouge.

It is recommended that, when electroplating a piece of jewelry where one bath will be hot (gold, for example) and the other cold (silver), the object be plated first in the hot plating bath, masked, and then plated in the cold bath.

An electroplating outfit that can be readily used by most craftsmen and jewelers consists of:

1. a 25 ampere rectifier
2. a double burner electric hot plate
3. two copper bus bars (one positive, one negative) used to suspend the anode and the cathode wires
4. a bus bar rack which can be made from a non-porous material
5. two 3-foot sections of 12 gauge stranded wire which are connected from the rectifier to the bus bars with alligator clips
6. pyrex and stainless steel beakers for electrocleaning, stripping, rinsing, and plating
7. stop-off lacquer
8. a pyrex funnel to pour plating solutions
9. filters to remove dust, dirt, and sludge from the plating solutions
10. glass stirring rods to help agitate the plating solutions
11. anodes and plating solutions
12. rubber gloves and rubber apron

Fig. 235 Electroplating set-up

SILVER PLATING Silver, probably the first metal to be plated successfully commercially (it replaced Sheffield plate about 1840) requires two silver formulas or solutions—a strike and a regular. Why the strike formula? Metals such as copper, brass, nickel silver, and Britannia (white metal), when dipped into the silver cyanide bath or solution, will have precipitated onto them by immersion a poorly adhering, powdery silver deposit. Further plating cannot be accomplished successfully onto this poorly adhering deposit. Silver strike baths contain (note the formula below)

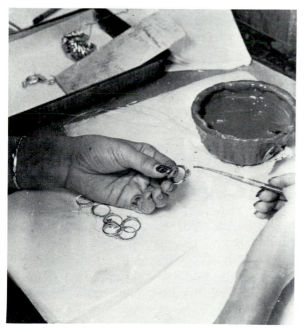

Fig. 234 Lacquering rings for two color effects

133

a small quantity of silver to a comparatively large cyanide content, and this bath will not precipitate silver onto the object being plated by immersion.

Note: Dipping wire must be connected to the cathode bar before dipping the object to be plated into any strike or plating solution, otherwise a poorly adhering immersion plate will form on object.

SILVER STRIKE

Silver cyanide . . . . . . 0.5 to 0.7 ounces (troy)
Potassium cyanide . . . . . . 10 ounces (avoir.)
Water (tap) . . . . 1 gallon
Temperature (room) . . . . 70° to 80°F.
Current density . . . . . . 15 to 25 amp./sq. ft.
Voltage . . . . 4 to 6
Anode . . . . stainless steel

A 10 to 20 second strike is sufficient. The object, when removed from the strike bath, should be placed immediately into the regular silver bath.

Note: It is good procedure to use a ⅓ smaller silver (fine) anode next to the stainless steel anodes to maintain the silver content of the strike solution.

REGULAR SILVER BATH

Silver cyanide . . . . 5.5 ounces (troy)
Potassium cyanide . . . . 10 ounces (avoir.)
Potassium carbonate . . . . 4 ounces (avoir.)
Water . . . . 1 gallon
Temperature (room) . . . . 70° to 80°F.
Current density . . . . 5 to 15 amp./sq. ft.
Voltage . . . . 1 volt
Anode . . . . silver (fine)

A ¼ to ½ hour silver plate is a good, adequate commercial plate. A one hour plate (wire brush after ½ hour) is an excellent and a comparatively inexpensive plate. When the plating time has been reached, remove the object from the bath and dip it into a bucket of cold water. Then wash it in running water. The object can be dried quickly by dipping it into hot water and then into (hot if possible) sawdust, or better yet, ground corn cobs.

RHODIUM PLATING Rhodium can be plated directly onto platinum and white gold jewelry, and many manufacturing jewelers are so do-

ing since, as previously stated, the plate is very durable, hard, brilliantly white, and is not affected by acids or perspiration.

Sterling silver, brass, copper, and white metal rhinestone jewelry should be given a nickel plate before being rhodium plated. The reason for this is simple. The rhodium plate is porous; thus sterling silver and the other metals will eventually tarnish under the plate and thus affect the finish. The nickel plate provides a dense protective coat that will not tarnish under the rhodium, and it also prevents soft solder and white metal from contaminating the rhodium solution.

Wash the jewelry object in cold water after nickel-plating and immediately rhodium plate. Cleanliness is of utmost importance. Rhodium solutions are very easily contaminated and spoiled. Any traces of polishing compound remaining on the article will contaminate the rhodium solution. Ferrous metals (tweezers) should not enter the solution.

Rhodium is purchased as a concentrated solution from which the plating solution is easily prepared by following the supplier's instructions. The anode must be platinum (platinumized titanium). A very thin piece will do since it does not dissolve into the solution. A stainless steel anode may be used in schools and by craftsmen who only plate occasionally.

Voltage . . . . 2 to 5 volts
Temperature . . . . room to 110°F.
Plating time . . . . 15 to 60 seconds

As the solution weakens, it is replenished by adding more rhodium concentrate.

A standard procedure for maintaining the strength of rhodium solutions is as follows: Put some rhodium solution (from the normal rhodium plating solution which is in the glass plating jar) into a small glass bottle (about 1 ounce of solution). Put this small bottle in a drawer so that it is not faded by sunlight. After rhodium plating for several days, compare the color of the rhodium solution in the glass plating jar with the color of the sample. If the color of the rhodium plating solution is noticeably lighter, then add rhodium replenisher to the rhodium solution until the rhodium solution is as dark as the sample. Add distilled water to compensate for evaporation and drag-out losses.

Rhodium baths have poor "throwing power". The objects should be turned slowly so that all portions are equally exposed to the anode. The solution should also be agitated. Remove the work every few seconds to check whether plating has been completed. After plating, rinse in running water and then dry.

NICKEL PLATING Nickel is very easy to plate. The following solution may be used or a solution may be purchased.

Nickel sulphate . . . . 14 oz.
Nickel chloride . . . . 8 oz.
Boric acid . . . . 5 oz.
Water . . . . 1 gallon
Temp. of solution . . . . 85-90°F.
Voltage . . . . 5 volts
Anode . . . . Nickel
Current density . . . . 20-40 amp./ft.^{2}

Since the nickel anode tends to disintegrate or dissolve rapidly, forming a sludge on the bottom of the plating tank, it is best to keep the nickel anode enclosed in a closely woven cotton bag which will catch the nickel sludge. Clean the bag occasionally, and, for best results, bags not purchased from plating dealers should be washed in boiling water to remove any starch from the cotton. Agitation is important. Nickel plating usually takes between three to ten minutes.

COPPER PLATING Below is a safe, practical and easy-to-prepare formula for copper plating and electroforming.

Copper sulfate . . . . 28 oz.
Sulfuric acid . . . . 7 oz.
Water . . . . 1 gallon
Temp. of solution . . . . 70-80°F.
Voltage . . . . 1 to 3
Current density . . . . . . 25 to 30 amp./ft.^{2}
Anode . . . . copper

Note: One volt should be used for small jewelry objects, for if a larger voltage is used the current density will be too high (too much amperage) and the copper will be deposited in a dark powdery form which will not adhere to the object being plated. High voltage and amperage also will "burn" the extremities (such as prongs) of the object being plated.

Since copper from the anode is added to the plating solution at almost the same rate as copper is plated onto the jewelry object, the solution maintains the same chemical composition; thus it can be used for long periods. Remove the copper anode when objects are not being plated. Copper plating solutions should be agitated. Immersion for two to five minutes will generally produce an adequate layer of copper.

AGITATION Slow mechanical agitation of the object being plated permits the use of higher current densities and thus faster plating time. Commercially, this is done by moving the cathode bar, from which the object being plated is hung, back and forth. Agitation is not necessary for plating a few objects at one time in schools and craft shops.

BRIGHTENERS The regular plating bath will leave a mat finish on the object. This finish can be polished and is sufficiently good for a plate in schools and craft shops. If a bright finish is desired, small quantities of special chemicals, known as brighteners, can be added to the silver bath. Carbon disulfide or ammonium thiosulfate in very small amounts(1 to 1½ cc to 10 gallons) can be added to a silver bath until a bright finish is obtained. Proprietary brighteners can be purchased from dealers. The compounds are not stable, and small amounts should be added occasionally.

RINSING AND DRYING Immediately after a final plating, the jewelry object is washed in clean cold and then hot water to prevent water spotting or staining. The object is then dried in clean hardwood sawdust or ground corn cobs that are warmed in a metal container, or by means of steam under pressure.

Craftsmen can dry plated objects by waving them over an electric heater or stove.

The appearance of the objects immediately after they have been removed from the plating bath, or after drying, may be disappointingly dull. However, a light buffing with jeweler's rouge will quickly give the objects a lustrous finish.

DRAG-OUT As the plated object is removed from the plating solution, some of the solution clings to the piece and is removed and lost. This loss, known as drag-out, can be rather expensive. It can be minimized by dipping the removed object into a container of clean tap water for gold and into distilled water for rhodium plating. This water is then added to the plating solutions as needed.

Brush plating can be used for the two-tone coloring of jewelry or for plating objects that cannot be tank-plated. The piece to be plated is suspended from or attached to the cathode wire.

A brush plater is made from a brush whose bristles are bound with copper, nylon, or stainless steel. Thin 28-30 gauge copper wire is wrapped around the bristles several times, bent so that it will extend through the bristles, and then cut so that it will not come in contact or directly touch the work. The thin copper wire is connected to 20 gauge wire, which is connected to the positive pole of the plater. Also, a small brush similar to the one described above can be inserted into the discharge end of a medicine dropper. The anode wire is pushed through the rubber bulb and connected to the plater. Wax can be used to seal the end. The medicine dropper is filled with plating solution and the dropper is squeezed so that one drop at a time is deposited on the work, or the brush is dipped into plating solution and the solution is painted on. A brush plater can also be made by inserting a sponge wrapped with wire into a glass tube, corking the opposite end of the tube, leading the wire through the cork to the plater, filling the tube with solution, and then dabbing the solution onto the piece. A slightly higher current density should be used when brush plating.

ELECTROFORMING

The process of plating thick deposits of metal onto non-conductive substances such as wax or styrofoam is known as electroforming. With this technique, jewelry craftsmen can:

1. Form and make unusual shapes, bulky or large, that are comparatively light in weight.

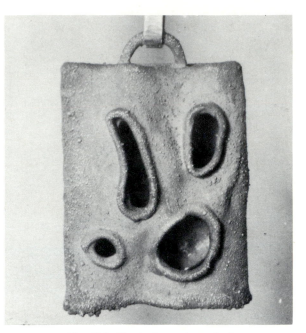

Fig. 236 Electroformed pendant

2. Form objects that are too large to be cast in the average craftsman's centrifugal casting machine.

3. By plating for extended periods with high current densities (higher voltages), create shapes and textures which cannot be obtained with other techniques.

FORMING Shapes for electroforming can be made from wax (see page 146), styrofoam or any other light material. When designing the object to be electroformed into a wearable jewelry object, size and final weight should be considered carefully.

CONDUCTIVITY To make a non-conductive substance such as wax conductive (able to carry electricity) metals such as brass powder or liquid silver are sprayed or painted onto the non-conductive substance. The painting method is inexpensive and is also the one that is practical for craft work.

Absorbent materials such as wood, leather, etc. may be first coated with shellac, plastic film, hot wax, or varnish that has been thinned with alcohol in order to make them impervious to the painting solutions. Experiment to see that the coating is not affected by the plating bath.

The silver paint (silver is the best conductor of electricity) is recommended. One coat applied with a camel's hair brush is sufficient. Several brands are on the market. Metaplast's can be painted on quickly and the object can be plated after a five minute drying period. Acheson Colloids Electrodag 416 can be plated after a very short drying period. Dupont's #4817 must be cured according to their instructions.

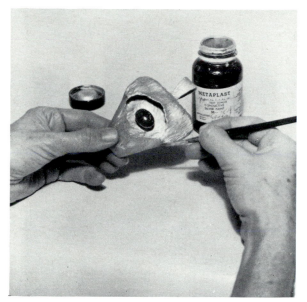

Fig. 237 Painting a model with conductive paint

The cathode wire should be inserted into the model before the conductive paint is applied. In this way the paint adheres to, and thus connects, the model and wire, thereby insuring a good contact. Square wire can be used. Sometimes a fork can be made on the end of the cathode before inserting it into the model to help sink the model into the solution. Excessively buoyant models may be weighted with acquired nuts and bolts that are either inserted into the model or suspended from the cathode. The cathode wire can also be attached to the model after it has been painted.

A conductive surface paint can be made by mixing bronze or brass powder (free of oil) with lacquer. Mix ½ ounce lacquer thinner and ½ ounce clear lacquer. Stir in ½ ounce (by volume) of very fine brass or bronze powder. Paint a coat of this mixture onto the object to be electroformed. The painting must

be done as soon as the lacquer hardens for brass oxidizes quickly and loses its conductivity. The mixture should contain just enough lacquer to make the powder adhere to the object. The surface should look frosty when dry. A shiny glazed surface indicates excess lacquer which will "stop off" the conductivity and should be corrected by adding more thinner to the mixture before a second coat is painted on the object. A second coat should be applied as soon as the first coat has dried.

ELECTROFORMING PROCEDURE The actual electroforming procedure is a plating process. The time required to obtain the required metal thickness can be determined from the charts listed previously. Observe the amperage being used and from the object's surface area calculate the current density. A low current density with slight agitation of the object being plated will give a smooth deposit. If a rough deposit with granular (treed) growths, especially on the edges of the plated object, is desired, increase the voltage to obtain larger amperage and thus current density.

It is good procedure, after silver painting the object to be electroformed, to first copper plate it. This way, one can observe if the plating is taking all over. Then the object may be silver or gold plated. Since gold is expensive, after the object has been silver or copper plated to the desired thickness, it can be gold plated for appearance.

If, in the beginning stages of electroforming, the piece develops a surface roughness in certain places (known as orange peel) the piece may have been too close to the anode, or the conductive coating may have been too heavy in spots. Any "orange peel" which develops should be smoothed down with fine emery cloth. The piece should then be electrocleaned and returned to the tank. The current can be periodically reversed for a short period of time. This helps to create a smooth surface when electroforming, especially with cyanide solutions.

Agitation and filtration are essential in successful controlled electroforming. More vigorous agitation will mean a faster deposition rate and thus smaller smoother crystals will form on the surface of the model. A high

Fig. 238 Electroformed ring   Robert Browning

rate of filtration, which eliminates metallic sediment and contaminants, prevents occlusions from forming as the metallic coating is being deposited on the model, and therefore facilitates the formation of a smoother plating surface. Batch filtration is a simple inexpensive way of filtering. Pour the material from one container into another through a filter.

Although there is theoretically no limit to the thickness of metal that can be deposited by the electroforming process, if the article has been in the plating solution for an extended period of time, the surface will start to become frosty and dull because of the formation of tiny nodules. When this occurs, the article should be removed from the plating solution and scratch-brushed with a soft brass wire wheel to burnish down the surface. It should then be electrocleaned, rinsed, and returned to the plating bath. This cycle may be repeated as many times as desired. Turning down the current will minimize the frequency of this operation. The article of jewelry should be polished to the desired luster, and then electrocleaned before the final plating is done.

After the electroforming process has progressed enough so that the piece is rigid, the expendable materials—wax, wood, styrofoam, etc.—that were used for the base models can be boiled or heated until they either melt out of the form or are reduced to ash. If the electroformed metal has completely enclosed the model, small holes should be drilled through the metal to allow the model material to escape during burnout. The piece should then be electrocleaned, whereupon electroforming can proceed until a sufficient deposit of metal has been achieved. Once the final layer of metal has been deposited on the piece, it is frequently lightly polished or scratch-brushed.

It is possible to electroform a setting around a gemstone (providing the gemstone is resistant to the plating solution) by securing the gemstone to the model, whereupon the metal will form around the edge; by painting certain areas of the gemstone with conductive paint; or by building the model around the gemstone and then securing the stone after the model has been removed.

Electroformed metal can be sawed, drilled, soldered, or enameled.

Fig. 238A Pendant   Barbara Skelly

138

CASTING

Jewelry can be reproduced quickly, exactly, and practically by several casting methods. The traditional methods of casting jewelry are: sand, charcoal, cuttle fish, tufa, gravity, pressure, vacuum, and centrifugal. The centrifugal or lost wax method is the most recent (since 1930) and is generally considered the best method of casting most jewelry objects since there is no limit to the intricacy of the wax model shapes which can be cast quickly and inexpensively. Centrifugal casting can also be used for casting platinum and other high melting alloys which cannot be cast in sand or cuttle fish. Sand and cuttle fish casting are rarely used commercially today; however they still have historical, educational, and therapeutic values, and for these reasons they shall be discussed first.

Fig. 239 Salt Cellars   Judith Reiss

NOTES ON CASTING In principle, casting is a very simple process. Any metal will become molten when sufficiently heated. Molten metal can be poured into the cavity of a refractory mold, where it will assume the shape of the cavity when it cools and hardens.

In all casting methods, reproductions are made from a model. The model must be made accurately and slightly (10%) larger than the desired casting, for allowances must be made for metal shrinkage and for filing and polishing.

The model for a ring should always be made one-half a size larger than what the finger measures (a model for a size 7 ring should be size 7½) because the molten metal shrinks that much when it cools.

The model should be polished or finished perfectly. Any imperfections will be trans-ferred to the metal casting, resulting in needless time and labor spent on removing imperfections in the metal casting.

The models for sand and cuttle fish casting cannot have undercuts, for if they do they cannot be removed without breaking the sand or cuttle fish. Models for centrifugal casting can be very intricate and have undercuts—the reason for the method's popularity.

For sand and cuttle fish casting, the metal may be melted in a hand crucible; for centrifugal casting, it is melted in the crucible attached to the machine or in a larger furnace-type crucible and then poured into the machine's crucible.

Keep water away from molten (melted) metals. Water hitting the hot metal will form steam and the metal will spatter. It is advisable to wear safety glasses when melting metals.

A more thorough description of the lost wax and centrifugal casting processes can be found in the author's book, "Centrifugal or Lost Wax Jewelry Casting for Schools, Tradesmen, Craftsmen".

1. SAND CASTING

Sand casting is done in a mold composed of fine casting sand. The sand used is very fine "French" sand (Albany No. 00). The sand is mixed (tempered) with water or glycerine to hold it together. Properly tempered sand when squeezed in one's hand should not ooze water or glycerine, and then when broken in half by hand should part sharply. The sand can be stored in a wooden box or a metal container after being used.

Water must be added constantly and mixed thoroughly with the sand to keep it properly tempered; oil will not evaporate from the sand and therefore should be added only occasionally. Water tempered sands are superior; oil sands are good for schools—more later.

The sand is packed into a flask. The flask has two parts: one with pins, the drag; one with holes to receive the pins, the cope. Packing is best done on a flat piece of steel or marble—called the mold surface.

The method of casting a ring will be explained from here on. It is comparatively easy with the following information to cast flat objects.

The model used for sand casting cannot have undercuts because the sand would be disturbed when the model is lifted from the mold, thereby destroying the mold cavity. Metal models of rings, pins, belt buckles, etc., or patterns fabricated from a hard, close-grained wood such as cherry or maple can be used.

When packing the flask, first place a half-round piece of rod or a piece of tubing cut in half on the steel or marble surface. The rod or tube should have a diameter equal to the diameter of the finger size of the ring being cast and its length should be approximately 2″. Place the cope section of the flask, hole side down, so that the half-round piece is in the center. Now pack the sand into the flask.

The sand is sifted through a sieve or riddle when packing, in order to remove all foreign matter and to get a fine layer of sand around the model. Ordinary screening can be used to make a riddle. Sift a sufficient amount of sand to completely cover the tube and then add unsifted sand until it is several inches above the height of the cope. Now pack the sand firmly into the cope, first with your fingers, especially in the corners, and then lightly with a hammer or a very small mallet. Smooth the sand by running a flat piece of steel over the top of the cope.

Turn the cope over and remove the half-round piece of metal. Place the ring to be cast on a round rod or tube whose diameter is the same as the ring size—in other words, the ring should just slip snugly on the rod. The rod's length should be slightly shorter (¼″ will do) than the length of the half-round piece. Now place the ring and rod over the depression in the sand formed by removing the half-round piece (fig. 240). The top of the ring should be up, and the shank down. Push the shank and the rod down into the sand until the rod is halfway down. If necessary, with a small spatula, add sand against the shank to eliminate any imperfections. For better adherence, with a small camel's hair brush, wet the sand near the shank before adding the extra sand.

Fig. 240 Half-round piece in sand (bottom of picture) and when removed ring on rod (top) is placed in position

Fig. 241 Ring impression and tube and rod for forming core in position

Dust a very light layer of powder over the sand and the ring. Talc powder may be used; lycopodium, however, is superior. It is best to keep the powder in a small, semi-porous cloth bag. By tapping the bag lightly it is easy to spread a thin, even layer of powder. The powder acts as a separator; that is, it prevents the sand in the drag from sticking to the sand in the cope.

Now place the drag part of the flask on the cope, sieve some sand into it, and finally pack it entirely with sand and smooth the top.

The flask must now be separated and the model ring removed. To separate, tap the sides of the flask lightly with a hammer to vibrate the model and thus release adhering sand from it. Then slowly lift the drag from the cope and remove the model ring. A sharp impression of the ring should remain in the sand (fig. 241).

A core—a round piece of sand the same diameter as the rod the ring fits on—must be made. It is made by packing sand into a small tube (2″ long) with the same inside diameter as the outside diameter of the rod. Push the packed sand out of the tube with a rod (fig. 241).

A sprue opening and gate is formed so that the molten metal may be poured into the flask. The easiest way to do this is to take the tang (back) of a needle file and push it through the sand from the shank impression side of the cope.

Enlarge the formed opening to the width of the shank, and on the outside part of the cope scrape away some of the sand to a funnel shape so that it will be easy to pour the metal in (fig. 242).

Finally, with a scriber, scratch several light lines from the ring impression to the edge of the flask in order to permit the air to escape from the hollow ring impression in the sand when the molten metal enters.

The flask is assembled by first blowing out any loose sand, then placing the core in position, and finally closing both parts with the cope section up.

The actual casting process is simple. The

Fig. 242 Gate and sprue opening in the sand

metal may be melted in a hand or furnace crucible. The hand crucibles are ideal for schools and small shops (fig. 245).

The weight of the required metal can be determined by weighing the model and then adding a little extra metal to this weight. When melting the metal add a little borax to keep it from oxidizing. Pour the molten metal as quickly as possible into the gate in the sand. The flask can be opened almost immediately to remove the cast ring. Nip or cut off the sprue and complete the ring as desired.

The finest castings are obtained from dried, water-tempered sands. After the flask has been assembled it is baked in a gas oven or over a gas stove until all the moisture in the sand evaporates. Whereas a wet sand will form steam when the molten metal enters and the steam will interfere with the castings, a dry sand will not and therefore a better casting can be had. If time is a factor, good castings can be obtained by merely heating the sand for a moment or two before the flask is assembled.

141

2. CUTTLE FISH CASTING

Cuttle fish casting was very popular before centrifugal casting was perfected. It still has educational values and occasionally it can be used for quickly casting rough models and simple pieces that haven't any undercuts. Castings that are made using the cuttle fish method are frequently engraved, or become the main section of a more complex piece of jewelry having a stone setting or applied ornamental decoration.

Fig. 243 Pendant made by cuttle fish casting and centrifugal casting   Ruth Goodman

The cuttle fish is actually the dried shell of a marine mollusk. One side of the shell is hard and the other soft. Cuttle fish can be used as a mold for casting jewelry because it will easily retain any impression made in its softer side, and because it has the ability to withstand high temperature. When purchasing, the larger shells are preferred.

The model for cuttle fish casting can be made from either metal, hard carving wax, or pre-formed "master ring blanks". Hard carving waxes are excellent for making models for cuttle fish casting since they can be easily carved, drilled, filed, sawed, etc. and yet will still make a sharp impression in the cuttle fish.

When selecting metal models for casting in cuttle fish, a commercial metal ring can be used as long as it has no undercuts. The model selected should be shaped so that it is possible to press it halfway into a cuttle fish easily without distortion. After the model is removed, there should be a true imprint of its actual shape.

To cast a ring, two shells are required. The cuttle fish should be thick enough at their midsection so that, after the model is pressed into place, approximately ½″ of cuttle fish material remains between the model and the shell's exterior.

Once two suitable cuttle fish have been selected, use a jeweler's saw and cut away the superfluous shell to get a rectangular shaped piece as shown in figure 244. A one half inch wall thickness from the ring to the edges of the fish and a three quarter inch wall thickness from the ring to the top and bottom is adequate. After cutting, file or rub

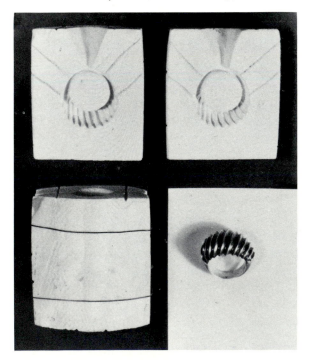

Fig. 244 Ring model, its impression in the cuttle fish, and two halves held together with binding wire

142

the sides on sandpaper to even them, and then, with a file, make diagonal grooves across them so that when the model is removed the two sections can be aligned properly.

The soft surfaces of the shells can be made perfectly flat and true by rubbing them on a rough piece of sandpaper or emery cloth. This is done so that no molten metal will seep from the mold. Press the side of the model ring halfway into one of the cuttle fish. Then take the other shell and squeeze it into the ring until it meets the first shell, keeping the edges of each shell aligned. The cuttle fish should be held between the palms of the hands in order to keep the pressure equally distributed over the outer surfaces of the mold. More pressure can be exerted by placing the clasped hands between the knees and then squeezing. Once the shells have been pressed together as firmly as possible, separate the two sections and carefully remove the model.

A layer of fine, powdered graphite can be lightly dusted on the mold after the model has been removed. The model is then placed back into its original position in the first cuttle fish, and both cuttle fish are once again pressed together. After the model has been carefully removed, a thin layer of graphite will remain affixed to the walls of the cuttle fish mold, leaving a smoother surface from which a casting with finer detail can be made.

Pegs made from toothpicks, metal pins, or matchsticks can be used as alignment pins. The pegs are inserted halfway into each of the corners of the cuttle fish mold after the model has been pressed into place. When the other half of cuttle fish is pressed over the model, the pegs also make an impression so that when the cuttle bones are reassembled, both halves of the mold are aligned perfectly.

A triangular, tapered sprue gate (opening for pouring in the metal) should be made with a file or cut with a knife into each section of the cuttle fish from the edge of the mold to the shank of the ring. The sprue gate should enter into the cavity in an area where there is no decoration. Near the ring the gate can be enlarged with the tang of

a needle file to the width of the shank. Several vent lines should be lightly scratched into the cuttle fish upward from the ring impression to the edges of the fish in order to permit air and gases to escape.

The two sections of the cuttle fish should be assembled and aligned by means of the filed guide lines on the sides and then tied tightly together with binding wire. Before pouring the metal into the mold, the mold should either be held upright with tongs or placed in a pan filled with sand. The mold is cast in a similar manner to sand casting. The metal is melted with a torch in a small pouring crucible. The flame of the torch is also kept on the metal in the crucible during pouring to keep it free flowing. The metal is poured into the gate of the mold until it fills the sprue gate. When the button metal has cooled sufficiently the mold is broken open, the casting is removed and pickled in acid, the sprue is sawed off, and then the casting is finished as desired.

Note: It is possible to change the width and/or depth of the casting by varying the depth that the model is pressed into the cuttle fish. In order to make a casting narrower than the original model, press the model slightly less than halfway into each

Fig. 245 Silver, melted in a hand crucible, being poured into a cuttle fish mold

143

half of the cuttle fish. To make a casting wider than the model, first press together the cuttle fish in the traditional manner. Open the mold and remove the model. Then insert the model into one half of the mold and press it slightly deeper than half its width. Remove the casting from the cuttle fish and repeat the process for the outer half of the cuttle fish mold. After the model has been removed and the mold reassembled, the casting will be larger than the original model. The ring size of the casting will remain the same.

If a sharp impression of the top of a ring is desired, a three section mold can be made (fig. 246). A three-piece sectional mold is also used if the top of the ring is designed in a way that would not permit the model to be released if a two piece mold were used.

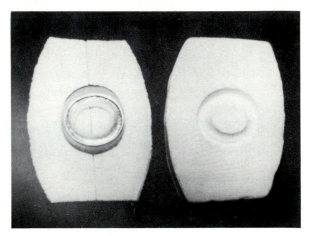

Fig. 246 A three-piece cuttle fish mold

A cuttle fish mold can only be used for one casting.

3. TUFA CASTING

Tufa is a lightweight, highly refractory, natural pumice stone that is used primarily by the American Indians to make molds for casting "flat back" silver jewelry such as pendants and belt buckles. As in cuttle fish casting, only relatively simple shapes that do not have undercuts or intricate detail can be cast successfully. However, it is possible to reuse the tufa mold for up to twenty castings, whereas a cuttle fish mold can be used only once.

The first step in tufa casting is to cut the tufa stone into two rectangular blocks with a back saw. The blocks should be large enough so that there is at least one-half of an inch between the outside dimensions of the model and the outside of the mold. A coarse file is used to file the two contacting surfaces of the mold until they are flat. In order to make sure that these two surfaces will butt perfectly together they should either be rubbed together or sanded against a sheet of sandpaper to remove any irregularities.

An outline of the article to be cast along with the sprue channel and gate is drawn on one of the flat surfaces with a pencil. Small knives, chisels, gouges, or riffler files can be used to carve out the cavity in the tufa, usually in a V-shaped or U-shaped depression. A straight U-shaped sprue channel should be cut leading away from the cavity to one end of the mold. Finally, a V-shaped pouring funnel is carved from the sprue channel to the top of the mold. **Note:** The mold cavity should not have any undercuts. To insure that the entire cavity is filled when the molten metal is poured, the diameter of the sprue channel should be as wide as the thickest cross-sectional part of the cavity and should be joined to a thicker part of the cavity.

Fig. 247 Tufa mold and casting

Several vents should be cut with a knife leading from the cavity to the outside of the mold so that gases are not trapped inside the cavity when the metal is poured into the mold. Heavy binding wire or wooden clamps should be used to hold the two parts of the mold together in order to prevent metal leakage. A better casting will result if the tufa is heated to approximately 500°F. so that any moisture in the mold will evaporate.

The metal is melted in a small crucible and then poured into the upright mold. It is important to continue heating the crucible as the metal is poured so that it remains molten. Once the metal has solidified and cooled in the cavity, the mold is opened and the casting is carefully lifted from the cavity with the aid of a sharp, pointed tool. A saw can be used to remove the sprue, and any fins or surface irregularities are then filed smooth.

4. CENTRIFUGAL CASTING

Centrifugal casting, the newest and most accurate method of casting intricate jewelry and industrial objects, is within the scope of the average craftsman. The required equipment is comparatively inexpensive and some of it can be made; the technique is mechanical in nature and can easily be developed; and the results are truly amazing and accurate. Centrifugal casting has literally revolutionized the manufacturing jewelry industry by means of its simple method of reproducing intricate jewelry pieces quickly.

The casting method itself is a development and refinement of the very old so-called Lost Wax Process of casting and the modern method the dentist uses for casting inlays and bridges. The Lost Wax Process was used by the ancient Greeks and Chinese over two thousand years ago. Benvenuto Cellini later used this same method to cast many of his famous works of art.

The name Lost Wax Process, owes its origin to the fact that an expendable wax model of the article of jewelry to be cast is made first. The model is fastened to a conical wax sprue and then encased in a mold of heat-resistant plaster of paris or some other refractory material. An opening is left in the mold leading from the pattern so that the wax can burn away. The wax is burned away by heating the mold slowly in a kiln as soon as the plaster of paris has hardened. When the wax has melted and burned away, a cavity is left in the mold. Molten metal is then poured into the cavity of the mold through the same opening that was used to eliminate the wax. After the metal has solidified, the mold is broken open and the casting is removed. Because the wax was burned away and the mold destroyed, each lost wax object is unique.

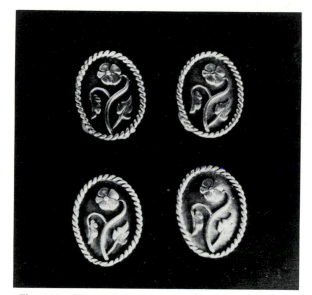

Fig. 248   One earring is handmade, the others cast. Can you tell which one?

In 1907, Doctor Taggert, an American dentist, perfected a method of restoring the shape of a tooth that was drilled to remove decay. Before Taggert's time, teeth were restored by malleting either gold or silver into the prepared cavity in the tooth. Taggert pressed wax into the cavity and then carved it until it assumed the shape of the original contour of the tooth. The wax pattern was removed, surrounded by a heat-resisting plaster compound, then the wax was eliminated from the plaster by heating, and finally gold was cast into the cavity formed by the elimination of the wax. The metal was forced into the plaster mold by means of an air pressure or centrifugal force casting machine. The machine most widely used today by the

145

dentist and the jewelry manufacturer is the centrifugal—hence the name of the process, Centrifugal Casting.

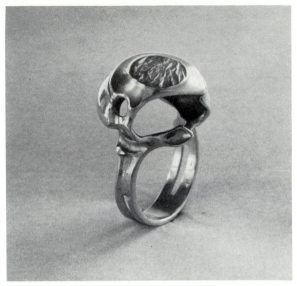

Fig. 249 Ring   **Randy Burns**

Though dentists successfully used the Lost Wax Process for over a quarter of a century, it wasn't until the 1930's that the manufacturing jewelers in this country discovered that they could use the process for casting jewelry. The factor that made the process adaptable to the jewelry industry was the devising of a means of rapidly duplicating a jewelry model in wax by means of a rubber mold. **Note:** Metal molds are used for some jewelry objects. In other words, the jewelers added another step to the dentist's lost wax process of centrifugal casting—a rubber mold—and this mold permits them quickly, accurately, and inexpensively, to duplicate almost any piece of jewelry, first in wax and then in gold, silver, or platinum.

The drawback to the lost wax technique is not that an intricate model cannot be reproduced, but that the original wax model is destroyed each time the piece is cast. The process is therefore too slow for mass producing identical pieces of jewelry.

The centrifugal casting process begins with the creation of an original model. Original models for casting can be made of either metal or wax depending on the skill and the intent of the jeweler. Metal models are usually made by commercial jewelers who need

to make duplicate castings from wax models produced from rubber molds. Wax models are usually used by craftsmen or jewelers who either produce one-of-a-kind jewelry pieces or as the original model for a metal model.

The advantage of using wax to create a model is that wax is relatively pliable and soft and thus can be easily worked. Wax model making therefore offers a wide range of design possibilities to an individual who might not be very skilled in metalworking techniques, but who possesses imagination and ingenuity. By working in wax, the designer can avoid making errors that could be very costly if executed in precious metal. Also, wax designers can obtain textures and shapes in a wax model that could never be achieved if the design were made in metal.

Casting waxes for producing models are formulated from combinations of mineral and organic waxes and gums such as carnauba, candelilla, beeswax, and paraffin. These commercial waxes are available in various colors, hardnesses, and shapes. The color is usually indicative of the different working characteristics of each wax. The varying hardnesses allow the different waxes to be bent, melted, filed, and sculpted by many tools. Prepared waxes are available in the form of flat sheets and round wire that correspond to the thicknesses of the Brown and Sharpe metal gauge. There are various hard waxes that can be filed, drilled, sawed (a spiral saw blade works best), or cut on a lathe.

Transparent waxes can be used as tracing sheets to transfer a paper design onto wax. Tube waxes can be used to quickly create a basic ring shape. There are waxes that can be easily stretched thin, waxes that can be used to weld two pieces of wax together, waxes that can be woven, and special waxes with very low melting points. This special wax can be used as a matrix to build up a hollow wax form and then dissolved away in hot water.

ONE-OF-A-KIND CASTINGS Although there are many methods of creating a wax model, the majority of the techniques fall into two

Fig. 250 Commercial wax shapes for model makers

basic categories. Either they are of a sub-tractive, or carving nature, or they are of an additive or building nature. In those techniques of working with wax that are considered subtractive, the design is achieved by beginning with a piece of wax and removing the excess wax by cutting, carving, engraving, sawing, or drilling.

The wax model for the cast pin in figure 251 was made by pouring melted wax into a plastic container to form a slab ¼″ thick. The slab was cut to shape with a jeweler's saw. The final shape was obtained by scraping and shaving the wax with the edge (sharpened) of a barrette file.

Fig. 251 Wax model and cast pin with pearl

The pin in figure 252 was made by heating a spatula and pushing it through 16 gauge sheet wax and then quickly blowing out the adhering melted wax. The pendant in figure 252 was formed by cutting the wax to shape with a mold knife (a hot spatula can be used) and then bending it to shape by hand. Both were given a smooth finish by passing a hot flame over them very quickly.

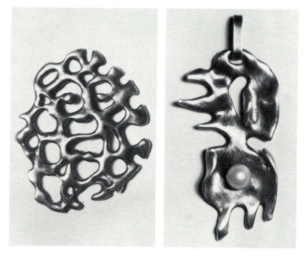

Fig. 252 Cast pin and pendant from sheet wax

Various textures can be applied to the surface of a wax model by means of a hot needle, spatula, or knife edge.

Fig. 253 Texturing wax model with a needle

The hard waxes, as previously stated, can be sawed, carved, drilled, and filed. They can

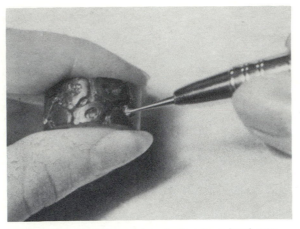

Fig. 254 Forming a ring design in a hard wax with a bur

also be shaped by burs held in a flexible shaft outfit (fig. 254) and with engraving tools.

In the additive process, a wax model is formed by either fusing various shapes of wax together, or by gradually building up a piece of wax with layers of molten wax that are deposited on the piece with a hot spatula, wire, awl, needle, or saw blade. Wax will melt and adhere to the hot tool (dental instruments can be used), and, with careful manipulation of the tool, the melted wax can be flowed onto other waxes to form many unusual shapes for casting.

Note the cast ring in figure 255. The wax model was made by warming over a flame or in warm water a piece of a soft red wax (dental type) and then by bending it over a mandrel to form a band. The ends of the band are fused by means of a spatula. A hard green wax is applied by means of a

spatula to the band to create the design shown. The small shot is formed and applied by gathering wax on a hot awl or wire and by then touching the awl or wire to the wax band.

The wax model for the pendant in figure 256 was made by fusing wax rods or wires. The wires can be fused neatly by heating the end of a jeweler's saw blade and applying the hot blade to the wax wires. Round wax wires can be flattened by rolling the top of a ring mandrel over them to form rectangular wires. A rough texture can be applied to one-of-a-kind wax castings by rubbing the wax models with a fine wire brush, or by spraying a fine wax mist over them by melting wax and using a mouth atomizer fixatif outfit of the type used by artists for charcoals and pastels.

Many times a wax model is both built up and carved away. These two methods are

Fig. 256 Wax model for pendant made by fusing wax wires

Fig. 255 Wax, model, and cast ring in gold

Fig. 257 Applying wax with spatula

148

frequently employed when making prong and bezel settings. Prongs and bezels are constructed in wax on the model so that they can be cast as one unit rather than made in metal and soldered to the piece after the casting has been made. Figure 257 shows a prong setting being built up directly around the gemstone so that it will closely match the shape of the gemstone. Figure 258 illustrates a bezel setting being formed by cutting down the wax model with a flat engraving tool.

Note: Designs and contours are more easily made in the wax bezel or prong setting when the gemstone is supporting it.

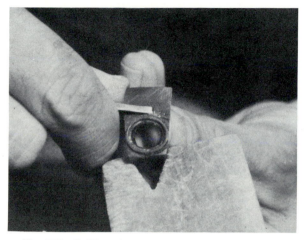

Fig. 258 Cutting down top wax to form a bezel with a flat engraving tool

SUGGESTIONS If decorative holes are to be made in the wax with a heated tool the gemstone should be removed. Spread a thin layer of vaseline or oil around the stone so that it can be easily removed from the wax model. Wax bezels should not be made too thick, since, after casting, it may be difficult to push the metal bezel over the gemstone. Prongs can be made by using wax wires or by trailing wax on the gemstone with either a wax pen or a spatula.

Observe the wax model for a pendant in figure 259. It was made from 16 gauge sheet wax by melting out wax, bending by hand, and fusing parts with a hot needle. Additional wax was added with a hot spatula.

Most wax models can be created with a few inexpensive forming and carving tools such as spatulas, files, saw blades, pointers,

Fig. 259 Wax pendant on sprue base

and needles. Many jewelers favor the hand instruments used in dentistry and wood carving. A dental tool with a tiny spoon is frequently used to deposit additional wax on the model. The end of this metal tool is held over a low flame for several seconds, removed from the flame, and immediately placed against a piece of wax. The wax will melt on the tool and the liquid wax is then deposited on the model. Warm metal tools work better than cold tools when cutting and manipulating wax. An alcohol lamp (fig. 260) or a bunsen burner are the standard equipment used for heating wax forming tools.

Fig. 260 Heating spatula over alcohol lamp

Some model makers use an electrically heated spatula (with interchangeable tips) which eliminates the manual heating of a spatula over a flame (fig. 261).

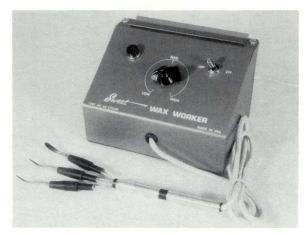

Fig. 261 Electric spatula with temperature control

Electric wax pens which extrude wax onto a model at a controlled rate are used by many model makers and jewelers, especially for making prongs.

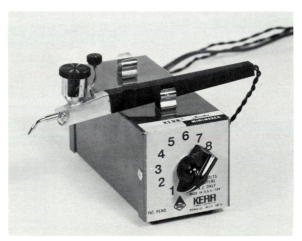

Fig. 262 Electric wax pen for extruding wax

Wax models for rings are usually formed on a special stepped ring mandrel. Mandrels for bracelets and necklaces can be constructed from aluminum or copper sheets. These support bases should be lubricated with a thin film of oil so that the completed wax pattern can be easily removed.

Weight and size should always be considered when making a wax model. The finished metal casting weighs approximately 10

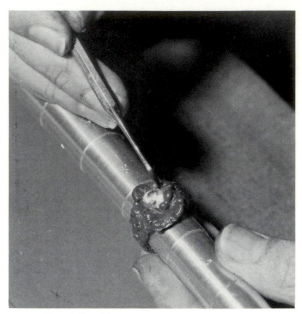

Fig. 263 Wax model being constructed on a ring mandrel

times more than the wax model if it is cast in sterling silver and approximately 15 times more than the wax model if it is cast in 18 karat gold. Note how the ring in figure 264 was made lighter by removing wax from the inside of the birds and from the back of the shank. The finished wax model should not

Fig. 264 Ring   Lee B. Peck

be excessively heavy and large because: the metal will cost more; it could be difficult to melt the required metal with the torches available; the object cannot be worn properly.

After the wax model has been completed, it can be cast in a refractory material by the lost wax process in order to create either a one-of-a-kind casting or a metal model for making a rubber mold for duplicate wax models. Wax models cannot be used as models when making a rubber mold because the model must have a melting point of approximately 150°F. above the vulcanizing temperature (310°F.) of the uncured rubber that is used to make a rubber mold.

RUBBER MOLDS are used extensively for the mass production of wax patterns from metal models. Since rubber molds are extremely elastic and flexible the wax patterns can be easily removed without breakage or distortion. Therefore, metal models that have undercuts can be used.

REQUIRED MATERIALS The following are required to make a rubber mold: an aluminum rubber mold frame, mold rubber, benzine, ⅛" brass rod, a cone-like gate-forming plug with a ⅛" hole drilled through it, and

Fig. 265 Ring model in one piece frame

an incising knife. The required aluminum frame can be purchased from casting supply houses. Craftsmen can cast or cut their own frames from an aluminum bar. One piece frames are currently used by commercial casters. Two piece frames may be used by craftsmen. A good size for rings is shown in figure 265. The opening is 1⅞" by 2⅞" with a depth of 1¼". For narrower rings, depths of ¾" and less can be used. Smaller and larger rubber mold frames are used for pins, brooches, and other jewelry objects.

MAKING THE MOLD A ring will be used to explain the process of making the mold. The ring model, if original, must be carefully made and polished, for all imperfections will be carried into the mold. Brass or silver (preferred) are recommended for making the original models and they are generally made by hand, using standard jewelry making techniques. Nickel silver can be used when making delicate prong settings since it has a high melting point. Remember that the model must be ten per cent larger to allow for shrinkage, filing, and polishing.

To proceed: Silver solder a 1½" piece of the ⅛" rod to the center of the shank of the ring. The sprue rod will form an opening so that wax can be injected into the rubber mold to form a wax model. It also eventually forms a wax sprue on the wax model so that molten metal can be cast into a plaster investment mold. The sprue former has two purposes: it creates a gate in the rubber mold so that wax can be easily injected into the mold; and later forms a button which is required when the molten metal is being injected into the investment. Note from figure 265 the shape of the sprue rod where it is attached to the ring model. The sprue rod was hammered (forged) to this shape before it was soldered to the ring. Note also in figure 277 how some sprues divide in order to obtain better wax flow and eventually metal flow to different parts of the casting.

EXPLANATION Originally two piece aluminum frames (fig. 266) separated by a thin (38 gauge) piece of copper or by the cloth covering the uncured rubber were used to make the rubber mold. The reason for the separator and the four square holes in the corners of the separator: it is easy to cut the mold into two halves after the mold rubber has been vulcanized, and the square holes are used to form locks (described later) to properly align the two halves of the finished mold.

Fig. 266 Two piece frame assembled

Now one piece molds are used commercially, and they are also recommended to craftsmen. The one piece method of forming a mold, since it is practical and comparatively easy to use, will be described in this book. Beginning craftsmen will have sufficient information to make two piece frames, if they desire, after reading the following chapter.

MOLD RUBBER The uncured rubber for making the mold is purchased in sheets 1/8 inch thick with a thin cloth separator on one side. The rubber must be absolutely clean since a slight trace of dirt, oil, or powder will keep the rubber sheets from flowing and adhering to one another. The rubber is cleaned with benzine as it is packed.

The rubber is cut with a shear or mold knife into rectangles to fit snugly into the aluminum frame.

PACKING THE FRAME Place two sheets of rubber in the bottom of the frame and then place the ring with the sprue rod and former in position so that it is held in the frame as shown in figure 267. A hole may be drilled into the frame so that the sprue may be inserted into it to hold the ring firmly in place. A layer of rubber is then cut so that it fits around the metal model, sprue, and gate former. Other smaller pieces of rubber are cut and inserted around the ring as shown in figure 267. Then two additional sheets are placed in the frame to complete the packing. The cloth covering should have been left or should be replaced on the outside sheets of rubber.

Fig. 267 One half of frame packed with rubber

VULCANIZING The uncured rubber in the mold is now ready to be vulcanized. Professional workers use a commercial vulcanizer (fig. 268) which consists of two electrically heated steel plates that can be squeezed together. Most vulcanizing presses have a thermostatic control so that a vulcanization temperature of 310°F. can be maintained for the forty-five to ninety minutes that it usually takes to vulcanize the rubber in the mold.

The required vulcanization temperature is 310°F. and the time is 15 minutes for each

Fig. 268 A commercial vulcanizer

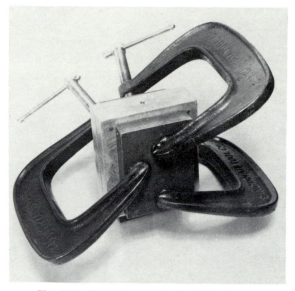

¼ inch of rubber thickness—45 minutes is required for a ¾ inch mold. The handle or clamps should be tightened as follows during the vulcanization period:

1. First tighten plates lightly.
2. After two minute periods—lightly.
3. After eight minutes (from start) tighten as firm as possible.
4. Do not tighten again during vulcanization period.

If a commercial vulcanizer is not available, the mold may be vulcanized by clamping steel or aluminum bars to the frame by means of "C" clamps (fig. 269). The entire frame, clamps and all, may be heated in a kitchen oven, or if available, in an electric furnace or kiln.

CUTTING THE RUBBER MOLD After the rubber has been vulcanized, the aluminum frame is removed from the vulcanizer or furnace and cooled in water, then the rubber mold is separated from the frame and cut into two sections. The cutting of the rubber

mold is one of the most important processes in industrial centrifugal casting. While the end result of cutting open the rubber mold and removing the metal model is the creation of a cavity for the wax impression (the exact duplicate of the metal model), it is of utmost importance that the mold be cut open skillfully so that when molten wax is injected into the mold, the delicate model that is formed can be removed without being damaged.

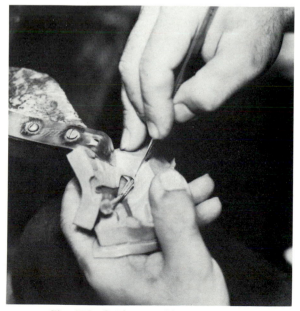

Fig. 270 Cutting a rubber mold held against a can opener

Note from figure 270 that an ordinary beer or soda can opener is used to hold the rubber mold while it is being cut.

Craftsmen can hold the rubber mold in a vise (fig. 271) while cutting. The fins around the edges of the mold formed by the required excessive amount of rubber are cut off with a pair of shears before or after the mold is cut into sections.

Fig. 272 Cut mold with wax pattern

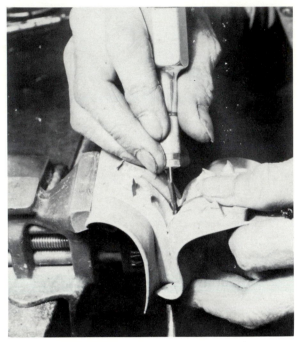

Fig. 271 Cutting the mold held in a vise

The rubber mold is cut into two sections with a very sharp mold knife. First a 1/8″ cut is made around the center of the entire side of the mold. Then the four locks for aligning purposes are cut into the rubber mold. Note the shape of the locks in figure 272. A lock is cut by spreading the rubber by means of the beer opener or while it is in a vise, and making the two outer edge cuts with a curved mold knife blade 1/8″ deep almost straight down into the rubber. Now the rubber is spread apart and the top flat cut is made. Finally, one or two back cuts are made.

From figure 272 one can observe how the entire rubber mold was cut into two sections. Use even strokes with a straight mold knife blade when cutting, and cut away from the sprue rod and from the ring model in order not to damage them. The knife continues to

make smooth cuts gradually away from the model until the rubber mold has been cut in half. The separation of the mold is completed by stretching and then cutting the joining rubber in the shank opening of the ring. The metal model is then carefully removed. When cutting rubber molds away from complicated models, the rubber is stretched to allow the knife to reach hard-to-cut areas.

Note that the core (center) of the rubber part of the ring was hollowed and several cuts were made partly into the rubber from the ring impression, not to remove rubber but to make it more flexible in order to remove the wax without breaking it. These release cuts have another important purpose—they form passages for air to escape when wax is injected into the mold.

Very complex rubber molds have removable cores and flexible or removable sections so that complicated one piece wax models can be made. These cores and cut sections are removed when the wax is being lifted from the mold and replaced again in the mold before the wax is injected.

Imperfections in the rubber mold can be touched up by means of a small spatula or steel modeling tool that has been heated until red hot.

Fig. 273 Rubber mold for ring with removable core

Fig. 275 A commercial wax injector

Fig. 274 Enlarging sprue with an electric spatula

WAX PATTERNS Once the rubber mold has been successfully cut open, wax patterns can be made from the rubber mold by means of a centrifugal machine or wax injector. The wax injector (fig. 275) consists of a covered aluminum pot filled with wax that is electrically heated to keep the wax molten and thermostatically controlled in order to keep the temperature of the wax constant. The casting temperature of most injection waxes is between 145° and 165°F.

Wax should be injected at its lowest possible molten-flow temperature in order to prevent excessive shrinkage of the wax model. Air or hydraulic pressure is used to force the wax into the mold. Use the least possible amount of air pressure when injecting wax into the mold. Usually 3.5 lbs. of air pressure is a sufficient amount of force to fill the cavities of a rubber mold with wax. 5.5 lbs.

of air pressure is recommended for thick wax patterns.

To make a wax model, the rubber mold is held tightly together between two flat and firm pieces of metal (⅛″ aluminum will do) and pressed against the nozzle of the injector, which then injects molten wax into the mold. When the wax cools, the mold is opened, the wax model is removed, the mold is put back together, and wax is once again injected into the mold. The wax injector shown in fig. 275 is used for production work.

The centrifugal method is preferred by craftsmen and small concerns that require a few castings at a time, since wax can be melted quickly in the machine's crucible or in a separate container and poured into the crucible. As can be seen from figure 276, the rubber mold is placed on the end of one of the arms, and the wax crucible, with its nozzle inserted into the sprue opening, is on the inner side. The melted wax is poured into the crucible, then the arm is relased so that it turns quickly, thus forcing the wax into the mold by means of centrifugal pressure. Very intricate and accurate waxes can be obtained from this method. With a little ingenuity, craftsmen can make a wax injector arm to fit onto the metal centrifugal casting machine's base.

Fig. 276 A centrifugal wax injector

Fig. 277 Wax patterns

The craftsman can melt wax in a small ladle held over a bunsen burner. Wax melted in a ladle must not be overheated when injected, for very hot wax will adhere to the rubber mold.

Injection waxes are available in different colors and also in varying degrees of hardness and flexibility for special uses. The green colored wax is preferred by many casters since the patterns made from it are easier to check for flaws.

The rubber mold must be powdered to facilitate removal of the wax. Talc powder, held in a small porous cotton bag so that it can be dusted onto the rubber, is used by practically all commercial casters. Use the powder sparingly, otherwise some of the sharp detail will be lost. Usually it is only necessary to dust talc on the rubber mold after three or four wax patterns have been made. When talcing the mold, bend the rubber in order to open the release cuts as much as possible.

The wax is removed from the mold just after it hardens, which usually takes a minute or two, depending on the thickness of the mold cavity. Often the rubber mold must be cut in spots where it is difficult to remove the wax without breaking it. It is really amazing how easy it is to obtain intricate shapes in wax (fig. 277) by means of judicious cutting of the rubber mold. Slight imperfec-

tions in the wax pattern can be corrected by applying melted wax (paraffin is recommended) with a fine brush, or by scraping the pattern with a razor knife.

Note: Intricate rubber molds can be brushed with a mixture of castor oil diluted with alcohol (50%) or sprayed with a silicon mist for wax removal. Talc powder also can

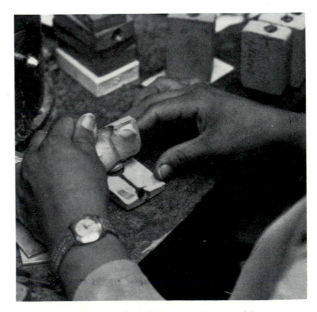

Fig. 278 Opening the rubber mold

be brushed on the rubber mold for wax removal with an ordinary one inch paint brush.

Note: It is essential that the top part of the rubber mold first be separated from the bottom while the bottom part is held down on a table. Then the bottom part of the model can be lifted while the mold is flexed and the wax model can be completely removed. This procedure avoids much wax pattern breakage due to an excessive bending of the rubber mold.

SPRUING After the desired degree of refinement has been achieved in the wax model, the next concern is with the process of spruing. Sprues are the wax wires used to support the wax models in the desired casting position when they are encased in the casting investment. When the sprues are burned out or "lost", passageways are left through which the melted wax can escape from the mold. Later during casting, the sprue system provides passageways through which the molten metal can flow into the mold, thereby duplicating the wax models in metal. Because of the important function of these channels, a sprue system is always carefully constructed so that poor, incomplete castings are avoided.

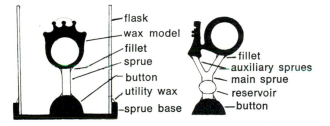

Fig. 279 Parts of a sprue system

Sprue size is largely determined by the size and shape of the wax model. Sprues are attached to the thick and non-decorative sections of the model. The sprues should always be as short (not longer than ¾") as possible in order to prevent the premature cooling of the metal during the casting process. The main sprue should also be thick enough so that the metal does not solidify before the rest of the casting. This is important because during the casting process the molten metal solidifies progressively back toward the main sprue. Furthermore, a thick

sprue system assures that the casting will have adequate molten metal to draw upon while solidifying, thus minimizing shrinkage and porosity. Sprues should be as straight as possible so that the molten metal can easily flow into the mold cavity.

Multiple sprues should be used when a wax pattern has a thick section running to a thin section and then to a thick section. The multiple sprues are attached to the thick sections of the wax pattern.

The model and the sprue must be firmly joined together so that they do not separate during the vacuuming process. A sprue wire can initially be tacked to the wax pattern with sticky wax. Then a heated spatula or needle can be used to apply additional wax to the joint so that the sprue and pattern are welded firmly together. **Note:** Where the sprue and the pattern meet, a fillet should be made so that the molten metal can flow quickly and smoothly into the cavity.

Round wax sprues can be formed by pouring wax into a tube of the desired diameter. Harden the wax by means of cold water. Warm the outside of the tube carefully and by means of a rod push the wax slowly out of the tube.

Fig. 280 Wax rings on sprues and bases

The wax patterns to be cast are mounted on a sprue base. The sprue bases that are used in commercial casting are made of rubber. A metal sprue base (fig. 280) has a center cone that rises from the center of its base and acts as a support for the wax

157

model. Rubber sprue bases have an elevated lip that allows them to fit snugly around a compatible stainless steel flask, which is used to hold the investment. The rubber sprue base will have either an elevated cone or an elevated cone with a recess in the center. In either case, the center portion of the base is filled with wax or plasteline, and the wax pattern is inserted into the plasteline or attached to the wax by means of a heated spatula or a small electric soldering iron.

Craftsmen can invest one wax pattern at a time several ways. If the pattern has an attached wax sprue, this sprue can be attached to a sprue base by warming the end of the sprue carefully and touching it to the base. Additional wax is added to the sprue at the base by applying melted wax with a small brush or with a hot spatula (fig. 280).

The shape of the sprue base was designed for an additional function. When the investment has hardened and the sprue base has been removed, the cone-shaped depression formed from the elevated cone is the beginning of the sprue system and acts as a reservoir (known as the button) for the excess metal that is cast into the flask.

Commercially, many wax patterns are cast at the same time. Note from figure 281 that the wax patterns can be very close to one another; a space of ⅛″ is sufficient. The

Fig. 281 Waxes sprued for casting commercial rings

waxes are either attached individually to the wax sprue base or mounted on a large central sprue. When many small wax models are attached to a large sprue the technique is referred to as "treeing".

After the waxes are attached to the sprue base, they may be dipped into a wetting agent. A good wetting agent reduces surface tension, permitting the water base investment to wet or adhere to the oil base wax. It also removes talc powder and perspiration from the wax. Today, many commercial casters use a wetting agent such as Kerr's vacufilm. Good castings, however, can be obtained by craftsmen without the use of an agent.

Note: A space of ¼″ between a wax pattern and the side of the flask and ½″ between a wax pattern and the top of the flask should be left so that "blow-outs" of the investment are avoided.

A flask cannot be larger than the holding capacity of the casting machine or require more metal than can be melted in the melting furnace.

Craftsmen can form cylinders from sheet metal by means of a grooved seam. A good size flask for rings is: diameter, 1⅜″; height, 2⅝″, as shown in figure 285.

After the wax models have been sprued, the stainless steel flask is snapped into the lip of the rubber sprue base so that the casting investment can be poured into the flask without leaking. The role of the casting investment is to form a heat resistant mold that will accurately reproduce in metal the wax models in the flask. A good investment possesses the power to withstand the high temperatures necessary for removing wax and the higher temperature and pressure of the molten metal without cracking, and is porous enough to let air escape when the molten metal is rapidly cast into the flask. Kerr's Satin Cast, a commercially prepared investment, is highly recommended.

When the investment powder is mixed with water, the resulting mixture is known as a slurry. The proportion of water to investment powder must be accurately controlled in order to obtain uniform and perfect castings. Manufacturers of investment will specify the water-powder ratio that should be used.

The investment is mixed with water by weight in the following proportion: 40 parts of water=100 parts of investment or 6½ ounces of water = 1 pound of investment. Room temperature water, 70°F., should be used, and after it is placed in the mixing bowl, the investment is added slowly and mixed until the batch is uniformly smooth.

The investment is mixed commercially by means of a heavy duty electric mixer; craftsmen can mix the investment with a spoon or with a hand mixer. The mixing time should be from 2 to 4 minutes in order to obtain a smooth batch.

For very fine, intricate castings, slightly more water (up to 2%) can be added to the investment in order to obtain a finer slurry that would flow into smaller crevices more smoothly. For heavier castings, slightly less water (2%) is used with the investment powder in order to obtain a slightly less fluid slurry that would be sturdier for heavier castings.

Fig. 283 Air removed by means of vacuum

ous, yet simple method is employed to remove the trapped air. Immediately after the investment is mixed in the bowl, the bowl is placed under a bell jar and the air is pumped out by means of a vacuum pump. By reducing the air pressure in the bell jar, the air in the bowl exerts enough pressure to force its way out of the investment. Much of the air, however, is eliminated by vapor pressure, for room temperature water will boil when the air pressure is reduced sufficiently. The boiling (vapor pressure) will completely eliminate all air. The slurry in the mixing bowl is vacuumed until it rises and then collapses—this takes from 30 to 45 seconds. 10 seconds after the investment collapses (breaks), the vacuum pump should be turned off and the vacuum should be released.

RECOMMENDED PROPORTIONING CHART FOR KERR INVESTMENTS

SATIN CAST 20/SUPERVEST/BRIL-CAST 20/ CRISTOBALITE INLAY

Wt. of Investment in Pounds	RECOMMENDED PROPORTIONING FOR HEAVY CASTING 38/100			RECOMMENDED PROPORTIONING FOR REGULAR CASTING 40/100			RECOMMENDED PROPORTIONING FOR EXTRA FINE CASTING 42/100		
	WATER		Yields Approx.	WATER		Yields Approx.	WATER		Yields Approx.
	cc.	oz.	Cu. In.	cc.	oz.	Cu. In.	cc.	oz.	Cu. In.
1 lb.	173	6	21.3	182	6.4	21.9	191	6.72	22.5
5 lbs.	862	30.4	106	908	32	110	953	33.6	112
10 lbs.	1725	60.8	213	1816	64	219	1907	67.2	225
15 lbs.	2588	91.2	320	2724	96	328	2860	100.8	338
20 lbs.	3450	121.6	426	3632	128	438	3814	134.4	450
25 lbs.	4312	152	532	4540	160	548	4767	168	562

NOTE— to determine flask content in cu. ins.

Volume of round flask = 0.7854 X dia.^{2} X height

Volume of square flask = width X length X height

Fig. 282

Above is a chart that is recommended by Kerr for mixing their Satin Cast powder. **Remember:** 40/100 is used for most castings.

After mixing, before and after the investment is poured into the flask, trapped air bubbles must be removed. If not removed, these trapped air bubbles will appear as small metal balls on the metal casting. An ingeni-

The bell jar rests on a base with a thin rubber top for an air-tight fit, and the entire base is vibrated (joggled) after the vacuum has been released to insure that all air bubbles are removed. The investment is then poured slowly down the sides of the flask until it rises a little above the wax patterns. It is very important that the investment is poured carefully into the flask so that the wax patterns are not disturbed or broken. The flask is placed under the bell jar again to completely pump out as much air as possible. It is a good idea to place a removable one inch high collar made from either masking tape or rubber tubing around the top of the flask before vacuuming in order to prevent the investment from bubbling out of the top

Fig. 284 Pouring investment into the flasks

of the flask during vacuuming. Again, after the vacuum is released, the base of the bell jar is joggled to insure that the investment flows into the crevices of the models and to loosen very small bubbles from the wax patterns. After vacuuming, additional investment is added to fill the flask, which is then vibrated to level the additional investment.

The setting, also called working, time of commercial investment powders is approximately nine (9) minutes. This means that from the time the investment is mixed to the time it begins to harden is approximately 9 minutes.

The "working time" of the investment process starts as soon as the investment powder is added to the water and ends when the flasks are totally filled (capped) with investment and left undisturbed to harden.

Although the best casting results are obtained with vacuuming, good castings can be made without a vacuum system, and schools and craftsmen should be encouraged to cast even if a vacuum system is not available. Flasks can be placed on a commercial vibrator or set on the table of a jig saw and then vibrated to remove air bubbles from the wax models.

Note: Single waxes, even intricate ones, can be invested by craftsmen without using the vacuum method by carefully painting the wax with the investment and then by pouring the rest of the investment around the wax. By carefully vibrating the flask, most of the air which would cause irregularities in the casting would be removed.

After the investment has hardened sufficiently (approximately one hour) the rubber sprue base can be removed from the flask.

WAX ELIMINATION The purpose of the burnout process is to eliminate the wax and moisture from the mold without disturbing the investment around the model chambers. A second function of the burnout process is to mature the investment so that the flask can withstand the thermal shock from the molten metal that rapidly enters it during casting. In order to melt, and then eliminate the wax in the flasks, a furnace or kiln capable of reaching a temperature of at least 1400°F. must be used.

The burnout process begins when the investment flasks that have been allowed to dry for approximately two hours (but have not completely lost all of their moisture) are placed in a burnout furnace. The investment should be heated when moist for dry investment tends to crack when heated. Also, water turns to steam when heated and the steam helps to eliminate the wax from the walls of pattern cavities in the investment. The flasks are placed in the burnout kiln with the sprue side down so that the wax may flow out easily when heated. The eliminated wax, since it contains waste materials, should not be used again.

The ideal burnout furnace is a front loading, gas fired, muffled kiln that has a spe-

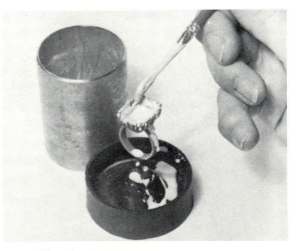

Fig. 285 Painting investment on model
with small brush

cially constructed floor which facilitates wax elimination and air circulation. Such a burnout furnace should have a pyrometer and a cam operated unit that automatically regulates the burnout cycle. Schools, craftsmen, and small manufacturing jewelers can use an electric burnout furnace like the one shown in figure 286. These furnaces should have a thermocouple connected to a pyrometer to indicate the temperature inside the furnace, and a rheostat to regulate the temperature. Small electric enameling kilns can also be used for burnout. If a furnace does not have a flue, the door of the furnace should be left open slightly to permit air to circulate throughout the furnace and to allow wax fumes to be eliminated during burnout. To promote wax elimination inside of the flasks, the flasks should be elevated by placing them on top of ceramic star stilts, triangular rods, or a wire mesh enameling rack, especially if the floor of the furnace is not ribbed.

Fig. 286 6" x 6" electric burnout furnace for schools and craftsmen

Successful castings have been made in school shops by heating and burning out the wax from small flasks with a torch. A furnace, however, is better.

The temperature of the burnout furnace must be raised gradually (from 3 to 6 hours) from room temperature until a temperature of 1350°F. is reached. While most of the

wax will melt out of the flasks at 300°F., the carbon residue is not eliminated until a temperature of 1350°F. has been achieved. This is usually the maximum temperature of the burnout cycle. The burnout time depends on the size and number of flasks in the furnace and also on the size of the furnace.

WAX ELIMINATION

SUGGESTED BURN-OUT CYCLES

The following burn-out cycles are recommended:

Select proper burn-out cycle according to size of flasks.

5 Hour Cycle	8 Hour Cycle	12 Hour Cycle
For flasks up to 2½" x 2½" preheat furnace to 300°F.	For flasks up to 3½" x 4" preheat furnace to 300°F.	For flasks up to 4" x 8" preheat furnace to 300°F.
1 hour- 300°F.	2 hour- 300°F.	2 hour- 300°F.
1 hour- 700°F.	2 hour- 700°F.	2 hour- 600°F.
2 hour-1350°F.	3 hour-1350°F.	2 hour- 900°F.
1 hour-See note	1 hour-See note	4 hour-1350°F.
		2 hour-See note

Note: During last hour the temperature must be adjusted so that flasks are at correct temperature for casting.

Note from the above chart that the temperature of the furnace is gradually raised until the wax is completely eliminated (1350°F.) and then lowered and held at the proper flask temperature of the metal being cast. The proper flask temperature is one that is high enough to keep the metal in a fluid condition as it travels through the sprues, yet cool enough to allow the metal to solidify once it has reached the cavity. Proper investment flask temperature is therefore very critical in the casting process. The proper flask temperature is approximately 1000°F.—1100°F. for white gold; 900°F.—1000°F. for yellow gold; 800°F.—850°F. for silver; and 900°F. for bronze.

The flask in the burnout furnace can be held for several hours, if necessary, at the required temperature before metal is cast into it. The flask should not be removed from the furnace until the metal is ready to be cast for if the investment is permitted to cool too much it will shrink and cracks will develop which will affect the castings; also, the molten metal will chill and harden before it could get into fine crevices.

One can tell if the burnout is complete without a pyrometer on a furnace by observing the color of the investment near the sprue opening. Dark gray spots on the surface of the investment around the sprue opening and a flame coming out of the sprue opening indicate insufficient burnout. When the investment is a chalky white without any flame from the sprue opening, the burnout is complete. **Note:** If the temperature in the burnout furnace exceeds 1500°F., the investment will start to deteriorate and poor castings will result.

Fig. 287   Flask with dark areas on investment surface has had insufficient burnout (Courtesy of Kerr Manufacturing Company)

While the heat of the oven burns out the wax, preparation should be made for the casting process. The casting metal should be cut and weighed; the crucibles that are to be used to cast and melt the metal should be cleaned; and, if the crucibles are new, the inside of the crucibles should be "glazed" with a coating of boric acid which will prevent small particles of the crucible from dropping into the molten metal.

Weight of Required Metals

14K Gold = 13 times weight of wax
Silver   = 10 times weight of wax
Platinum = 21 times weight of wax

There are two methods that are used for determining the amount of metal that is needed for the casting process. The first method is to weigh all of the wax that comprises the models and sprue system of the flask on a triple beam scale. This weight is then multiplied by the specific gravity of the metal to be cast. The second method

is to measure the amount of water that is displaced by the wax models and their sprue systems when they are immersed into a graduated cylinder; and then to add an appropriate amount of metal to a second cylinder that contains the same amount of water until the water is brought up to the same level as in the first cylinder.

Extra metal (20%) is added for the button (metal in the sprue base after casting) which will force and feed metal into the cavities in the investment during the casting cycle.

CASTING PROCEDURE The easiest phase of the entire operation is the actual casting procedure. The centrifugal machine used in schools and by craftsmen for most gold and silver jewelry casting is similar to the one the dentist uses (fig. 288). A heavy spring in the base of the machine is employed to develop the necessary centrifugal force. The force developed is tremendous and is dependent on the speed of rotation, length of the arm, and the weight of the metal.

Note: Craftsmen and schools can use the same centrifugal machine for casting the wax and metal. A special arm can easily be made to fit onto the base for wax casting. The machine should be guarded by a metal band.

The casting machine in figure 289 was bolted to a cement block poured two thirds the height of the can. This is an ideal arrange-

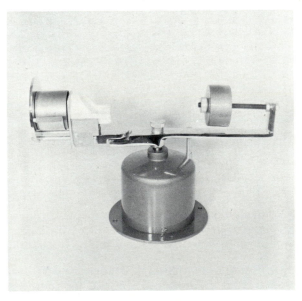

Fig. 288   "Kerr" centrifugal machine

Fig. 289 Centrifugal machine set in an ash can

ment for schools and small shops since the ash can forms a safety guard, a minimum of space is used, the casting machine can be moved to where the metal is to be melted; then the machine can be stored where desired when not used.

The spring-driven horizontal turning centrifugal casting machine must be mounted so that it is perfectly level in order to prevent unnecessary and dangerous vibrations when the casting arm spins.

A metal shield should surround the casting machine to protect the operator from the spinning action of the arm and from molten metal and parts of the machine that may fly out and away from the center of the machine. The shield also will help recover any gold or silver which may accidently spill or fly out of the crucible when the arm revolves.

Note from figure 289 that the flask is placed on the end of one arm of the machine and the nozzle of the crucible to hold the molten metal is placed into the sprue opening of the flask. The other end of the machine's arm has adjustable weights to balance the arms.

A heavy spring or, for commercial casting machines, an electric motor in the base of the machine is employed to turn the arm in order to develop the necessary centrifugal force, which is out or away from the center; and this force injects the molten metal into

the flask. All the metal in the crucible enters the flask on the first rotation, and the arm continues to spin so that the metal remains in the flask until it solidifies.

It is easy to use the spring-operated casting machine. To wind the arm, merely turn two or three revolutions in the opposite direction from the spring-driven rotation. The arm is then held from turning by a rod in the base of the machine which is dropped when the arm is ready to be released. The metal, gold or silver, may be melted, as it is in commercial plants, in a graphite or silicon carbide crucible in a gas operated furnace and then poured into the casting machine's crucible, or it may be melted directly in the machine's crucible with a gas blowpipe or by means of electricity. **Note:** To check oxidation of the metal when it is being melted, a small amount of powdered borax flux is added.

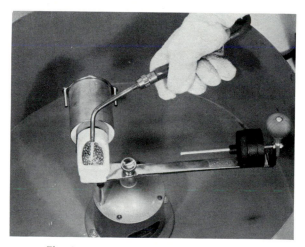

Fig. 290 Melting metal in a spring-driven centrifugal casting machine

Immediately after the metal in the machine's crucible has become molten, the flask is removed from the burnout kiln with tongs and placed in position on the flask cradle of the machine. Carefully slide the crucible and crucible shield against the flask so that the hole in the crucible is aligned with the sprue opening of the flask. Continue to apply heat to the crucible with a torch once the flask is in position. When the metal shines and begins to spin, its fluidity should be checked with a carbon stirring rod. Once the metal begins to "roll" like mercury, the torch should be lifted away from the molten metal, and the casting arm released so that it spins and the developed centrifugal force injects the molten metal into the flask. The casting formed, due to a continuous application of strong pressure by centrifugal force, is very dense, more so than castings made using other methods.

The arm of the machine must be balanced. This is done by placing a cool flask, crucible and metal in position on a straight arm and then loosening the center retaining nut. Adjust and tighten the weights on the arm so that only a slight tap is required to tilt it. Note that the casting arm rotates on a horizontal plane for casting gold and silver.

Note also that the arm pivots (is "broken") on the end where the flask and crucible are. Why? This prevents molten metal from sliding out of the side of the crucible before the rotating arm develops sufficient speed to create a centrifugal force strong enough to force the molten metal straight out into the flask.

The flask and crucible end of the arm is held in the "broken" position shown in figure 290 when the metal is melted in or poured into the machine's crucible.

The vertical rotating arm type of casting machine (fig. 291) is preferred by commercial jewelers for casting platinum. The crucible and flask are assembled as shown in the picture. The platinum is melted directly in the crucible by means of a gas-oxygen torch. The arm, due to four powerful coil springs, has the very quick starting speed necessary for platinum casting, and the fact that the arm rotates vertically eliminates the possibility that the arm may hit the torch.

IMPORTANT: The temperature to which the metal is heated before entering the flask is critical if flawless castings are to be achieved. Underheating of the metal will cause it to solidify before it has filled all of the crevices of the mold. Overheating of the metal will increase shrinkage during cooling and make it more likely that the castings will be porous. The molten metal is cast when it has turned into a clear liquid with a mirror-like surface. 18 karat gold is cast at approximately 1800°F., silver at 1710°F., and platinum at 3200°F.

Many large casting manufacturers use casting machines that are designed for a higher rate of production and greater efficiency than

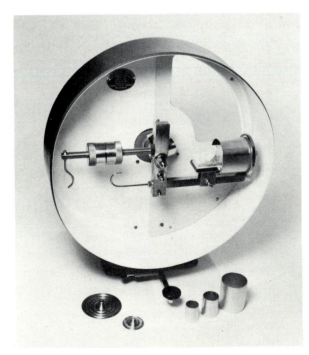

Fig. 291 Vertical rotating arm machine for platinum casting

Fig. 292 Ultra Cast high frequency centrifugal induction casting machine with electric eye for metal melt control

is possible with a conventional centrifugal casting machine. A high frequency induction-melting casting machine utilizes an immersion pyrometer that will accurately read the temperature of the metal as it is being melted. The metal is melted by an induction coil which encircles a crucible mounted on a rotating casting arm. When the metal has reached its proper casting temperature (which is constantly being recorded on a digital display panel), a flask is placed on the casting arm, the induction coil is retracted by means of a lever, and a motor that rotates the casting arm is activated by a switch. Some machines can also cover the melting crucible with a layer of argon gas. The argon gas keeps air out of the crucible in order to prevent oxidation of the metal while it is being melted.

Vacuum casting machines have become very popular and are recommended for casting heavy rings and large objects. The flasks that are used in vacuum casting are perforated. As soon as the metal to be cast is molten, the flask is placed in the vacuum chamber of the machine, a suction valve is opened, and a strong vacuum is created around the flask. When the molten metal is poured into the flask it is immediately sucked into the model cavities of the mold by the pull of the vacuum.

After the metal has been cast, the flask is removed from the casting machine with metal tongs. In order for the cast metal to crystallize properly for less brittle and easier to work castings, flasks, after the casting opera-

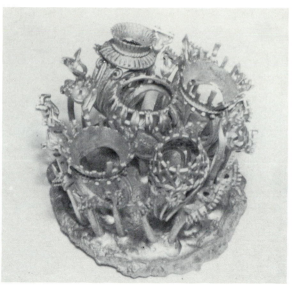
Fig. 294 Gold rings removed from investment

tion, should be left to cool in air as follows: yellow gold—5 minutes; white gold—10 minutes; platinum—10 minutes; silver—5 minutes.

The flask is then immersed in a bucket of cold water. This sudden change of temperature will usually loosen the investment from the flask, and the castings can be separated from the investment. Small pieces of investment can be removed with a stiff brush or an air pressured water gun. Next the base of the castings (the button) and then the individual sprues of the castings are cut off with a sprue cutter. Then the castings are pickled (cleaned in acid), washed in water, and then dried. The castings require very little filing to complete.

INFORMATION FOR MODEL COPIES Commercial manufacturers and model makers have developed a method (somewhat unethical) of copying other manufacturers' cast objects. This is done by obtaining, often by purchasing in a retail store, a jewelry object which the model maker or manufacturer desires to copy. All stones are removed from rings and the joint and catch are also removed from pins.

The thickness of the metal on jewelry objects to be copied must be increased. Why? When a jewelry object is cast, the metal shrinks when it solidifies. If rubber molds,

Fig. 293 Metal being poured into small vacuum caster

165

Fig. 295 A small plating outfit for model copying

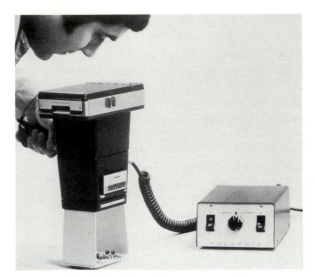

Fig. 296 Polaroid camera used for
jewelry documentation

waxes, and then castings were made from the purchased jewelry object, the castings obtained would be too thin.

The metal in the jewelry object is increased by plating with copper. Figure 295 shows the type of small plating outfit that is used commercially. The outfit will deposit metal on the model at the rate of approximately .0005 to .001 inches per hour. A slow plating deposit is necessary for a smooth surface—14 to 20 hours is usually sufficient to add the necessary metal.

After plating, a rubber mold is made as explained previously in this chapter and as many pieces of jewelry as desired can be cast and manufactured.

Many jewelers take pictures of their finished models or jewelry for catalogues and for their own records.

Fig. 296A Ring, pendant, earclips   Takashi Wada

STONES AND SETTINGS

1. PRECIOUS AND SEMI-PRECIOUS STONES

Precious and semi-precious gemstones have traditionally been an intregal part of the design and construction of jewelry. Although jewelry is frequently made solely of metal, most fine precious jewelry is composed of both metal and gemstones. Beauty, value, rareness, texture, color, transparency, and tradition are the reasons why certain minerals have been classified as gemstones and are incorporated with precious metals to create pieces of precious jewelry.

The diamond is known for its brilliance, fire, and hardness; rubies and emeralds are very rare and have very distinctive and beautiful colors; a fine opal is prized because of

Fig. 297 Pendant   **Legg Brothers Limited**

its fiery display of colors; aquamarines exhibit an alluring blue-green transparency; and the golden tiger-eye is valued because of its fine fibrous luster.

Many of the gemstones set in jewelry have long been credited with possessing magical powers and the ability to give protection against certain illnesses and misfortunes. The sapphire prevents poverty and death by poison. Pearls bestow purity and innocence. The diamond gives the wearer long life and joy. The Chinese have a great belief in the fortune-bestowing powers of jade. According to the laws of astrology, there is a stone for each sign of the zodiac.

The precious gemstones are the diamond, ruby, sapphire, and emerald. In lieu of a better term, the word "semi-precious" has become the accepted classification for all other gemstones. The value of a gemstone is determined by its beauty of color, rarity, hardness, type and quality of its cut, and its size. In most cases, an increase in the size of a stone means a much more than arithmetical increase in its unit value. The rarity and subsequent value that is placed on a gemstone is usually the most crucial variable in determining the price of a piece of jewelry.

NATURAL STONES Natural stones, as the name indicates, have been formed by nature and are found as minerals in or on the earth's surface.

SYNTHETIC STONES The scarcity and high price of precious gemstones have been an incentive for the manufacturing of synthetic gemstones. Most synthetic stones are formed by fusing the same chemicals the natural stones are composed of by means of the intense heat of the oxygen and hydrogen flame. Though manufactured, they are essentially the same as natural stones since they contain the same chemicals and possess identical physical properties; that is, they are just as hard and have practically the same specific gravity and index of refraction. Synthetic stones can be distinguished from the natural by slight uneven distribution of color, structure lines, and the presence of air bubbles under a microscope.

Rubies, sapphires, and spinel are manufactured synthetically successfully and by adding various colors to the above, many other stones, such as the emerald and aquamarine, can be copied. Even the star sapphire and ruby can be made synthetically. Since 1948, a Californian scientist, Carroll Chatham, has perfected a secret process for making truly remarkable synthetic emeralds by a synthesis process.

The ultimate achievement: February, 1955, General Electric announced that their scientists were able to make synthetic diamonds. Synthetic diamonds are now being used in industry, and for many purposes (drills, dies) they are superior to natural diamonds.

IMITATION STONES Imitation stones are manufactured from glass or plastic. They are comparatively inexpensive, and they can be detected easily by means of a file since they can be filed, whereas most stones cannot.

DOUBLETS Two pieces of stone are glued together with an invisible cement to form a larger, more expensive-appearing stone. A true doublet consists of a genuine material; a false doublet consists of a genuine crown (top piece) and a glass or less expensive material as the pavilion (bottom). The two sections are usually joined at the girdle (center) or slightly below in order to make detection difficult. Rubies, garnets, opals and diamonds are used for doublets.

TRIPLETS is the name given to stones made by gluing three sections together.

WEIGHTS Most natural and synthetic stones are weighed and sold by the carat. One carat equals 1/5 of a gram or 3 and 1/16 grains. One pennyweight contains approximately 7.9 carats.

The diamond carat is subdivided into 100 parts or points; thus, a fifty-point diamond is equal to ½ of a carat and a twenty-five point diamond equals ¼ of a carat.

Note: The carat as a unit of weight is not related to the term karat as used as a unit of the fineness or purity of gold.

Strands of cultured pearls are weighed by the momme (Japanese). 1 momme = 18.75 carats.

SIZES The diamond point and carat are also used to designate the diamond's size. Other round stones are sized by numbers (See chart, fig. 298). A number 30 stone equals the size of a one carat diamond. Rectangular and oval stones are sized by millimeters. Thus, a 10/8 stone is 10 millimeters long and 8 millimeters wide. Pearls are sized by millimeters.

HARDNESS Hardness of a stone may be defined as the resistance that the stone offers to abrasion or scratching. If the polished surface of a gemstone is soft enough to be easily scratched, it will soon lose its attractiveness. The harder stone will scratch the softer. Dust is largely sand which is a form of quartz (hardness 7). Stones above hardness 7 will not be scratched by dust and are considered very hard. Hardness sets containing fragments of stones are available for testing purposes.

The hardness of different stones and minerals has been arranged by a mineralogist, Moh, in the following scale.

1. Talc	6. Feldspar
2. Gypsum	7. Quartz
3. Calcite	8. Topaz
4. Fluorite	9. Ruby or Sapphire
5. Apatite	10. Diamond

A steel file has a hardness of 6½ and glass 5½. Thus a file can be used to identify glass imitation stones since the file will scratch the glass. The file, however, will not scratch quartz (hardness 7) and stones above quartz on Moh's scale.

The diamond, hardness 10, is much harder than the ruby or sapphire, hardness 9, than the Moh scale indicates. In a more scientific scale (the National Bureau of Standards scale) the diamond is listed as 6200-6500, sapphire as 1400-1450, topaz as 1250, and quartz as 710-790.

TOUGHNESS Toughness is the ability of a stone to withstand breakage. Hardness and toughness are very different properties and

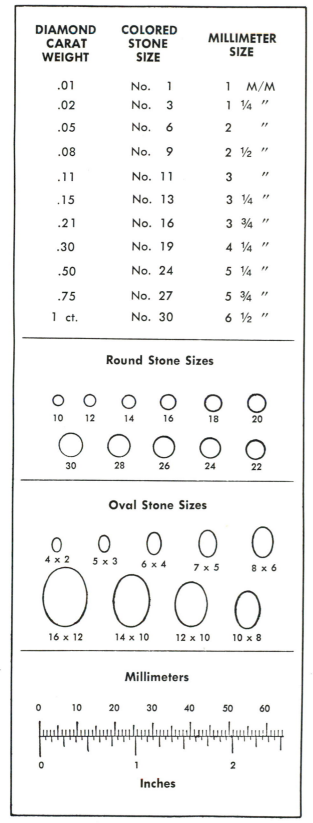

DIAMOND CARAT WEIGHT	COLORED STONE SIZE	MILLIMETER SIZE
.01	No. 1	1 M/M
.02	No. 3	1 ¼ "
.05	No. 6	2 "
.08	No. 9	2 ½ "
.11	No. 11	3 "
.15	No. 13	3 ¼ "
.21	No. 16	3 ¾ "
.30	No. 19	4 ¼ "
.50	No. 24	5 ¼ "
.75	No. 27	5 ¾ "
1 ct.	No. 30	6 ½ "

Round Stone Sizes

10 12 14 16 18 20

30 28 26 24 22

Oval Stone Sizes

4 x 2   5 x 3   6 x 4   7 x 5   8 x 6

16 x 12   14 x 10   12 x 10   10 x 8

Millimeters

0 10 20 30 40 50 60

0   1   2

Inches

Fig. 298 Diamond carat weights, colored stone sizes, millimeters and inches

each may vary within any given stone. The diamond, the hardest material known, is not considered a very tough material for it may be cleaved or fractured easily, sometimes by dropping or by the prongs of a setting. Jade, a comparatively soft stone, is the toughest of all stones since it resists breakage.

CUTS AND SHAPES Stones are cut and shaped to enhance their beauty and to match the design of the jewelry object. The simplest and oldest type of cut is the cabochon (fig. 300). The shape of cabochon stones may be round or oval. Opaque and many translucent stones are generally cut cabochon. Examples: turquoise, star sapphire, ruby, opal, quartz (many varieties), garnet, moonstone, cat's eye.

Fig. 299 Ring   **Allan Lindsay**

All other cuts are based on facets, that is, smooth plane surfaces symmetrically placed of pleasing geometric outline. Several faceted cut stones are shown in figure 300. Facets create reflecting planes so that light rays entering the stone from the crown (top) will be reflected back also through the crown to give the stone maximum fire and color.

A cameo has a raised carved design; an intaglio has a design cut or engraved into the stone; and a cuvette has a hollow background with a raised design.

169

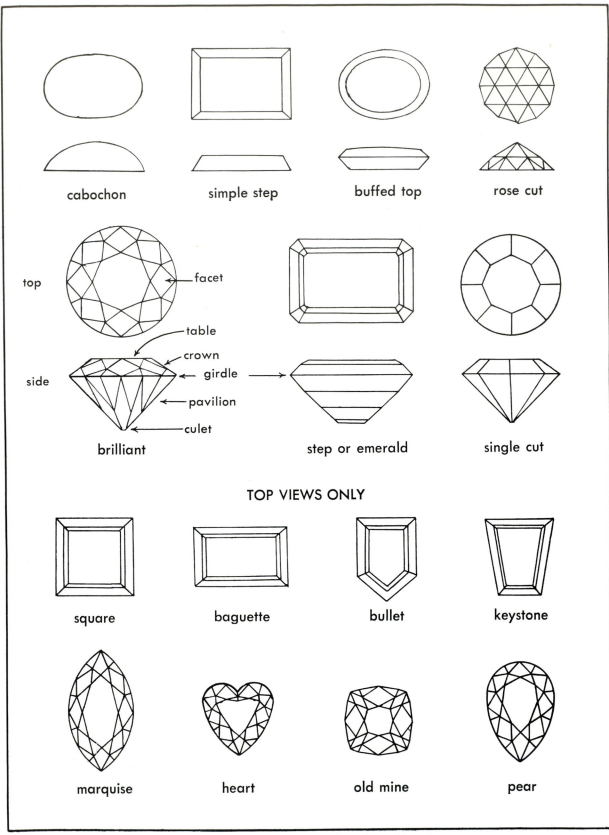

cabochon   simple step   buffed top   rose cut

top

facet

table

crown

side

girdle

pavilion

culet

brilliant   step or emerald   single cut

TOP VIEWS ONLY

square   baguette   bullet   keystone

marquise   heart   old mine   pear

Fig. 300 Shapes of precious and semi-precious stones

SPECIFIC GRAVITY The specific gravity of a stone is the comparison of the weight of the stone to the weight of an equal volume of water. Thus a stone with a specific gravity of 2.5 will be 2½ times heavier than an equal volume of water.

REFRACTIVE INDEX A ray of light going into a stone is bent. The degree of bending is the same for similar stones and is called the refractive index. The diamond has the greatest refractive index of all natural stones—2.42. Stones with high refractive indexes also reflect (throw back) greater amounts of light. Thus, most light which penetrates and is bent by the upper (crown) facets of the well-cut diamond will also be reflected by the lower (pavilion) facets of the stone and returned to the eye of the observer—the reason for the diamond's brilliance. Synthetic titania has a refractive index of between 2.62 and 2.90.

The refractive index (R.I.) number, 2.42, 2.62, etc., is found by dividing the speed of light in air (V) by the speed of light in the stone (V'); or mathematically speaking:

$$R.I. = \frac{V}{V'} = \frac{\sin i}{\sin r}$$

REFRACTION When a ray of light passes through a stone and emerges as a single ray, the stone has single refraction. If the light emerges as a double ray, the stone has double refraction. The diamond, glass, spinel, and garnet are the only transparent stones with single refraction; all other transparent stones have double refraction. The zircon and peridot are so strongly double refractive that their base edges appear double when viewed through the top or table facet.

CHROMATIC DISPERSION White light passing through a prism or facets of a stone is separated into its component colors: namely, red, orange, yellow, green, blue, and violet. This separation in the diamond is very great, so great that often practically pure colors (fire) can be seen. Chromatic dispersion of white light by synthetic titania is six to eight times greater than it is in the diamond.

PLEOCHROISM The garnet, spinel, and diamond (isotropic minerals) have the same color when observed from any direction. All other stones have different shades of the same color and sometimes many different colors when viewed from different directions

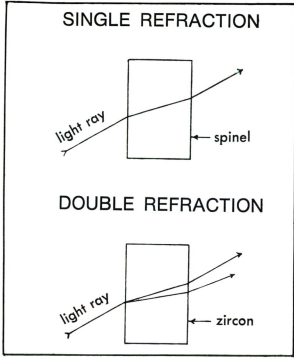

Fig. 301

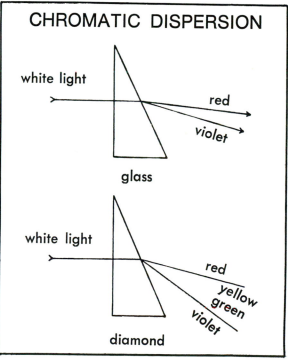

Fig. 302

171

—this is known as pleochroism. Dichroism is the name given to stones with only two color effects.

Fig. 303 Pendant　　　　**Donald Wright**

DESCRIPTION OF THE STONES

Mineralogists arrange stones that have the same chemical and physical properties into families. Below is a practical description of the important commercial stone families and also a description of the valuable independent stones.

H . . . . hardness
Sp. Gr. . . . . .specific gravity
R. I. . . . . .refractive index

QUARTZ H. 7 Sp. Gr. 2.76 R.I. 1.54-1.55

Quartz, the most abundant of all minerals, chemically is silicon dioxide (the same as white sand). Its hexagonal crystals are found in almost every color, in the pure colorless form, and also transparent, translucent, and opaque. Some of the better known varieties of quartz with their associated colors are:

Crystal . . . . colorless
Jasper . . . . dull reddish
Carnelian . . . . reddish
Chrysoprase . . . . green
Black onyx . . . . black
Chalcedony . . . . blue

Amethyst—pale violet to dark purple in color. Clear, dark faceted stones are scarce, popular, and expensive.

Tiger's-eye — banded yellow and reddish brown fibers. The wavy, silky sheen in tiger's-eye is known as **Chatoyancy.**

Bloodstone — dull greenish, opaque, with spots of red jasper.

Agates — banded or striped, sometimes mossy and occasionally with imbedded insects.

Petrified wood — quartz that displaced the cellular structure of wood.

Citrene — light brown and is sometimes called Topaz-Quartz.

CORUNDUM H. 9 Sp. Gr. 4.0 R.I. 1.76-1.77

Corundum chemically is aluminum oxide and its crystals are hexagonal. After the diamond, corundum is the hardest natural stone. Good quality stones are rare and very expensive.

Ruby is the red variety.

Sapphire is the blue variety.

Sapphire is the name also given to yellow (yellow sapphire), green (green sapphire) and other colored corundums.

Occasionally, due to very small inclusions of rutile arranged in a hexagonal pattern, a star-like effect, called **Asterism,** is created in sapphires and (very rare) rubies.

BERYL H. 8 Sp. Gr. 2.6 R.I. 1.57-1.58

Beryl is chemically beryllium aluminum silicate. It is a hard but also a brittle mineral.

Emerald is the green variety.
Aquamarine is the blue to sea-green variety
Morganite is pink.
Golden Beryl is golden-yellow.

CHRYSOBERYL H. 8.5 Sp. Gr. 3.5 R. I. 1.75

Chrysoberyl is chemically beryllium aluminate. It is harder and more durable than beryl.

Alexandrite is bluish-green in daylight and purplish-red in artificial light. First found in the Ural mountains and given the Russian Czar's name in 1830.

Cat's Eye is a greenish, fibrous, chatoyant variety which when cut cabochon resembles a cat's eye. The stone is rare and expensive. **Note:** An inexpensive stone in the quartz family, tiger's-eye, should not be mistaken for cat's eye.

JADE Jade consists of two very tough minerals of almost similar appearance, jadeite and nephrite.

Jadeite H. 6 to 7 Sp. Gr. 3.3 R.I. 1.66-1.68 Jadeite (often called Chinese Jade) is semi-transparent to opaque; the color varies from greenish-white to emerald green.

Nephrite H. 6 to 6½ Sp. Gr. 3 R.I. 1.60-1.63 Nephrite (often called New Zealand Jade) is translucent to opaque and the color varies from white to dark green.

GARNET H. 7-7.5 Sp. Gr. 3.4-4.3
Garnets are found in nearly every color but blue. The transparent red variety is accepted as the usual garnet, and, though it is very attractive, it is not highly prized since it is very abundant.

Pyrope (Bohemian garnet) the ruby red variety is the most popular garnet.

Almandine is a deep red variety which is usually cut cabochon. Carbuncle, a once popular name for a high cabochon-cut almandine garnet, occasionally is found with a four ray star, an interesting type of asterism.

Demantoid is a grass green variety of the mineral andradite. It is rare and good specimens are expensive.

ZIRCON H. 7.5 Sp. Gr. 4-4.8 R.I. 1.79
Zircons rival diamonds in brilliance and fire and are used in inexpensive jewelry to imitate diamonds. It is the heaviest transparent stone known. The popular colors, white, golden brown and blue, are produced by heating the natural brown or yellow stone. Zircons are very brittle and highly double refractive.

Hyacinth is a reddish-brown zircon.

DIAMOND H. 10 Sp. Gr. 3.5 R.I. 2.42
The diamond is the hardest and generally acknowledged as the most precious of all stones. Pure white or bluish-white transparent flawless diamonds (which are perfectly cut) are known as gems. Diamonds that are slightly tinted brown or yellow are known as off-color. Chemically diamonds are composed of pure carbon. Since the stone is an excellent conductor of heat it is cold when touched. It is not attacked by acids.

Fig. 304 Diamond earrings

The beautiful fire of the diamond is due to its high dispersion; that is, white light entering it is broken up into its separate parts and when the light emerges, practically pure colors can be seen. To bring out its maximum brilliance and fire, the brilliant (round) diamond is usually cut with 58 facets; 33 on top or crown, 25 on base or pavilion.

In 1919, Marcel Tolkowsky, a European cutter and mathematician, developed the ideal proportions for a brilliant cut diamond (fig. 305) to yield maximum brilliancy with a high degree of fire. Today, most diamond rough is sawed, not cleaved, with circular diamond saws into sections parallel to the table. The tendency is for the cutter to obtain more total weight from the rough by making the crown thinner than the 16.2% thickness shown in figure 305. This produces a diamond with a wide table and shorter crown facets; however, it also sacrifices some of the diamond's fire.

Note: The girdle of a diamond is not sharp —it would chip if it were. The thickness of

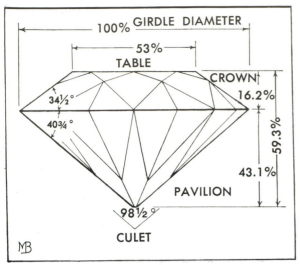

Fig. 305 Ideal proportions for brilliant diamond

the girdle should average approximately 1½% of the girdle diameter of the stone.

"Fisheye" is the name given to a diamond whose crown (top) lacks brilliancy. This is due to a thin pavilion.

"Dark center" is a diamond with a thick pavilion. Light escapes from the pavilion facets and the crown appears dark or black.

"Melee" is the name of small full cut (58 facets) diamonds — from 5 to as many as 35 to the carat.

Single cut stones are very small diamonds with 17 facets. They are sized from 5 points (1/20 of a carat) down to ¼ point (1/400 of a carat).

SPINEL H. 8 Sp. Gr. 3.6 R.I. 1.72

Spinel is chemically magnesium aluminate.

Spinel occurs in almost all colors. It was often mistaken for the ruby and sapphire since it is found in the same gravel; however, spinel is softer, has a lower specific gravity and has single refraction. The mineral is now made synthetically.

TOPAZ H. 8 Sp. Gr. 3.5 R.I. 1.61-1.62

Almost any yellow stone was formerly called topaz and even today citrine is sometimes called topaz-quartz. Though the stone is found in many colors and colorless, the deep, yellow variety, called precious topaz, is mainly used as a stone. It can easily be distinguished from citrine by its deep yellow color and by its greater hardness, brilliancy and specific gravity.

TOURMALINE H. 7-7.5 Sp. Gr. 2.9-3.2 R.I. 1.63

Tourmaline is a complex borosilicate. It has a vitreous (glass-like) lustre. Its dichroism is very strong. Green is the color commonly associated with the stone.

Indicolite is blue.

Rubellite is rose-red or pink

Tourmaline is found in more colors than any other stone and its hexagonal crystals are often multi-colored.

PERIDOT H. 6.5-7 Sp. Gr. 3.2-3.6 R.I. 1.68

Peridot is the yellow to greenish variety of the mineral olivine. It is strongly double refractive. Since the natural stone is too soft to be used in rings, synthetic spinel with a peridot color is used as the August birthstone in rings.

LAPIS LAZULI H. 5.5 Sp. Gr. 2.85 R.I. 1.50

A rich blue opaque stone, spotted with desirable silvery white specks of iron pyrite. Afghanistan is the source of the best quality stone. Swiss lapis is an imitation dyed jasper (quartz).

MALACHITE AND AZURITE H. 3.5 Sp. Gr. 3.7 to 4.0.

Malachite and Azurite are hydrated copper carbonates. Malachite is green and azurite is blue. Both minerals are sometimes intimately associated. Malachite is cut cabochon and is popular in bandings of different shades of green, which sometimes are mixed with blue.

MOONSTONE H. 6 Sp. Gr. 2.55 R.I. 1.53-1.54

Moonstone is a variety of the mineral feldspar with a bluish, pearly reflection. Cut cabochon. The finest moonstones are found in Ceylon.

HEMATITE H. 6

A coal-black appearing stone that is chemically iron oxide. Cut cabochon and faceted, it is very popular for intaglios.

SIMULATED DIAMONDS is the name (unethical too) given to a group of synthetic stones that are advertised and sold as low priced diamonds. Three such stones, in order in which they appeared on the market are:

Titania (1949) is synthetic rutile which is titanium dioxide. Properties: fire superior to diamond, highly double refractive, scratches easily, color is pale-yellow and almost colorless.

Fabulite (1953) is stromtium titanate. It is the first synthetic stone with no counterpart in nature that has been accepted by jewelers. Its fire is less than titania's but more than diamond's. Fabulite is transparent, practically colorless (resembles the diamond), single refractive, and scratches easily since its hardness is only 5 to 6.

YAG (1970) is synthetic yttrium aluminum. It is classified as a garnet since it contains aluminum, is single refractive, and has the same internal and external form of natural garnets. Though not as brilliant, it has a close appearance to a diamond when cut with the same facets of a diamond.

In water, YAG becomes transparent, diamond retains its brilliance. YAG is not brilliant when looked at through its table at an angle. When the bottom (pavilion) of YAG becomes dirty its resemblance to a diamond is greatly diminished.

COMPARISON CHART

	Hardness	Dispersion	Refr. Index	Sp. Gravity
Diamond	10	.044	2.417	3.53
Titania	6½-7	.330	2.62 -2.90	4.25
Fabulite	5-6	.190	2.409	5.13
YAG	8.5	.028	1.833	4.65

OPAL H. 6. Sp. Gr. 2.15 R.I. 1.45

Opal's popularity is due to its fiery brilliant colors. The colors are produced by white light which is broken up into its component colors by the minute cracks of "watery" patches in the stone. Cut cabochon. The finest opals come from Australia; they are expensive since they are becoming scarce.

TURQUOISE H. 6 Sp. Gr. 2.7 R.I. 1.63

A soft but fairly durable stone that is very popular with the American Indians. Sky-blue turquoise, usually from Persia, is the most valuable. The color is not stable and is affected by dirt, grease, and perspiration. The undesirable green variety is often dyed blue.

Turquoise matrix contains specks of associated rock. Cut cabochon.

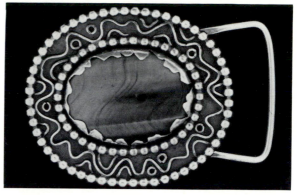

Fig. 305A Belt buckle   **Nancy Finelli**

PEARL H. 2.5-3.5 Sp. Gr. 2.5-2.7

Natural pearls are found within the shells of oysters or mussels. The pearl is formed by a foreign body such as a sand grain or dead minute organism which enters the shell and irritates the animal. The animal deposits a secretion (nacre—a form of calcium carbonate) about the irritating foreign body, and layers and layers of the secretion eventually, after several years, form the pearl.

Cultured pearls are made by artificially depositing a foreign body—usually a small bead made from another oyster—in the oyster or mussel, which is then returned to water. Nacre is deposited around the inserted bead (called a nucleus) at the rate of 3/10 of a millimeter a year. Thus it takes over 3 years to produce a pearl one millimeter larger than the inserted bead or nucleus. A cultured pearl can be differentiated from the natural by means of X-rays or when drilled; the dust from the core of the cultured pearl is a bright white; whereas, the dust from the natural pearl has the same pearlish color.

Imitation or simulated pearls are made by dipping hollow spheres of glass into a solution made from fish scales. This imparts a pearly luster to the glass.

Pearls are soft, easily scratched, and can be damaged by acids and perspiration. The color of pearls varies from white to tints of yellow, blue, red, green, and black. The silvery white round pearls free from blemishes are the most popular. **Baroque** pearls have irregular shapes. **Mobbe** pearls have flat bottoms.

BIRTHSTONES Below are the currently accepted natural and synthetic birthstones. The synthetic stones are produced from synthetic corundum (C) or spinel (S) which are colored to imitate the natural stones.

Month	Natural	Synthetic
January	Garnet	Garnet (C)
February	Amethyst	Amethyst (C)
March	Bloodstone or Aquamarine	Aquamarine (S)
April	Diamond	White Sapphire (C)
May	Emerald	Green Spinel (S)
June	Pearl or Moonstone	Alexandrite (C)
July	Ruby	Ruby (C)
August	Sardonyx or Peridot	Peridot (S)
September	Sapphire	Sapphire (C) or (S)
October	Opal or Tourmaline	Rose Zircon (S)
November	Topaz or Citrine	Golden Sapphire (C)
December	Turquoise or Lapis Lazuli	Blue Zircon (S)

2. DESIGNING JEWELRY AROUND STONES

The manner in which a gemstone is mounted in a piece of metal is influenced by the type and shape of the gemstone, determined by the design of the jewelry, and governed by the fact that the purpose of the setting is to hold a gemstone securely while displaying it to the best possible advantage. Simple settings can be made by wrapping wires around gemstones. Cabochons, opaque gemstones, gemstones that have flat bases, and soft and/or fragile gemstones are usually set in a bezel, surrounded by metal, or placed on top of a flat seat and then secured with prongs. A gypsy setting may be used to set cabochons firmly in place so that the stone is protected from shock.

Transparent faceted gemstones depend more on light entering the stone and reflect-

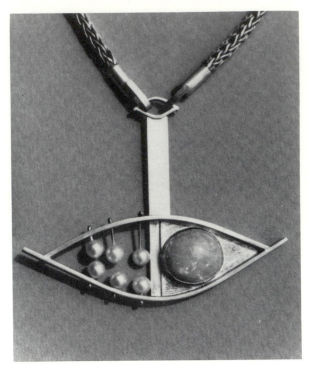

Fig. 306 Neckpiece   Grace Carmody

ing back through the facets to show their color and beauty than opaque cabochon gemstones. Consequently, the setting of faceted gemstones is done so as to interfere as little as possible with light reflection, while still securing the stone in a pleasing and tasteful manner. Open prong settings best fulfill this requirement, since the metal prongs

Fig. 307 Ring   Fretz

176

hold the gemstone only at the widest point (the girdle) and all sides of the gemstone are visible. The classic example of the open prong setting is the Tiffany setting, which is used for engagement rings.

Not all faceted gemstones are mounted in raised prong settings. Some jewelry designs or settings do not lend themselves to the upward projection of a dominating gemstone. Methods have been devised for setting gemstones lower than or flush with the surface of the metal to which they are mounted. Many variations of this type of setting are made, the most popular of which are the diamond, pavé, and star settings.

Fig. 308 Ring   **Christine Thrower**

There are other mountings that are used in the setting of gemstones. Emeralds are set in box prong settings. A channel setting is used for baguette gemstones. The fishtail setting is a popular variation of the prong setting. Illusion settings make a gemstone appear larger due to reflected light from the rim of the metal setting. Small pavé mountings (similar to the open prong settings) are often soldered close together on an article of jewelry to create a cluster setting. Pearls are secured to jewelry objects by a pearl prong setting or by means of a peg that is fitted into a hole that has been drilled into the pearl.

Although most gemstones are cut to standard sizes and shapes and set in traditional settings, contemporary jewelers frequently work with unusually shaped gemstones and then design a unique setting that enhances and compliments it. It should be noted that cast and stamped bezel, prong, box-frame, and coronet settings can be, and often are purchased in standard sizes, different metals, and various styles by jewelers and then soldered to pieces of jewelry. Nevertheless, handmade settings are still preferred by most craftsmen.

Fig. 309 Pendant   **Anne Krohn Graham**

3. UNCUT STONES AND WIRE WRAPPING

Uncut and barrel tumbled stones have become popular in recent years. Their varied colors and abstract shapes make them especially adaptable for informal jewelry.

Suitably sized stones for jewelry (fig. 310) are found naturally or are obtained by crushing or hammer chipping larger stones. Tumbled stones are natural stones that have had their edges and other surfaces polished smooth in a tumbling barrel with abrasive or polishing compounds added. The barrel is rotated slowly for many hours and eventually the sharp edges of the stones will wear off

177

from the stones sliding against one another; the abrasive compounds and the polishing compounds will leave them bright and polished.

The following are some of the stones (and their colors) which can be purchased uncut from dealers: amethyst (purple), citrine (yellow), aquamarine (light blue to green), rose quartz (pink).

The following are some of the stones that are available polished: chrysocalla (green to blue), tiger's-eye (yellow, also blue), obsidian (black), bloodstone (green with red specks), jasper (brown), amethyst (purple), torantilla agate (gray with white shell circles), rhodonite (pink and black), sodolite (blue), aventurine (green with white specks).

Fig. 311 Wire wrapped earrings

Fig. 310 Uncut and tumbled stones

WIRE WRAPPING Wire wrapping is the ideal method of attractively holding the uncut and tumbled polished stones. Round or square wire can be used. 20 gauge wire is used for the earrings in figure 311. The earrings are wrapped as follows:

Earrings number 1 and 2 are wrapped as shown in figure 312. After wrapping, the wire is tightened around the stones by means of snipe or round-nose pliers by gripping the wire where shown and twisting it. No solder-

ing is required. Earrings number 3 and 6 are wrapped as shown. Number 4 earring has a previously hard soldered link bent around the stone, and a smaller link is then inserted to attach the stone to the earwire.

Number 5 earring is made in a similar manner to number 1 with the wires, however,

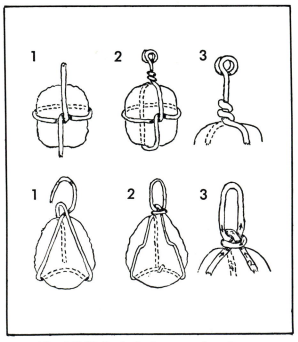

Fig. 312 Method of wire wrapping stones

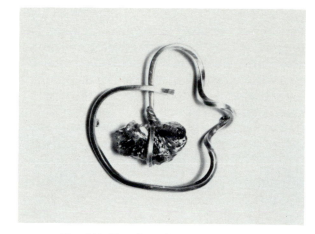

Fig. 313 Pin-wire with uncut amethyst

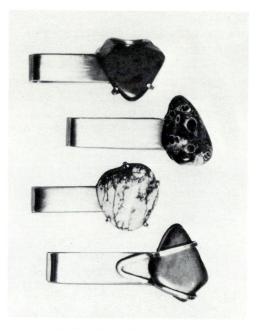

Fig. 315 Tie clips with tumbled stones

crossed at the bottom and the top ends of the wires hard soldered together.

The simple wire settings (fig. 314) for tie clips number 1 and 3 (fig. 315) are first hard soldered where shown, bent and wrapped around the gemstone, cut to length, and then finished by rounding the ends with a file. The stones are removed, the settings are soft soldered to the tie clips, and then the stones are reset in the wire settings.

An epoxy pearl cement (see page 202) is used to cement the stone to tie clip number 2. The epoxy cement also can be used to cement earwires and pins directly to small uncut and tumbled stones.

Number 4 tie clip is made as shown in the picture. The above can be used for cuff links. The tie clips are bent to shape (see fig. 470) and polished before the wires are soft, or hard soldered to them.

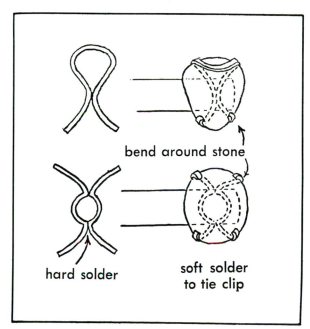

bend around stone

hard solder

soft solder to tie clip

Fig. 314 Simple wire settings

Fig. 316 Wire wrapped pendants

The top and bottom chains in the bracelet group (fig. 317) are made as described on page 231. The links of the center chain—"bird cage" type—are made by forming open spirals (fig. 90) at both ends of pieces of wire. The wires are bent in the center so that both spirals touch one another. Then the ends of the wires are pulled apart to form the bird cages.

Fig. 317 Bracelets with uncut and tumbled stones

4. BEZEL SETTINGS

Bezel is derived from the French word "biseau" which means "slanted edge." Stones with slanted edges—cabochon cut stones—were the first to be ground and polished by man; thus settings for these stones —bezel settings—were one of the first to be developed and used. Today, bezel settings are very popular with craftsmen and, even though they are comparatively easy to make, they are also used commercially for precious stones set in quality gold and platinum jewelry.

Note: The thickness of the material—silver, gold, or platinum—required to make a setting depends upon the size of the stone and the type of setting. By studying completed settings, the craftsman should be able to determine quickly the proper metal thickness. Holes are usually drilled into the metal by the modern jewelry craftsman by means of a flexible shaft; however a hand drill may be used. When soldering, use a higher melting solder first, and as other parts are added, use a lower melting one.

SETTING TOOLS The tools shown in figure 319 are used for setting stones. The fitting tools can be ground to shape from square and round engraving tools. Beeswax is used to pick up the stones for testing and placing purposes. The use of the other tools is described where used. The setting tool is made of steel. Its rectangular tip may be 1/8″ by 3/16″ or smaller. The pushing and rocking tools may be steel or brass. The pushing tool's tip may be a 1/8″ or 3/16″ square. The rocking tool is 3/16″ wide and of any desired length. A burnisher is an oval-shaped polished and hardened piece of tool steel which can be purchased with a straight or curved tip.

Fig. 318 Cast rings with bezel settings   Peter Blodgett

BEZEL OR BOX SETTING The bezel setting is used primarily for cabochon and simple step cut stones, though occasionally it is used for the other cuts. There are three common versions: box, bearing, and rectangular.

BEZEL SETTING The recommended metal thickness for small, round and oval cabochon stones is:

sterling silver . . . . 28 gauge
yellow gold . . . . 30 gauge (.010)

Pure (fine) or sterling silver for bezels? Some craftsmen prefer pure silver to sterling. The reason: pure silver has a higher melting point—it will not melt as easily and, since it is softer, it is easier to push (set) over the stone.

Beginning craftsmen, however, should encounter no difficulty, by following the instructions in this book, in using sterling silver. Since sterling silver is used commercially, it is easier to obtain, and, since it wears better, it is recommended that sterling silver be used for all silver settings.

To make a bezel setting, wrap a thin strip of metal around the girdle of a cabochon cut stone (fig. 321). Cut strip to the required length. File and fit the edges until they meet perfectly and then solder with hard solder to form a band. Strip should be cut the right length or a hair line smaller, for if the band (bezel) that it forms is too small it may be stretched by hammering on a small, round tapered mandrel; if it is too large, it must be cut smaller and resoldered.

Note: Bands (bezels) for oval stones are stretched on a round mandrel; the sides of the round band are squeezed together carefully to form an oval band.

The band may be shaped with pliers and it should fit the stone perfectly but not tightly. If a stone is forced into a tight fitting bezel, it is liable to crack. Level one side of the band on a smooth, flat file or on an emery rubbing stone. Now solder the band to a flat piece of metal to form the bezel.

The solder (medium) should be placed along the inside edge of the bezel. The flat

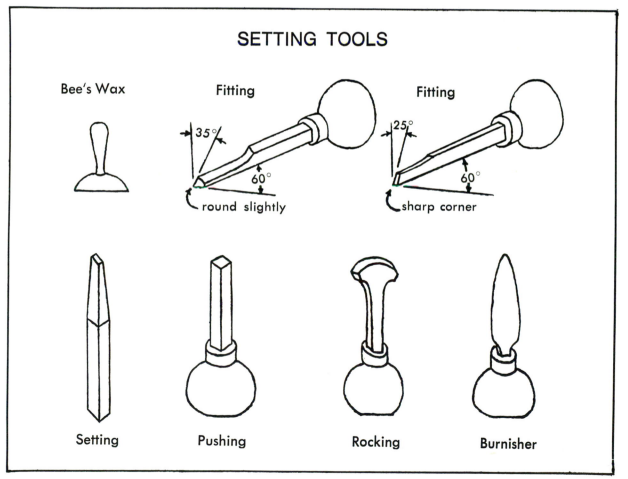

SETTING TOOLS

Bee's Wax

Fitting
35°
60°
← round slightly

Fitting
25°
60°
← sharp corner

Setting

Pushing

Rocking

Burnisher

Fig. 319

piece of metal is heated until the solder starts to flow under the bezel and then the torch is immediately lifted away. If the bezel is heated, the solder will only flow up onto the bezel.

If the stone is transparent, saw out most of the metal inside of the bezel and leave just enough metal, as shown in figure 321, to form a bearing. File the bezel to the required height, just sufficiently high to set the stone. Occasionally the stone may be raised by dropping in a loose flat inner bezel. When all soldering is completed, the stone is set.

The stone may be set in a bezel setting by means of a burnisher, pushing or rocking tool, or setting tool. The burnisher is rubbed back and forth over the bezel's edge until it is forced down over the stone. The pushing tool is pressed to force the edge of the bezel over the stone. The rocking tool is rocked back and forth to press the edge of the bezel over the stone. The setting tool is preferred by many craftsmen for setting stones in bezel settings. While the gemstone is being set, the piece can be securely held by a ring clamp, mandrel, engraving block, or a shellac stick.

Note from figure 321 the position of the tool. Don't hammer directly against the stone, for the vibration from the hammer blow will be transmitted to the stone and is apt to crack it. Start by hammering the top edge of the bezel in at an angle of 45° and on alternate sides to ensure centering the stone. Continue hammering until the bezel is firmly against the stone. As one proceeds, however, the angle of the setting tool should be raised until the tool is hammering almost straight down on the edge of the bezel. With all methods, smooth the edge of the bezel with a fine barrette (safety edge and back) file after the bezel has been forced against the stone.

Beginners often encounter the problem of fitting a cabochon stone into a bezel that is slightly too small. The solution is: grind the girdle (edge) of the stone very lightly on a carborundum wheel, or, with a fitting tool, remove some of the metal from the inside of the bezel.

Twisted wire is often soldered around a bezel setting. The trick to fitting the wire is:

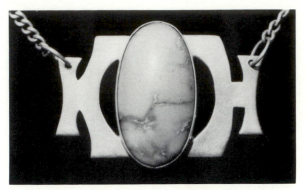

Fig. 320 Pendant with bezel setting made for Katy Hanson   Peter Bovin

first, solder the wire to form a band a little smaller than required; taper the top edge of the bezel slightly with a file; then, stretch the band, if necessary, on a mandrel until it can be forced onto the bezel; finally, solder the twisted wire to the bezel or base metal (fig. 321).

BEZEL BEARING SETTING The bezel bearing setting differs from the previously described bezel setting in that the bezel is usually not soldered to a flat piece of metal and also contains a metal strip soldered on the inside (fig. 321) to form a bearing (or seat) for the stone. The inner bearing is used to raise the level of a stone for high bezel settings for pins, or to provide a flat base for a stone when the bezel is soldered to, or formed to fit, a curved shank of a ring. Make the bezel the same way as the plain bezel setting. Then form a band from another piece of metal, generally a little thicker, so that it fits inside the bezel. File one side of the band, after it has been soldered, until it is perfectly flat. Now fit it into the bezel, smooth side up, to form a bearing for the stone. Leave it sufficiently from the top of the bezel to allow enough metal to set the stone. Solder the band to the bezel and then file the bottom to the desired shape. The bezel and bearing can be soldered together by flowing solder on their bottom edges. In this way, no clean up of solder is necessary on the bearing. The stone is set in the same way as the bezel setting.

BEZEL RECTANGULAR SETTING This setting is ideal for simple step stones. The bezel can be made from thicker metal than the box

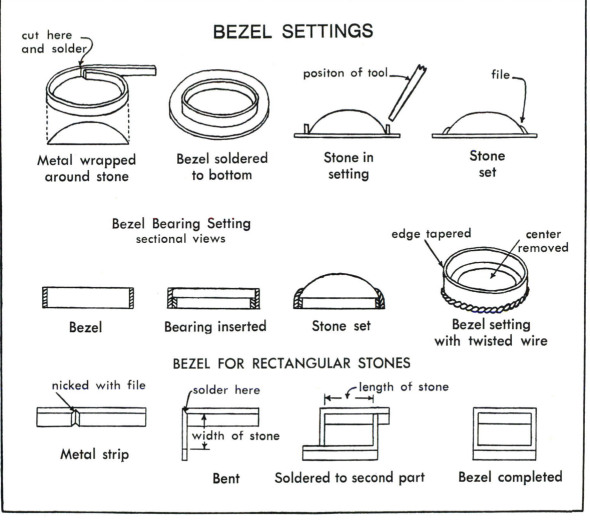

BEZEL SETTINGS

cut here and solder

Metal wrapped around stone

Bezel soldered to bottom

positon of tool

Stone in setting

file

Stone set

Bezel Bearing Setting
sectional views

Bezel

Bearing inserted

Stone set

edge tapered   center removed

Bezel setting with twisted wire

BEZEL FOR RECTANGULAR STONES

nicked with file

Metal strip

solder here

width of stone

Bent

length of stone

Soldered to second part

Bezel completed

Fig. 321

setting, as thick as 16 gauge in sterling silver. The height of the metal should be just a little less than that of the stone. Two strips of metal are required.

One strip is nicked or grooved, first with a three square file and then the edge of a rectangular file to ⅞ of its thickness, and then bent in towards the nick to form a right angle (fig. 321). Solder the metal in the inner corner where it has been bent to reinforce it. The two sides of the bent metal should be a little longer than corresponding sides of the stone. Then the stone is placed in the corner of the piece and one end of the metal, usually the shorter, is filed so that it is exactly the width of the stone. The other strip of metal is treated similarly. The two strips are now put together (fig. 321) so that the inside space

Fig. 322 Rings with rectangular box bezel settings
Peter Blodgett

183

is the exact size of the stone. The pieces are then soldered together, and, after soldering, the protruding ends are cut off. A little filing on the sides and bottom is all that is necessary to complete the rectangular bezel setting. Though the setting can be made from one strip of metal, the method described above is much faster and more accurate, and is the method used by commercial jewelers. The stone is set, after the bezel has been soldered in position, the same way as the other bezel settings.

Note: When thick metal, 20 gauge or thicker, is used for bezel rectangular settings, it is advisable to file all sides of the setting at a 30° angle away from the stone. This will permit the metal to be hammered against the stone easier. Commercially, an electric hammer (fig. 323) is often used to set stones in bezels.

Fig. 323 Stone being set in bezel with an electric hammer

5. PRONG SETTINGS

SIMPLE PRONG SETTINGS This setting is exceptionally easy to make, yet very practical. It is often used for gold and silver link bracelets, pins, and earrings. Occasionally it is used in platinum jewelry for settings for small diamonds. Though the cabochon cut stone is especially adapted for its use, it is used with the other cut stones. There are several ways of making the setting and soldering the prongs.

Fig. 324 Ring with prong setting   Maurice Abramson

The bearing or base piece is made from rectangular wire or from tubing. The wire is bent with the aid of pliers, cut to size, and soldered to form bands to match the shape of the stone. Sections may be cut from tubing with a jeweler's saw to form the bands for round stones. In either case, the band should be slightly smaller than the base or girdle of the stone so that when the stone rests on it, it should not be seen when looking straight down.

The placement, number, and size of the prongs is determined by the size and shape of the stone. Generally four prongs are used. The prongs are made from round, rectangular, or half-round wire, and the shape of the wire is determined by the relationship of the setting to the design of the jewelry.

The prongs are soldered to the base as follows: Cut the prongs a little longer than required. Place the bearing or base on a smooth charcoal block. With pliers, force the prongs against the side of the base and slightly into the charcoal (fig. 325). The prongs now can be easily soldered to the base without fear that they will move. Many craftsmen prefer to solder one prong to the base first. This prong keeps the base from moving when the other prongs are placed in their proper positions. When soldering is completed, the setting is removed from the charcoal block, the bottom ends of the prongs are nipped off, then the

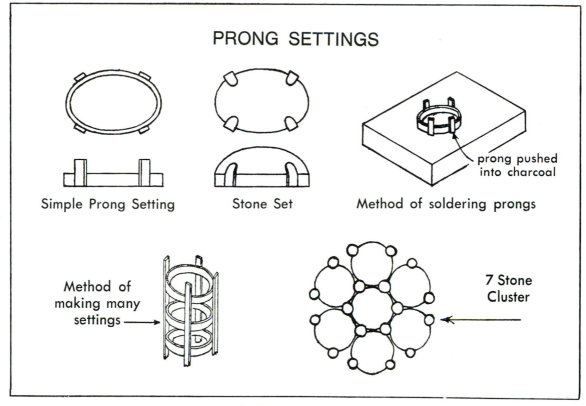

PRONG SETTINGS

Simple Prong Setting

Stone Set

Method of soldering prongs

prong pushed into charcoal

Method of making many settings →

7 Stone Cluster

Fig. 325 Prong settings

bottom is filed and rubbed smooth on a flat emery stone. Finally, the prongs are cut and filed to the proper height to complete the setting.

When many identical, simple prong settings must be made, there is a trick way of making them much faster than the above method. The bearing or base pieces are made from wire or tubing, though usually tubing, the same way as they are made above. The prongs are made from two wires of the proper thickness and shape. Each wire is bent in the center to form a long U. The inner width of the U should be the same as the outer width of the band. Cross both U's at the bottom, solder them together, and adjust the prongs so that they are equal distances apart. Place one of the bases in position between the prongs and solder. Repeat the operation, leaving just sufficient room between the bases for the proper height of the prongs.

Fig. 326 Tanzanite ring with prong setting
Courtesy of Tiffany & Co.

Fig. 327 Brooch with prong settings   **Gene Pijanowski**

185

When all the bands have been soldered (fig. 325), the wires are nipped to form individual, simple prong settings.

Cabochon stones are set in simple prong settings by merely pushing the prongs in and down on the stone with a pushing tool and occasionally by hammering lightly on a setting tool. The ends of the prongs are filed to shape.

SMALL PRONG SETTINGS Small four prong round bottom settings for holding faceted stones can be made as follows: With a divider, scribe a circle onto the metal (22 gauge) as shown in figure 328. The diameter of the circle and the thickness of the metal depends upon the stone's size. Cut the metal to shape with a jeweler's saw.

With a dapping tool, hammer a depression into a lead block the size of the desired small prong setting. Place the cut metal over the hollow and with the dapping tool hammer the metal down into the hollow to form the setting. If a small hole is desired in the bottom of the setting, it can be drilled or punched through the metal. The small punch (fig. 328), ground from a piece of tool steel, is used over a lead block. A little filing and adjustment of the prongs is required to complete the small round bottom prong setting. If a straight sided small four prong setting (called a circlet setting) is required, it can be made by punching through the hole in the round bottom setting with the tapered punch shown in figure 328. Six and eight prong settings (called Tiffany settings) can be made the same way as the above.

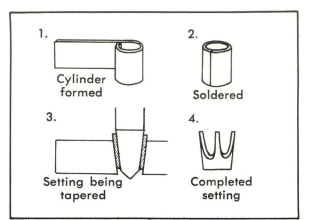

Fig. 329 Forming a round closed prong setting
Courtesy of Janet Vitkavage

CLOSED STONE SETTINGS are similar but more complex settings that can be used for both cabochon and faceted gemstones.

A cylinder can be formed from 20 gauge sheet that has a diameter slightly smaller than that of the stone. After soldering, the cylinder is then tapered by placing it in a special bezel plate (the back of a drawplate can be used) and then forcing it open with a punch until the wide end of the setting is larger in diameter than the stone. The stone should not be able to drop into the setting. It should rest on the edge of the cylinder, since metal will be removed to form a seat during the setting process.

If the cylinder is left closed, it can be used to set cabochon stones (tube setting). A pointed cone or setting bur is used to enlarge the opening to the correct seat diameter. Approximately 30% of the tube wall is removed when the seat is made so that the stone will fall in and rest on it. The stone is tacked in place with parallel pliers and then set as in a bezel setting.

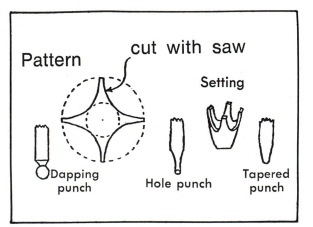

Fig. 328 Pattern for small prong setting

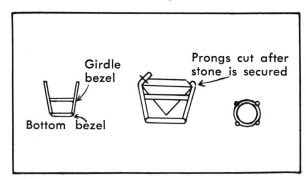

Fig. 330 Wire prong setting Courtesy of Janet Vitkavage

For faceted stones, the cylinder can be cut to form a prong setting. Equally spaced guide lines are scribed on the top edge of the cylinder for the number of prongs desired. The shape of the prongs is then sketched and scribed on the outside of the cylinder. The metal between the prongs is removed with a saw. **Note:** The saw is held at an angle so that only one side of the setting is being cut. This also results in the beveled edge at the bottom of the U-shaped cuts which is typical of this type of setting. Final finishing is done with a file.

The delicate wire prong setting can be made as follows: The top bezel, which is the same diameter as the girdle of the stone, is made from 22 gauge round wire. The bottom bezel is made slightly smaller (it must sit on top of the girdle bezel without falling through). A correct proportional taper angle is thus formed when the prongs are soldered to the upper and lower bezel. The bezels are soldered with hard solder after they have been formed round on a mandrel (small drill, bezel mandrel). A cylindrical bur or a joint file is then used to make grooves in the bezel links for the prongs. The grooves are cut to a depth that allows the prongs to be inserted at least ⅓ the way into the wire links so that the stone can be properly set. The prongs are inserted into the grooves of the bezel links, the links are properly spaced, the bottoms of the prongs are pushed into a charcoal block, and the bezels are soldered to the prongs to form the setting. The excess prong metal is cut from underneath so that the prongs and lower bezel are flush.

The stones are set with a snipe nose plier as shown in figure 332. Craftsmen who do not

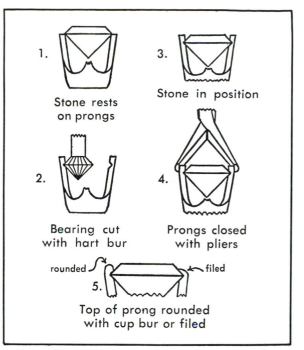

Fig. 332 Setting a stone in small prong setting

possess a flexible shaft outfit can use a swivel tool handle for holding and rotating the hart bur. The bearing can also be cut with a small 2/0 bur. If a small ball or bud bur is used it is good procedure to push the bur from its front across the prong to form the bearing, as shown in the picture.

A hart or a round bur is used to individually cut the bearings in a prong setting. Care must be taken since the bur is difficult to control and can easily "walk" on the prong.

A setting bur can be used (fig. 334) to quickly and simultaneously cut the bearing (creating a seat) in a prong. A millimeter

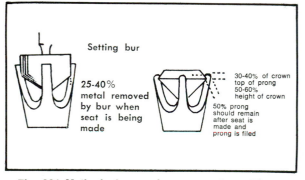

Fig. 331 Method of preparing prongs for setting
Courtesy of Janet Vitkavage

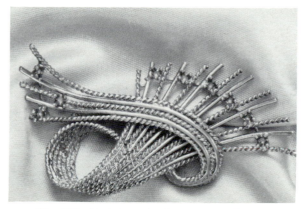

Fig. 333 Cast brooch with prong settings

187

Fig. 334 Bearings being cut with a setting bur

Fig. 335 Bearing being cut with bud bur

Fig. 336 Stone held by beeswax, being positioned

Fig. 337 Prongs being closed over gemstone
with pliers

Fig. 338 Prongs being finished with cup bur
Courtesy of the Gemological Institute of America

Fig. 339 Cast ring   Michael Jerry

gauge can be used to determine the diameter of the stone's girdle and the proper bur size. The amount of metal that will be removed from the prongs by the setting bur (25% - 40% of the original thickness) is determined by the thickness of the prongs, the position of the prongs, and the size of the bur. If necessary, the prongs can either be bent inward or dapped outward so that the correct prong thickness will result when the seat is cut.

Before the stone is set, the inside of each prong should be lightly filed. The stone should then be placed inside the setting and its alignment checked to make sure that the girdle is level. The stone is set by first tacking down the prongs with parallel pliers and then securing the prongs with a stone pusher. The prongs should not be cut to length or shaped until the gemstone has been secured. A knife edge file can be used to finish the prongs.

Commercially, small prong settings are purchased by jewelers by sizes, and the sizes are matched with the colored faceted stone sizes—a number 2 prong setting is used for a number 2 stone. Prong settings can also be made in wax as part of the piece to be cast.

PRONG CLUSTER SETTINGS (from plate)

This is an extremely attractive prong setting that is especially suited to round faceted rubies and sapphires. The cluster is often used in the center of modern pins and earrings. A seven stone cluster (fig. 325) will be used to explain the making of the setting. A circle is cut to the required size and then domed up slightly to form the base piece. The prongs are made from round wire and are cut a little longer than required. The prongs for the center stone are placed first as follows: In the center of the base piece, with a pencil, draw a circle the same size as the girdle of the stone. Mark off the positions for the six required prongs. Note (fig. 325) that the prongs are spaced equally and that they are placed approximately ⅓ the thickness of the wire inside the circle. Center punch the prong positions (an engraving tool may be used) and then drill holes, the same size as the prong wire, right through the base piece. Place the prong wires right through the holes so that they protrude slightly. Now solder the prongs, from the back side, to the base piece with a high melting solder.

Repeat the operation for the other stones. Note that only four prongs, though some craftsmen use six, are required for these stones. After all the prongs have been soldered into position, the parts that protrude through the back of the base are ground flush. Holes, as large as possible (á jours), are now drilled between the prongs where the stones are to fit. Finally, the outer edge of the base piece is filed smaller until it touches the prongs to complete the setting.

PRONG CLUSTER SETTINGS (from wire)

Some jewelers use wire rather than plate to create a diamond cluster setting. The layout of the cluster is drawn precisely, and all measurements are taken from the sketch. Links made of wire must be formed to support the stones. The links should be the exact diameter of the girdle of the stone and can be made from 22 gauge wire. They are closed and arranged on a soldering block in the desired pattern and soldered with hard solder or soldered together in investment. Then they are domed slightly in a dapping block, since the outside stones are usually set at an angle to the center stone. A cylindrical bur is then used to make grooves in the links for the prongs. Prongs are placed between the links and must be inserted at least ⅓ the way into the thickness of the wire link to allow for metal to be removed for setting. The prongs are set up in place in a charcoal block and soldered simultaneously. Excess metal is cut from underneath so that the prongs and the links are flush. A supporting bezel can be soldered inside and underneath the cluster to add strength to the setting.

The stones are set in the prong cluster by cutting a bearing on the prongs for the stones with a hart bur or setting tool. The center stone is set first by hammering or pushing the prongs in and down upon it with a pushing tool or snipe nose pliers. Then the other stones are set. The prongs can be rounded off by a cup bur.

EMERALD CUT PRONG SETTINGS

This setting, one of the most beautiful of all settings, is made by hand only for the most expensive

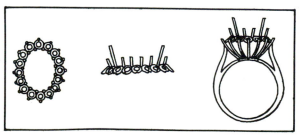

Fig. 340 Wire prong cluster setting
Courtesy of Janet Vitkavage

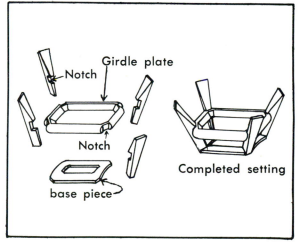

Fig. 341 Prong setting for emeralds and brilliant cut stones

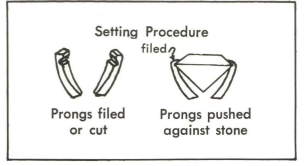

Setting Procedure

Prongs filed
or cut

Prongs pushed
against stone

Fig. 342 Setting the stone

gold and platinum jewelry and for models. Good craftsmanship is required to make it properly and every little detail must be studied carefully. There are several fundamental methods of making the setting, and the method that the individual craftsman uses depends on his background and training. In all methods, the setting is made to fit an individual stone.

The method described below is preferred by many jewelers. The girdle bezel is made first from a piece of flat metal by marking off the proper opening to match the rectangle of the stone at the first horizontal plane below the girdle. **Note:** The corners are marked to match the small octagonal corners of the stone. The opening is cut out with the jeweler's saw, and the saw is held at the same angle as the slope of the stone. The opening is then filed so that the stone fits into it perfectly. Next, the proper thickness of the crossbars is marked off with the aid of a divider, and the metal is cut along this

line with the jeweler's saw, inclined at the same angle as the opening. The frame that is formed (fig. 341) becomes the crossbars of the setting. The outside is filed, and a notch, which matches the thickness of the prong, is filed into each corner of the frame.

The prongs are made from a rectangular piece of metal and they are cut a little longer than required. They are now filed on the wide sides in order to taper them properly (fig. 341). The bottom of the prong now should be square. A notch is filed in each prong so that the inside edge of the prong reaches the inside opening of the bezel.

The prongs are then soldered to the frame with a very high melting solder. A piece of metal is curved to form the base, and the prongs are cut and filed to the proper height and then soldered to the base. The opening is then cut in the base, and finally the outside of the base is cut to shape to complete the setting.

After the setting has been soldered in position, and the jewelry object completed, the stone is set. Each prong is notched with a file or cut with a hart bur (fig. 332) to form a bearing (fig. 342). The prongs are then pushed and if necessary hammered to set the stone. The top of the prongs must be filed to complete the setting.

WIRE MOVEMENTS. Individual prong settings can be attached together with wire so that they will be able to move and flex. A post is first soldered to the setting between the girdle and bottom bezel. Round wire, usually slightly smaller than the distance between

Fig. 342A Ring   Klaus Kallenberger

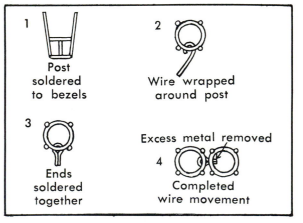

1
Post
soldered
to bezels

2
Wire wrapped
around post

3
Ends
soldered
together

Excess metal removed

4
Completed
wire movement

Fig. 343 Wire movement construction

the upper and lower bezel (the smaller the wire, the more the flex), is wrapped around the post. After shaping and closing, the ends of the movement are soldered together. **Note:** The diameter of the wire loop will determine the amount of movement. Then the end of the movement is usually soldered to the lower bezel of the next setting. Any protruding metal inside the setting should be removed. A post can be soldered to the opposite side of this next setting and the process repeated to add additional prong settings to the movement.

SPLIT SHANK FOR PRONG SETTINGS. Start with a square rod of metal approximately ½ millimeter larger in width than what the widest measurement of the shank will be after it is rolled and forged. The center of the rod is rolled through a mill to form the thin bottom portion of the shank. The rod is then hammered over a mandrel to form the shank. The top of the shank is placed on its side on an anvil and the ends are flared and made thinner by forging. The shoulder area is formed after the shank has been formed. With a 5/0 or 6/0 sawblade, saw into the shank to create the shoulders. The shoulders are pried up with a knife. After the shoulders and shank have been filed, the setting is inserted and then soldered to the shank.

To determine the length of rod needed for the shank: Calculate the circumference of the ring size needed by obtaining the diameter of the ring size and multiplying by π. Add 1 millimeter for tolerance. Deduct the size of the bottom bezel or plate. **Note:** The thickness of the metal used for the lower bezel

Fig. 345 Soldering a prong setting to a shank
Courtesy of A. R. "Rick" Shalburg

is usually 16 gauge and the lower shoulder should be filed to the same thickness.

The setting can be soldered to the shank by holding them together with a pair of special stainless steel tweezers that have been heated and forged to match the curve of the shank.

6. DIAMOND SETTINGS

The fundamental operations in diamond setting are not too difficult to master. However, due to the value of the diamonds, perfection is essential for appearance and for safeguarding the stone; perfection can be had only through considerable practice and study.

The following additional tools are required:

BRASS PUSHING TOOL The brass tool is used to force stones into position. A 3/16″ rod, 3″ long, set in a round engraving handle will do. The tip of the tool is made slightly concave so that it will not slip on the stones.

EYE LOUPE Most setters use the loupe after, not during, the setting operation for inspection and touching up purposes.

POWDER BAG Powder is dusted onto the setting occasionally to eliminate any glare so that the setting can better be observed. Talc powder wrapped in a cloth or in a bag will do.

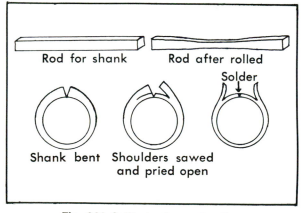

Rod for shank   Rod after rolled

Solder

Shank bent   Shoulders sawed and pried open

Fig. 344 Split shank construction

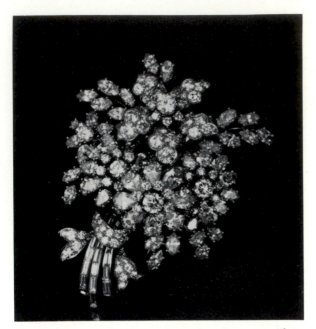

Fig. 346 Diamonds in bead, channel, and prong settings
Courtesy of Tiffany & Co.

MILGRAIN WHEELS (fig. 351) The milgrain wheels are used to roll the fine milgrain border around the edge of the box of the setting. Light machine oil is touched to the wheel when used.

BEADING TOOLS (fig. 351) Beading tools are used to form the beads around the stone. The tool is made by hammering a tool steel rod into a beading block. The block has various sized beads set into it and the hammering produces a concaved beading tool. The tool is not hardened after it has been formed, for hardened steel would tend to chip the stones. When used, the beading tool is held in a ball handle. It must be reshaped occasionally on the beading block.

ENGRAVING TOOLS The engraving tools used for setting stones are held in round

Fig. 346A   Sliding millimeter gauge

handles and are shortened for sturdiness and manipulation purposes. Of the many different shapes used, the following are the important ones:

Number 51 and 52 round (fig. 351) for raising the metal to form the beads.

Number 1 onglette (point) or knife for cutting sharp corners and straight lines.

Number 1 or 2 onglette or knife tool sharpened to cut on the side for rough and bright cutting. The tool is first sharpened with the regular engraving tool at a 45 degree angle, then it is leaned at an angle of 60 degrees to the right and sharpened so that it will cut on its right side. Another tool is sharpened so that it will cut on its left side.

BEARING TOOLS Bearing or fitting tools are ground from flat or round tools. The tool is sharpened as described above, but it is shaped so that it will cut on the right side and bottom at the same time (fig. 319). The right side edge of the tool is rounded slightly.

BURS A set of round and bud burs are required to properly prepare drilled holes for

Fig. 347   Platinum brooches ready to be set
with diamonds

the stones. To help determine the correct bur size, measure the girdle of the gemstone with a sliding gauge (fig. 346A). Use the bur whose diameter at its widest point is the same as the girdle of the gemstone or the next sized (either smaller or larger) bur. Be careful not to use an oversized bur.

HOLDING OBJECTS Rings may be held in a ring clamp as shown in figure 348. Brooches

Fig. 348 Enlarging a hole with a bud bur

and irregular shaped objects are held in shellac—see page 82.

METAL PREPARATION A hole is drilled through the metal a little smaller than the stone, and then with a bud bur it is enlarged so that the girdle of the stone will rest slightly above the surface of the metal. With a ball bur, the same size or slightly larger than the girdle of the stone, the opening is enlarged so that the girdle of the stone will rest a little below the surface of the metal. The burs are dipped into oil of wintergreen occasionally to help the cutting operation. The stone is placed in position with the aid of beeswax and is then leveled and pushed down firmly with the brass pushing tool.

Á JOUR CUTTING An important aspect of diamond setting that is often neglected is the cutting of an á jour, or opening on the under-

Fig. 349 Holes being arilled for diamond settings

side of the metal, so that light can enter the gemstone through the culet (bottom) and thus enhance its beauty. The easiest method for creating an á jour is to partially cut into the back of the hole already drilled with a conical bur. With more expensive jewelry, sketch the placement of the á jours on the back of the piece and then mark with a scriber. Keep in mind that the same amount of metal should be left between each á jour. The á jours are formed by sawing the metal from the back. A constant angle should be maintained while sawing. Removing the corners first will permit the saw blade to move freely and cut a straight mitered edge. The saw should be tilted forward slightly so that as the á jour is being cut no metal is removed from the setting.

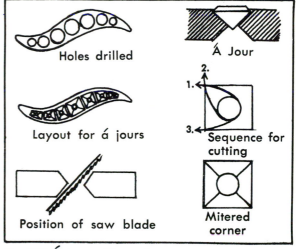

Fig. 350 Á jour cutting   Courtesy of Janet Vitkavage

CUTTING A SEAT For the best quality work, especially for the larger stones, a seat is cut with a fitting tool (fig. 319) after the bud bur has been used. The tool is spun around the opening for the stone in order to smoothly remove metal. The seat is cut (fig. 354) so that the stone fits snugly. **Note:** The seat can be cut with a number 2 bevel edge (fig. 359) and a number 40 flat graver. The bevel edge tool is first used to form the upper part of the seat; then the flat tool is used to remove metal below to complete the seat.

MARKING THE BOX Though in many cases the shape of the box for the setting is indicated, often it must be marked. It may be

193

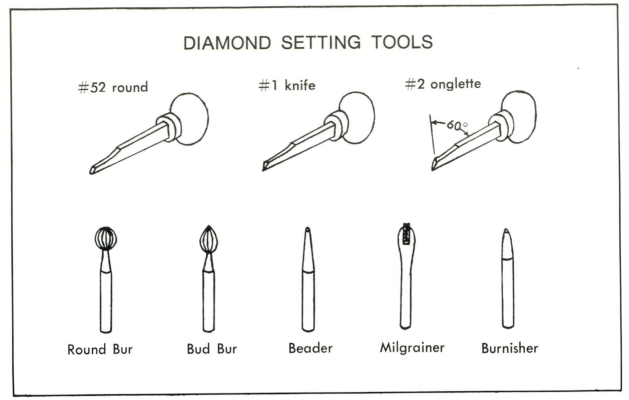

DIAMOND SETTING TOOLS

#52 round #1 knife #2 onglette

60°

Round Bur   Bud Bur   Beader   Milgrainer   Burnisher

Fig. 351   Diamond setting tools

marked with a pencil and then a light engraving cut. Popular shapes for setting round stones are the square, triangular, and the hexagon. The square four bead setting will be described.

RAISING THE METAL (BEAD) Starting approximately 1/16″ from the gemstone, the metal is raised in one of the corners with a #51 or #52 round tool or a #3 point tool (see fig. 354). This raised metal is eventually formed into a bead. The tool is held at an angle of approximately 45 degrees to begin the cut. The cut is made from the corner towards the stone by pushing and slightly rocking the tool into the metal. The graver is stopped just before it reaches the stone. Then the tool is raised forward slightly so that the point of the raised metal sticks up to form a little triangular shaped bead which

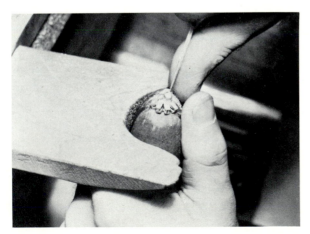

Fig. 352   Raising a bead on a ring

Fig. 353   Close-up of raising a bead
Courtesy of the Gemological Institute of America

overlaps the stone slightly. Repeat this operation from the opposite side of the square and then from the other corners to form four beads. As can be seen from the diagram, the beads now hold the stone permanently in position (fig. 354-6). Note also that by raising the bead, metal has been pushed against the girdle of the gemstone so that it does not vibrate. The subsequent operations are done primarily to accentuate the size and the beauty of the stone.

ROUGH CUTTING OR CARVING The purpose of rough cutting is to remove the metal around the bead and the stone. The metal is removed at an angle from the girdle of the stone to the edge of the box. First, the corners must be cut to leave them sharp in order that

a clean, square picture frame corner can be cut. This is done by cutting straight down to the bead to form a "V" (with a number 1 knife tool or a number 00 point tool) directly over the round cut that was left when the round graver formed the bead.

The metal is now rough cut with a slicing motion from one corner to the other corner in the direction shown by the arrow in figure 354-7. Small pieces of metal are actually sliced out. No attempt is made to remove all the metal in one cut. Metal is removed by cutting a straight line from one corner of the box (starting at the "V" cut) directly behind the bead and continuing the cut past the girdle and behind the next bead to the next "V" cut. A number 1 onglette or point tool sharpened to cut on the right side can be used.

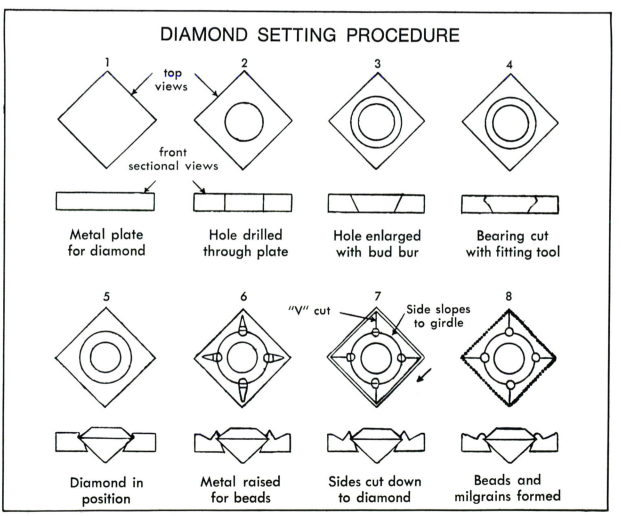

Fig. 354

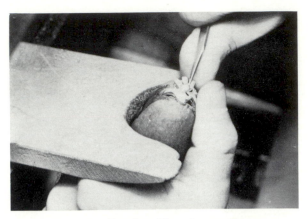

Fig. 355 Rough cutting at an angle

Now the metal is sliced in the other direction (back to the corners) to complete the rough cutting on each side. An onglette tool sharpened to cut on the left side is used. Dab the setting with powder to remove glare and to better observe the work.

Touch up spots around the beads or diamond where necessary. **Note:** Always cut away from the girdle of the stone and/or towards the bead when cleaning metal from a setting. Never cut below the girdle of the gemstone.

Note: Many setters prefer to remove the metal with one graver by slicing in one direction.

BRIGHT CUTTING Bright cutting is done with the same shaped tools as used for rough cutting, but sharpened for bright cutting as previously explained in the chapter on engraving. The purpose of bright cutting is to obtain a smooth, even, bright surface around the stone in order to properly reflect the stone's brilliancy. One long smooth cut is made, generally from right hand corner to left hand corner. Many experienced setters prefer to use a flat tool for bright cutting.

COMPLETING THE SETTING The beading tool is used on the raised triangular-shaped bead to form a neat round bead. When forming the bead, the tool is pressed and rotated in the general direction of the stone in order to hold the stone more firmly. **Note:** A cup bur with a flexible shaft outfit may be used instead of the beading tool to form the round bead.

Finally, if necessary, cut straight lines to form a raised surface around the setting for milgraining. The milgrain tool is rolled back and forth to form neat milgrains.

PAVÉ SETTING is a type of diamond setting in which multiple rows of diamonds are set closely together in a plate of metal. After the stones have been set, the piece of jewelry should look like it is paved with diamonds.

The size, shape, and number of diamonds, the distance between the stones, and the

Fig. 356 Pavé setting   Courtesy of William Klein

placement of the holes will dictate the type of pavé setting. In an expensive pavé setting, the holes for the diamonds are usually laid out so that after the stones have been set, they will rest girdle to girdle. In a less expensive pavé setting more metal is usually left between the stones. Although four beads are usually raised around each diamond to hold it securely, sometimes a single bead is raised between three diamonds, if the stones are very close together. If there is an excessive amount of metal between the stones, a decorative non-functional bead can be raised between the beads, or metal can be cut away between two adjacent diamonds until a raised diamond design has been formed.

When designing a piece of jewelry that will have a pavé setting, it is important that the jeweler work closely with the setter. Pavé setting is an art unto itself, and most jewelers

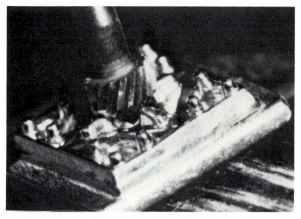

Fig. 357 Opening the metal with a setting bur
Courtesy of the Gemological Institute of America

will send their pavé work to an experienced setter.

When preparing the metal for pavé work, the design for stone placement is laid out, holes are drilled through the metal, and ajours are cut, as previously described in the section on diamond setting. Each hole is then individually opened with a bud bur so that the stone sits in the metal slightly below its girdle. The stone can be secured with a brass pushing tool. The holes should be opened so that the girdles of the stones are level with each other.

If the holes have been drilled close together, a setting tool, known as a box foot, can be used to push metal against the girdles to help further secure the diamonds and thereby facilitate the raising of the beads. A box foot tool can be made from the handle of a barrette file. After each stone has been fitted, the tool is placed inside and against the top edge of an adjacent hole and then pushed toward the stone.

The beads are raised as previously described with either a number 1 or 3 point graver or a number 52 or 53 round tool. A 0 or 00 point tool is preferred by most setters for cutting away excess metal from between the stones and from around the beads to define their shape; and for forming an outside linear border around the setting, which is known as a thread. **Note:** When cutting and cleaning, never cut below the girdle of the gemstones. After the metal around the settings has been cut and cleaned, it is bright-cut, and then the beads are finished with a beading tool.

GYPSY SETTING FOR DIAMOND Often the brilliant cut diamond is set in a gypsy type of setting. As previously described for the other diamond settings, a hole is first drilled through the metal, enlarged with a bud bur, and then a bearing or seat is cut for the stone. After the stone has been snapped into position, it may be set by hammering or burnishing. The hammering method is the same as the one described for the regular gypsy setting. To burnish the setting, a round piece of tool steel, shaped and highly polished as shown in figure 351, is held at a slight angle away from the stone and then rotated around the stone. After several turns the tool is raised so that it is practically perpendicular to the stone as it is rotated. Eventually, the pressure from the tool will burnish the metal over the edge of the girdle and hold the stone.

ILLUSION SETTINGS The diamond appears larger in the illusion setting due to reflected light and can be set quicker—thus cheaper.

Illusion settings have four main narrow supports for holding the diamond and forming a prong or "bead". The diamond is set as follows: if necessary, enlarge the opening with a bud bur so that the diamond's girdle rests just above the opening. With a hart

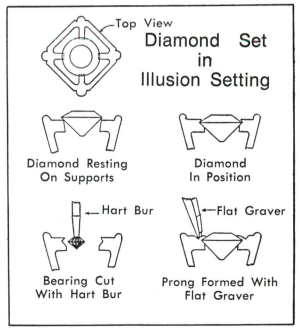

Fig. 358

197

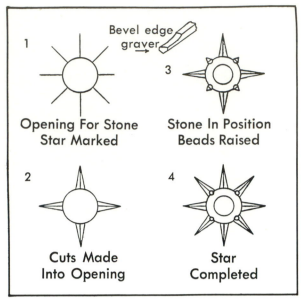

Fig. 359 Method of cutting star setting

1 — Opening For Stone Star Marked
2 — Cuts Made Into Opening
3 — Stone In Position Beads Raised
4 — Star Completed

bur (fig. 358) cut bearings into the four supports. Push the diamond down so that it snaps into the bearing. With a flat engraving tool, cut down into the support pieces directly behind the diamond to raise a prong or "bead", which is forced against the stone as described on page 193. The diamond is now set—no beading tool is used.

STAR SETTINGS The opening for the stone is prepared as described on page 193. Then the points (usually 6 or 8) are marked on the metal with a pencil or light scratch of the

Fig. 360 Pendant with a star setting

graver. With a bevel edge graver, half the points are cut right into the opening for the stone. The cut is light at first, and deeper and wider at the opening (fig. 359).

Now the stone is placed in position. The beads are raised as described on page 193. **Note:** The beads may be raised with the bevel edge graver. Finally, with the bevel edge graver, cuts are made behind the beads to complete the setting.

The preferred method to round the top of the bead is to use a cup bur.

FISHTAIL SETTING FOR DIAMOND The fishtail box setting for the brilliant cut diamond is very popular for engagement rings. The diamond is set as follows. Cut a bearing with a hart bur (fig. 361). Then with a jeweler's saw (or a small circular saw) make two cuts

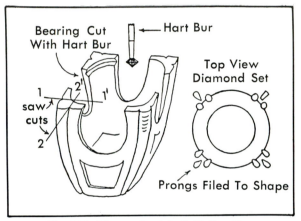

Fig. 361 Diamond set in fishtail setting

in each corner down to the bearing. File the prongs to a desirable shape; the tear drop and other shapes shown in figure 361 are attractive.

Note: The hart bur is also called a bearing bur by some jewelry supply concerns.

After the diamond is placed on the bearing, the eight inner prongs are pressed over it with a pushing tool or with pliers. Touch up the individual prongs with a file to complete the setting. **Note:** The four outer prongs are purely decorative.

CHANNEL SETTING WITH BAGUETTES (fig. 362) Channel set marriage rings are very attractive. The bearing in the ring is cut with an onglette graver sharpened as shown in

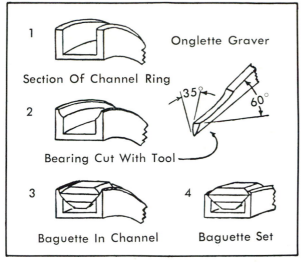

Fig. 362 Channel setting with baguettes

figure 362, and it is cut so that the girdles of the baguettes will rest below the top edge of the channel. Finally, the thin top edge of the channel is forced over the stones with a pushing or setting tool.

Jewelers and setters purchase rings for channel settings from supply houses. Large manufacturers cast their own settings. Quality jewelers for large diamonds (5 to 7 mm baguettes) will make a channel ring in platinum by hand from a rectangular piece of metal.

Today, small (3 points) brilliant cut stones are used only in guard bands.

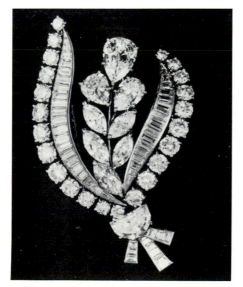

Fig. 363 Diamond brooch   Cartier, Inc.

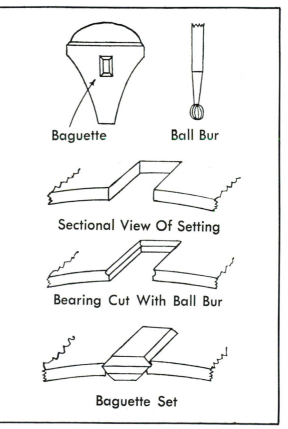

Fig. 364 Channel setting

Note: Usually when setting diamonds, no metal should be visible between the gemstones. They should appear to be girdle to girdle.

BAGUETTE SETTINGS A single baguette may be set in a ring as follows. If the opening for the stone isn't in the ring, cut it with a jeweler's saw. The bearing is cut with a flat and onglette graver—a small 2/0 ball bur can be used especially in the corners of the setting—so that the stone can snap into the setting. Then, with a setting tool (fig. 319) fitted into

Fig. 365 Baguette set in a ring

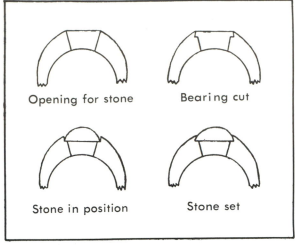

Fig. 366 Method of making a gypsy setting

Opening for stone

Bearing cut

Stone in position

Stone set

Fig. 368 Ring with gypsy setting

a flexible shaft hammer handpiece, the metal around the baguette is tapped over the girdle of the stone. A little filing is necessary to complete the setting.

Note: It is best to cut the bearing or seat in one or more sides of the setting so that the baguette fits perfectly into these sides; thus these sides require very little hammer setting.

7.   GYPSY SETTINGS

GYPSY SETTING This is a popular setting for men's cast rings with cabochon cut stones.

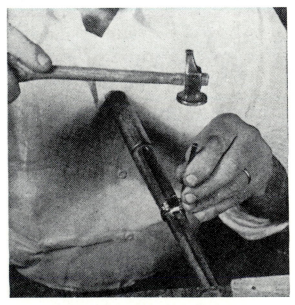

Fig. 367   Hammering a flat setting tool

Figure 366 shows a sectional view of a cast ring. A bearing or seat is cut into the tapered opening for the stone. The opening is usually made by means of a core when the ring is cast; however, it may be cut into the ring with the jeweler's saw. The bearing is cut with a fitting tool (fig. 319) or with an inverted cone bur.

Note that the bearing or seat is undercut slightly so that the stone can be snapped into position and the metal can then more easily be hammered down to hold the stone. The stone is set by hammering on a flat setting tool until the metal is pushed against the stone. Professional setters use an automatic hammer which fits onto the flexible shaft. The setting tool is inserted into the hammer. The ring being set may be held in a ring clamp or on a ring mandrel. The ring clamp may be held in a vise when the ring is being set by hammering on a hand tool. The ring mandrel is held by inserting its tip into a previously drilled hole in the work bench and pressing against the other end of the mandrel with one's chest (fig. 367). This method is preferred since it is faster and the mandrel provides a solid foundation for the ring while it is being hammered.

8.   PEARL SETTINGS

Pearls are secured (set) to jewelry objects by means of pearl prong settings or by means of pegs and pearl cement. Commercial jewelers purchase pearl prong settings (picture)

Fig. 369 Drilling a pearl

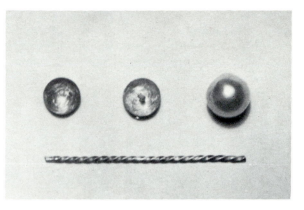

Fig. 371 Concave base, twisted peg, and pearl

Fig. 370 Pendant   Donna Matles

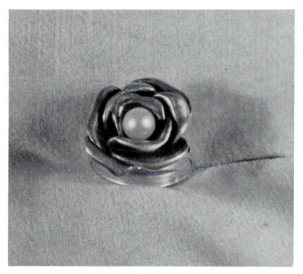

Fig. 372 Ring with pearl peg setting
Carol Schneider

from setting and finding concerns. When a special size is desired, the setting can be made in a similar manner to the small prong setting described on page 186. The prongs have this disadvantage—they can be seen from the top, thus marring the beauty of the pearl. The peg setting permits one to set the pearl without any metal showing from the top, and therefore, it is used for the finest gold and platinum jewelry. The setting is made as follows:

DRILLING A hole is drilled into the pearl 2/3 of its thickness. The pearl is held in one's hand (fig. 369) or in a commercial jig, and the drilling is done by means of the flexible shaft outfit, though it can be done with a drill press. Carbon steel drills can be used; high speed drills last longer. The thickness of the drill depends upon the size of the pearl and peg.

Note: The peg to be formed slips into the hole; it is not threaded or forced into it. A number 55 drill can be used for a 7 millimeter pearl.

CONCAVE BASE A concave base to support the pearl is made from a flat circular piece of metal (fig. 371). The diameter of the circle should be less than the diameter of the pearl so that no metal can be seen from the top. The metal is formed (concaved) to the pearl's shape by means of a dapping punch and a lead or dapping block.

Note: Many jewelry objects are designed and made without the concave base. A thicker peg is used.

THE PEG The peg is made from square wire. The wire is twisted, as shown in figure 371, and the twisted wire should just fit into the drilled hole in the pearl. Now drill a hole, the same diameter as the twisted wire, through the center of the concave base piece. Insert the twisted wire and then, from the back of the base, solder it to the base. With nippers, cut the twisted wire so that it is slightly shorter than the depth of the hole drilled into the pearl. File, emery, and polish the back of the base and then solder it to the jewelry object. When the jewelry object has been completed and polished, the pearl is cemented (set) as follows.

CEMENTING THE PEARL In recent years epoxy type pearl cements have become popular with most commercial jewelers and craftsmen. These cements are sold in two separate tubes or small jars and they must be mixed thoroughly in equal proportions. The cement is packed into the hole in the pearl with a jeweler's saw blade and then the pearl is put on the peg. The pearl may be clamped to the peg with a cross lock tweezer or with a clothespin.

The cement hardens chemically in about 8 hours. The hardening process can be hastened by placing cemented pearl objects near an electric heater, or a 250 watt heat lamp, or by heating in an electric furnace at 175°F.

Before the epoxy cements were used, pearls were cemented with a white solid pearl cement as follows.

The cement is broken into small pieces by crushing with a plier. The small pieces are inserted into the hole in the pearl. The pearl is warmed over an alcohol lamp flame until the cement melts and adheres to the inner walls of the hole. The peg of the jewelry object is warmed slightly and the pearl is pressed onto it until the cement hardens.

Caution: The pearl is moved continuously over the alcohol flame and heated just sufficiently to melt the cement, otherwise the pearl will be damaged.

Note: Since 1968 a new, almost instantaneous, high strength, no mixing cement has been marketed under the name of Aron Alpha. The cement is recommended; however, handle it carefully — it sticks to the skin. It can be dissolved by acetone.

PEARL STRINGING The required cord (preferably silk) and needles for stringing pearls can be purchased from supply houses. Before stringing the pearls, arrange them in the order desired. Tie a length of cord to the catch so that two ends extend. A pearl is passed onto the two cords by means of a pearl needle; a knot is then tied and this knot is pushed towards the pearl by means of a long needle or awl (fig. 373). Another pearl is passed down along the cords. This pearl is used to push the knot firmly against the first pearl. The process is repeated until the stringing is completed. Ends of the cord are glued to the catch so they do not unravel.

Fig. 373 Method of stringing pearls

Fig. 374 Pearl necklace   **Ole Lynggaard**

JEWELRY OBJECTS & THEIR CONSTRUCTION

1. JEWELRY DESIGN

The designing of jewelry is a highly specialized and important branch of the jewelry industry. Large manufacturing concerns and smaller ones that specialize in expensive jewelry employ their own designers. Many jewelers subscribe to a monthly design service which consists of a group of designs mailed out each month by a design organization. The designs are interpreted and varied slightly and thus become "original" pieces. It is also customary for small jewelry concerns to send out their special order work to be designed by a specialist.

Jewelers are always conscious of design and style developments and are constantly seeking new and innovative ideas. Jewelry designs, just as clothing and furniture, are subject to style trends and do change periodically. Contemporary art, current fashions, economic conditions, and social circumstances influence the jewelry that is made. For example, prevailing hairstyles often dictate whether or not earrings are worn, and changing mores determine what types of jewelry can be worn and by what sex. It is not, however, valid to believe that jewelry design changes with the same rapidity as do fashions. Good design is timeless, and the basic principles of jewelry design have remained the same for centuries. The design and craftsmanship of Egyptian, Greek, Byzantine, and Renaissance jewelry has yet to be surpassed.

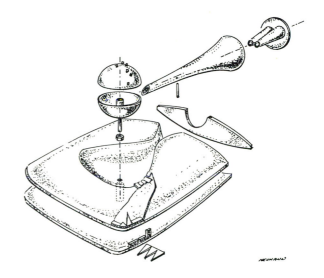

Fig. 376 Diagram of gold pendant William A. Neumann

Fig. 377 Gold pendant   **William A. Neumann**

Fig. 375 Contemporary ring   **Jacklyn Davidson**

Fig. 378 Jewelry designs by Angela Cummings of Tiffany & Co.

It is essential that all jewelry workers, commercial and hand craftsmen, give considerable thought to the design of the jewelry objects which they make, for an object is only as good as its design. The jewelry designer must think of the visual design possibilities of the materials used, and of the use the wearer will make of the jewelry object. As the designer arranges the various parts, he must consider the total size and weight of the metal, gems, and findings, must look at the spacing of the individual pieces, and decide on the methods of connecting them.

Although jewelry making techniques, materials, methods, and processes do not impose many restrictions on what can be made, there are certain tacit rules regarding the economics and regulating the technical design of a piece of jewelry. The cost of the metal, gemstones, and labor must always be considered. Try to use as little material as possible, while simultaneously trying to create a visual image that shows as much metal as possible. Contemporary designers have been greatly influenced by the fluctuating price of gold. In developing designs for jewelry that contain gemstones, the primary consideration is usually the number and placement of the stones and gems. Many times the treatment of the metal is minimized and the designer concentrates on ways that will most effectively display the gemstones.

Good design is not restricted to machine or handicraft. New techniques, such as centrifugal casting and machine chain making, also can influence jewelry design since the techniques can permit freer and less expensive use of materials. A jewelry object made by hand or machine may be well or poorly designed. If an object is made by hand and is designed poorly it can be a piece of junk; if an object is made by machine and is designed well it can be a work of art, and vice versa. In other words, the design of the jewelry object, not necessarily the method of making it, is the important consideration.

Though good artists are not necessarily the best jewelry designers, it is essential that jewelry craftsmen constantly refer to the artistic principles of design. Art terms such as symmetry, balance, proportion, and composition, should be understood and applied. It is

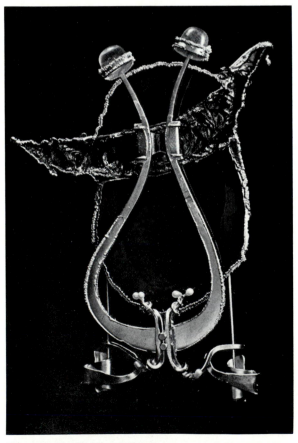

Fig. 379 Electroformed brooch   Stanley Lechtzin

suggested that a contemporary art book be referred to for definition and significance of art terms.

Knowing one's current ability as a designer and craftsman is very important. A designer must be aware of what skills will be needed to construct a piece of jewelry. Metal is not a very forgiving material. Mistakes are often very difficult, impossible, or expensive to correct. It is wise to practice new techniques on copper or brass before working with the precious metals. Working with wax models has an advantage in that wax can be easily carved or bent into any shape, and gemstones can be readily pressed into place to see how they will look.

Hopefully, jewelers will continue to develop new designs and integrate new techniques into their work by examining both past and contemporary jewelry, studying books and magazines on jewelry making, taking part in workshops and seminars, enrolling in classes, and experimenting with new methods and processes.

Though some jewelry (hat pins, cuff links) is functional (serves a useful purpose) most jewelry can fall into an ornamental classification; that is, the jewelry is molded into a shape which is primarily decorative in nature. Even the functional jewelry depends for the most part on applied ornamentation for its eye appeal.

There are two important rules of design that are worthy of note:

1. Appropriate design and ornament arises naturally from the physical nature of a material and the processes of working the material. In other words, designs and ornaments that are suitable for clay are not necessarily satisfactory for metal nor can some of them be made in metal.

2. Ornament and design must fit the form and function of an object. The ornament on a ring must be suitable for a ring, yet it may not be suitable for a pin.

There are several types of ornament and design that are also worthy of note:

1. Geometric: Ornament or design composed of straight lines, curves, dots, domes, etc., to which no pictorial significance can be assigned.

Fig. 380 Pendant　　　　　　**Elsa Peretti**

2. Conventionalized: Ornament or design which though based on naturalistic objects (animals, plants, etc.) departs from the exact representation of such objects in the interests of linear rhythm, simplification, and formal significance generally.

Fig. 381　Jewelry designs and prototype
Courtesy of Tiffany & Co.

205

3. Abstract: Abstract, non-figurative, and free-form design calls for an arrangement of lines, shapes, colors, and material into forms which should have an intellectual and aesthetic appeal. Any one, or combinations of more than one of the above may be repeated to form an "all over" pattern. Repeated patterns are commonly found in the links of bracelets and necklaces, and borders of pins.

Note: Simple design principles can be effectively combined to create beautiful pieces of jewelry.

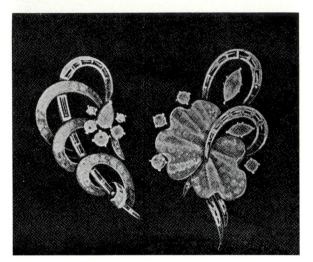

Fig. 382 Commercial designs

Frankly, just reading the above and understanding it does not make one a jewelry designer. The purpose in presenting the above is to give the average jewelry craftsman a little art information for background. It is hoped that hand craftsmen especially will be stimulated sufficiently to attempt to work out their own thoughts logically in the metal they are working with so that they can develop a truly creative jewelry art. Good designing takes time, requires thought, and is often hard work; but it can pay high dividends both economically and emotionally.

PRACTICAL DESIGN PROCEDURE

1. Do the original sketch on a good grade of paper with a hard, sharp pencil.
2. Trace the design onto tracing paper.
3. For a realistic effect, the design on the tracing paper or, better yet, frosted plastic may be tinted with water colors.

4. Commercial designs are painted on dull black cardboard with white and other water colors (fig. 382).

2. TRANSFERRING DESIGNS

After a jewelry object has been designed, it is necessary to transfer the design to the metal. Below are listed several important methods that may be used.

Method 1 This is the method used by most jewelers. Trace the design with a sharp, hard (No. 3) pencil onto a piece of tracing paper. Heat the metal slightly to warm it, and while it is still warm rub a piece of yellow beeswax over it to leave a thin layer. Let the metal cool to room temperature. This can be done quickly by placing the metal on a thick piece of steel, which will conduct the heat from it.

Now place the tracing paper on the wax, graphite side down. With a smooth surface, such as a burnishing tool or the handle of some pliers, rub the tracing paper until the wax shows through and then slowly remove the tracing paper. A graphite design should be on the wax.

Scratch the design onto the metal through the wax with a scratch awl, warm the metal again, and wipe the wax off with a rag to com-

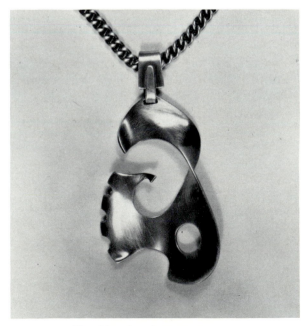

Fig. 383 An abstract pendant

206

plete the transfer of the design to the metal. **Note:** If monograms or letters are transferred, the design must be retraced on the opposite side of the tracing paper for it to appear properly.

Method 2 Trace the design onto tracing paper. Clean the metal with steel wool. Place a piece of carbon paper face down on the metal and the tracing paper on top of it. With a sharp pencil, retrace the design on the tracing paper, pressing firmly, and a carbon impression will appear on the metal. Scratch or engrave the design into the metal. Some craftsmen prefer to cover the metal first with a thin coating of Chinese white. The carbon and tracing paper can be held in position with paper clips.

Other Methods For piercing, the tracing paper can be glued or cemented to the metal, and the metal can then be cut with a jeweler's saw.

For production work, thin brass (22 gauge) patterns are made perfectly. It is comparatively easy to retrace the patterns onto the metal.

A rubber stamp can be made of the design so that it can be stamped onto the metal.

PLASTER COPIES If an exact three dimensional inexpensive replica of the shape of a completed jewelry object is desired for future reference or reproduction, a plaster of paris copy (fig. 384) can be made. This is done as follows: Press the jewelry object into plasteline (modeling clay) and then remove it carefully, thus leaving a negative imprint of the jewelry object in the plasteline. Wrap a piece of thick paper or thin sheet metal around the plasteline to form a wall at least ½" higher than the plasteline.

The plaster of paris is mixed as follows: To obtain the proper amount of water, pour water into the enclosed wall around the plasteline and then pour the water into a mixing vessel. Slowly add plaster of paris to the water (do not mix) until the plaster appears slightly above the level of the water. Now mix the plaster to a thin, cream-like consistency and then pour it over the plasteline impression. Vibrate the plasteline in order to remove any trapped air pockets.

Fig. 384 Plaster copies

When the plaster of paris hardens—2 to 5 minutes—the plasteline is removed, thus leaving a positive of the object in the plaster.

3. RINGS

RING SIZES Ring sizes (fig. 386) run from number 1, the smallest, to number 13, the largest.

The average woman's size is 6; the man's is 9.

Fig. 385 Sterling silver rings   **Katia Kamesar**

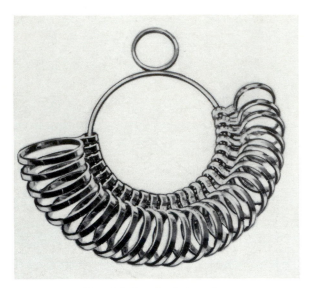

Fig. 386 Standard ring sizes

TO DETERMINE LENGTH OF METAL FOR RING SIZE

Craft Method Wrap a piece of paper around the finger on which ring is to be worn and cut paper to size. Cut the metal slightly smaller than the length of paper, for after the metal has been bent and soldered to form a band it may be stretched to the proper size; if the band is too large, it must be cut and resized.

Professional Method A standard ring stick or gauge is used. With a divider take the required ring size length off the stick or gauge (fig. 387) and then cut the metal to that length.

0 1 2 3 4 5 6 7 8 9 10 11 12 13

Fig. 387 Lengths for ring sizes

TO BEND A FLAT STRIP INTO A RING

Method 1 The ends of the strip can be bent in and together with half-round or round nose pliers. This method is recommended and can be used for practically all rings but those with very heavy bands. When bending, grip the very ends of the strip with the pliers and bend the ends in only (fig. 388). The strip does not have to be formed into a perfect

ring; only the ends should be bent to approximate the curvature of the ring and also to meet properly. After soldering, the strip is hammered on the ring mandrel to become a perfectly round ring.

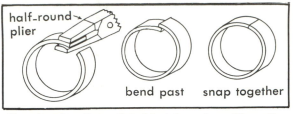

Fig. 388 Bending a flat strip into a ring with a plier

Method 2 The strip can be placed over a semi-circular grooved piece of wood. A ring mandrel is placed over the strip (fig. 389). A few blows on the mandrel with a mallet will quickly curve the metal. Move the mandrel and strip to different positions to form a perfect ring. Grooved steel blocks can be purchased.

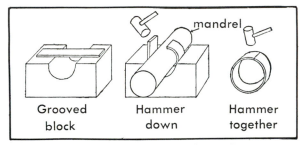

Fig. 389 Method of forming a ring

A simple bending machine (fig. 390) is available for professional jewelers. The machine is used to bend very thick bands or shanks.

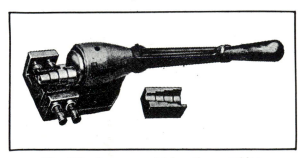

Fig. 390 A commercial bending machine

TO FILE ENDS OF BAND

The ends of the strip or band must fit perfectly before they are soldered. No space should be allowed for the solder.

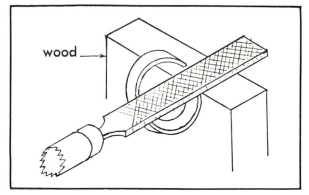

Fig. 391 Method of filing ends of band

Craft Method Hold the band as shown in figure 391. Note that one end of the band, the lower, is pressed against the top edge of the wood (held in a vise) and up against the file. The file is always held in a horizontal position and as close to the back of the band as possible. While pressing the file down as hard as possible against the wood and the end of the band, push the file forward; this will file a smooth end on the band. File the other end similarly.

To get the ends of the band to snap together, overbend them with a plier and then force them slowly back into position. No binding wire should be required to hold the band together while soldering.

Professional Method Hold the band against the bench pin and with your fingers squeeze

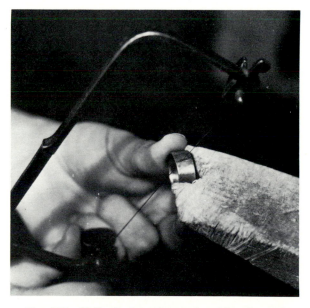

Fig. 392 Method of sawing ends of band evenly

the band to force the ends together. With a jeweler's saw, make one or more cuts between the ends as they are pressed together to even them perfectly (fig. 392). No filing is required.

When soldering, the solder usually used for silver work is placed inside the band over the seam; for gold and platinum work, it is placed on the outside of the band. No space should be allowed for the solder. **Suggestion:** Review method of soldering a band on page 57.

TO STRETCH A RING

Place the ring on a ring mandrel and then hammer straight down on the shank. Reverse the ring occasionally on the mandrel while hammering to avoid tapering the shank. A rawhide hammer may be used to stretch the ring slightly. A steel hammer will stretch a ring considerably, especially if the shank or band is annealed.

Carved or engraved marriage bands which cannot be hammer-stretched and also all plain band rings can be stretched as follows:

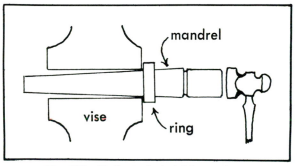

Fig. 393 Method of stretching a ring

Place the band on a ring mandrel and then place the mandrel between the jaws of a vise as shown in figure 393. By hammering the end of the mandrel the ring can be pushed onto the mandrel. It is best to rotate the mandrel and also to reverse the ring on the mandrel while it is being stretched to avoid tapering it. Commercial ring stretchers are available at dealers.

TO SHRINK A PLAIN BAND

This sounds almost impossible, but it can be done as follows: Place the ring in a dapping block opening that will just take the ring.

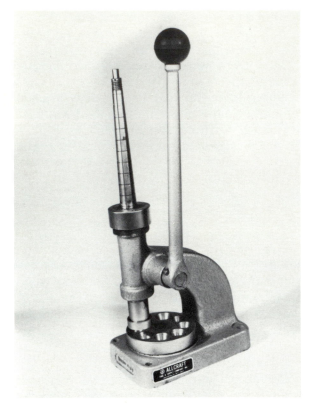

Fig. 394 Combination ring enlarger and reducer

Hammer the ring down so that it will be forced into the dapping block. Reverse the ring and repeat. Since the sides of the hollow in the dapping block slope in gradually, the band will be pushed in, thus forming a smaller sized ring.

RING CONSTRUCTION

The rings have been carefully selected in order to explain different construction techniques.

Fig. 395 Ring stretcher for rings with settings

LOVER'S KNOT Material: 14 gauge sterling silver round wire, 2 pieces, each 4″ long.

By hand, tie a knot in one wire and tighten it by placing ¼″ of one end in a vise and then pulling the other end with a flat jaw plier.

Place second wire through the loop of the first, tie knot, and tighten the same way. The wires must be tied as shown in figure 396.

Bind wires together with binding wire and then silver solder to hold them together; however, do not solder knot. Now remove the binding wire, cut ends to ring size, bend wires to form a ring, file ends perfectly, and finally silver solder ends together.

Finish ring by pickling, shaping on ring mandrel, filing soldered parts, emerying, and polishing. The lover's knot ring is very attractive with an antique finish or in gold. 12 gauge wire can be used for a man's ring.

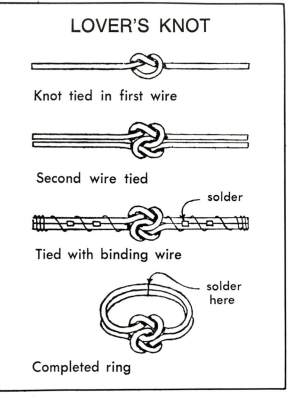

Fig. 396

SIMPLE INITIAL RING (fig. 397) Material: 14 gauge wire 7″ long, small piece of 18 gauge sheet.

The simple initial ring is an ideal elementary project for a school or camp program. The ring is made as shown in the diagram. Shot is made as described on page 45. Heavy block initials are the easiest to cut to shape by beginners and also look best. Shape the initial to the ring's curvature before soldering in place.

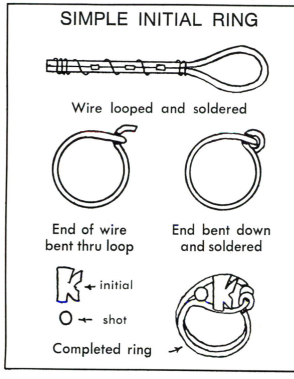

SIMPLE INITIAL RING

Wire looped and soldered

End of wire bent thru loop

End bent down and soldered

← initial

← shot

Completed ring ↗

Fig. 397

TWISTED WIRE Material: One piece of 12 or 14 gauge wire, 8″ long.

Bend the wire in half (fig. 398), place the loose ends in a vise, and then twist the wires tightly with a hand vise or hand drill. Flatten the twisted wire slightly on an anvil or flat piece of steel with a hammer. A rolling mill may be used to flatten the wires. Anneal the wire and then form into a band of the required ring size. The ends of the twisted wire must be filed so that they match perfectly before they are soldered.

There are many novelty twisted wire rings that can easily be made. See the chapter on twisted bracelets for more suggestions.

BELT RING The belt ring (fig. 399) can be made without the use of a jeweler's saw, and for this reason and because of its popular appeal, it is an ideal project for beginners and schools and camp programs.

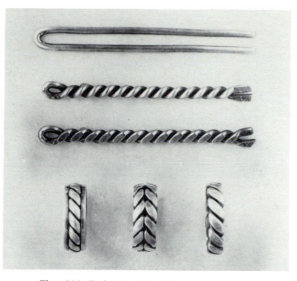

Fig. 398 Twisted wire ring construction

Material: 1 piece, 18 gauge sterling silver, ⅝″ by 2½″.

With a shear, cut a strip ¼″ wide from the main piece, size, form into a band, and solder. The sides of the band are evened by rubbing them on a smooth, flat file.

The overlapping piece (¼″ x 1″) is now cut to shape, bent, and soldered to the band over the band's previously soldered seam. After soldering, rub the sides of the ring even again and file the end of the overlapping piece so that it appears to arise from the band.

Place a piece of metal in a vise to make the buckle, and with a hand file, file in a "U" shaped notch, the width of which should be the same as the band. It is a simple matter to cut the outside of this piece to a buckle shape with a shear. Curve the buckle slightly and solder it to the band at the end of the overlapping piece.

The little strap is made from a thin strip of metal. The metal is nicked with a file and bent in towards the nick to form a right angle bend. Another nick is required to form a "U" shaped piece the width of which should be the same as the band. Solder this piece to the band where desired and then cut off the ends of the "U" with a saw.

The pin is cut to the shape shown and then soldered to the ring. The holes may be punched or drilled into the metal. File and finish the ring as desired.

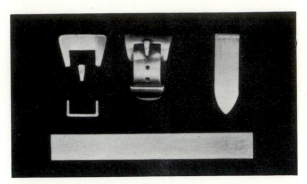

Fig. 399 The belt ring and its parts

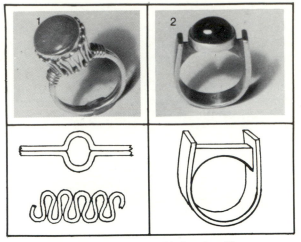

Fig. 401 Two rings with bezel settings

SIMPLE WIRE RING WITH A STONE Two pieces of 14 gauge wire are soldered together as shown in the top of figure 400. After soldering, the wires are bent, sized, and soldered to form a ring of the proper size. Flatten the top of the wire ring by filing so that the setting can be soldered to it.

The bezel (28 gauge sheet) soldered to 22 gauge sheet, and twisted wire (18 gauge) are made and assembled as explained in the chapter on bezel settings. The ornamental wire (20 gauge) is bent to shape by hand. Parts are assembled as shown in the picture.

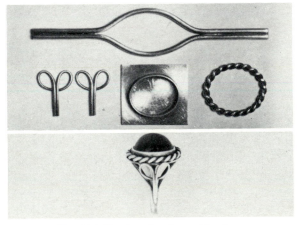

Fig. 400 Simple wire ring with stone

TWO RINGS WITH BEZEL SETTINGS (fig. 401) **Ring 1** was constructed to show how a simple high-domed ring can be made. Note that the shank (14 gauge) is formed similarly to the ring above. By means of a fine flat plier, 20 gauge round wire is bent to the shape shown. One side, the bottom, of the bent wire is soldered together and then the wire is bent, cut to size, and soldered to form

an oval shape, the size of which should fit around and be soldered to the oval top of the previously formed ring. The tops of the wire are bent out so that the bezel setting fits within, and then the setting is soldered in position. Four turns of 20 gauge round wire are soldered to each side of the shank and, after soldering, these wires are filed flush with the inside of the ring.

Ring 2 is made from 16 gauge metal which is bent to the shape shown. Another piece of 16 gauge metal is cut and soldered to the first piece, and then the bezel setting is soldered to this piece.

TWO RINGS WITH RAISED SETTINGS The two rings were made to show how long tapered pieces of metal can be bent to make practical shanks and unusual rings (fig. 402)

Ring 1 This ring was made in gold. The semicircular shaped setting is slightly longer than the stone and is tapered down almost to the width of the support part of the shank. A groove is filed or cut with a setting tool on both sides of the setting for the girdle of the stone. After all soldering has been completed, the top edge of the metal is forced over the stone by means of setting tools. Some of the metal is also hammered over the octagonal edges of the stone to keep it from slipping out sideways.

Ring 2 The stone in ring 2 is a turquoise. The ring is made as shown in the diagram and the picture.

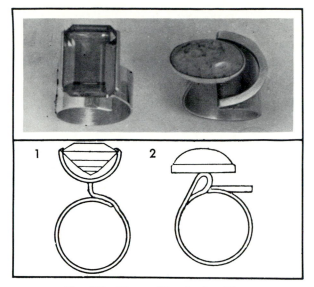

Fig. 402 Rings with raised settings

FOUR EASY-TO-MAKE RINGS (fig. 403) All four rings are made with plain or slightly tapered bands as shanks.

Ring 1 A circular disk is formed in a dapping block into a half sphere. The sphere is squeezed in a vise or hammered, and then it is filed until the top edge is oval. The bottom of this piece is now filed to match the shape of the band to which it is then soldered.

After the setting has been made, a piece of 8 gauge round wire is soldered to its bottom. A hole, very slightly smaller than the soldered wire, is drilled through the bottom of the concave oval piece and the shank of the ring.

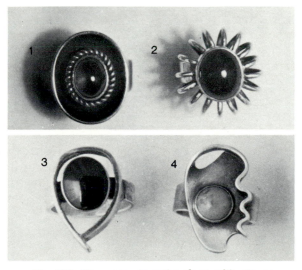

Fig. 403 Four easy-to-make rings with stones

The wire is forced through the hole, and, after the setting has been adjusted from the top, the wire is soldered to the shank.

Ring 2 A bezel is made for the stone, and it is soldered to an 18 gauge base. 16 gauge wire is wrapped around a 3/16″ rod. The wire is spread and bent so that the setting will fit on top of it as shown in the picture. The setting is soldered to the wire and the wire to the band.

Ring 3 A strip of 16 gauge metal is bent and soldered to the shape shown, and then it is soldered to a band. The setting is made and treated similarly to ring two.

Ring 4 The top of ring four is made from a sheet of 18 gauge metal. The long end is bent with half-round and round nose pliers to the shape shown, and then it is soldered in position. The exterior metal is cut and filed to the required shape. After the bezel is soldered to the top, the top piece is soldered to the band.

SNAKE RING There are many versions which can be worked out if the following ring is made.

Material: 1 piece, 8 gauge half-round wire, 10″ long.

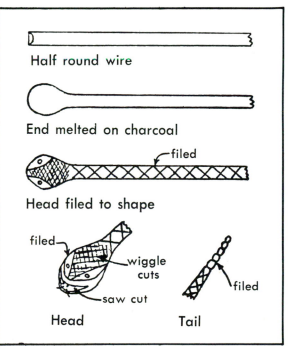

Fig. 404 Method of forming snake rings

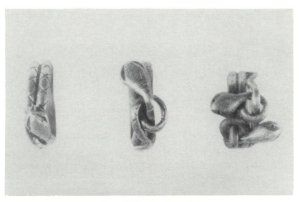

Fig. 405 Snake rings

The head of the snake is formed first by heating one end of the half-round wire on a charcoal block until it melts. Place the charcoal so that one end is higher; thus when the metal melts it will roll back on itself into an elliptical shaped form. The mouth is filed in with a three-square file, and then the head is shaped with a crossing file to form the hollow for the eyes and the shape of the nose (fig. 404). The eyes may be punched in with a beading tool or, better yet, small rubies may be used.

Scale effects can be had by means of hammer, or stamp marks, or triangular markings can be filed in. The end of the wire is tapered, and then the rattles are formed with a file. Wrap the snake around a ring mandrel several times to form a ring of the proper ring size and solder where necessary. If desired, fangs and teeth may be added to the mouth by first enlarging the mouth with a jeweler's saw and then opening it with a chasing tool.

BEZEL BEARING SETTING (fig. 406). The setting is made as described under Bezel Bearing Setting (page 182). The wire (20 gauge) is coiled around a rod and then spread sideways. Accurate soldering is required to solder it into position. The shank is made from 18 gauge metal. The leaves are cut from 22 gauge metal and chased over a lead block.

RING WITH A HOLLOW BASE This conventional ring with a hollow base for a rectangular setting has been selected to show how a setting can be built up for a ring. The rectangular setting is made as described under settings (page 182). It is then soldered to a flat or slightly domed-up base piece. A piece of metal slightly larger than the base piece is domed in a lead block to the shape shown in figure 407. The corners of the domed piece may be sharpened by hammering over the

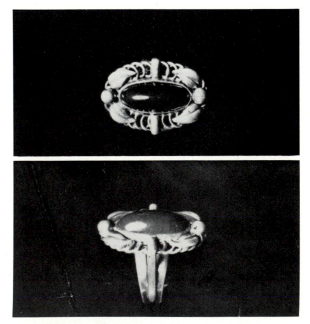

Fig. 406 Ring with bezel bearing setting

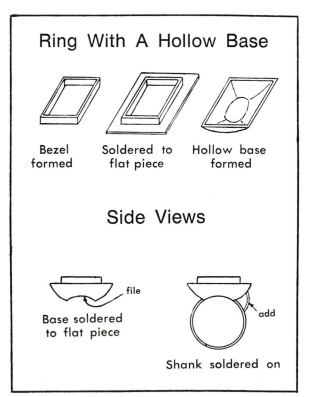

Fig. 407 Ring with a hollow base

corners of a lead block. The center of the piece is cut out as shown, and its bottom is filed to fit the finger. Its top is now filed flat, and then it is soldered to the setting. Many appropriate shanks can be made for this type of ring. Oval settings can be treated similarly.

ELEMENTARY RINGS WITH ONE PEARL

(fig. 408) All rings but the first have pearls which have been drilled ½ the diameter so that they can be glued to pegs (see page 201).

Ring 1. Forged square wire—pearl held with wire looped ends. **2.** Long triangular piece of metal—pearl glued to bent up end. **3.** Ends of notched rectangular strip bent up —pearl glued to peg. **4 and 5.** Forged from

RING FORMED FROM A PATTERN An attractive, heavy-appearing man's ring, suitable for a monogram or stone, can be formed from sheet metal cut to the shape of the pattern shown in figure 409. The pattern is best made by folding a piece of paper in four parts and then drawing one fourth of the pattern. After being cut with scissors, the paper is opened, and the pattern is traced onto a piece of metal, usually 16 gauge. When cut to shape, the metal is domed lightly where shown and then bent, with the aid of pliers, to form a ring. The sides are soldered together and eventually a top piece is soldered on. The side walls of the ring may be shaped for an oval, round, or rectangular top.

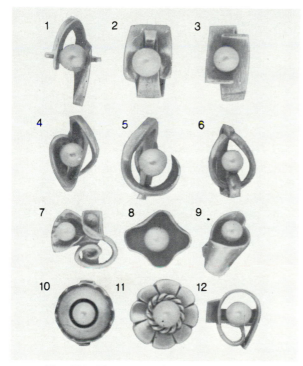

Fig. 408 Elementary rings with one pearl

square wire. **6.** Formed from one piece of half-round wire—pearl glued to peg. **7.** Flower formed from disc—pearl glued to spiraled wire. **8.** Disc domed in dapping block into a sphere—sides hammered in. **9.** Ring bent to shape by means of round nose pliers from long triangular strip of metal. **10.** Domed disc with center cut out soldered to crimped disc. **11.** Slightly domed chased disc soldered to domed chased base. **12.** Strip formed as shown with end bent up as peg for pearl.

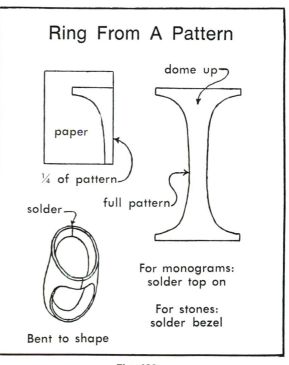

Ring From A Pattern

dome up

paper

¼ of pattern

full pattern

solder

For monograms: solder top on

For stones: solder bezel

Bent to shape

Fig. 409

MASCULINE RING WITH RECTANGULAR STONE This masculine appearing handmade ring is recommended for buffed top rectangular stones such as 16/12 or 14/12 hematite intaglios, black onyx, sapphires, or for tiger's eye cameos. The rectangular bezel is made from 16 or 18 gauge metal as explained on page 182. A rectangular bearing is made the same way as above and then soldered inside the bezel as shown in figure 410. Then file the bottom of the rectangular setting to match the finger curvature.

The shank for the ring can be made from a bar of 8 gauge metal 7/16″ wide. The length of the bar is the ring size length minus the width of the setting plus about ¼″. The center of the shank metal is forged (hammered) thinner. After cutting the shank metal to shape, bend it around a ring mandrel, file the sides and the top of it flat and the ends so that the setting fits into it; thus it can be soldered in place.

The alternate shank is easier to make. Cut the metal (16 gauge) the same as above but almost the width of the setting. The tapered groove is filed into the shank.

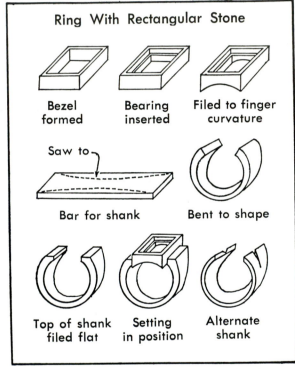

Ring With Rectangular Stone

Bezel formed

Bearing inserted

Filed to finger curvature

Saw to

Bar for shank

Bent to shape

Top of shank filed flat

Setting in position

Alternate shank

Fig. 410 Masculine ring with rectangular stone

MASCULINE RINGS Most commercial masculine rings are cast in order to obtain the bulky appearance of a man's ring. The following eight rings were made to show craftsmen how different construction styles of masculine rings can be made by hand.

All rings in figure 411 were made with bezel bearing settings (see page 182). **Ring 1** Rectangular wire soldered to 16 gauge tapered band; disc cut from 8 gauge wire. **Ring 2** 10 gauge square wire bent like wire in figure 400. Ornament made from 14 gauge square wire. **Ring 3** Shank similar to one in figure 410. **Ring 4** Setting soldered inside 16 gauge elliptical ring.

Fig. 411 Masculine rings with stones

The top and shank of the **PB** monogram ring (fig. 412) is one piece of 16 gauge metal. A "U" piece is soldered to its underside. This is cut and filed to finger curvature shape. **MB** ring is made as shown. Initials made from one piece of 16 gauge rectangular wire.

Fig. 412 Masculine initial rings

Fig. 413 Masculine initial rings

MB ring with small stone (fig. 413): Piece of 16 gauge metal bent to outside shape, notched for side pieces which are cut and filed to finger curvature after being soldered in position. Top piece then soldered to complete ring shape. **DS** ring made as shown in figure 413.

TWO RINGS WITH EMERALD-CUT STONES

On page 189, commercial methods of making prong settings for emerald-cut stones are explained. The two rings in figure 414 were made to show beginning craftsmen that these stones can be held in rings with easy-to-make settings. **Ring A** The long strip (1—fig. 414) is bent with flat nose pliers to form a seat or bearing (2) slightly smaller than the stone. The corners are then filed flat and the prongs (3) are soldered to them to form the setting (4). The shank (5), after being bent to shape, and the ornamental wire (6) are then soldered to the setting.

Ring B The shank is made from two rings (1) and two pieces of twisted wire (2) soldered together. The prongs are made from two "U" pieces (3) soldered to the shank (which has been notched for them), and the crossbar (4) (bent from round wire) is soldered to the prongs. The ring is completed by soldering the forged tapered twisted wire (5) to the shank and crossbar.

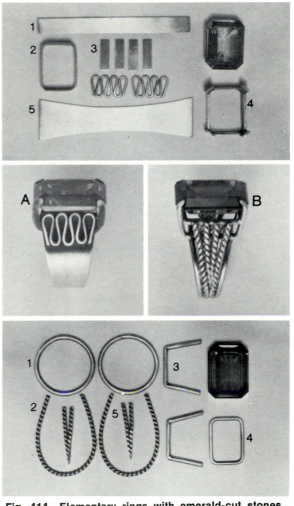

Fig. 414 Elementary rings with emerald-cut stones

ROSE PETAL RING An easy way to assemble the rose petal is by cutting the metal (24 gauge) as shown in figure 415. This piece is then shaped in a dapping or lead block. The edges are rolled over with a round nose plier. A smaller piece of metal is cut for the inner petals. Ring and ornamental wire are made as shown in the picture.

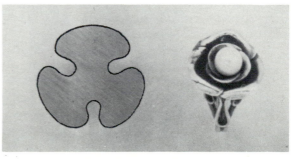

Fig. 415 Rose petal ring

EASY-TO-MAKE RING SUGGESTIONS

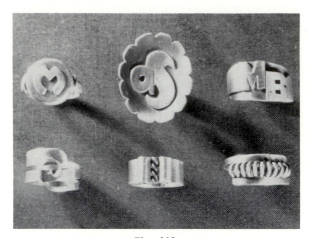

Fig. 416

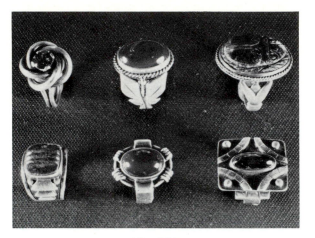

Fig. 417

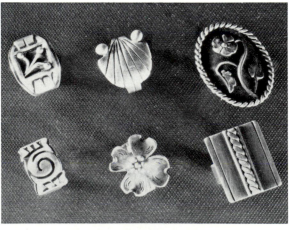

Fig. 418

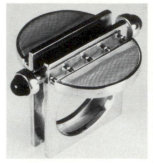

Fig. 419 Ring
Hannelore Gabriel

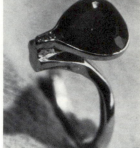

Fig. 420 Ring Natalie Paul

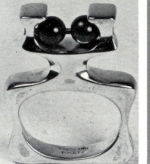

Fig. 421 Ring Fretz

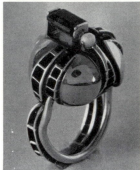

Fig. 422 Ring Randy Burns

4. EARRINGS

Earrings should be designed with comfort as the primary consideration. They should be constructed from thin gauge metals for lightness.

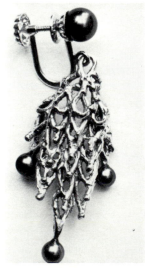

Fig. 423 Earring
Robert Natalini

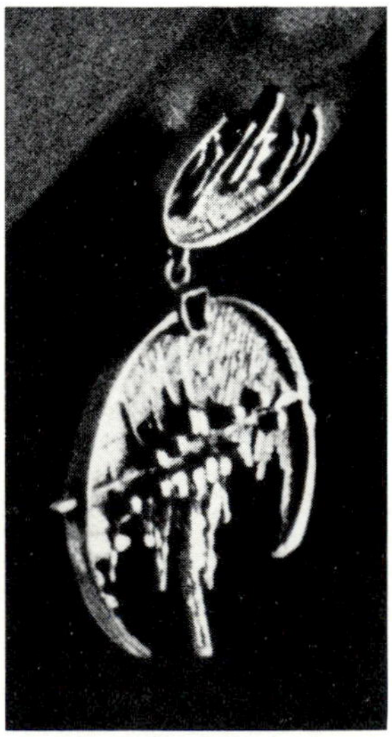

Fig. 424 Earring
Sylvia Falkove

ELEMENTARY EARRINGS The shape of the required metal is shown next to each earring. Note how simple the constructions are. In the triangular group (fig. 425), with the exception of the ear wires, no soldering is required. In order to conserve material, it is better to form the triangles by cutting a rectangle diagonally in half and then slightly cutting the bases of the cut pieces to form two triangles. 24 gauge sheet copper or silver is recommended for these earrings.

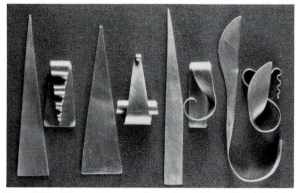

Fig. 425 Elementary earrings based on the triangle

In the rectangular group (fig. 426), the slotted earring is cut with a shear and bent to shape with round-nose pliers. The flower earring calls for elementary chasing techniques which can be accomplished quickly over a dapping and a lead block. A rivet is required for one of the earrings, and it is not soldered but forced into the loop of the bent piece. The earring with the twisted wire is made by rolling the ends of the rectangular piece of metal with round-nose pliers until the space left is just wide enough for the twisted wire. The twisted wire may be soldered permanently in position.

In the circular group (fig. 427) the circles can be purchased cut to shape in silver or they can be cut with a shear. All parts, ear wires excepted, are silver soldered together. The first earring, top left, is cut as shown, chased over a lead block, and then formed with a round-nose plier. The small disc in the center earring is formed in a dapping block, and then it is soldered with the small shot in the center to the larger disc. The crimped wire in the top right earring is soldered to a disc that has been chased and curved slightly.

The bottom left earring is chased. The leaf in the center one is line chased and soldered as shown to a disc that has been domed slightly after the hole has been cut. The last earring is formed in a dapping block, the small piece is curled in with a plier, and the flattened twisted wire is bent and soldered where shown.

Fig. 427 Elementary earrings based on the circle

In the wire group, the first earring is made from a coil of wire; the other earrings are bent to shape with pliers. The first earring in the lower group is made from half-round and

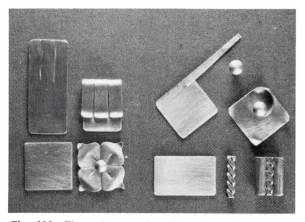

Fig. 426 Elementary earrings based on the rectangle

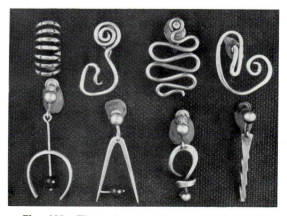

Fig. 428 Elementary earrings made from wire

round wire; the other earrings are forged from square and round wire.

EARRING SUGGESTIONS (fig. 429) The coiled spring earring is made from 14 gauge wire. The tip of the wire in the next earring is enlarged by heating it so that it melts and rolls back upon itself. The leaf earring is made by soldering a rectangular wire to the leaf. The crimps are formed with round-nose pliers. The top right earring is made from 12 gauge wire.

The bottom left earring is made from 24 gauge sheet metal. The spiral earring is made from 14 gauge wire and a small silver ball or shot. Twisted wire is silver soldered to the next earring. The slots in the small earring are cut with a jeweler's saw. The leaf earring, bottom right, is chased in pitch or a lead block. The appropriate finish for these hand-made earrings is the antiqued; they can be given a high polish.

Fig. 429 Earring suggestions

DROP EARRINGS (fig. 430) This is a group of easy to make drop earrings. 22 or 24 gauge sheet metal can be used. 16 gauge wire is used in the top left earring. The slits in the

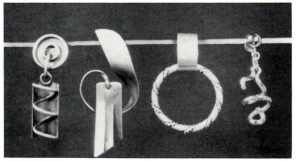
Fig. 430

next earring are cut with a shear. The hoop in the gypsy earring is made as described in the chapter (page 236) on twisted wires. The abstract wire earring, top right, is made from 14 gauge wire.

The holes in the center earrings are punched through the metal with an awl (see page 39). The small links in the end earrings are silver soldered together. The middle earrings are bent to shape with round and half-round pliers.

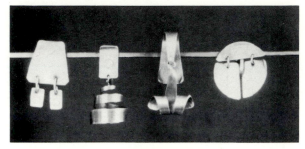
Fig. 431

The earrings in figure 432 are made from round, square, and rectangular wires.

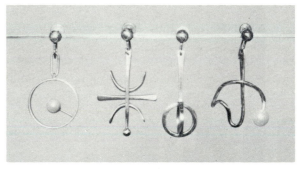
Fig. 432 Drop earring suggestions

PIERCED EARRINGS (fig. 433) This group was made to offer to beginning craftsmen design suggestions for easy-to-make small earrings for pierced ears. All earrings were made in gold. Commercial pierced earring stems were soldered to the backs of the earrings.

ATTACHING EAR WIRES Ear wires and clips are soft soldered to copper and silver earrings. A method of soft soldering an ear wire to an earring is described under Soft Soldering on page 60. Gold ear wires are usually soldered to the earrings with 8 karat solder. The construction of a simple but practical ear

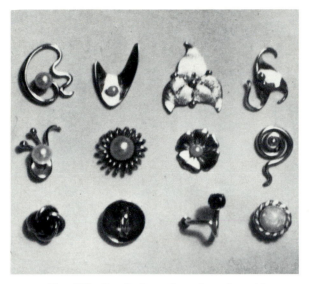

Fig. 433   Small pierced earrings in gold

clasp for pendant earrings is described on
page 249. **Note:** In order for button earrings
to hang properly, the earring back should be
soldered to the earring above its midpoint.

Fig. 434
Atelje Sundahl

Fig. 435
Sam Kramer

5.   PINS

ELEMENTARY PINS The pins (fig. 437) are
made from 22 or 20 gauge copper. The wire
for the brushes and treble clef is 14 gauge.
The clef is soft soldered to the disc. The
ends of the brushes are flattened by squeezing the wires in a vise. The three wires are
silver soldered together and then soft sol-

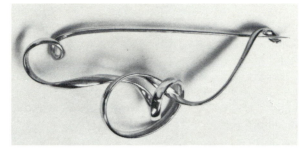

Fig. 436   Abstract pin   Courtesy of Georg Jensen

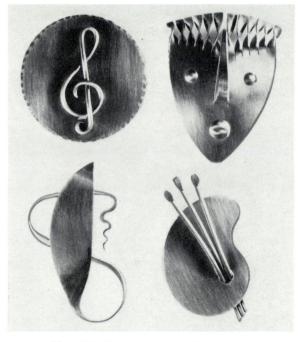

Fig. 437   Elementary pins in copper

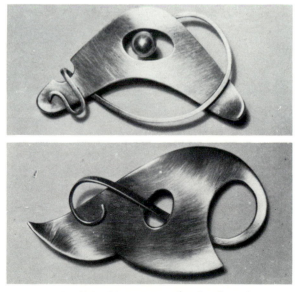

Fig. 438   Elementary pins in silver

dered to the palette. The eyes and mouth of the mask are formed in a dapping block. The slits for the hair and nose are cut with a shear.

ELEMENTARY PINS IN SILVER The two pins in fig. 438 are examples of contemporary design trends in silver. They can be made by using elementary techniques.

Square wire and a hollow ball are used for the top pin.

The stem going through the hole of the leaf pin is an extra piece of silver.

ELEMENTARY PINS IN GOLD (fig. 439) Gold is a sturdier metal than copper or silver; thus thinner gauges can be used. **Note:** Since gold is expensive, gold filings should be saved.

Fig. 440 Parts of monogram   **Fig. 441 Parts soldered together**

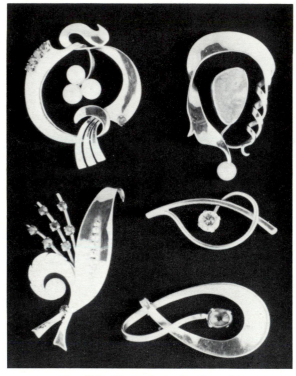

Fig. 439   Elementary pins in gold

Fig. 442 Pin completed   **Fig. 443 Abstract pin**

PIN SUGGESTIONS The pins in figures 444 to 450 are examples of objects that can be made by employing elementary jewelry making techniques. The pins in figures 444, 445 and 446 are approximately one-half size.

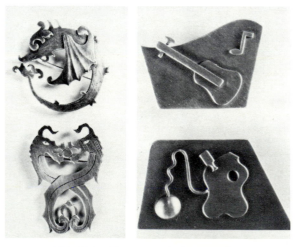

Fig. 444   Pierced and abstract pins

TWO INITIAL MONOGRAM This original style has a three dimensional effect. It is made as follows. The first and second initials are cut to shape as shown in figure 440. Note that metal is left on the second initial so that the first one may be soldered to it. After the soldering operation (fig. 441), the metal is cut away from the first initial, leaving the pin shown in figure 442.

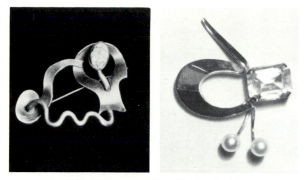

Fig. 445 and 446   Abstract pins

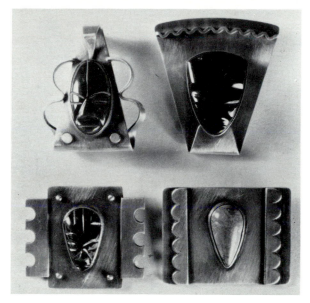

Fig. 447   Pins with Mexican stones

BOWKNOT PIN

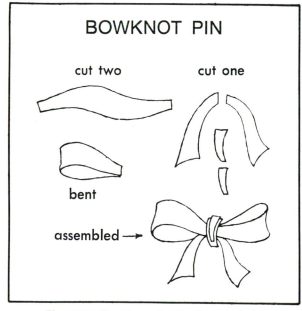

cut two

cut one

bent

assembled →

Fig. 448   How to make the bowknot pin

THE BOWKNOT The bowknot is a popular inspiration for many silver and gold pins. If desired, one piece patterns for both sides of the bow can be made. The center piece is usually set with stones.

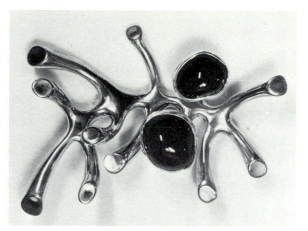

Fig. 449   Pin   Mary Nelson

Fig. 450   Pin   George van Duinwyk

ATTACHING JOINTS AND CATCHES

Pin backs of the combination or bar type are soft soldered, whereas individual joints and catches are usually hard soldered to pins.

PIN BACKS Soft solder flux is applied to the base of the pin back and to the pin. The pin back is held in position with a tweezer or plier. Small pieces of soft solder are applied to the holes in the pin back or along the sides of the pin back, and then the pin, not the pin back, is heated until the solder melts. Craftsmen may perform the soldering operation by holding the pin over a bunsen burner (fig. 451). If desired, the solder may be melted onto the base of the pin back before it is clamped in position. It is advisable to leave the pintong sticking straight up so that it is not heated, and thus softened, when the pin back is soldered to the pin.

Fig. 451 Soldering a pin back over a bunsen burner

SILVER PINS It is best to melt a small piece of solder onto the bases of individual joints and catches. The joint and catch may be held in a charcoal or asbestos block. When cool the joint and catch are placed in position, and the pin is heated around the joint and catch until the solder remelts. If necessary, the joint and catch can be pushed to proper positions with a poker.

COMMERCIAL METHOD Melt solder onto the bases of the joint and catch. Apply flux to the pin where required. Hold the joint with a tweezer. Heat the pin where the joint is to go until it turns light red and then apply the joint while the metal is still red. The solder on the base of the joint will melt, and, if the torch is lifted at that moment, the joint will adhere to the pin. The catch is soldered to the pin the same way.

The above commercial method of soldering calls for perfect timing when heating the metal and placing the joint and catch. With a

little practice, however, the average craftsman should be able to master the technique.

Wire solder is used commercially to apply the solder quickly to many joints and catches. The joints and catches are lined up on an asbestos board. Flux is applied. The joints and catches are heated individually, and, when light red, the wire solder is touched to them.

GOLD PINS A small piece of gold solder, usually 8 karat, is melted onto the pin where the joint and catch are to be placed. The joint and catch are then placed in position and the pin is reheated around them until the solder melts. An old pin or a piece of wire may be placed between the joint and catch to align them properly.

PINTONGS Some pintongs are manufactured with rivets attached. They are placed, open as far as possible, between the holes in the joint. The joint is then squeezed together with a plier to hold the pintong permanently in position.

Pintongs that require rivets are superior and are used for finer jewelry. The pintong is attached by placing it in position and inserting the rivet wire through the holes in the joint and itself. Often the holes must be aligned with a broach or reamer. The broach is turned through the holes of the joint and pintong at the same time and from opposite sides. It is best that the hole in the pintong should be very slightly larger than the holes in the joint. This way, the pintong can turn on the rivet without eventually breaking the rivet, as it would do if it could not turn freely.

Note: A pintong, or wire for a pintong, can be hardened by placing one end of the wire in a small hand vise, pin vise, or plier; holding the other end of the wire with one of these tools; and then turning the tools in opposite directions while pulling on the wire to keep it taut. Planish and file if necessary.

If a rivet wire is not available, the front end of a different pintong can be used. Cut the rivet so that it projects slightly (1/64″) on each side of the joint. The rivet is hammered lightly on a steel block with a riveting hammer to spread the ends, which keeps the pintong in position permanently.

If necessary, the pintong is cut so that it projects slightly (1/64") beyond the catch and then a new point is filed on it. The pintong point must be sharp in order not to damage the clothing, and it must not project too much for safety's sake.

Fig. 451A   Pin   J. Fred Woell

A plier with parallel flat jaws can easily be adapted for flaring the ends of the rivet when attaching the pintong to the joint. With a small round bur attached to a flexible shaft, open a small round depression in one of the jaws. Position the bur so that its side sits in the hole, close the pliers, and then rotate the bur so that a mark is made in the other jaw of the pliers. The holes are now aligned. Open each hole individually with the bur until their diameters are slightly larger than the diameter of the rivet wire. Insert the rivet wire through the joint and pintong (the pliers can be used to push the rivet through the holes) until it projects slightly on each side of the joint. Then, grip the rivet with the pliers, using the holes in its jaws, and rotate the pliers back and forth until the ends of the rivets are compressed and spread into flared semispherical shapes.

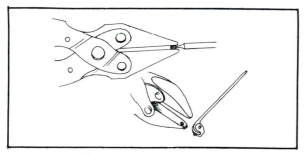

Fig. 452   Rivet setting plier

6. PENDANTS & NECKBANDS

The terms pendant, neckband, neckpiece, collar, choker, and necklace are difficult to define as the differences between them are often negligible. Although pendants are generally thought of as objects that hang freely from a chain or wire, many contemporary jewelers will integrate the pendant with the chain, neckband, or neckpiece. Chokers, collars, and neckpieces may be forged or shaped from a single piece of metal, or consist of many pieces and/or other materials

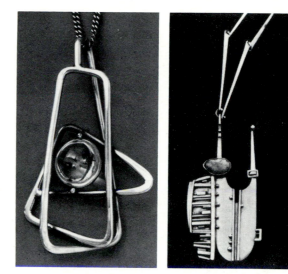

Fig. 453 Pendant
Henry Steig

Fig. 454 Pendant
Ruth Goodman

Fig. 455 Pendant   Jacklyn Davidson

that might be joined together by rivets or links so that they move or flex. Chains and necklaces can be very similar in design, both having repeated link motifs.

Suggestions for constructing bails, rings, loops, and hooks for attaching a pendant to a chain are shown in fig. 463. The opening, or loop, for the chain can also be integrated into the body of the pendant. The loop must be placed so that the pendant is balanced and hangs properly from the chain.

Fig. 459   Elementary pendant suggestions

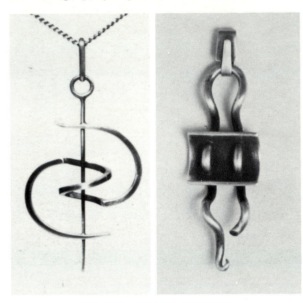

Fig. 456 and 457 Pendants

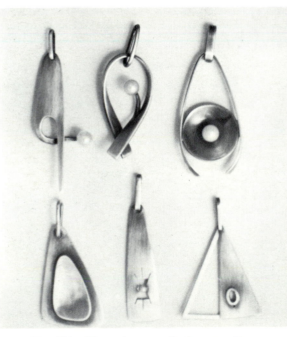

Fig. 458   Elementary pendant suggestions

Fig. 460 Fused pendants   David Yurman

226

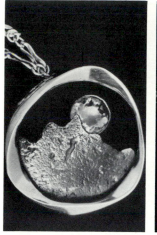

Fig. 461 Pendant
Ross Coppelman

Fig. 462 Pendant
Roberta Phay

Square wire and sheet metal wire were used to make the neckband in figure 466; the back pivots on the side piece by means of a wire rivet.

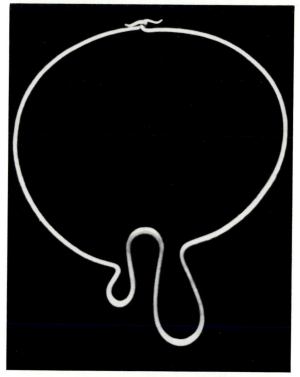

Fig. 464 One piece wire neckband

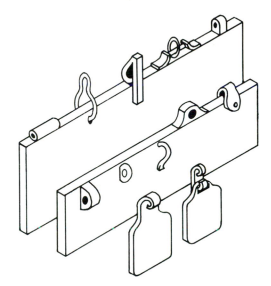

Fig. 463 Suggestions for ways to attach pendants
Courtesy of Jan Mainzer

NECKBANDS

The three neckbands shown were made to give beginning craftsmen construction techniques and design possibilities for a popular jewelry item. The one piece neckband (fig. 464) was made from 14 gauge round wire. The loops were bent to shape with half-round pliers; their ends were forged. The neckband was planished (hammered).

The sides of the center piece in figure 465 were made from 16 gauge rectangular strips through which holes were drilled for the band.

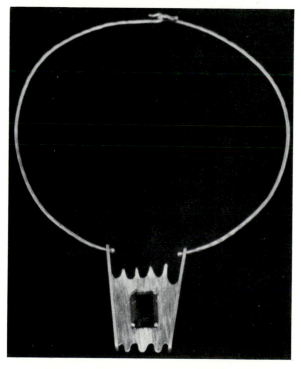

Fig. 465 Wire neckband with center piece

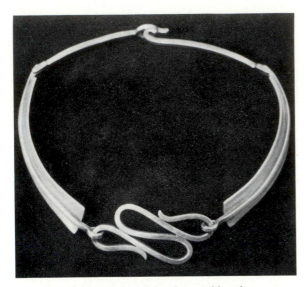

Fig. 466 Flexible wire neckband

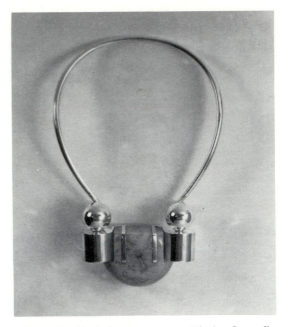

Fig. 468   Neckpiece   Hiroko Swornik

Fig. 467 Torso neckpiece   Mary Ann Scherr

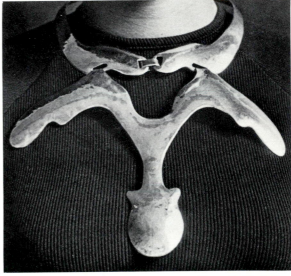

Fig. 469   Neckpiece   Alyse B. Tartell

7. TIE CLIPS

Hard copper or spring sterling silver (see Metals) should be used for the tie clips since annealed copper and silver are too soft and haven't sufficient spring to maintain their shape. The required metal thickness depends upon the type of clip being made. 18 gauge metal, ¼″ to ⅝″ wide, can be used. 16 gauge metal, ¼″ to ⅝″ wide, is sturdier, thus superior, for monogrammed, filed, and narrow tie clips. A good length for the metal is 4" to 5", and in schools where a foot squaring shear is available, it is best to buy the metal that long and then cut it to the required width.

BENDING PROCEDURE The metal can be bent to form the clip as follows:

1. Place the metal between the jaws (smooth with a filed round edge) of a vise and bend to a right angle as shown in figure 470. In school shops, the metal can be bent in a sheet metal worker's brake.

2. Again, in the vise, bend metal back 30 degrees at position shown and then bend up end of the metal with round-nose pliers.

3. Place metal on flat surface and continue bending process with the aid of a round-nose plier.

4. Finally, form the completed clip shape by squeezing the metal slightly in the vise until it assumes the shape shown in the diagram. Note that the clip is a little narrower at A-A than it is at B-B. The reason for this is simple: when the clip is inserted into the tie and shirt, an allowance must be made for the thickness of the fabrics.

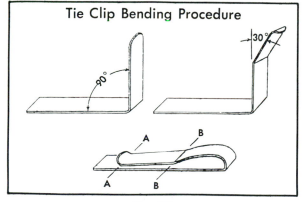

Fig. 470

Caution: It is best to heat spring sterling silver to a very light brown only where the right angle bend is to be made in order to anneal it slightly; otherwise it may break as it is being bent. Soft solder all parts to the clip after it has been bent.

Note: The inside metal of the tie clip should be polished before it is bent to shape, for if the metal, especially its edge, is rough or sharp, it will damage the tie.

TIE CLIP SUGGESTIONS

1. Parallel Lines: The lines are filed into the metal with a three-square needle file.

2. Small Ball: The line is filed with a three square file. The texture is hammered into the metal with a line chasing tool; the metal is cut to shape with a jeweler's saw. A small hollow ball or shot is soft soldered to the clip.

3. Belt Buckle: 1/16" holes are drilled into the clip. The buckle is cut to shape with the jeweler's saw. The pin is silver soldered to the buckle, which is then soft soldered to the clip. The strap is bent to shape and also soft soldered to the clip.

4. Rectangle: Lines are filed and a hole is drilled through the rectangular piece of metal. The rectangle is soft soldered to the clip after the clip has been bent to shape.

4a. Abstract: A hole is drilled through and the abstract design is cut into the metal with a jeweler's saw. Then the metal is soft soldered to the clip.

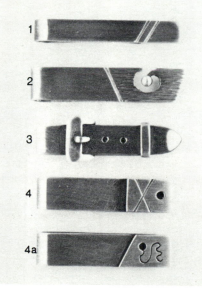

Fig. 471   Tie clip suggestions

229

5. Ball and Wire: Square wire is bent to the shape shown and the ends are silver soldered together. The wire and ball are soft soldered to the clip.

6. Forged: Square wire is forged and filed and then soft soldered with a hollow ball to the clip.

7. Filed: The sculptured effect is achieved by filing the clip with a half-round needle file.

8. Monogram: The top, side edge, and space between the initials, is beveled with a file in order to obtain a three dimensional effect. The letters are cut to shape with a saw. The letters are shaped before the metal is bent to form the tie clip.

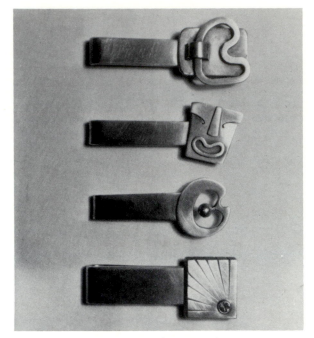

Fig. 473   Tie clip suggestions

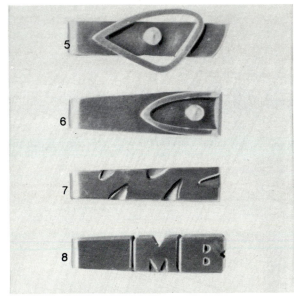

Fig. 472   Tie clip suggestions

karat is used for gold tie clips. After all soldering has been completed, the gold is tapped with a smooth hammer in order to harden it. Hammering will harden silver and copper, though not as hard as the rolled metal. Too much hammering will distort the tie clips.

Figure 473: The tie clips shown in figure 473 were made to match and form sets with the cuff links described on page 243. The small end pieces are made first and all parts should be silver soldered to them. After the small pieces have been pickled, they are soft soldered to the clips.

SOLDERING PROCEDURE Do not attempt to hard solder pieces to the main part of the tie clip, for the heat required for hard soldering will soften the metal. Individual parts may be silver soldered together and then soft soldered to the clip. Gold solder of the proper

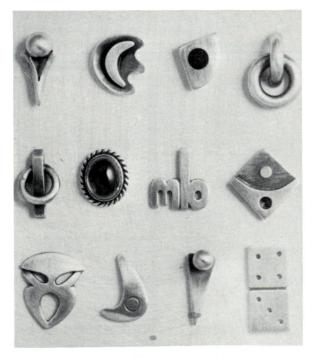

Fig. 474   Tie tac suggestions

FINISHING The tie clips can be given a high polish or, for informal wear, an antique finish (page 72). In both cases, remove all nicks with files and then the file marks with fine emery paper (page 63).

TIE TACS

In recent years, tie tacs have become very fashionable. The top left tie tac in figure 474 was made by first bending a half-round piece of wire in half and then forging, soldering, and filing it to shape. A hollow ball is then silver soldered to the wire where shown. The second tie tac (top, left) was designed and made by Sigi in Taxco, Mexico. The tac with the black circle (3rd from left) was made by drilling a hole part way through the metal and melting enamel in the hole. The other tacs illlustrate design possibilities that can easily be made by beginning craftsmen.

Excellent clutch backs (picture) are available from commercial finding houses. Posts for them are made that can be soft or hard (preferred) soldered to the tie tacs.

Fig. 474b

A post can be silver or soft soldered to a tie tac by first melting a small piece of solder directly onto the tac or onto the back of the post. Then with the aid of a tweezer, hold the post against the tie tac. Preheat the metal (see Soldering) and then, by heating the metal around the post, remelt the solder so that when the flame is removed the post will adhere to the tac.

It is good procedure to solder the post as high as possible on the tie tac; otherwise the tacs tend to turn when worn.

8. CHAINS AND CHAIN MAKING

FORMING THE LINKS The links for most chains are formed by first wrapping wire of the required thickness around a rod or mandrel and then cutting across the formed coiled wire with a jeweler's saw in order to get individual links. The shape and diameter of the rod or mandrel should correspond to the shape and inside diameter of the required link.

The wire can be wrapped around the mandrel by hand, or the mandrel and one end of

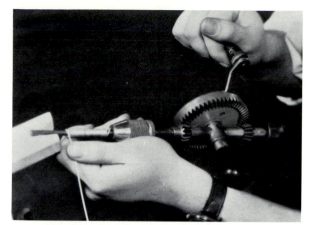

Fig. 475 Wrapping wire with a hand drill

the wire can be placed in the chuck of a hand drill and the wire can be wrapped quickly by turning the hand drill (fig. 475).

Heavy (9 gauge) links suitable for identification bracelets are formed around a ¼″ rod with a slot on one end; the other end of the rod can be formed into a handle, or it can be held in the jaws of a wood worker's brace. The rod is squeezed between two soft pieces of wood held in a vise so that it can be turned easily without slipping. The wire is placed in the slot in the rod and formed by turning the rod.

When elliptical links are desired, it is best to wrap one or two layers of paper around the elliptical mandrel first and then to wrap the wire. After the wire has been formed, burn the paper off with a torch and thus the wire can be removed easily.

CUTTING THE COILED WIRE Hold the coiled wire by hand against the bench pin and cut down one side with the jeweler's saw (0/2 blade) to form individual links (fig. 476). A rod may be inserted part way up the coiled wire and moved down as the cutting proceeds to facilitate holding the wire. Heavy links can be cut by placing the coiled wire in a vise as shown in figure 477.

CLOSING THE LINKS The links are closed by first squeezing each one individually with a plier in order to eliminate the gap created by the jeweler's saw. Then with two pliers, the link is twisted sideways to complete the closing operation. One half of the links are closed and then soldered individually.

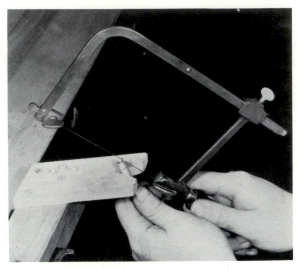

Fig. 476 Cutting the coiled wire

SOLDERING THE LINKS The soldering and assembling process is comparatively easy. As many as possible of the closed links are lined up on an asbestos or charcoal soldering block with the seam to be soldered furthest away. Flux and solder are applied to each seam and then the link is heated until the solder melts. Often it is easier to apply the solder by means of a poker (see Soldering). For silver chains, low melting silver solder will do except for chains that are to be twisted, which require medium melting solder. The proper gold karat solder should be used for gold chains.

Two soldered links are now joined by one unsoldered link to form a group of three links. After closing the unsoldered link with pliers, it is placed as shown in figure 478

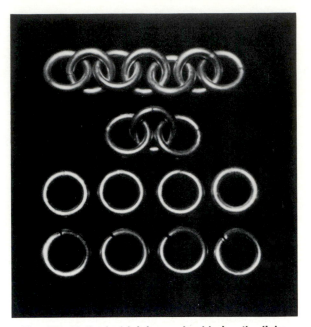

Fig. 478 Method of joining and soldering the links

and soldered. Groups of three's are joined to form a chain of seven links (fig. 478) and so on until the chain of the required length is formed.

TWISTED CHAINS Twisted chains are made from round or oval link chains. Make the chain of the required length as described above and then twist it. The twisting is done by placing one end of the chain in a vise and holding and twisting the other end with a hand vise (fig. 479). Lean back on the chain as it is twisted and all the links will twist and line up evenly (fig. 480). **Note:** Medium melting silver solder must be used for silver twisted chains, for the easy melting silver solder is too weak and is apt to break as the chain is twisted. The chain should be annealed before it is twisted.

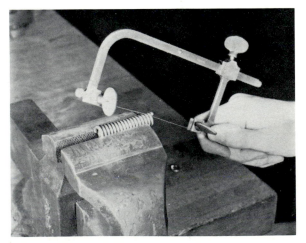

Fig. 477 Cutting heavy links in a vise

Fig. 479 Method of twisting a chain

Fig. 480 Chain twisted

HANDMADE CHAIN POSSIBILITIES Chains with innumerable link possibilities can be made by hand. All round and all oval chains are made as described above. Twisted, combinations of round and oval links, and several popular novelty chains, as shown in figure 482 and 484, are described below. With a little ingenuity, many other variations can be worked out. The thickness of the wire and the size of the links depend upon the use of the chain.

1. The chain consists of oval links.

2. A good, easy way to make key chains for men. Long oval links are twisted as shown and then combined with small round links.

3. A chain for charms. Round wire is bent with pliers and then soldered as shown to form links. They are then connected with round links.

4. A popular handmade key chain. Long oval links are cut in half, placed together as shown, and after their ends are squeezed together slightly for better contact, they are soldered together. Additional sections are added similarly.

5. A delicate chain consisting of groups of three long and three short oval links.

6. A chain of 8 gauge sterling silver for an identification bracelet made as described under twisted chains. The top of the chain can be filed flat.

7. A rope chain—very popular for chokers and bracelets, especially in gold. It is made from round rings. The rings are opened so that the gap is slightly wider than the metal thickness. Two rings are then soldered together to form a link as shown in fig. 481. Another link is formed through this and then a third through both of them. From here on the procedure is the same as the last link. The rings are held together with tweezers while being soldered.

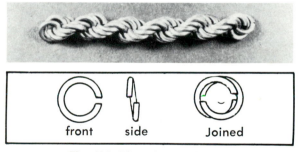

front   side   Joined

Fig. 481 Rings for rope chain

8. A chain made of three turns of half-round wire interlocked with three more turns of wire. The ends of the interlocked pieces are soldered together.

9. A simply constructed but effective chain for charms, etc. A long oval link is bent in half around a rod or with round-nose

233

pliers, and the bent part is squeezed together as shown. The links are then inserted through one another to form a chain.

10. A chain of two round rings combined at right angles to form a link. Additional links are added as shown in the picture.

11. This spiral chain is very popular in gold. It is made by wrapping wire around a rod to form a long, open spaced coil. The coil is cut every second turn. Two sections are interlocked as shown in the picture, and the ends only are soldered together. After all links have been added, the chain is flattened lightly with a mallet and then each link is filed on the top to flatten.

12. The chain is made from long oval links. The first link is given a half turn by gripping its ends with flat nose pliers. Note from fig. 483-3 that a rod (flattened on top and bottom) is held inside the link when it is twisted.

   Now the next link is placed on the first link and then twisted in a similar fashion. This is continued until the desired length of chain is obtained. The top of the chain can be flattened by hammering on the rod used when the links are twisted. This chain is often made commercially from hollow wire or tubing. See page 279 for the method of forming a hollow wire chain.

Fig. 482 Handmade chain possibilities

234

13. This chain is made by wrapping wire around a rod to form a link as shown in figure 483-1. Two links are soldered together as shown in figure 483-2. Two more links are inserted between these to form a single unit as shown in the picture.

   Now four links are placed on the first group to form a new section of the chain. By holding the first group up in the air with a tweezer or wire, the four new links will align themselves and thus can be soldered. Soldering is best done by means of a poker as described on page 58.

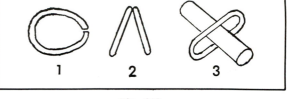

Fig. 483

14. This interesting chain is very popular in gold as an individual chain or when used in combination with other chains to form wide bands. Concaved rectangular wire (convexed can be used) is formed into oval links. One link is soldered and, by means of pliers, it is given a quarter turn to the right. Another link is soldered through the first link and given a quarter turn to the left. The next link is soldered through both links and given a quarter turn to the right. The process is continued by always soldering and twisting another link through the last two links until the desired chain length is obtained.

   Note: Both ends of all individual links can be filed slightly thinner and narrower so that they can easily be woven together.

15. This chain can be used to make a link bracelet. Long links are formed from half-round wire. An oval link, made from rectangular wire, is inserted into the long link and then soldered in position. Round wire is used to form the small connecting links.

16. The chain is made by cutting coiled wire to form links of 1½ turns. These are slipped through one another and the ends are pushed into the holes of beads to hold them together as shown in the picture. After soldering the ends to the beads, another unit is inserted and so on until the desired length is obtained.

17. This chain, popular for ladies' watch bands, is made by coiling lengths of wire clockwise and counterclockwise around a rod of the required thickness. Even spacing is obtained by winding wire with one turn of separate wire (shown in picture) on a rod. Sections are nipped off the long coils of the required length.

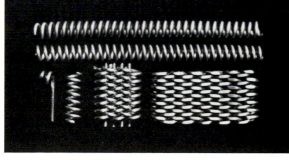

Fig. 484 Handmade chain

Clockwise and counterclockwise sections are put together to form a band. Wires, a little longer than the width of the band, hold sections together by the means of a poker. Very small pieces of solder (page 58) are used to solder wires to the ends of coils. After soldering, the ends of wires are nipped off and the sides are filed until smooth. Width can be tapered by hammering.

Fig. 485 "Memorial to a Would-be Mariner"
Barbara Skelly

9. BRACELETS

LINK BRACELETS The three link bracelets in figure 486 were designed and made in silver to illustrate link bracelet possibilities. The top bracelet is chased. The center bracelet is made from square wire. Small prong settings (see page 186) are used to hold the stones. The end of the center wire is forged to a taper so that it can be bent to form a link. Each link in the bottom bracelet was cut to shape from one piece of metal.

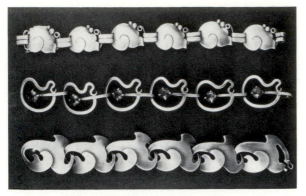

Fig. 486 Silver link bracelets

RECTANGULAR BRACELETS Rectangular link bracelets (fig. 487) are comparatively easy to make. 18 or 20 gauge metal can be used. Each link is curved slightly over a stake or baseball bat and, if stones are used, the curving should be done before settings are applied.

The top and center bracelets are chased and then matted with a small doming or dapping tool. The second bracelet has appliquéd strips of metal and stones held with bezel settings. Twisted wire is soldered to the bottom bracelet.

The shape of an easy-to-make effective catch for the bracelets can be seen in figure 514.

BANGLE BRACELETS Bangle bracelets (fig. 488) are made from twisted wires, usually sterling. The wires and bracelets can be made quickly and with very little equipment. These

wires (14 gauge or thinner) can be twisted with a hand drill (fig. 490); the thicker wires are best twisted with a hand vise (fig. 489) or brace. The wires should be annealed.

To make a bangle bracelet from a twisted wire, bend the ends of the wires with a plier to form a band. **Note:** The band does not have to be perfectly round at this stage. Cut off the end pieces of the wire with a shear or jeweler's saw to leave the band the proper

Fig. 488 Bangle bracelets

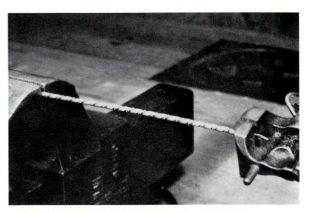

Fig. 489 Twisting wire with a hand vise

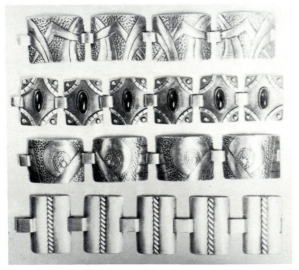

Fig. 487 Rectangular link bracelets

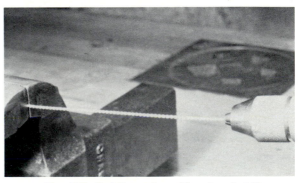

Fig. 490 Twisting wire with a hand drill

size for a bangle bracelet. File the ends of the band so that they meet and match perfectly. Join the ends with hard solder, and, after soldering, a little filing may be necessary to smooth the seam. Round the bracelet around an old baseball bat or silversmith "T" stake with the aid of a mallet.

There are innumerable twisted wire possibilities. The ones shown in figure 491 and described below are popular. The gauges and lengths specified are for bangle bracelets.

1. Flat strip (6 by 18 gauge, 10″ long) twisted to the right.

2. Round wire (14 gauge, 22″ long) bent in half and twisted to the right. After twisting, the wire is flattened by hammering or rolling through a mill.

3. Square wire (8 gauge, 10″ long) twisted to right and then hammered or rolled slightly.

4. Square wire (8 gauge, 10″ long) twisted alternately to the left and to the right by means of a hand vise.

5. Material: Round wire—18 gauge, 28″ long. Half-round wire — 8 gauge, 11½″ long. Round wire bent in half and twisted to right, then placed on flat part of half-round wire and twisted to right.

6. Material: the same as above. Round wire bent in half and twisted to right, then placed on round part of half-round wire and twisted to right.

7. Material: Square wire—12 gauge, 12″ long. Round wire—18 gauge, 28″ long. Round wire bent in half and twisted to right, then placed against square wire and twisted to right.

8. Round wire (18 gauge, 28″ long) bent in half and twisted to right, then placed with two pieces of round wire (14 gauge, 12″ long) and twisted to the right.

Note: The wires can be twisted to the left for different effects.

SLAVE BRACELETS Slave bracelets are usually made from 18 gauge metal, 6″ long. The three bracelets shown (fig. 492) are offered as design suggestions. In the top bracelet, 12 gauge square wire is filed and bent as shown and silver soldered to the center of the bracelet. A hollow silver ball is soldered to the end of the wire. The spiral in the center bracelet is formed from 10 gauge square wire. The wire is bent in at a right angle and soldered across the end of the bracelet. Two

1 2 3 4 5 6 7 8
Fig. 491 Twisted wire possibilities

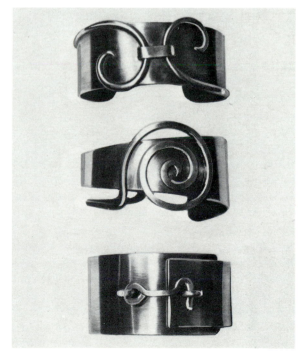

Fig. 492 Slave bracelets

rectangular strips are soldered together to form the bottom bracelet. The hook, which can be opened, is 10 gauge square wire; the joint and catch are made from 10 gauge round wire.

It is advisable to bend the bracelet strip to shape before soldering the other parts to it. Do the bending with a mallet over a baseball bat or metal stake. When bending, start from the ends and work in towards the center.

Fig. 493 Bracelet   **George Jensen**

10. FLAT AND HOLLOW BRACELETS

Flat and hollow bangle bracelets are made commercially in silver and gold. Both types are made by hand and both are recommended as challenging projects for advanced craftsmen.

FLAT BRACELETS Flat bracelets can be made with parallel or tapered sides and as wide as 1½ inches or more if desired. The recommended gauge for the top of the bracelet in silver is 20 gauge; in gold, 22 gauge (.025) or 24 gauge (.020). The length of the flat top piece of metal averages 7½ inches. Longer or shorter metal strips are used for thicker or thinner wrists.

To make the bracelet, the flat top piece of metal is bent to an oval shape over an art metal or sheet metal stake, or over a piece of wood such as an old baseball bat. After

the metal is bent, the ends are soldered together and the band is now shaped perfectly (fig. 495-1) over a stake or, if available, a bracelet mandrel.

Note that the flat outside piece is made from one strip of metal, not two, for it is easier to shape and fit parts this way. After several other parts are soldered to this band, the band is cut into two sections.

Two bands or rings (fig. 495-2) made from square (1/16″) or rectangular (1/16″ x ⅛″) wire are formed so that they fit perfectly inside the oval bracelet. After soldering, if the bands are too small, they can be stretched as shown in figure 495-3. The rings are soldered to the inside edges of the bracelet (fig. 495-4). Cross lock tweezers can be used to hold the rings to the bracelet during the soldering operation.

Notes on soldering: Commercial jewelers use easy flow gold solders; 10 karat for the rings and 8 karat for most other parts. Recommended to craftsmen: Use 14, 12, and 10 karat for better color match. For silver bracelets: Use medium solder for the rings and easy flow for all other parts.

Now a piece of metal (24 gauge in silver, 26 in gold) is formed as shown in figure 495-7 so that it fits inside the bracelet and across

Fig. 494 Bracelet   **Peter Blodgett**

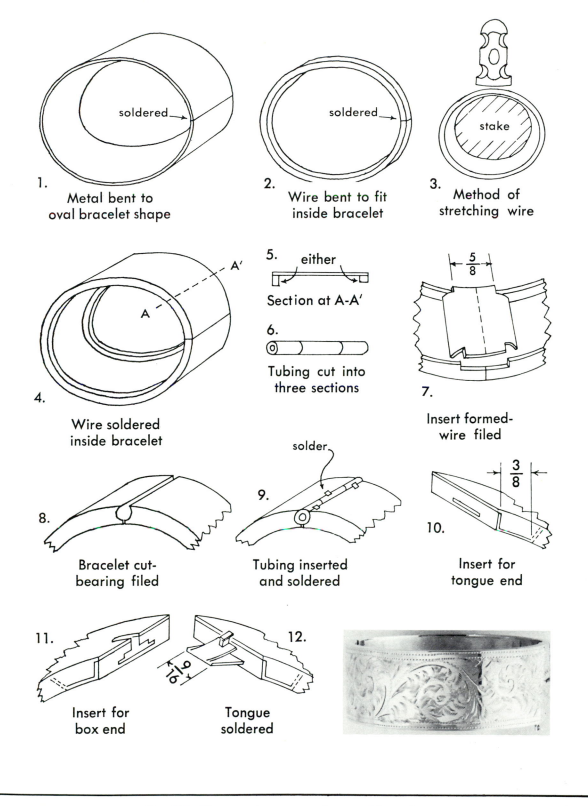

1. Metal bent to oval bracelet shape

2. Wire bent to fit inside bracelet

3. Method of stretching wire

4. Wire soldered inside bracelet

5. either

Section at A-A'

6. Tubing cut into three sections

7. Insert formed-wire filed

8. Bracelet cut-bearing filed

9. Tubing inserted and soldered

10. Insert for tongue end

11. Insert for box end

12. Tongue soldered

Fig. 495 Diagrams for constructing a gold or silver flat bracelet by hand

the bracelet where the hinge is to be. Note that the wires are filed down to the thickness of the metal insert and that the insert is curved to the bracelet shape. This piece of metal is soldered to the bracelet and then filed flush on the outside edge.

Notes on filing: Do not file the sides of the bracelet perfectly until all soldering is done, for if the filing is perfect some of the solder may flow out of the seam while the other soldering is being done.

For less expensive and easier construction, the insert metal may fit directly over the wires —the wires do not have to be filed down.

Next, the bracelet is cut in half right through the metal insert. With a round file, preferably one with a parallel edge, a bearing is filed (fig. 495-8) across the bracelet the exact width of the tubing which is to be inserted to form the hinge. The bearing is filed so that when the tubing is inserted it will be, as shown in figure 495-9, slightly above the top edge of the bracelet. After the soldering operation, the tubing is filed flush with the top edge.

The tubing can be made as explained on page 28. Seamless tubing (3/32″ will do) can be purchased from dealers. The tubing is cut into three sections—the length of the center section should be slightly shorter than the combined length of the end sections.

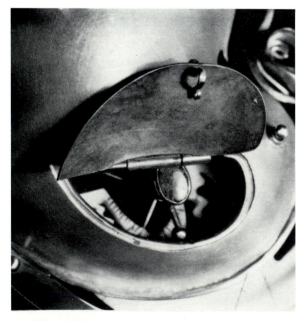

Fig. 496   Detail of a hinge   Marilyn Davidson

To solder the tubing to the bracelet, first tack solder with a small piece of solder as shown in figure 495-9. When the front or catch part of the bracelet is completed, the bracelet can be separated, and then the tubing can be soldered perfectly without any danger of soldering the hinge together.

Note: If a wide (⅛″ or more) rectangular wire is used to construct the bracelet, a bearing for the tubing should be made. The construction of the bearing is explained in the following chapter on hollow bracelets.

A wire is inserted through the tubing to complete the hinge, then the front end of the bracelet is cut in half. The construction of the box and tongue is explained on page 249 under Findings. Note that the rectangular wire is filed down for the thickness of the insert metal. A figure "8" safety catch (fig. 514) or a chain guard can be added to the side of the bracelet.

After all soldering has been completed, the bracelet is pickled, filed, emeried, and polished. It may be ornamented as desired.

Fig. 497   Hollow bracelet

HOLLOW BRACELETS Commercially, the top and inside part of the hollow bracelet are curved by rolling the flat metal through forming wheels somewhat similar to the forming wheels used in a sheet metal shop for bending metal. Craftsmen can make the top and inside part by hand.

Commercially, 28 gauge (.012) gold is used for the low-priced hollow bracelet. The metal is very thin and the bracelets are dented easily. Recommended for craftsmen: In gold, 24 gauge (.020) for outer strip and 26 gauge (.016) for inner strip. In silver, 22 gauge and

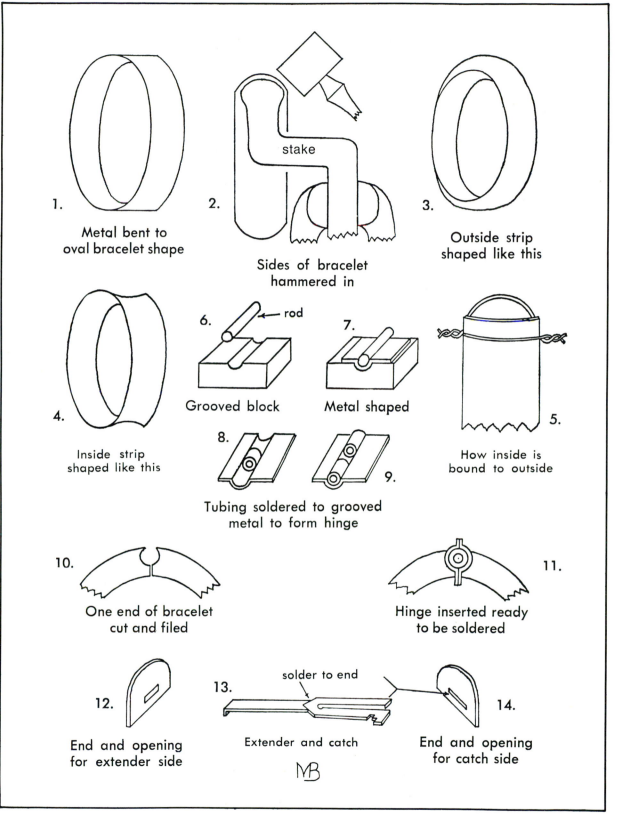

1. Metal bent to oval bracelet shape

2. Sides of bracelet hammered in
stake

3. Outside strip shaped like this

4. Inside strip shaped like this

5. How inside is bound to outside

6. Grooved block
rod

7. Metal shaped

8. 9. Tubing soldered to grooved metal to form hinge

10. One end of bracelet cut and filed

11. Hinge inserted ready to be soldered

12. End and opening for extender side

13. Extender and catch
solder to end

14. End and opening for catch side

MB

Fig. 498 Diagrams for constructing a gold or silver hollow bracelet by hand

24 gauge. An outside strip 7¾″ long and ¾″ wide can be formed into an oval band, after hammer shaping, of approximately 2⅛″ x 2⅜″ and 11/16″ wide inside dimensions.

To form the convex outer band, first bend the metal into a flat oval band (fig. 498-1) and solder the ends together. Place the band over a stake as shown in figure 498-2. Several art metal stakes can be used or one can be forged and filed from a steel bar. Tap down on the edge of the band lightly with a smooth-faced mallet or planishing hammer, and while hammering rotate the band continuously. It is best to form one side of the band and then the other. It may be necessary to anneal the metal once to obtain the final shape.

The inside strip is made from a piece of metal ⅛″ wider than the bracelet. Note from figure 498-4 that it is slightly concave. The strip can be bent to the required shape by first curving the entire piece of metal over a long rod so that it is concave. Anneal the metal and then bend it over a round piece of wood such as a baseball bat that has a concave groove filed or turned around it. The metal strip after bending does not have to be soldered to form a band. It is best to hold the strip to the bracelet in many places with binding wire as shown in figure 498-5. A very small space (1/64″) should be left at the ends of the inner band so when this band is being soldered to the bracelet, air can escape with the heat and also can re-enter when the metal cools.

After the inside is soldered to the bracelet, the excess side metal is best removed by cutting with a small (7″) curved shear, and then the edge is filed until it matches the shape of the bracelet. The bracelet is now cut in half, and with a round file, a bearing is filed for the hinge (fig. 498-10).

The hinge is made from 28 gauge metal as shown in figures 498-6,7,8,9. The rod (3/32″ is a good size) should be the same width as the tube to be used for the tubing. The block can be made by drilling a hole (⅛″) through two metal bars clamped together. The metal for the hinge should be slightly larger than the width of the bracelet. Place the metal as shown in figure 498-7 and hammer firmly straight down on the rod. Remove the rod, and hammer down lightly on the metal to straighten it.

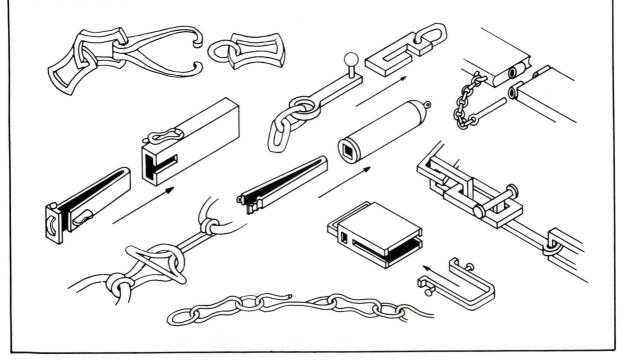

Fig. 499 Clasps for necklaces, chains and bracelets
Courtesy of Jan Mainzer

Note that a small section (⅛″ to 3/16″) of tubing is soldered to one grooved piece of metal and two larger sections are soldered to the other, as shown in figure 498-8, 9. The small section of tubing should fit as tightly as possible between the other sections. The hinge is pickled. The two sections are warmed very slightly and India ink, the type used in mechanical drawing, is brushed only onto the surfaces with the tubing until they are completely black. The hinge is assembled, the outside surfaces are emeried clean, it is inserted into the bracelet as shown in 498-10, and then it is soldered to the bracelet. Why the India ink? The black carbon residue left by the ink will keep the tubing and inner surfaces of the hinge from soldering to one another.

After soldering, the excess metal is trimmed from the hinge and it is filed to the shape of the bracelet. A wire is inserted through the tubing, then the front of the bracelet is cut in half. The end piece for one side is made as shown in figure 498-12; the other side as shown in figure 498-14. Both pieces are cut slightly larger than the outside of the bracelet.

The extender and catch are made from 22 or 20 gauge metal. Note that the catch part with the notch and depressor is slightly wider near the notch than it is near the extender. For greater strength, note that a "V" joint was used where the entender is soldered to the catch. The side of the bracelet is cut out for the depressor part of the catch. The long end of the catch is inserted through the end piece and the short end is soldered to this piece. After pickling, the other end piece is slid onto the catch and then the inner surfaces are covered with India ink. Now the catch unit is placed in position and soldered to the bracelet. Finally, the bracelet, after polishing, is ornamented as desired.

11. CUFF LINKS

CUFF LINK SUGGESTIONS Note: All parts are hard soldered together.

1. Mask: The mask is 16 gauge metal and the nose is 18 gauge. The mouth is made from 18 gauge square wire. The eyes are cut into the metal with a jeweler's saw.

2. Abstract: 16 gauge metal is cut as shown, drilled, and then soldered to an

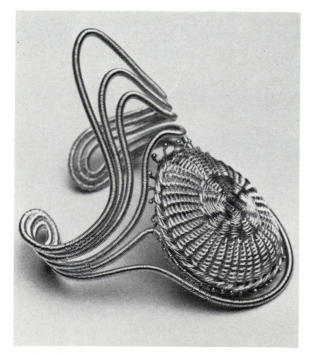

Fig. 501 Bracelet   **Mary Lee Hu**

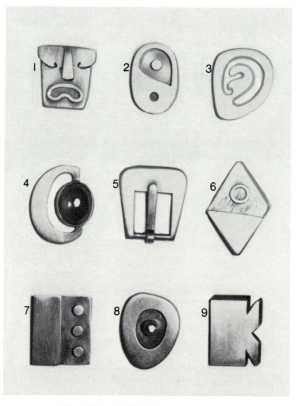

Fig. 502 Cuff link suggestions

18 gauge base. The round disc is made by cutting off a section of a piece of round wire.

3. Abstract: 20 gauge sheet is pierced and soldered to an 18 gauge base piece.

4. Stone: The oval stone is set in a bezel setting. The stone is set after all soldering has been completed.

5. Buckle: 16 gauge metal is cut, filed, and soldered together as shown.

6. Diamond: Base metal is hammered. Ring and triangular piece are then soldered to it.

7. Three Dots: A rectangular strip is soldered to the base piece. The three dots are made by cutting off sections of a piece of round wire.

8. Small Ball: Top piece is pierced and then it and a small ball are soldered to a base piece.

9. Block Initial: The initial is cut and filed from 16 gauge metal.

10. Link and Loop: Link is soldered to a base piece. Loop is made from 18 gauge metal.

11. Three Links: Three 8 gauge links are soldered together as shown. The bottom of the center link is flattened so that the cuff link back can be soldered to it.

12. Modern: 18 gauge strip and a ball (or shot) are soldered to a base piece, which is then cut and filed to shape.

13. Monogram: The two initial monogram is made as explained on page 222. The top initial is cut from twenty gauge metal. It is soldered to the bottom piece, 18 gauge, which then is cut to shape.

14. Bent Wire: Rectangular wire, 16 gauge, slightly less than ⅛″ wide, is bent as shown. The center strip is a long strip that forms the metal for the swivel back. Two other little loops are soldered in position on opposite sides of the center loop.

15. Rectangular: Rectangular 16 gauge sheet is bent as shown. Twisted wire is then soldered to it.

16. Triangular: 12 gauge square wire is bent, filed, and then it and a ball are soldered to the triangular piece.

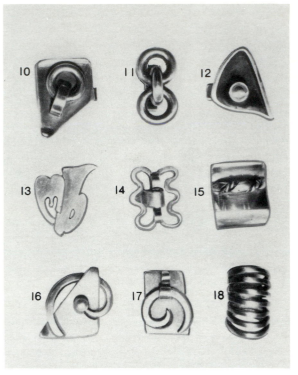

Fig. 503 Cuff link suggestions

17. Spiral: Square wire, 12 gauge, is bent as shown and soldered to a rectangular base. 18 gauge metal is looped twice and soldered in the position shown.

18. Ring: Square wire is formed around a rod. The rings are soldered together on the back only. They are then hammered until they are oval in shape.

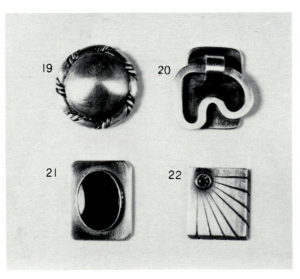

Fig. 504 Cuff link suggestions

244

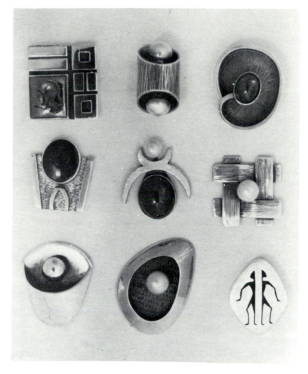

Fig. 505 Cuff link suggestions

19. Domed Disc: Twisted wire (fig. 504) is soldered around a domed disc.

20. Abstract: Square wire, 11 gauge, is soldered to a rectangular base. The loop, 16 gauge, is formed to go over but not touch the square wire.

21. Stone: The oval stone is set in a bezel setting. The stone is set after all soldering has been completed.

22. Radiating Lines: The base piece, 14 gauge, is beveled on two edges to give a three dimensional effect. The radiating lines are engraved into the top of the base piece and they are filed into the beveled edges.

    The cuff links in figure 505 were made to give beginners design suggestions for easy to make cuff links with stones and pearls. The bottom right cuff link is a Mexican design.

HANDMADE CUFF LINK BACKS Practical handmade cuff link backs are shown in figure 506. All parts should be hard soldered together. The back pivots, and it may be ornamented with twisted wire, file marks, etc. These backs can enhance the appearance

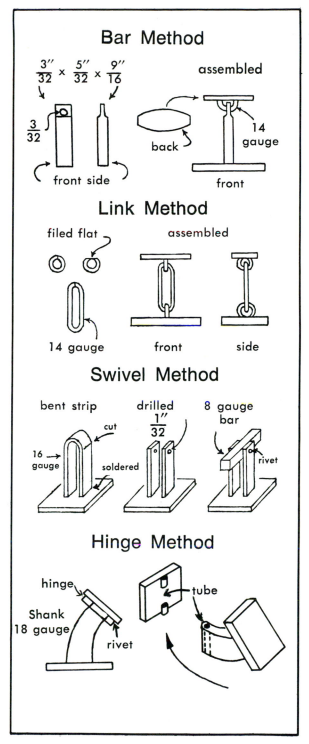

Fig. 506 Handmade cuff link backs

and increase the value of cuff links. The commercial type of cuff link back is shown in figure 513. An inexpensive commercial cuff link back that can be soft soldered to the cuff link is also available.

245

12. MONEY CLIPS

The four money clips in figure 507 are made from spring sterling silver. Hard copper, brass, and gold can be used. The money clips are cut to shape before they are bent.

If spring hard or hard metal is not available, the softer metals can be hardened by carefully planishing — hammering with a smooth-faced hammer.

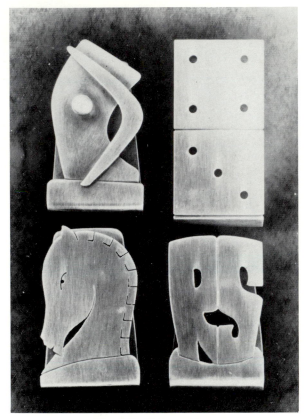

Fig. 507 Money clips

BENDING PROCEDURE It is essential that spring sterling silver be heated to a light brown where the right angle bend is to be made in order to anneal it slightly; otherwise it may break as it is being bent. Parts should only be soft soldered to the clip; hard solder will soften (anneal) the metal, and it then will not retain its shape.

1. Place the metal between the jaws of a vise or two pieces of angle iron and then bend it to a right angle (fig. 508-1). It is best to round the edge of the vise or angle iron slightly where the metal is to be bent.

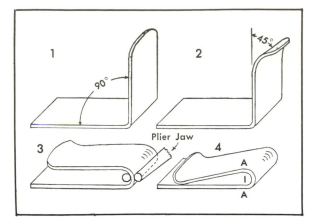

Fig. 508 Money clip bending procedure

2. Hammer the back part of the money clip to the shape shown in figure 508-2.
3. Place the clip on a flat surface and continue the bending with round nose pliers.
4. Finally, complete the bending process by squeezing the metal at A - A' between the jaws of a vise until it assumes the money clip shape shown in figure 508-4.

In school shops, the money clips can be bent in a sheet metal worker's brake.

13. BELT BUCKLES

The three belt buckles shown in figure 510 are typical of conventional shaped belt buckles. With a little ingenuity many design variations can be worked out; for example, the elementary buckle can be converted by means of appropriate etched, chased, or appliqué designs to the cowboy or school type of buckle.

Fig. 509 Belt buckle   Yonny Segel

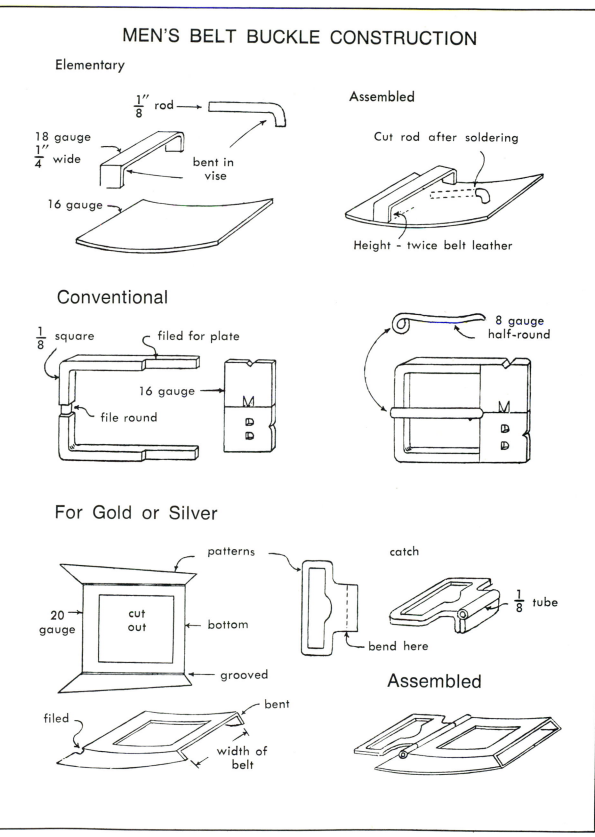

MEN'S BELT BUCKLE CONSTRUCTION

Elementary

$\frac{1}{8}''$ rod

18 gauge $\frac{1}{4}''$ wide

bent in vise

16 gauge

Assembled

Cut rod after soldering

Height - twice belt leather

Conventional

$\frac{1}{8}$ square

filed for plate

16 gauge

file round

8 gauge half-round

For Gold or Silver

patterns

catch

20 gauge

cut out

bottom

bend here

$\frac{1}{8}$ tube

grooved

bent

filed

width of belt

Assembled

Fig. 510   Men's belt buckle construction

The conventional shaped monogrammed buckle, since it can be made quickly and is popular as a personalized gift item, has commercial possibilities. The square wire part of the buckle may be filed down where shown to one half or to the entire monogrammed plate thickness. It is best to curve the parts of this buckle to body curvature before they are assembled. By curving and even twisting the square wire part of the buckle, attractive buckles for ladies' belts can be made.

The amount of time required to make the last buckle by hand warrants the use of gold or silver. The flat surface of this buckle can be pierced for monograms, or designs may be engraved or appliquéd onto it effectively. Solder is melted into the grooves of the sides after they are bent to reinforce them.

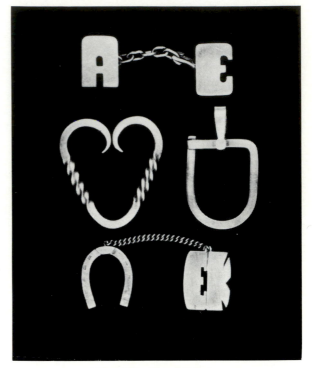

Fig. 512   Key holders

The square wire (9 gauge) is bent to the shape shown. The loops are made from 20 gauge metal and are held to the square wire by means of a rivet (made from wire) so that they can swing. The key chain is attached to the upright loop. A rectangular notch is filed into the square wire near its end so that the other loop snaps into it and thus stays in position. The square wire is bent in in order to release the loop when keys are inserted or removed.

A commercial twist chain is used on the horseshoe and monogram key holder. The keys are inserted by wrapping the chain along one end of the horseshoe. The keys are slipped on the other end, and then along the entire horseshoe, until they emerge from the opposite end.

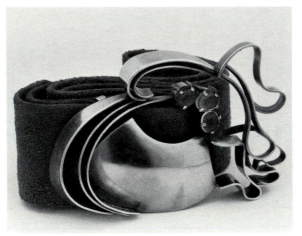

Fig. 511   Belt buckle   Debra Lynn Gold

14. KEY HOLDERS

The initials, in the top key holder, are made from 18 gauge silver. The oval chain is made as described in the previous chapter on chain making. The links (one half part) are soldered to the bottom of the initials. A small sister hook is used to open the chain so that the keys may be inserted.

The heart-shaped key holder is very practical and comparatively easy to make. 9 gauge square wire is twisted, bent, and then filed to the shape shown.

The key holder to the right of the heart-shaped one is ideal for men's key chains.

15. FINDINGS

The term findings is thought to have been derived from the "findings" a jeweler would make or adapt after searching through his scrap or stock for some part in order to finish a piece of jewelry. Today the term is used in the precious jewelry manufacturing industry to denote unassembled jewelry parts and stock shop products such as settings, beads, safety catches, pin backs, and jump rings.

Manufactured clasps, catches, and other findings (fig. 513) for jewelry are so comparatively inexpensive and well-made that they are generally accepted and used for most jewelry. Most findings are available in either sterling silver, gold filled, or 14 karat gold. However, occasionally for a handmade item, the craftsman must make his own clasp or catch. This is particularly true when one of the items becomes an integral part of the design. It is the intent of this chapter to explain how simple and more complex clasps and catches can be constructed for handmade jewelry.

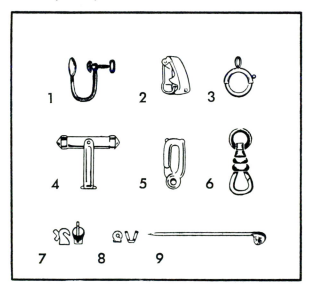

Fig. 513 Manufactured findings. 1. Ear wire, 2. Bracelet clasp, 3. Spring ring, 4. Cuff link back, 5. Sister hook, 6. Swivel, 7. Safety catch, 8. Joint, 9. Pintong

SIMPLE EAR CLASP A piece of 20 gauge metal, hammered slightly to harden, and 3/16″ wide is bent as shown in figure 514. The clasp is soft soldered to the earring. This actually makes a simple but practical and comfortable clasp that is worth trying.

SIMPLE CATCH FOR LINK BRACELETS— Material: 18 or 20 gauge metal. The width of the catch should be slightly less than the length of the slot in the bracelet. The metal is bent with round nose pliers to the shape shown in figure 514. The round part is opened slightly, placed through the slot on one side of the bracelet, and closed again to complete the catch. No soldering is required. See bracelets in fig. 487.

BOX CLASP The box clasp can be made many ways. Of the two ways described here, the first method is a simple, quick one; the second is a superior one for better jewelry. The material to use is 20 or 22 gauge for the box and 24 gauge for the tongue.

Method 1 The box is marked out as shown in figure 514, cut to shape with a jeweler's saw, and then bent to shape with pliers. The tongue is marked out, cut to shape, and then bent as shown in figure 514. The very edge of the bent part is hammered to give the tongue a little spring.

The top or open part of the box is soldered to the jewelry object, and the object is notched to receive the little knob on the tongue. The back of the tongue is soldered directly to the other half of the jewelry object.

Method 2 A strip of metal for the sides of the box is nicked with a file and bent to the shape shown in figure 514. After bending, the metal strip is strengthened with solder. The front of the strip is then cut and filed to the shape shown. The narrow gap should be the thickness of the metal used for the tongue, and the wider gap should be just a hairline wider than twice the thickness of the metal used to make the tongue.

The bent strip is then soldered to a flat piece of metal, and, after soldering, the flat piece of metal is filed flush to become the bottom of the box. The completed box is soldered to the jewelry object, which is first notched for the knob on the tongue.

The tongue is marked out, cut to shape, bent, and after the knob has been soldered on, the edge is hammered slightly to give the tongue spring. On gold and platinum work, after bending, the bent part of the tongue is straightened by a little solder or better yet, wire rivets.

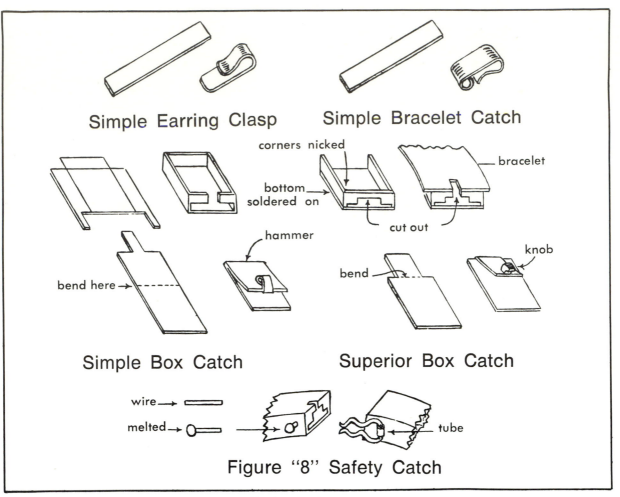

Simple Earring Clasp   Simple Bracelet Catch

corners nicked

bottom soldered on

hammer

bend here →

cut out

bracelet

bend

knob

Simple Box Catch   Superior Box Catch

wire →

melted →

tube

Figure "8" Safety Catch

Fig. 514 Handmade clasps and catches

FIGURE "8" SAFETY CATCH FOR BRACE-LETS This is a simple but effective additional catch that is used as a safety guard, usually on the side of a bracelet.

It is made by first heating a small piece of wire (18 gauge) on one end until the rod melts to form a small round knob. A hole is drilled in the side of the bracelet, and the wire is inserted and soldered in position with the knob projecting slightly.

A small tube is soldered on the other side of the bracelet as shown in figure 514. A piece of 18 gauge wire is inserted and bent to the figure 8 shape. The ends are cut even and soldered together. Slight adjustments with pliers may be necessary to complete this effective safety catch.

EARWIRES Although most craftsmen prefer not to make earwires by hand, figure 515 il-

lustrates how to construct various earwires for pierced ears. After the stem has been hard soldered to either a setting, pad, or pearl cup, it should be hardened by the same method as pintongs (see page 224). The friction nut should be given a spring or hard

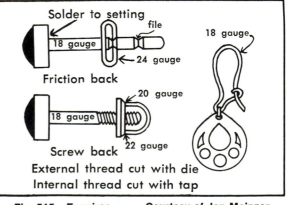

Solder to setting

file

18 gauge

24 gauge

Friction back

20 gauge

18 gauge

22 gauge

Screw back

18 gauge

External thread cut with die
Internal thread cut with tap

Fig. 515   Earwires   Courtesy of Jan Mainzer

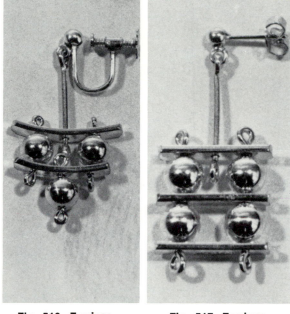

Fig. 516 Earrings
Theodor Olsens

Fig. 517 Earrings
Theodore Olsens

temper. The groove for the nut can be made with a triangular file. A threaded post and screw back can be made with a number 0-80 threads per inch tap and die.

Pintongs, joints, and catches are other examples of findings that are not commonly

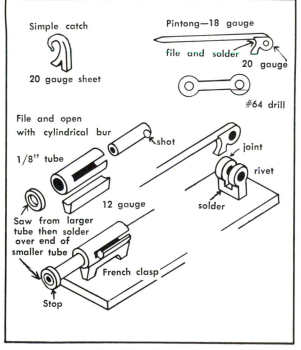

Fig. 518 Pin backs

made by jewelers. If a specialized piece of jewelry calls for a specialized pinback, figure 518 shows how one can be constructed.

16. JEWELRY REPAIRING

The repairing of jewelry—costume, silver, gold, or platinum—calls for techniques that are practically identical with those required to make a jewelry object by hand. In other words, if one has mastered the techniques previously described in this book, one should not encounter difficulty in repairing jewelry objects.

The repairs can be classified into different groups and, for the sake of clarity, they are classified as follows: white metal, silver, gold, and platinum.

Care must be taken to determine the type of metal the jewelry item is made from before it is classified and repaired. This can be done by means of the tests for metals, pages 16 to 24.

WHITE METAL Replacing defective or broken off joints and catches is one of the more frequent types of repairs on white metal jewelry. To replace, if necessary, melt a small piece of low melting bismuth solder onto the bottom of the joint or catch. Then place the joint or catch, with a little soft solder flux applied, in the proper position. Apply the heat with a soft flame. Heat for a fraction of a second and remove the torch or heat quickly. Repeat the process until the solder melts. One must be very quick and careful with the torch and heat, for if the metal is heated for a fraction of a second too long, it will melt, since white metal (page 23) has a comparatively low melting point (app. 400°F.). However, with a little practice, one should encounter no difficulty in soldering the joints, catches, and other parts to white metal jewelry.

An electric soldering copper can also be used for the soldering operation. Soft solder is melted onto the joint. It is then held in the proper position with a tweezer. The hot soldering copper is touched to the joint. The heat will melt the solder. Don't forget the soft solder flux.

251

SILVER JEWELRY Before silver soldering, check to see that the object being repaired has no soft solder on it, for soft solder when heated to red heat will burn into the silver.

It is best, as a rule, to remove all stones, except rubies and sapphires, from jewelry objects that require silver solder repairs, otherwise the stones will crack. If careful, soft solder repairs can be made without ruining the stones.

Stones may be removed from bezel settings with a flat engraving tool. The engraving tool is pushed down between the stone and the bezel and then twisted to open the bezel. This is continued around the stone until it can be removed.

Occasionally, a stone can be protected from the heat required for silver soldering by wetting powdered asbestos and then forming it into a ball around the stone (see page 58).

When repairing a jewelry object with silver solder, the object's polished finish can be protected; that is, oxidation of the metal can be prevented by covering the metal with boric acid (see page 34) before soldering.

GOLD JEWELRY If necessary, determine the karat of the gold object requiring repairs by means of the method described on page 19. Use the same color solder as the gold in the jewelry object. Though it is best to use the highest karat solder possible, if in doubt about the solders previously used, use a low karat solder (12, 10, or 8) for repairs.

Occasionally, it is advisable to plate a gold jewelry object that has been repaired in order to obtain a uniform color.

Joints and catches are soldered to pins as described on page 223. 8 karat solder is usually used for them and for earwires.

Diamonds, sapphires, and rubies do not have to be removed from gold jewelry objects which require repairs to be made by soldering. Do not dip the gold into water after soldering for the stones are liable to crack.

While stones are immersed in water, often repair soldering can be done with the hot flame of an oxygen-gas soldering torch.

Polished parts can be protected from discoloration or oxidation by means of boric acid as described on page 34.

Engraved or carved marriage bands can be stretched without damaging the carved or engraved surface by means of the method described on page 209.

It is best to hammer-stretch a ring with a large brilliant, emerald, etc., cut stone in a ring mandrel that is grooved; otherwise the stone may be forced out of the setting if the bottom of the stone presses against the mandrel.

If a ring must be stretched one or more sizes, it is best to anneal the shank so that the metal will stretch easily.

PLATINUM Though the self-pickling fluxes can be used for soldering platinum, it is best to use a specially prepared commercial platinum flux.

Diamonds can be left in settings while soldering, and a missing bead can be soldered to a bead setting directly on the diamond and to the setting without fear of ruining the stone.

Do not attempt to stretch marriage rings with channel or fishtail settings, for the diamonds will snap out of the settings. If necessary, cut the ring and spread it sufficiently to solder in a section to make the ring the proper size. The new section is then drilled, enlarged with burs, and cut to make the required settings to blend with the others in the ring.

Platinum objects, after being repaired and polished, are often rhodium plated to hide the solder discoloration and to give the jewelry object a new sparkle.

17. REFINING GOLD

The recommended way to handle scrap gold is to send it to a commercial refiner for cash or for credit for purchasing fine or karat gold. Commercial refiners have the necessary equipment and know-how to economically refine small and large quantities of gold.

Craftsmen who wish to can refine small quantities of gold as follows:

1. Remove ferrous metals by means of a magnet.

2. Weigh the scrap and to it add 5 times the weight in copper. This lowers the karat of the gold so that nitric acid will react with it.

3. Melt this batch in a crucible and, from a height, pour the melt onto a piece of metal in order to obtain a thin slab. Cut the slab into small pieces.

4. Place the pieces into a glass (pyrex preferred) container or test tube and then carefully pour a 15% nitric acid solution into the container or test tube. Let stand. When chemical action ceases after several hours, pour out the blue solution (contains copper nitrate) and add more acid. Repeat until chemical action almost ceases. Then add a 25% nitric acid solution. When chemical action stops, heat the solution with new acid (25 to 35%) until all chemical action ceases.

5. Wash the metal, while still in a glass container, until all traces of acid disappear.

6. Place gold and black-appearing soft sponge-like remains into a crucible, add a little borax powder, and heat with a torch or in a furnace until it melts and fuses together. This gold will be approximately 99% pure.

A thorough discussion on refining gold is in the author's book on jewelry casting.

18. FORMULAS FOR ALLOYING GOLD

Fine gold (24K) and the necessary alloys (base metals) properly proportioned for alloying different colored golds can be purchased from refiners. When a lower karat is desired from a higher karat or fine gold, the following formula is used.

FORMULA FOR LOWERING THE KARAT —

$$A = \frac{G\,(K - W)}{W}$$

A = weight of alloy metal needed to lower the karat
G = weight of the gold
W = karat wanted
K = karat of the gold

EXAMPLE 1: A jeweler has 70 dwts. (pennyweight) of fine (24K) gold which he wants to alloy down to 14K. How many dwts. of alloy must be added?

$$A = \frac{70\,(24 - 14)}{14} = \frac{70\,(10)}{14} = \frac{700}{14} = 50$$

Thus, 50 dwts. of alloy added to 70 dwts. of fine gold will give (50 + 70) 120 dwts. of 14K gold.

EXAMPLE 2: How many dwts. of alloy must be added to 120 dwts. of 14K gold to lower it to 12K?

$$A = \frac{120\,(14 - 12)}{12} = \frac{120(2)}{12} = \frac{240}{12} = 20$$

FORMULA FOR RAISING THE KARAT When it is necessary to raise the karat of gold (usually scrap) the following formula is used.

$$FG = \frac{S(KW - KS)}{24 - KW}$$

FG = fine gold
KS = karat of scrap
KW = karat wanted
S = weight of scrap

EXAMPLE: A jeweler has 20 dwts. of 10K scrap which he desires to raise to 14K. How much fine gold must be added?

$$FG = \frac{20\,(14 - 10)}{24 - 14} = \frac{20\,(4)}{10} = \frac{80}{10} = 8$$

Thus, 8 dwts. of fine gold added to 20 dwts. of 10K gold will give 28 dwts. of 14K gold.

PRACTICAL CHARTS In actual practice most jewelers do not use 10, 14, or 18 karat gold, but a gold content ½ karat lower; thus a jewelry item stamped 10K usually has a gold content of 9½K and, similarly, 14K is usually 13½K, 18K is 17½K. The reason—the law permits a variation of ½K (see page 277) and most manufacturing jewelers therefore, due to the money saving factor, alloy their gold accordingly.

Note: Quality jewelry concerns such as Tiffany do use the actual gold karat content (14K or 18K) stamped on their jewelry items.

PROPORTIONS FOR ALLOYING GOLD

9½ KARAT

Wanted	Fine Gold		Alloy	
dwts.	dwts.	gr.	dwts.	gr.
20	7	22	12	2
40	15	20	24	4
100	39	14	60	10
500	197	22	302	2

13½ KARAT

20	11	6	8	18
40	22	12	17	12
100	56	6	43	18
300	168	18	131	6

17½ KARAT

20	14	14	5	10
40	29	4	10	20
100	72	22	27	2

The alloy composition for Handy and Harman's 13½ karat yellow gold alloy #2 is:

Silver 20.11%, Copper 70.11,% Zinc 9.72%.

To prepare a ten ounce batch of alloy the following can be used:

Silver 2 ounces, Copper 7 ounces, Zinc 1 ounce.

This alloy, very ductile, is recommended by L-S Manufacturing, Woodside, New York: Silver 11.86%, Copper 73.12%, Zinc 15.02%.

The following is recommended for white gold by Rodman and Yarus:

Nickel 30%, Copper 54%, Zinc 16%.

This alloy is recommended by L-S Mfg.: Nickel 25.15%, Copper 58.85%, Zinc 16%.

The alloy is melted in a graphite crucible with the zinc on the bottom. When melted, the alloy can be cast in an ingot mold, or if small pellets are desired, it is poured slowly and permitted to drop from a height into cold water.

Red gold is obtained by lowering the silver content and increasing the copper content.

Green gold is obtained by lowering the copper content and increasing the silver content.

COMPOSITION OF HANDY AND HARMAN'S KARAT GOLDS

COLOR	NAME	KARAT	GOLD%	SILVER%	COPPER%	ZINC%	NICKEL%
Yellow	No. 2	9.5	39.60	12.08	42.28	6.04	——
		13.5	56.25	8.75	30.65	4.35	——
		14.	58.33	8.31	29.19	4.17	——
	No. 8	18.	75.00	15.00	10.00	——	——
White	No. 60	9.5	39.60	——	34.00	8.70	17.70
		13.5	56.25	——	24.63	6.30	12.82
		14.	58.33	——	23.47	5.99	12.21
	No. 5	18.	75.00	——	2.23	5.47	17.30
Green	No. 350	13.5	56.25	36.70	6.80	.25	——
Red	No. 6	13.5	56.25	2.20	41.55	——	——

JEWELRY OBJECTS
by Contemporary Craftsmen

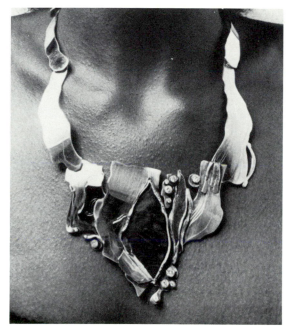

NECKPIECE   Glenda Arentzen

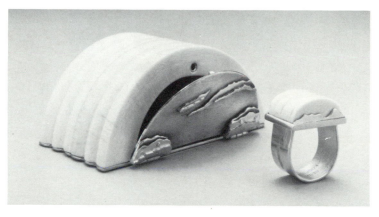

CONTAINER AND RING   Rena B. Koopman

RING   Harold O'Connor

NECKPIECE   Marci Zelmanoff   PIN   Holly Sparkman

NECKLACE   Dena Todd

NECKLACE   Bent Gabrielsen P.

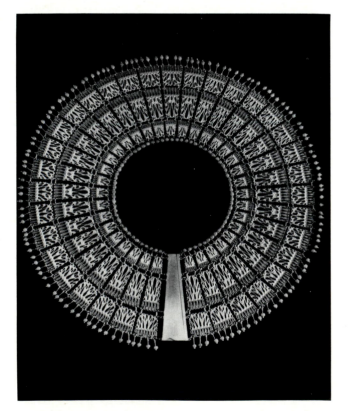

NECKLACE   Michael Croft

PENDANT   Thomas R. Markusen

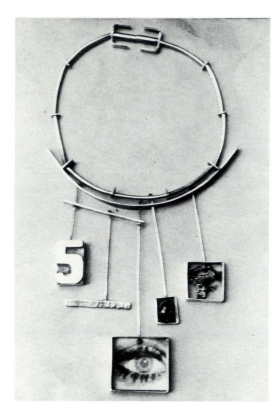

NECKPIECE   Carl Podszus

NECKPIECE   J. Hammond

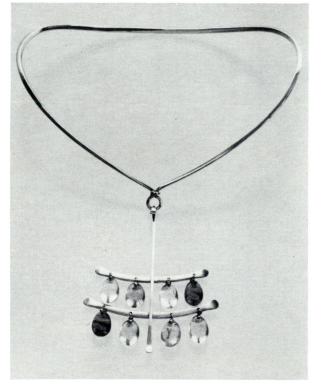

PENDANT G. Page   Courtesy of Georg Jensen, Inc.

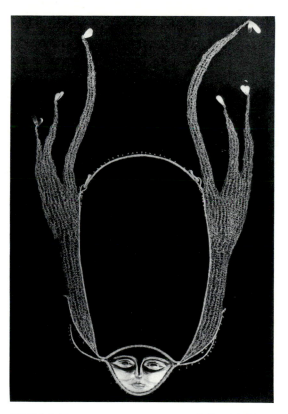

NECKLACE   Arline M. Fisch

PENDANT William A. Neumann

PIN Louis Mueller

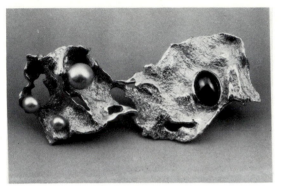

BROOCH Harold O'Connor

NECKPIECE Lynda Watson

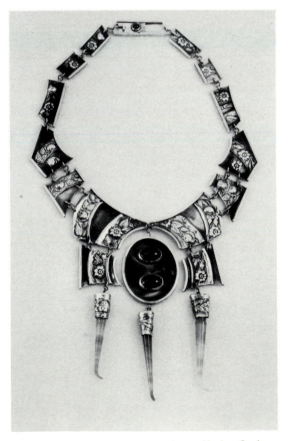

NECKLACE Anne Krohn Graham

BROOCH   Judith Reiss

BROOCH   Edwin Pearl

BRACELET   Jean Schlumberger   Courtesy of Tiffany and Co.

BRACELET   Harry Winston

NECKLACE   Jean Schlumberger   Courtesy of Tiffany & Co.

PENDANT   Eric Lowry FLYING PIN   Pahaka   PENDANT
Hiroko Sato, Gene Pijanowsky

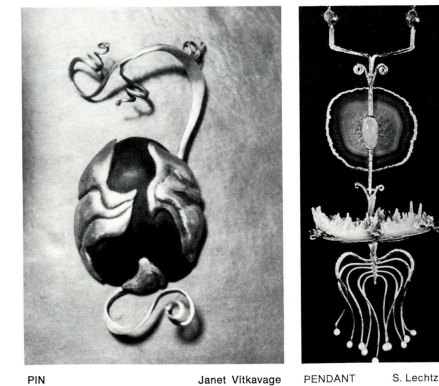

PIN   Janet Vitkavage PENDANT   S. Lechtzin PENDANT   Chuck Evans

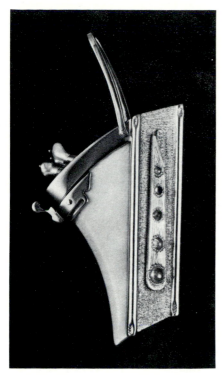

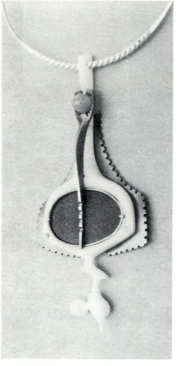

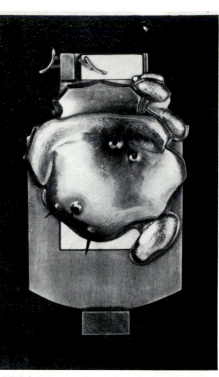

PENDANT   Claudia Kuehnl   PENDANT   Chuck Evans   BROOCH   Jem Freyaldenhoven

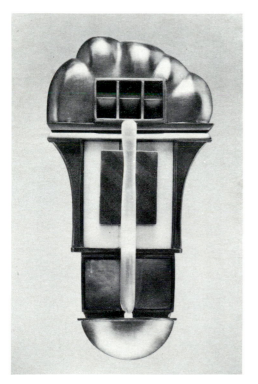

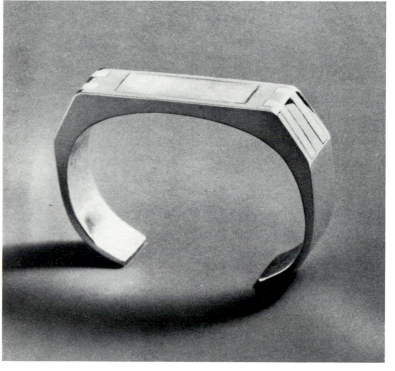

PIN   Richard Mafong   BRACELET   Bruce Keiser

EARRINGS   Ross Coppelman

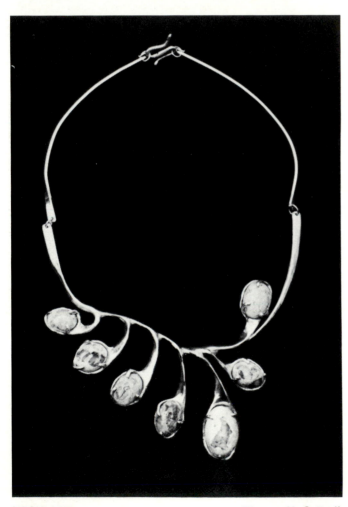

NECKLACE   Eleanor H. Cottrell

PIN   Etta Kaplan

PENDANT   Klaus Kallenberger

PIN   Etta Kaplan

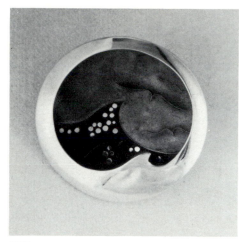

PIN   Kathryn Gough

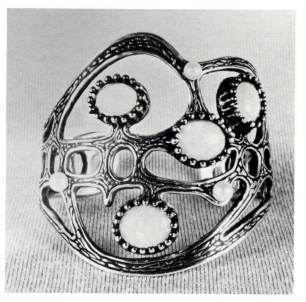

BRACELET   Robert Dhaemers

PENDANT   Dvora Horvitz

PIN   Yoshiko Yamamoto

COLLAR   Ellen Kaufman

PENDANT   Poul Warmind

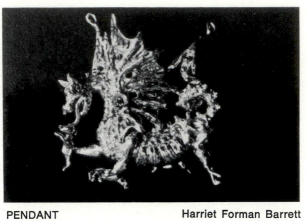

PENDANT   Harriet Forman Barrett

PIN   Dvora Horvitz

PIN   Castillo

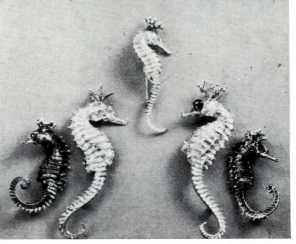

PINS   Judith Reiss

PENDANT   Ellen Greenfield

PICTURE FRAME   Tom Ambrosina

BELT BUCKLE   Jo-An Smith

PENDANT   Poul Warmind

PENDANT   Harriet Forman Barrett

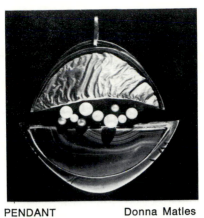

PENDANT   Donna Matles

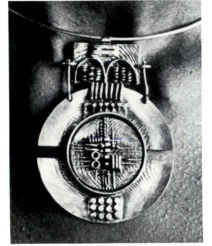

PENDANT   Robert Natalini

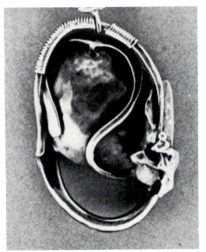

PENDANT   David Yurman

PENDANT   Dvora Horvitz

PENDANT   Virginia Julyan

PENDANT   Gertrude Fish

PENDANT   Bjorn Weckstrom

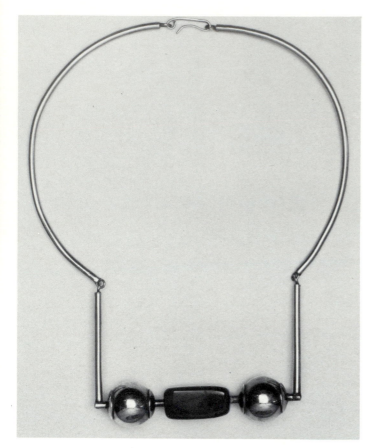

NECKLACE   Adda Husted-Andersen

BRACELET   Ruth S. Roach

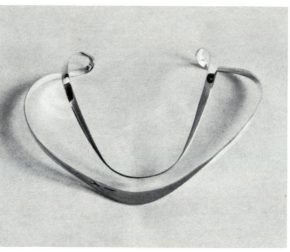

NECKBAND   Jo-An Smith

NECKLACE   Claudia Kuehnl

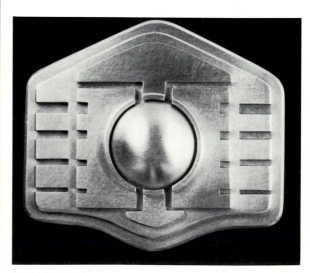

BELT BUCKLE   Frances Welles

PENDANT   Henry Steig

RING   Dvora Horvitz

RING   Fretz

PIN   Ralph Murray

PIN   Ralph Murray

RINGS   Ed Weiner

PIN   R. Mawdsley

RING   Hannelore Gabriel

PENDANT   Christopher Darway   NECKLACE   Pat Garrett

NECKBAND   Frank Patina

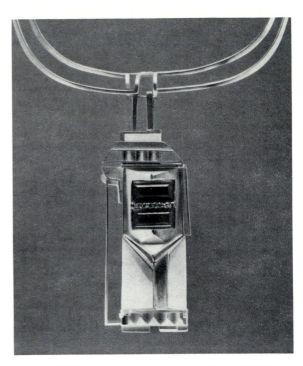

NECKLACE   Richard Mafong

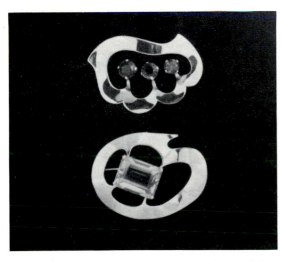

PINS   Etta Kaplan

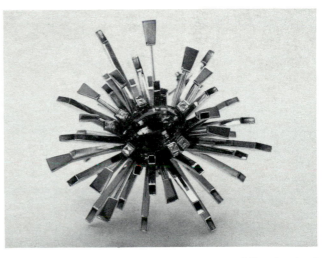

PIN   Gilian Packard

BRACELET   Georg Jensen   BRACELET   Wiltz Harrison

RING   Fretz

BANGLES AND CHOKERS Angela Cummings   Courtesy of Tiffany & Co.

RING   John Wescott

NECKPIECE   Lynda Watson   COLLAR   Arline M. Fisch

PENDANT   Poul Warmind

BROOCH   Harold O'Connor

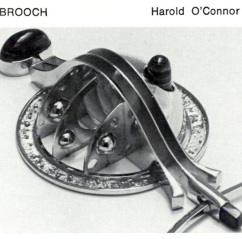

NECKPIECE   Hal Ross

PENDANT   Bev deJong

RING   Harold O'Connor

BELT BUCKLE   Pamela J. Burroughs   NECKLACE   Mary Ann Scherr

RING   Diana Penna   RING   Friedrich Becker   RING   Allen Lindsay

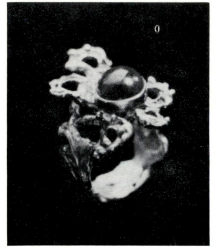

RING   Susan Bovin   RING   Peter Sauer   RING   Ross Coppelman

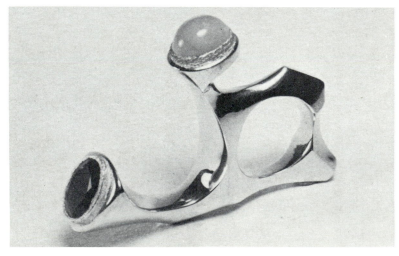

RING   Linda Weiss   RING   Fretz

MASK   Paul Lobel

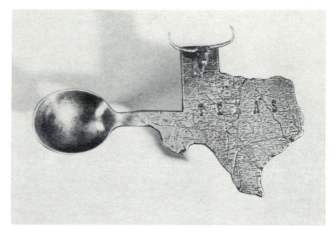

SPOON   Jim Cotter

CARRIAGE   Edward Higgins

TRANSPORTER   Earl Krentzin

TRACKED VEHICLE   Hal Ross

APPENDIX
COMPARATIVE WEIGHTS AND MEASURES

TROY WEIGHT

Used in Weighing the Precious Metals

24 grains	1 pennyweight
20 pennyweights (dwt.)	1 ounce troy
12 ounces	1 pound troy
5760 grams	1 pound troy

The troy ounce is about 10% heavier than the commonly used avoirdupois ounce.

Avoirdupois ounces x 0.9115 = troy ounces.

AVOIRDUPOIS WEIGHT

Used in Weighing the Base Metals

27-1/3 grains	1 dram (or drahms)
16 drams	1 ounce avoir.
16 ounces	1 pound
16 ounces	700 grains

The avoirdupois pound is about 21½% heavier than the troy pound.

Troy ounces x 1.0971 = avoirdupois ounces.

GRAM WEIGHT

1 gram	15.432 grains troy
1.555 grams	1 pennyweight dwt.
31.104 grams	1 ounce troy
28.35 grams	1 ounce avoirdupois

CARAT WEIGHT

Used in weighing precious stones and semi-precious gemstones

1 carat	3086 grains troy
1 carat	.007 ounce avoirdupois
1 carat	= .20 grams
1 gram	= 5 carats

The carat is further divided into points for simple measurement:

1 carat	100 points
½ carat	50 points
¼ carat	25 points
⅛ carat	12.5 points

DOUZIEME GAUGE

The gauge is divided in 72 sections or douziemes

1 douzieme = gauge = .0074 inch   ligne = 12 douziemes = .0888 inch

LINEAR MEASUREMENT (LENGTH)

1 meter = 1.0936 yards	1 decimeter = 3.937 inches	1 inch = 2.54 centimeters
1 meter = 3.2808 feet	1 centimeter = .3937 inch	1 inch = 25.4 millimeters
1 meter = 39.37 inches	1 millimeter = .0393 inch	1 foot = 304.8 millimeters
1 meter = 10 decimeters	1 micron = .000039 inch	1 foot = 30.48 centimeters
1 meter = 100 centimeters		1 foot = 3.048 decimeters
1 meter = 1,000 millimeters		1 foot = 0.3048 meter
1 meter = 1,000,000 microns		1 yard = 0.9144 meter

FLUID MEASUREMENT

1 ounce (fluid) = 29.57 cubic centimeters = 1.8 cubic inches

1 dram = 1/16 ounce (fluid) = 1.85 cubic centimeters

1 quart = 32 ounces (fluid) = 2 pints = ¼ gallon = 57 cubic inches

1 gallon = 4 quarts = 128 ounces (fluid) = 3.78 liter and 231 cubic inches = 0.134 cubic feet

1 liter = 1,000 cc (slightly more than 1 quart U.S.) = 0.264 U.S. gallons

1 cubic foot = 7.481 U.S. gallons = 1.728 cubic inches

1 imperial gallon = 1.2 U.S. gallons = 4.59 liters = 277.27 cubic inches

Specific Gravity, Melting Point, and Weight of Metal and Alloys

Metal	Melting Point °F.	Melting Point °C.	Specific Gravity	Weight in Troy ozs. per cu. in.	Metal	Melting Point °F.	Melting Point °C.	Specific Gravity	Weight in Troy ozs. per cu. in.
Aluminum	1220	660	2.70	1.423	Iridium	4449	2454	22.40	11.802
Antimony	1167	630	6.62	3.488	Iron (pure)	2795	1535	7.86	4.141
Beryllium	2462	1350	1.82	.959	Lead	621	327	11.36	5.985
Bismuth	520	271	9.80	5.163	Magnesium	1204	651	1.74	.917
Cadmium	610	321	8.67	4.568	Manganese	2273	1245	7.2	3.793
Carbon	....	....	2.22	1.170	Molybdenum	4748	2620	10.20	5.374
Chromium	3326	1830	7.14	3.762	Nickel	2645	1452	8.85	4.663
Cobalt	2696	1480	8.90	4.689	Osmium	4892	2700	22.48	11.844
Copper	1981	1083	8.94	4.710	Palladium	2831	1555	12.00	6.322
Gold	1945	1063	19.36	10.200	Phosphorus	111	44	1.82	.959
18 Kt. green	1810	988	15.90	8.375	Platinum	3224	1773	21.45	11.301
18 Kt. yellow	1700	927	15.58	8.211	15% Iridio Plat.	3310	1821	21.59	11.373
18 Kt. white	1730	943	14.64	7.712	10% Iridio Plat.	3250	1788	21.54	11.349
18 Kt. red	1655	902	15.18	7.998	5% Iridio Plat.	3235	1779	21.50	11.325
14 Kt. green	1765	963	14.20	7.482	Rhodium	3551	1955	12.5	6.586
14 Kt. yellow	1615	879	13.07	6.885	Ruthenium	4442	2450	12.2	6.428
14 Kt. white	1825	996	12.61	6.642	Silicon	2588	1420	2.40	1.264
14 Kt. red	1715	935	13.26	6.986	Silver	1761	961	10.53	5.548
10 Kt. green	1580	860	11.03	5.810	Sterling	1640	893	10.40	5.477
10 Kt. yellow	1665	907	11.57	6.096	Coin	1615	879	10.35	5.451
10 Kt. white	1975	1079	11.07	5.832	Tin	450	232	7.30	3.846
10 Kt. red	1760	960	11.59	6.106	Zinc	787	419	7.14	3.762

Comparative Weights of Equal Volumes

Coin Silver is	.995	times as heavy as	Fine Silver
Sterling Silver is	.998	" " " "	Fine Silver
	.796	" " " "	14 K Yellow Gold
	1.163	" " " "	Copper
	3.852	" " " "	Aluminum
Copper is	.895	" " " "	Sterling Silver
	3.311	" " " "	Aluminum
14K Yellow Gold is	1.257	" " " "	Sterling Silver
Platinum is	2.063	" " " "	Sterling Silver

RING SIZES

Each full ring size is .032 inches larger in diameter than the previous size. A ring shank is measured by determining the ring size, the inner diameter, and the circumference based on the inner diameter. Shank length = the circumference + 1½ times metal gauge thickness.

Ring Size	Inch	Ring Size	Inch	Ring Size	Inch	Ring Size	Inch	Ring Size	Inch	Ring Size	Inch
0	0.458 dia.	2	.522 dia.	5	.618 dia.	8	.714 dia.	11	.810 dia.		
¼	.466 dia.	2½	.538 dia.	5½	.634 dia.	8½	.698 dia.	11½	.826 dia.		
½	.474 dia.	3	.554 dia.	6	.650 dia.	9	.714 dia.	12	.842 dia.		
¾	.482 dia.	3½	.570 dia.	6½	.666 dia.	9½	.730 dia.	12½	.858 dia.		
1	.490 dia.	4	.586 dia.	7	.682 dia.	10	.746 dia.	13	.874 dia.		
1½	.506 dia.	4½	.602 dia.	7½	.698 dia.	10½	.794 dia.	13½	.890 dia.		

CIRCLE CIRCUMFERENCE

Circumference of a circle = Diameter x 3.1416

Diameter (Inches)	Circumference (Inches)	Diameter (Inches)	Circumference (Inches)	Diameter (Inches)	Circumference (Inches)	Diameter (Inches)	Circumference (Inches)
1/16	13/64	½	1-37/64	1¼	3-15/16	2	6-9/32
⅛	25/64	¾	2-23/64	1½	4-21/32	2½	7-55/64
¼	25/32	1	3-9/64	1¾	5½	3	9-27/64

CONVERSION TABLE
WEIGHT

To Convert

Grains to grams	multiply by	.0647989
Grams to grains	"	15.4324
Pennyweights to grams	"	1.55518
Grams to pennyweights	"	.64301
Ounces troy to grams	"	31.1035
Grams to ounces troy	"	.0321507
Ounces avoirdupois to grams	"	28.3495
Grams to ounces avoirdupois	"	.0352740
Ounces avoirdupois to grains	"	437.5
Grains to ounces avoirdupois	"	.0022857
Ounces troy to grains	"	480.0
Grains to ounces troy	"	.0020833
Ounces troy to ounces avoirdupois	"	1.09714
Ounces avoirdupois to ounces troy	"	.911458
Ounces troy to pounds avoirdupois	"	.06857
Pounds avoirdupois to ounces troy	"	14.583328
Pounds avoirdupois to kilograms	"	.4535924
Kilograms to pounds avoirdupois	"	2.20462
Pounds avoirdupois to grains	"	7000.0
Grains to pounds avoirdupois	"	.0001428
Kilograms to ounces avoirdupois	"	35.2740
Kilograms to ounces troy	"	32.1507

LENGTH

To Convert

Millimeters to inches	multiply by	.0393701
Inches to millimeters	"	25.4
Centimeters to inches	"	.393701
Inches to centimeters	"	2.54
Meters to inches	"	39.3701
Inches to meters	"	.0254
Feet to meters	"	.3048
Meters to feet	"	3.28084
Yards to meters	"	.9144
Meters to yards	"	1.09361

AREA AND VOLUME

To Convert

Square inches to square millimeters	multiply by	645.16
Square inches to square centimeters	"	6.4516
Square centimeters to square inches	"	.1550
Square millimeters to square inches	"	.00155
Cubic inches to cubic centimeters	"	16.3871
Cubic centimeters to cubic inches	"	.061024

TEMPERATURE

To Convert

°Fahrenheit to °Centigrade (Celsius) = Subtract 32 from degrees Fahrenheit, multiply remainder by 5, divide the product by 9

°Centigrade to °Fahrenheit = Multiply degrees Fahrenheit by 9, divide product by 5, and add 32

SUMMARY OF UNITED STATES STAMPING LAWS

Concerning Gold, Silver and Their Alloys

UNITED STATES GOLD STAMPING LAW OF 1906
If a jewelry article is made of gold and is stamped gold, it must also bear a quality mark such as "10 karat" (10K), "14 karat" (14K).

If an article of gold is given a quality mark, the fineness by assay must not be lower than:—

Watch Cases and Flatware .... .003 less than stamped quality.

Other articles, not including solder .... .0208 (½ karat) less than the stamped quality.

However, the assay of a complete article, including solder, must not be more than .0417 (1 karat) under the stamped fineness per karat. **For example,** the gold in a 14-karat watch case, free from solder must be at least .5803 by assay. The entire case, including solder, must assay at least .547 (13 karat). A gold ring, not soldered, stamped "14K" must assay at least .5625 (13½ karat). The gold in a brooch stamped "10K" must assay at least .3958 (9½ karat) and the entire brooch, solder and all, must assay at least .3750 (9 karat).

SILVER The silver in any article stamped "Sterling Silver" should assay .925, and the silver in an article marked "Coin Silver" should assay .900. The silver in an article, not including solder must not be less than this by more than .004. **For example,** an article marked "Sterling Silver" free from solder, must assay at least .921.

Soldered parts must not reduce the assay of the entire article, including solder, by more than .010 under the standard assays of .925 and .900, respectively, for sterling silver and coin silver. For example, an article marked sterling silver when melted, including solder, must assay at least .915.

GOLD AND SILVER USED WITH INFERIOR METAL —

An article made of an inferior base metal combined with gold may be marked "Rolled Gold Plate," "Gold Plate," "Gold Electroplate" or "Gold-Filled" as the case may be. If a mark is used to indicate the fineness of the gold, it must be accompanied by one of these terms. **For example: — "10K Rolled Gold Plate," "14K Gold Filled."**

The words "Sterling" or "Coin" alone or in combination with other metals cannot be used to describe a plated article. **For example: —** "Sterling Plate" is prohibited.

AN AMENDMENT TO THE STAMPING LAWS. Effective July 1, 1962. All articles which are stamped, tagged or labeled to indicate gold or silver content must also bear the trademark or name of a domestic (U.S.) concern.

The purpose of the amendment is to identify clearly a domestic firm responsible for the quality of a finished product bearing a gold or silver quality mark.

Imported gold or silver articles also must carry the mark or name of the importer, retailer, or other firm or person who will be responsible for the quality of the article.

PENALTIES Violators may be fined up to $500 or be imprisoned up to three months, or both at the discretion of the court.

NEW AMENDMENT TO THE STAMPING LAW. November 1, 1970. The new amendment is to put "teeth" in the enforcement of the law. Since 1907, when the original Stamping Act was passed by Congress, no action has ever been taken to enforce the act though many violations have occurred. The new amendment permits manufacturers and associations (vigilance committees) to take unscrupulous violators to U.S. district courts.

THE NEW GOLD ACT — GOLD LABELING ACT OF 1976 — AMENDS THE NATIONAL STAMPING LAW OF 1906 This bill reduces the permissable deviations in the indicated karat quality of articles made in whole, or in part, in gold. Enacted in October 1, 1976. Manufacturers have five years (October 1, 1981) to comply. All articles of merchandise made in whole or in part, of gold or any of its alloys, offered for sale, imported, exported, transported, mailed, or otherwise distributed in interstate or foreign commerce, shall not when tested, assay less than .003 parts than the fineness indicated by the mark stamped, engraved, or printed on the article. If an article contains solder, and/or an alloy of gold of inferior fineness, which is used to braze or unite the parts of such article, all such gold, alloys of gold, and solder shall be assayed as one piece, and the actual fineness of such article, considered in its entirety shall not be less, by more than .007 parts than the fitness indicated, or by more than .003 parts in the case of a watchcase or flatware.

STATE PLATINUM STAMPING LAWS

In effect in New York, New Jersey and Ill.
SUMMARY OF THE MAIN PROVISIONS

Articles must contain, if made **without** solder, 98½% Platinum metals; if made with solder, 95% Platinum metals.

A soldered article containing 95% or more of Platinum metals, of which over 90% is pure Platinum, may be stamped "Platinum".

A soldered article containing 95% or more of Platinum and Iridium, provided the Iridium is over 5% of the whole, may be stamped "Iridium Platinum." On such articles the percentage of iridium may be shown in thousandths. **Example,** (if 10% Iridium) .900 Platinum .100 Iridium.

Platinum on Gold articles containing 5% more of Platinum (by weight) may be stamped with the karat of gold followed by the words "and Platinum." **Example:** 14K Gold and Platinum.

No quality mark can be used without an accompanying trade mark.

STANDARDS OF GOLD

The history of gold and silver quality standards goes back to the early uses of these metals as money. Legal regulations governing the marking of gold jewelry began in England in the year 1239 and in one form or another have existed ever since in practically all civilized countries.

Penalties for violation of these laws have varied with prevailing conditions. History records that in England in the year 1397, a report was made on the false counterfeit stamps of two goldsmiths who were sentenced to be placed in the pillory at Westminster with their ears nailed to it and with a ticket over their heads upon which their offenses were written. From Westminster they were brought to the pillory at Chapside, where each offender had an ear cut off, after which they were conducted to Foster Lane to the bleak prison. In addition to all this disgrace and suffering, they had to pay a fine of 10 marks. This was typical punishment in most countries for similar offenses. In later years, punishment consisted of fines and imprisonment up to one year, or confiscation of all articles falsely stamped, plus fines and a forfeiture of the right to stay in business after repeated violations.

It is interesting to note that these severe penalties have been invoked to protect the jewelry industry as a whole. It is bad enough for a violator to defraud the public and take dishonest advantage of competitors, but the trade has always recognized the greater evil and danger of a general breakdown of public confidence in quality markings on jewelry.

In many foreign countries there is provision for the government regulation of Hall marks which are used in connection with quality marks as an added safeguard.

The established principle even in early days was that the buyer had only himself to blame if he purchased an unmarked piece of jewelry which proved to be inferior to the quality being claimed. On the other hand, if an article stamped under the provisions of a government law was found to be less than the quality indicated the seller was felt to have abused a privilege, violated a law, and endangered the reputation of the trade.

Stamping laws in the United States are of comparatively recent origin. They go beyond those of some other countries and regulate the marking of gold in combination with other metals. This permits the sale, at lower cost, of articles such as gold filled and rolled gold plate which have been produced under the safeguard of quality standards.

The moral influence of the trade at large, organization activities, and trade associations have combined to preserve and strengthen our stamping laws and to deter unscrupulous manufacturers from violating them.

Courtesy of Handy & Harman

USEFUL INFORMATION

PRECIOUS METALS Gold, silver, platinum, and palladium are known as the Precious Metals in the jewelry industry. They are also called the Noble Metals by some craftsmen.

BASE METALS Copper, zinc, and brass are called the base metals in the jewelry industry.

KARAT is a measure of fineness—24 karat is fine gold. One karat equals 1/24 (.0417). Thus 14 karat is 14/24 fine gold and the balance (10/24) alloy. If the gold content of an object is less than 10/24 the object can not be represented as karat gold.

COLORS OF GOLD Yellow, green, red and white are produced by variations in the alloy. Silver and zinc tend to give a green color, copper—red, and nickel—white.

SOLID GOLD The term "gold" and "solid gold" mean fine gold or gold of 24 karat and should not be applied to articles of a lesser quality.

GOLD FILLED is made by joining a layer (or layers) of gold alloy to a base metal alloy and then rolling or drawing to the thickness required. See page 18.

ROLLED GOLD PLATE is the same as gold filled, but usually of lower quality.

GOLD ELECTROPLATE is usually made by electrolytically depositing fine gold on a base metal. The plate thickness must be at least 0.000007 inches of fine gold. Items with a gold thickness less than 0.000007 can be labeled gold washed or colored.

FINE SILVER is commercially pure silver — contains no alloy material.

STERLING SILVER is 925/1000 (92½%) fine silver and 75/1000 (7½%) copper. This proportion is fixed by law.

COIN SILVER is 900/1000 (90%) fine silver and the balance copper. This alloy was used for U.S. silver coins before 1966. New (from 1966) dimes and quarters contain no silver and half dollars contain 40% silver.

COMMERCIAL SILVER is a term applied to silver that is 999 fine or higher.

FOREIGN SILVERWARE contains varying percentages of silver. In some cases, the fineness is as low as 700/1000 (70%).

DANISH SILVER Silverware made in Denmark is 830/1000 fine silver if made to minimum Danish standards. 925/1000 fine silver is made for export.

SILVER PLATED WARE is made by electroplating fine silver on a base metal alloy— usually nickel silver or Britannia metal, sometimes brass or copper. This inexpensive process was perfected for industrial purposes around 1840.

SHEFFIELD PLATE (originally) was made by bonding sheet silver to copper, rolling, and manufacturing into hollow-ware. The original process was abandoned about 1840 due to the introduction of electroplating. Imitations are made by electroplating silver on copper and are sometimes erroneously advertised as Sheffield Plate.

NICKEL SILVER, so-called, is a composition of nickel, copper and zinc. (It contains no silver).

BRITANNIA METAL is a composition of tin, copper and antimony. (See page 23).

PEWTER (original) was primarily a tin-lead alloy. It is now made in a tin, copper, antimony composition similar to Britannia metal (See page 23).

HIGH BRASSES run from 55% copper in the extruded brass to 70% copper in the deep drawing brass, the balance being zinc.

LOW BRASSES contain 80% or more copper, the balance being zinc.

GRAIN originally meant the weight of a grain of wheat. It was later standardized for trading purposes but is little used now, most weighing of gold, silver, and platinum being done in troy ounces and decimal (100ths) parts. See page 16.

A PENNYWEIGHT is the twentieth part of a troy ounce. The name originally applied to the weight of an Anglo-Norman penny.

AN OUNCE (troy) is about 10% heavier than the common avoirdupois ounce. There are 14.583 ounces troy in an avoirdupois pound.

HANDMADE The term handmade can only be applied to jewelry objects made entirely by hand without the use of machine tools.

HANDWROUGHT implies that the jewelry article was made partly by machine and partly by hand.

CARAT is a unit of weight. One carat equals 3.086 grains or 1/5 of a gram. The diamond carat is subdivided into 100 parts or points. Thus, a fifty point diamond equals ½ of a carat and a 25 point diamond equals ¼ of a carat.

"PERFECT" DIAMOND The word "perfect" or expressions of similar import should not be used to describe any diamond which discloses flaws, cracks, carbon spots, clouds or other blemishes or imperfections when examined by an expert under a 10-power magnifier.

"BLUE WHITE" No diamond should be described as "blue white" which shows any color or trace of any color other than blue or bluish.

MISLEADING TERMS It is improper to use the name of a less expensive stone (spinel) with a more expensive stone (ruby) to attempt to give the impression that the less expensive stone is related to the more expensive. Improper: Ruby Spinel, Topaz Quartz, Titania Diamond. Proper: Synthetic Corondum—Amethyst color; Synthetic Spinel — Peridot Color.

HOLLOW CHAIN Hollow chain is made as follows. Gold sheet of the proper width and thickness, is drawn through a draw plate into a tube (see page 28) of the required diameter. Before the tube is closed entirely, aluminum wire is inserted into the gold tube, then the tube is drawn through the plate until it is closed perfectly and is the required diameter. The diameter of the inserted aluminum wire should be the same as the required inside diameter of the gold tube.

By carefully heating the gold tubing with a soft flame, the gold may be annealed without melting the aluminum. The tube now can be bent around a mandrel as if it were a solid wire (see page 231) to form links for chain. After the bending operation, the links are cut apart with a jeweler's saw.

The aluminum is removed from the links by placing them into a sodium hydroxide (lye) solution, for sodium hydroxide dissolves aluminum. The gas that is given off from the chemical action is hydrogen. It is best to handle the solution in a well-ventilated room. Heating will hasten the chemical action.

After the aluminum has been removed, the gold links are washed and then they may be soldered together to form a chain.

SHEET METAL

Weight Per Square Inch by B & S Gauge

B & S Gauge	Thickness in inches	Fine Silver Ozs.	Sterling Silver Ozs.	Coin Silver Ozs.	Fine Gold Dwts.	10K Yel. Gold Dwts.	14K Yel. Gold Dwts.	18K Yel. Gold Dwts.	Platinum Ozs.	Palladium Ozs.
1	.28930	1.61	1.58	1.58	59.0	35.3	39.8	47.5	3.27	1.83
2	.25763	1.43	1.41	1.40	52.6	31.4	35.5	42.3	2.91	1.63
3	.22942	1.27	1.26	1.25	46.8	28.0	31.6	37.7	2.59	1.45
4	.20431	1.13	1.12	1.11	41.7	24.9	28.1	33.6	2.31	1.29
5	.18194	1.01	.996	.992	37.1	22.2	25.1	29.9	2.06	1.15
6	.16202	.899	.887	.883	33.1	19.8	22.3	26.6	1.83	1.02
7	.14428	.800	.790	.786	29.4	17.6	19.9	23.7	1.63	.912
8	.12849	.713	.704	.700	26.2	15.7	17.7	21.1	1.45	.812
9	.11443	.635	.627	.624	23.3	14.0	15.8	18.8	1.29	.723
10	.10189	.565	.558	.555	20.8	12.4	14.0	16.7	1.15	.644
11	.09074	.503	.497	.495	18.5	11.1	12.5	14.9	1.03	.574
12	.08080	.448	.443	.440	16.5	9.85	11.1	13.3	.913	.511
13	.07196	.399	.394	.392	14.7	8.77	9.91	11.8	.813	.455
14	.06408	.356	.351	.349	13.1	7.81	8.82	10.5	.724	.405
15	.05706	.317	.313	.311	11.6	6.96	7.86	9.37	.645	.361
16	.05082	.282	.278	.277	10.4	6.21	7.00	8.35	.574	.321
17	.04525	.251	.248	.247	9.23	5.52	6.23	7.43	.511	.286
18	.04030	.224	.221	.220	8.22	4.91	5.55	6.62	.455	.255
19	.03589	.199	.197	.196	7.32	4.38	4.94	5.89	.406	.227
20	.03196	.177	.175	.174	6.52	3.90	4.40	5.25	.361	.202
21	.02846	.158	.156	.155	5.81	3.47	3.92	4.67	.322	.180
22	.02534	.141	.139	.138	5.17	3.09	3.49	4.16	.286	.160
23	.02257	.125	.124	.123	4.60	2.75	3.11	3.71	.255	.143
24	.02010	.112	.110	.110	4.10	2.45	2.77	3.30	.227	.127
25	.01790	.0993	.0980	.0976	3.65	2.18	2.46	2.94	.202	.113
26	.01594	.0884	.0873	.0869	3.25	1.94	2.19	2.62	.180	.101
27	.01419	.0787	.0777	.0773	2.89	1.73	1.95	2.33	.160	.0897
28	.01264	.0701	.0692	.0689	2.58	1.54	1.74	2.08	.143	.0799
29	.01125	.0624	.0616	.0613	2.29	1.37	1.55	1.85	.127	.0711
30	.01002	.0556	.0549	.0546	2.04	1.22	1.38	1.65	.113	.0633
31	.00892	.0495	.0489	.0486	1.82	1.09	1.23	1.46	.101	.0564
32	.00795	.0441	.0435	.0433	1.62	.969	1.09	1.31	.0898	.0503
33	.00708	.0393	.0388	.0386	1.44	.863	.975	1.16	.0800	.0448
34	.00630	.0350	.0345	.0343	1.29	.768	.868	1.03	.0712	.0398
35	.00561	.0311	.0307	.0306	1.14	.684	.772	.921	.0634	.0355
36	.00500	.0277	.0274	.0273	1.02	.610	.689	.821	.0565	.0316
37	.00445	.0247	.0244	.0243	.908	.543	.613	.731	.0503	.0281
38	.00396	.0220	.0217	.0216	.808	.483	.545	.650	.0448	.0250
39	.00353	.0196	.0193	.0192	.720	.430	.486	.580	.0399	.0223
40	.00314	.0174	.0172	.0171	.641	.383	.432	.516	.0355	.0199

The weight of a square times .7854 equals the weight of the circle cut from the square.

The weight of a circle times 1.273 equals the weight of the square with a side the circles' diameter.

ROUND WIRE

Weight in Pennyweights or Ounces Per Foot in B & S Gauge

B & S Gauge	Thickness in inches	Fine Silver Ozs.	Sterling Silver Ozs.	Coin Silver Ozs.	Fine Gold Dwts.	10K Yel. Gold Dwts.	14K Yel. Gold Dwts.	18K Yel. Gold Dwts.	Platinum Ozs.	Palladium Ozs.
1	.28930	4.38	4.32	4.30	161.0	96.2	109.	130.	8.91	4.99
2	.25763	3.47	3.43	3.41	128.	76.3	86.1	104.	7.07	3.94
3	.22942	2.75	2.72	2.70	101.	60.5	68.3	81.5	5.61	3.19
4	.20431	2.18	2.15	2.14	80.3	48.0	54.2	64.6	4.45	2.42
5	.18194	1.73	1.71	1.70	63.6	38.0	43.0	51.2	3.53	1.97
6	.16202	1.37	1.36	1.35	50.5	30.2	34.1	40.6	2.80	1.56
7	.14428	1.09	1.07	1.07	40.0	23.9	27.0	32.2	2.22	1.24
8	.12849	.863	.852	.848	31.7	19.0	21.4	25.6	1.76	.984
9	.11443	.685	.676	.673	25.2	15.1	17.0	20.3	1.39	.780
10	.10189	.543	.536	.533	20.0	11.9	13.5	16.1	1.11	.619
11	.09074	.431	.425	.423	15.8	9.46	10.7	12.7	.877	.491
12	.08080	.341	.337	.335	12.6	7.50	8.47	10.1	.695	.389
13	.07196	.271	.267	.266	9.96	5.95	6.72	8.01	.552	.309
14	.06408	.215	.212	.211	7.89	4.72	5.33	6.36	.437	.245
15	.05706	.170	.168	.167	6.26	3.74	4.23	5.04	.347	.194
16	.05082	.135	.133	.133	4.97	2.97	3.35	4.00	.275	.154
17	.04525	.107	.106	.105	3.94	2.35	2.66	3.17	.218	.122
18	.04030	.0849	.0838	.0834	3.12	1.87	2.11	2.51	.173	.0968
19	.03589	.0674	.0665	.0662	2.48	1.48	1.67	1.99	.137	.0767
20	.03196	.0534	.0527	.0525	1.96	1.17	1.33	1.58	.109	.0609
21	.02846	.0424	.0418	.0416	1.56	.931	1.05	1.25	.0863	.0483
22	.02534	.0336	.0331	.0330	1.23	.738	.833	.994	.0684	.0383
23	.02257	.0266	.0263	.0262	.979	.585	.661	.789	.0543	.0304
24	.02010	.0211	.0209	.0208	.777	.464	.524	.625	.0430	.0241
25	.01790	.0168	.0165	.0165	.616	.368	.416	.496	.0341	.0191
26	.01594	.0133	.0131	.0131	.489	.292	.330	.393	.0271	.0151
27	.01419	.0105	.0104	.0103	.387	.231	.261	.312	.0214	.0120
28	.01264	.00835	.00825	.00821	.307	.184	.207	.247	.0170	.00952
29	.01125	.00662	.00653	.00650	.243	.145	.164	.196	.0135	.00754
30	.01002	.00525	.00518	.00516	.193	.115	.130	.155	.0107	.00598
31	.00892	.00416	.00411	.00409	.153	.0914	.103	.123	.00847	.00474
32	.00795	.00330	.00326	.00325	.122	.0726	.0820	.0978	.00673	.00377
33	.00708	.00262	.00259	.00258	.0964	.0576	.0651	.0776	.00534	.00299
34	.00630	.00208	.00205	.00204	.0763	.0456	.0515	.0614	.00423	.00238
35	.00561	.00165	.00162	.00162	.0605	.0362	.0408	.0487	.00335	.00188
36	.00500	.00131	.00129	.00128	.0481	.0287	.0324	.0387	.00266	.00149
37	.00445	.00104	.00102	.00102	.0381	.0228	.0257	.0306	.00211	.00118
38	.00396	.000820	.000809	.000806	.0302	.0180	.0204	.0243	.00167	.000934
39	.00353	.000652	.000643	.000640	.0240	.0143	.0162	.0193	.00133	.000742
40	.00314	.000516	.000509	.000507	.0190	.0113	.0128	.0153	.00105	.000587

Copper is .895 the weight of sterling silver.

Square Wire is 1.27324 times as heavy as round of the same gauge.

To convert inches to millimeters:—inches x 25.4 equals millimeters.

To convert millimeters to inches:—millimeters x .0354 equals inches.

STERLING CIRCLES

Weight in Ounces for Various Diameters in B & S Gauge

Dia in Inches	B & S GAUGE 15	16	17	18	19	20	21	22	23	24	25	26
1/4	.0153	.0137	.0122	.0108	.0097	.0086	.0077	.0068	.0061	.0054	.0048	.0043
1/2	.0614	.0547	.0487	.0433	.0386	.0344	.0306	.0273	.0243	.0216	.0193	.0171
3/4	.138	.123	.109	.0975	.0868	.0773	.0689	.0613	.0546	.0486	.0433	.0386
1	.245	.219	.195	.173	.154	.137	.122	.109	.0971	.0865	.0770	.0686
1 1/4	.384	.342	.304	.271	.241	.215	.191	.170	.152	.135	.120	.107
1 1/2	.552	.492	.438	.390	.347	.309	.275	.245	.218	.195	.173	.154
1 3/4	.752	.669	.596	.531	.473	.421	.375	.334	.297	.265	.236	.210
2	.982	.874	.779	.693	.618	.550	.490	.436	.388	.346	.308	.274
2 1/4	1.24	1.11	.985	.878	.782	.696	.620	.552	.492	.438	.390	.347
2 1/2	1.53	1.37	1.22	1.08	.965	.859	.765	.681	.607	.540	.481	.429
2 3/4	1.86	1.65	1.47	1.31	1.17	1.04	.926	.824	.734	.654	.582	.519
3	2.21	1.97	1.75	1.56	1.39	1.24	1.10	.981	.874	.778	.693	.617
3 1/4	2.59	2.31	2.06	1.83	1.63	1.45	1.29	1.15	1.03	.913	.813	.724
3 1/2	3.01	2.68	2.38	2.12	1.89	1.68	1.50	1.34	1.19	1.06	.943	.840
3 3/4	3.45	3.07	2.74	2.44	2.17	1.93	1.72	1.53	1.37	1.22	1.08	.964
4	3.93	3.50	3.11	2.77	2.47	2.20	1.96	1.74	1.55	1.38	1.23	1.10
4 1/4	4.43	3.95	3.52	3.13	2.79	2.48	2.21	1.97	1.75	1.56	1.39	1.24
4 1/2	4.97	4.43	3.94	3.51	3.13	2.78	2.48	2.21	1.97	1.75	1.56	1.39
4 3/4	5.54	4.93	4.39	3.91	3.48	3.10	2.76	2.46	2.19	1.95	1.74	1.55
5	6.14	5.47	4.87	4.33	3.86	3.44	3.06	2.73	2.43	2.16	1.93	1.71
5 1/4	6.77	6.03	5.37	4.78	4.26	3.79	3.37	3.00	2.68	2.38	2.12	1.89
5 1/2	7.43	6.61	5.89	5.24	4.67	4.16	3.70	3.30	2.94	2.62	2.33	2.07
5 3/4	8.12	7.23	6.44	5.73	5.10	4.55	4.05	3.61	3.21	2.86	2.55	2.27
6	8.84	7.87	7.01	6.24	5.56	4.95	4.41	3.93	3.50	3.11	2.77	2.47
6 1/4	9.59	8.54	7.60	6.77	6.03	5.37	4.78	4.26	3.79	3.38	3.01	2.68
6 1/2	10.4	9.24	8.22	7.32	6.52	5.81	5.17	4.61	4.10	3.65	3.25	2.90
6 3/4	11.2	9.96	8.87	7.90	7.03	6.26	5.58	4.97	4.42	3.94	3.51	3.12
7	12.0	10.7	9.54	8.49	7.56	6.74	6.00	5.34	4.76	4.24	3.77	3.36
7 1/4	12.9	11.5	10.2	9.11	8.11	7.23	6.43	5.73	5.10	4.54	4.05	3.60
7 1/2	13.8	12.3	10.9	9.75	8.68	7.73	6.89	6.13	5.46	4.86	4.33	3.86
7 3/4	14.7	13.1	11.7	10.4	9.27	8.26	7.35	6.55	5.83	5.19	4.62	4.12
8	15.7	14.0	12.5	11.1	9.88	8.80	7.84	6.98	6.21	5.53	4.93	4.39
8 1/4	16.7	14.9	13.2	11.8	10.5	9.36	8.33	7.42	6.61	5.88	5.24	4.67
8 1/2	17.7	15.8	14.1	12.5	11.2	9.93	8.85	7.88	7.01	6.25	5.56	4.95
8 3/4	18.8	16.7	14.9	13.3	11.8	10.5	9.37	8.35	7.43	6.62	5.90	5.25
9	19.9	17.7	15.8	14.0	12.5	11.1	9.92	8.83	7.86	7.00	6.24	5.55
9 1/4	21.0	18.7	16.7	14.8	13.2	11.8	10.5	9.33	8.31	7.40	6.59	5.87
9 1/2	22.0	19.7	17.6	15.6	13.9	12.4	11.0	9.84	8.76	7.80	6.95	6.19
9 3/4	23.3	20.8	18.5	16.5	14.7	13.1	11.6	10.4	9.23	8.22	7.32	6.52
10	24.5	21.9	19.5	17.3	15.4	13.7	12.2	10.9	9.71	8.65	7.70	6.86

TROY AND AVOIRDUPOIS WEIGHT EQUIVALENTS

Ounces Troy to Pounds and Ounces Avoirdupois

Ozs Troy	Lbs. & Ozs Avoir	Ozs Troy	Lbs. & Ozs Avoir	Ozs Troy	Lbs. & Ozs Avoir
1	1.1	39	2-10.8	77	5- 4.5
2	2.2	40	2-11.9	78	5- 5.6
3	3.3	41	2-13.0	79	5- 6.7
4	4.4	42	2-14.1	80	5- 7.8
5	5.5	43	2-15.2	81	5- 8.9
6	6.6	44	3- 0.3	82	5-10.0
7	7.7	45	3- 1.4	83	5-11.1
8	8.8	46	3- 2.5	84	5-12.2
9	9.9	47	3- 3.6	85	5-13.3
10	11.0	48	3- 4.7	86	5-14.4
11	12.1	49	3- 5.8	87	5-15.5
12	13.2	50	3- 6.9	88	6- 0.6
13	14.3	51	3- 8.0	89	6- 1.7
14	15.4	52	3- 9.1	90	6- 2.8
15	1- 0.5	53	3-10.2	91	6- 3.9
16	1- 1.6	54	3-11.3	92	6- 5.0
17	1- 2.7	55	3-12.4	93	6- 6.1
18	1- 3.8	56	3-13.5	94	6- 7.2
19	1- 4.9	57	3-14.6	95	6- 8.3
20	1- 6.0	58	3-15.7	96	6- 9.4
21	1- 7.1	59	4- 0.8	97	6-10.5
22	1- 8.2	60	4- 1.9	98	6-11.6
23	1- 9.3	61	4- 3.0	99	6-12.7
24	1-10.4	62	4- 4.1	100	6-13.8
25	1-11.5	63	4- 5.2	200	13-11.5
26	1-12.6	64	4- 6.3	300	20- 9.2
27	1-13.7	65	4- 7.4	400	27- 6.9
28	1-14.8	66	4- 8.5	500	34- 4.6
29	1-15.9	67	4- 9.6	600	41- 2.3
30	2- 1.0	68	4-10.7	700	48- 0.0
31	2- 2.1	69	4-11.8	800	54-13.8
32	2- 3.2	70	4-12.8	900	61-11.5
33	2- 4.3	71	4-13.9	1000	68- 9.2
34	2- 5.4	72	4-15.0	2000	137- 2.3
35	2- 6.4	73	5- 0.1	3000	205-11.5
36	2- 7.5	74	5- 1.2	4000	274- 4.7
37	2- 8.6	75	5- 2.3	5000	342-13.8
38	2- 9.7	76	5- 3.4		

Avoirdupois Ounces and Pounds to Ounces Troy

Avoir Ozs	Troy Ozs
1	.9115
2	1.823
3	2.734
4	3.646
5	4.557
6	5.469
7	6.380
8	7.292
9	8.203
10	9.115
11	10.026
12	10.937
13	11.849
14	12.760
15	13.672

Avoir Lbs	Troy Ozs	Avoir Lbs	Troy Ozs	Avoir Lbs	Troy Ozs
1	14.583	41	597.917	81	1181.250
2	29.167	42	612.500	82	1195.833
3	43.750	43	627.083	83	1210.417
4	58.333	44	641.667	84	1225.000
5	72.917	45	656.250	85	1239.583
6	87.500	46	670.833	86	1254.167
7	102.083	47	685.417	87	1268.750
8	116.667	48	700.000	88	1283.333
9	131.250	49	714.583	89	1297.917
10	145.833	50	729.167	90	1312.500
11	160.417	51	743.750	91	1327.083
12	175.000	52	758.333	92	1341.667
13	189.583	53	772.917	93	1356.250
14	204.167	54	787.500	94	1370.833
15	218.750	55	802.083	95	1385.417
16	233.333	56	816.667	96	1400.000
17	247.917	57	831.250	97	1414.583
18	262.500	58	845.833	98	1429.167
19	277.083	59	860.417	99	1443.750
20	291.667	60	875.000	100	1458.333
21	306.250	61	889.583		
22	320.833	62	904.167		
23	335.417	63	918.750		
24	350.000	64	933.333		
25	364.583	65	947.917		
26	379.167	66	962.500		
27	393.750	67	977.083		
28	408.333	68	991.667		
29	422.917	69	1006.250		
30	437.500	70	1020.833		
31	452.083	71	1035.417		
32	466.667	72	1050.000		
33	481.250	73	1064.583		
34	495.833	74	1079.167		
35	510.417	75	1093.750		
36	525.000	76	1108.333		
37	539.583	77	1122.917		
38	554.167	78	1137.500		
39	568.750	79	1152.083		
40	583.333	80	1166.667		

SOURCES OF SUPPLY It is advisable to consult local classified telephone directories for local suppy houses.

JEWELRY TOOLS AND FINDINGS

Gordon's
1850 E. Pacific Coast Hwy.
Long Beach, Calif. 90804

J.J. Jewelcraft
4959 York Blvd.
Los Angeles, Calif. 90042

Sungem
900 W. Los Vallecitos Blvd.
San Marcos, Calif. 91105

Grieger's
900 S. Arroyo P'kway
Pasadena, Calif. 91105

Swest Inc.
1725 Victory Blvd.
Glendale, Calif. 91201

Friedheim Tool Supply
412 W. 6th St.
Los Angeles, Calif. 90014

Bourget Bros.
1626-11th St.
Santa Monica, Calif. 90404

Jeweler's Workshop
451 Coddingtown Center
Santa Rosa, Calif. 95401

Louis Jeweler's Supply
607 S. Hill St.
Los Angeles, Calif.

Craftools, Inc.
1421 W. 240th St.
Harbor City, Calif. 90710

Paul Gesswein
255 Hancock Ave.
Bridgeport, Conn. 06605

Seabrook
135 3rd St.
San Rafael, Calif. 94901

D.J.S.
2403 Ogletown Rd.
Newark, Del. 19711

Rosenthal Jewelers Supply
117 N.E. 1st Ave.
Miami, Florida 33132

Bartlett & Co.
5 So. Wabash Ave.
Chicago, Ill. 60603

Alessi
322 W. St. Charles Rd.
Villa Park, Ill. 60181

Trowbridge Crafts
9 N. Elmhurst Rd.
Prospect H'ts, Ill. 60181

Marshall-Swartchild
2040 N. Milwaukee
Chicago, Ill. 60647

Central Supply
223 W. 4th St.
Davenport, Iowa 52805

Macmillan Arts & Crafts
9520 Baltimore Ave.
College Park, Md.

C.W. Somers & Co.
387 Washington Ave.
Boston, Mass. 02108

Terra-Cotta
765 Mass. Ave.
Cambridge, Mass. 02139

C.R. Hill Co.
2734 W. Eleven Mile Rd.
Berkley, Mich. 48072

Gager's Handicraft
3516 Beltline Blvd.
St. Louis Park, Minn. 55416

Rutlader Co.
8247 Wornall Rd.
Kansas City, Mo. 64114

Jules Borel & Co.
1110 Grand Ave.
Kansas City, Mo. 64106

Bergman Co.
1510 Howard St.
Omaha, Nebr. 68102

Anchor Tool
231 Main St.
Chatham, N.J. 07928

William Dixon Co.
Carlstadt, N.J. 07072

McKilligan Supply Co.
494 Chenango Street
Binghamton, N.Y. 13901

Niagara Jewelry Supply
Ellicott Sq. Bldg.
Buffalo, N.Y. 14203

Abbey Materials Corp.
116 W. 29th St.
New York, N.Y. 10001

Allcraft Tool
22 W. 48th St.
New York, N.Y. 10036

Gamzon Bros.
21 W. 46th St.
New York, N.Y. 10036

I. Shor
50 West 23rd St.
New York, N.Y. 10010

Borel
15 W. 47th St.
New York, N.Y. 10036

Woodstock Craft Tools
21 Tinker St.
Woodstock, N.Y. 12498

Montana Assay Office
610 S.W. Second Ave.
Portland, Oreg. 97204

Meiskey's Inc.
301 W. King St.
Lancaster, Pa. 17604

Keystone Jewelers Supply
710 Sansom St.
Phila., Pa. 19106

Phila. Jewelry Finding
140 So. 8th St.
Phila., Pa. 19107

Swest
10803 Composite Drive
Dallas, Texas 75221

Ascot Silver Mine
4214 Oak Lawn
Dallas, Texas 75219

Primrose Sonntag
180 W. 4 South
Salt Lake City, Utah 84110

ARE Supplier
Box 155, N. Montpelier Rd.
Plainfield, Vt. 05667

TSI, Inc.
105 Nickerson St.
Seattle, Wash. 98109

Cape Watchmakers
41 Burg St.
Capetown, So. Africa

LAPIDARY SUPPLIES AND EQUIPMENT

Mueller's
1000 E. Camelback
Phoenix, Ariz. 85014

Casa de Plata
1259 W. Miracle Mile
Tucson, Ariz. 85705

Lonnie's
7153 E. Apache Trail
Mesa, Ariz. 85208

Wright's Rock
Rt. 4, Box 462
W. Hot Springs, Ark. 71901

Terry's Lapidary
3616 E. Gage St.
Bell, Calif. 90201

O'Brien's Lapidary
1116 N. Wilcox Ave.
Hollywood, Calif. 90038

Allcraft Tool
204 No. Harbor Blvd.
Fullerton, Calif. 92632

W.H. Haney Co.
240 Castro St.
Mt. View, Calif. 94040

Frazier's Minerals
1724 University Ave.
Berkeley, Calif. 94703
Redondo Gems
1426 Aviation Blvd.
Redondo Beach, Calif. 90278
Bowsers'
3317 State St.
Santa Barbara, Calif. 93105
U.S. Lapidary
1605 W. San Carlos St.
San Jose, Calif. 95128
Silver City
4688 Convoy St.
San Diego, Calif. 92111
Shipley's
Bayfield, Colorado 81122
Colorado Lapidary
5818 E. Colfax
Denver, Colo. 80220
Ryder's Gold & Gem
1216 E. Colonial
Orlando, Fla. 32803
Rock & Shell Shop
2036 S.W. 57th Ave.
Miami, Fla. 33155
Weidinger
P.O. Box 39
Matteson, Ill. 60443
Spragg's Rocks & Gems
1228 Washington St.
Davenport, Iowa 52804
Ebersole Lapidary Supply
11417 W. Hwy. 54
Wichita, Kans. 67209
Friend's Lapidary Supply
Hikes Point Plaza
Louisville, Ky. 40220
Brad's Rock Shop
911 W. 9 Mile Rd.
Ferndale, Mich. 48220
Rozema's Rockpile
776 E. Leonard
Grand Rapids, Mich.
Baskin & Sons
732 Union Ave.
Middlesex, N.J. 08846
Crystal Gem Co.
1440 Willowbrook Mall
Wayne, N.J. 07470
Indian Jewelers Supply
601 E. Coal
Gallup, N.M. 87301
International Gem
15 Maiden Lane
New York, N.Y. 10038
New England Diamond Corp.
66 W. 47th St.
New York, N.Y. 10036
Max Stern & Co.
22 W. 48th St.
New York, N.Y. 10036

Technicraft Lapidaries Corp.
2248 Broadway
New York, N.Y. 10024
Janison & Haertel
102 Canal St.
New York, N.Y. 10002
Allen's Rocks
19133 Hilliard
Cleveland, Ohio 44116
Arrowhead Lapidary
330 S.W. 28th
Oklahoma City, Okla. 73109
Lapidabrade
8 E. Eagle Rd.
Havertown, Pa. 19083
Gilman's
Hellertown, Pa. 19083
King's Gem Center
5510 N. Freeway
Houston, Texas 77076
Rock's Lapidary
2211 S. Hackberry
San Antonio, Tex. 78210
Lathrop's Gem Shop
6702 Ferris St.
Bellaire, Tex. 77401
Ken Stewart's Gem Shop
143 Pierpont
Salt Lake City, Utah
Ovgem Ltd.
2487 Kaladar
Ottawa, Ont. Canada
Marshall's Lapidary
2090 W. 41st Ave.
Vancouver, B.C. Canada
Capilano Rock & Gem
1644 Bridgman
No. Vancouver, B.C. Canada
Green's Rock & Lapidary
1603 Centre St. N.
Calgary, Alta., Canada

GOLD AND SILVER

Handy and Harman
850 3rd Avenue
New York, N.Y. 10022
Wildberg Brothers
349 Oyster Point Blvd.
San Francisco, Calif. 94102
Swest, Inc.
10803 Composite Drive
Dallas, Texas 75220
Goldsmith Brothers
111 N. Wabash Avenue
Chicago, Ill. 60603
Rodman & Yaruss
17 West 47th Street
New York, N.Y. 10036

SILVER

Myron Toback
23 West 47th Street
New York, N.Y. 10036

T.B. Hagstoz & Son
709 Sansom Street
Philadelphia, Pa. 19106
Rio Grande Jewelers Supply
6901 Washington N.E.
Albuquerque, N.M. 87109

GOLD FILLED & GOLD

L-S Plate and Wire
70-17 51st Avenue
Woodside, N.Y. 11375
Vennerbeck & Clase Co.
150 Chestnut Street
Providence, R.I. 02903

PEWTER

White Metal Rolling & Stamping
80 Moultrie Street
Brooklyn, N.Y. 11222

BRASS, BRONZE, ALUMINUM

A.J. Oester Co.
50 Sims Ave.
Providence, R.I. 02909
Belmont Metals
330 Belmont Ave.
Brooklyn, N.Y. 11207
T.E. Conklin Brass & Copper
324 W. 23rd St.
New York, N.Y. 10011

FINDINGS

Eastern Findings Corp.
19 West 34th Street
New York, N.Y. 10001
Costa Findings, Inc.
45 West 47th Street
New York, N.Y. 10036
Long Island Jewelry Supply
18 Roselle Street
Mineola, Long Island 11501
Metal City Findings Corp.
450 West 31st Street
New York, N.Y. 10001
Myron Toback, Inc.
23 West 47th Street
New York, N.Y. 10036

ENAMELS

C.R. Hill Company
2734 W. Eleven Mile Rd.
Berkley, Michigan 48072
Thomas C. Thompson Co.
1539 Old Deerfield Rd.
P.O. Box 127
Highland Park, Ill. 60035
Allcraft Tool & Supply
100 Frank Road
Hicksville, N.Y. 11801

WOOD

Craftsman Wood Service Co.
2727 So. Mary St.
Chicago, Ill. 60608
Albert Constantine & Son, Inc.
2050 Eastchester Road
Bronx, N.Y. 10461